B
MAT   Edelman, Rob
EDE
                  Matthau

                                K214   25.95

DUE DATE

East Canton Branch
488-1501

SEP - - 2002

MATTHAU

MATTHAU

A Life

ROB EDELMAN AND AUDREY KUPFERBERG

Taylor Trade Publishing   *Lanham • New York • Oxford*

First Taylor Trade Publishing edition 2002

This Taylor Trade Publishing edition of *Matthau: A Life* is an original publication.
It is published by arrangement with the authors.

Published by Taylor Trade Publishing
A Member of the Rowman & Littlefield Publishing Group
4720 Boston Way
Lanham, Maryland 20706

Distributed by National Book Network

Book design and composition: Barbara Werden Design

Library of Congress Cataloging-in-Publication Data

Edelman, Rob.
  Matthau : a life / Rob Edelman and Audrey Kupferberg.
       p.   cm.
  Includes bibliographical references and index.
  ISBN 0-87833-274-X (alk. paper)
  1. Matthau, Walter. 2. Actors—United States—Biography. I. Kupferberg,
Audrey E. II. Title.

PN2287.M543 E33 2002
792'.028'092—dc21

                                                                    2002006110

∞ The paper used in this publication meets the minimum requirements of American
National Standard for Information Sciences—Permanence of Paper for
Printed Library Materials, ANSI/NISO Z39.48–1992.
Manufactured in the United States of America.

To Rae

CONTENTS

CONTENTS

ACKNOWLEDGMENTS

Charlie Matthau opened the doors to many of those who were interviewed for this book, yet he never intruded in the process of researching and writing. For his kindness and cooperation, we are grateful.

We would like to thank the following individuals who graciously agreed to be interviewed: Virginia Adams; Artoro Alfaro; Tige Andrews; Richard Benjamin; Anna Berger; Alex and Gloria Berger; Milt Berger; Jack Berger; Leon Birns; Burt Bloom; Pat Boone; John S. Bowman; Sylvia Brook (Syd Preses); the late Heywood Hale Broun; Alex Brounstein; Kirk Browning; Dr. Norman and Sandra Burg; Robert Carradine; Christina Collins; Rabbi Jerry Cutler; Al Dallmeyer; Asher Dann; Ossie Davis; Maxie Eisenberg; Verna Petty Fitzpatrick; Nina Foch; Dan Frazer; Ellen Geer; Ike Goldschlager; Herbert Green; Louis Guss; Linda Harrison; Mother Dolores (Dolores Hart); Arthur Hiller; Cy Hoffman; Marlene Iglitzen; Marty Ingels; Anne Jackson; Graham Jarvis; Georgann Johnson Tenner; Murray Juvelier; Aviva Kempner; Sylvan Kessler; Larry King; Shirley Knight; Sam Kweskin; Piper Laurie; Jean Longacre; Carlos Lopez; Ruby Ludwin; Lillian Lux; Judith Malina; Charlie Matthau; David Matthau; Arlene Mazerolle; Patty McCormack; Jayne Meadows; Nancy Mehta; Zubin Mehta; Rene Mendez; Dina Merrill; Radley Metzger; Bob Mills; Lana Morgan; Howard Morris; Patricia Neal; Tom Neilan; Don Olds; Betsy Palmer; Dr. Neil Parker; Sol Parker; Austin Pendleton; Paula Prentiss; Seymour Rexite; Beryl Richmond;

the late Michael Ritchie; Yvonne and Melvin Rogow; Rachel Rosenthal; Joanna Sanchez; Joseph Sargent; William Schallert; Les Schecter; Charlotte Haverly Scherz; Milton Schnur; Grace Schneider Sealine; Marian Seldes; William Shatner; Bea Shecter; Carole Shelley; Marvin Silbersher; Mark Stein; Max Stein; Judy Stone; Phyllis Thaxter; Paul Tripp; Norman Tulchin; Joyce Van Patten; Lia Waggner; Barney Weiner; Murray Weissman; Laura Winkler; Lana Wood; and Louis Zorich. Interviews conducted prior to the project's inception also proved helpful: the late Ben Bonus; Brian Garfield; the late Joseph Green; the late Robert Preston; and the late Molly Picon. We also wish to thank those who responded to our queries: George Roy Hill; Howard W. Koch Jr.; and Janet Leigh.

Plenty of individuals and organizations offered invaluable assistance during the preparation of this book. They are: Bob Addison; Cathleen Anderson; Melissa Andruski of the Southold (New York) Free Library; Monty Arnold; Arlie C. Aukerman; Jeanine Basinger; Jim Beaver; Evelyn Begley; Nadine Bloom; The Bohman-Fannings; Doug Bredt; Jack Carter; Maryann Chach of The Shubert Archive; Joe Chiplock of City Center; Dan Davis; Barbara DeMetz of Jalem Productions; Ginny Donnelly; Geoffrey Mark Fidelman; Terence Geary; Larry Glaser; Rabbi Samuel Glaser; Gene Golombek; Bob Goudy; Ted Hathaway; Fred Hess; Naomi Hyman; Shirley and Harry Hyman; Leith Johnson of The Cinema Archives, Wesleyan University; Judy and Milt Kass; Wolf Krakowski; Arieh Lebowitz; Masha Leon; Nachum Lerner of The Workmen's Circle; Richard Lerner of Tranquillity Camp; Bob Malatzky; Bob Marx; Dan McCarthy of the Southold (New York) Traveler Watchman; John McCarty; Hunton L. Morgan; Lloyd Morris; Doris Myers; Bill Ndini; Ken Nellis; The New York Public Library at Lincoln Center; Caraid O'Brien; James Robert Parish; Dick Phillips; Kate Phillips; Art Pierce; Lloyd Prang; Howard Prouty and Barbara Hall of the Margaret Herrick Library, Academy of Motion Picture Arts and Sciences; David Rhodes; Stephen Riordan; Eve Robbins; Rick Scheckman; Heather Seltzer of the Office of Alumnae Affairs, Barnard College; Phil Serling; Ron Simon and the staff of the Museum of Television and Radio; R. Lea Singer; Stanley Sludikoff of *Gambling Times* magazine; The Society for American Baseball Research; Daniel L. Stockton; Yale Strom; Eddie

Richmond and Dan Einstein of the UCLA Film and Television Archive; The University at Albany Library; Max Wilk; Sally Willis; Stuart Wright; Ric Wyman; Neil Zagorin; and Dr. Alex and Inge Zimmerman.

We wish to thank Roger Ebert, Larry King, and Leonard Maltin for providing us with pre-edited material, or manuscripts of their Matthau interviews. Extra-special bows go to Sylvia Brook (Syd Preses); Lana Morgan; Leonard, Alice, and Jessie Maltin; Michael Dorr, Ginger Strader, Nancy Rothschild, Mary Sestric, Barbara Werden, and Ross Plotkin for their spirit and helpfulness; and Camille Cline, our first editor. If not for Camille, this book would not exist. We could not begin to thank Charlie Matthau and David Matthau, who generously answered all our questions regarding their father. Finally, a special bow to Anne Jackson, who quipped, with regard to researching the life of Walter Matthau, "I'll bet that you're having more fun than a barrel of monkeys."

MATTHAU

CHAPTER I

Matuschanaskayasky?

In 1966, one year after he won everlasting stardom by creating the role of Oscar Madison on stage in *The Odd Couple*, Walter Matthau was profiled in *Current Biography*, a celebrity who's who.

Based on information culled from press clippings, the publication noted that his father "had been a Catholic [Eastern Rite] priest in Czarist Russia, but he ran afoul of Orthodox authorities there by his preaching of papal supremacy." Matthau had his father leaving Russia and abandoning the ministry, and then residing in Finland and Lithuania, where he met his wife, a Jew. The anecdote ended with the couple emigrating to New York.

This account illustrates Matthau's legendary penchant for fabricating his past, for taking delight in expressing himself with tongue planted firmly in cheek. The truth was that Matthau's father, Melas, was a Jew, as was his mother, Rose, whose maiden name was Berolsky.

Furthermore, *Current Biography* dutifully reported that one of Matthau's favorite hobbies was collecting "such appliances as mechanized hospital beds and massage chairs."

John S. Bowman, a freelance writer/editor, put together the piece. "I went through the mass of clippings," he recalled thirty-five years later. "Well, at least a couple of the 'sources' [that were] little more than gossip columns claimed that Matthau's mother had been a Romanian gypsy or circus performer or some such thing. What did I know? So I started my draft with this information. Then one night I happened to be looking at Johnny Carson and Matthau was his guest. And somehow their conversation opened up the subject that Matthau got a kick out of playing practical jokes or whatever he called them—[and], in particular, that he liked to tell weird stories about his life and past. And he tells Johnny that he's actually got people to believe and print his tales about his mother being a gypsy, or some such thing. And there were Matthau and Carson guffawing at the fools who fell for such stories.

"Guess what I did with my bio the first thing next morning?"

Yet Bowman did not catch the other fibs. "How could I have been so naive as to accept the story about his father?" he admitted.

Next, there is the matter of Matthau's surname. The most reputable film encyclopedias list it as Matuschanskayasky; it occasionally has been spelled Matasschanskayasky—and heaven knows what else. All are designations that would cause even the sturdiest theater marquee to wilt. And all are bogus. When he was born, his surname was Matthow; after World War II, while an acting student in New York at the New School for Social Research, he altered it to Matthau.

However, "Matthow" was shortened from some now-forgotten longer name. "You hear so many versions of what our last name was," noted David Matthau, Walter's firstborn. "I've heard my dad talk about what our last name was. [He pronounced it] two or three different ways: Matachansky, Mashayansky. I wouldn't even attempt to spell them. We never really sat down and had a serious discussion about what the name actually was." One time, after spelling it "M-a-t-u-s-c-h-a-n-s-k-y," Walter admitted, "I make up things about it . . . 'Son of great pirate general . . .'"

One thing is certain: it *never* was Matuschanskayasky. The story goes that Matthau, in a typically mischievous mood while sitting through an interview soon after becoming a major movie star, told the journalist that he was born Walter Matuschanskayasky. The writer printed the information, and the name was associated with the actor for the rest of his life. Matthau gleefully went along with the gag. In *Earthquake*, a 1974 disaster opus, he made a cameo appearance as a drunk. In the credits, he is billed as Walter Matuschanskayasky.

Back on December 3, 1936, when he was two months past his sixteenth birthday, Matthau applied for a Social Security card. The number he was assigned was 065-03-9840. For years, he claimed he listed his middle name as "Foghorn" on the application. He never bothered to correct the fib, he asserted, and it remained in his Social Security file.

This is yet another example of Matthau's passing off fabrication for fact. On the application, which survives in Social Security annals, he first listed his middle name as "John." The name "Jake" is written in script to the left of "John." Above "Employee's Signature as Usually Written," there is the florid signature "Walter Jake Matthow."

Larry King, on whose CNN talk show Matthau was a frequent guest, offered as good an explanation as any of why the actor relished fibbing. "A lot of it was play to him," King noted. "He said he enjoyed it because it made interviews so much more interesting. With Walter, you never knew when he was really being serious. Even in the deepest interviews, you never were quite sure."

Matthau once explained his rationale for fictionalizing his past by declaring, "That's my defense mechanism against pompous and ludicrous questions." That may be so, but it also was a way of distancing himself from a childhood that might have been conjured up by Dickens.

What is indisputable is that the actor was born in New York City on October 1, 1920. ("I was very young when I was born," he remarked when he was well into his seventies. "I was about nine months old.") Also unquestionable is the Lower East Side community in which he came of age, and the cruel fact that his childhood was, as Matthau admitted, "a nightmare, a dreadful, horrible, stinking nightmare."

For four decades beginning in the early 1880s, Eastern European Jews, seeking to escape from persecution and pogroms, abandoned their shtetls and crossed the Atlantic Ocean to America, where they hoped to live free from anti-Semitism. The flow of newcomers ceased in 1924, when tough laws were passed that ended this cycle of immigration. By then, two million poverty-stricken Jews had come to the United States. More than one-half million settled on the Lower East Side, a four-square-mile urban enclave.

If any of these greenhorns believed the cliche that the streets of New York were paved with gold, they quickly realized the fallacy of this notion. The Lower East Side was no North American Garden of Eden, but instead a dreary, pushcart-filled slum. The smells of fresh hot bagels and bialys, and home-cooked delicacies such as matzoh balls, briskets, and apple strudel, may have tempted the tastebuds, but the equally potent stench of poverty, with its sewage and animal droppings, did its share to discourage the appetite. Jobs were arduous; to eke out a meager existence, an immigrant toiled for endless hours, often in non-unionized sweatshops. As Leon Birns, Matthau's childhood friend, noted, "We grew up on the East Side at a time when it was very difficult to get along. Our folks didn't make much of a living."

But the immigrants did manage to meld as a community. They founded synagogues, schools, Yiddish-language theaters and newspapers, and settlement houses, which were the equivalent of YMCAs/YMHAs.

It was into this milieu that Walter Matthau was born, and in which he lived the first two decades of his life.

Matthau's father Melas, who called himself Milton in his adopted country, purportedly hailed from Kiev, in the Ukraine, where he was a peddler. He came to America during the twentieth century's first decade. The specifics of his origins are as imprecise as the spelling of his surname. Melas Matthow might have been Meilach Matuszanski, age twenty-two, of Bialycerkow, Russia, who arrived at Ellis Island on June 7, 1908. Bialycerkow, also spelled Bielayatserkov, is right outside Kiev. If indeed Melas and Meilach are one and the same, Walter's "great pirate general" wisecrack would not have been far off: "Meilach" is Yiddish for "King." Or he could be Moishe Matushansky, age seventeen, of Tochinowitzy, who arrived on December 27, 1906. Similarly, Rose Berolsky, born on a farm in Lithuania, may have been Rachel Brelsky, age eighteen, of Kelvoric, Russia, who came to Ellis

Island on June 10, 1913. Kelvoric, also spelled Kalvarija and Kalvar-
ijos, is located in Lithuania, approximately fifty miles from Vilna, the
capital city.

In another bit of whimsy, Matthau once testified that Milton was
the lone Jewish cowboy who roamed the American West. From this,
one conjures up the image of a Yiddisher wearing chaps, sporting six-
guns, and sliding off a horse. The fact was that Milton arrived in New
York, settled on the Lower East Side, and took any odd job he could
find, eventually toiling as an electrician, a photographer, and a
process server for a law firm. In the 1922–1923 "Trow's General
Directory of the Boroughs of Manhattan and Bronx, City of New
York," there is a listing for a "Milton Matthow." His profession: "electrician." His address: "120 Suffolk."

In 1961, Matthau noted that his father "loved music and art and
debates, and spent his money on classical records." He savored a
melting pot of music, including the voices of Enrico Caruso, the great
operatic tenor, and Josef Rosenblatt, the legendary singer of religious
cantorials. Six years later, Walter described Milton as "a sensitive,
intelligent man who was completely crushed by the competitive
system." However, in the mid-1980s, Matthau dubbed him "a con
man from Kiev."

On July 14, 1918, Milton and Rose became the parents of a son,
Henry, Walter's older brother. Henry would spend his life in the New
York area, where he owned several stores in which he sold Army-
Navy surplus goods.

Then Walter came along, two years and two-and-a-half months
later. In 1923, when Walter was three, Milton Matthow abandoned
his wife and sons. The reason remains unclear. He might have left
because of the pressure of supporting a wife and two young children.
Perhaps he did not get along with Rose, or he may have met another
woman.

"He never had a father, really," Matthau's second son, Charlie,
recalled. "I think he saw his own father just a couple of times. They
posed for a picture, and he took [Walter and Henry] out to lunch."
Walter once noted that Charlie, in fact, looked like his father. David
Matthau amplified his half-brother's comment by adding, "I think he
met his father a couple of times, as a young boy. It was, 'Oh, that man

is your father.' My dad was young, about age five or six. He met him a few times, and that was basically it." The actor himself stated that he had no memory of his father residing at home: "He must have lived there for some time—maybe a day or two."

Milton divorced Rose, remarried, and in 1932 reportedly fathered a third son: Marvin Matthow, Walter's and Henry's half-brother, who never was allowed entry into the Matthow-Matthau family circle. While in Chicago promoting *The Sunshine Boys* in 1975, Matthau whimsically declared that his father was ninety-one years old and "a technical advisor for Hughes Aircraft." However, when Walter was fifteen, he learned that his father, then in his mid-forties, had passed away. "I still don't know what he died of," Matthau declared decades later. "He died in the psychiatric ward in Bellevue Hospital. I think he died of TB." In the years preceding his demise, Milton Matthow made no effort to support his first family; Walter once remarked that his mother, brother, and he often "didn't have seventy-five cents between us."

Rose Matthow placed her sons in the Daughters of Israel day nursery on East Fifth Street, at a cost of one dollar per week, while she went off to labor in sweatshops, sewing ladies' rayon under-wear—a particularly difficult material on which to keep an even stitch. Her salary: a paltry eight dollars per week. "We never knew whether she was coming home," Matthau somberly recalled. "We'd play and hang around the stoop. That first cold spell used to fill me with terror because soon it would be getting darker and I'd have to wait on the street in the dark and cold." Rose finally arrived to pick up her boys, and took them to a nearby cafeteria where they dined on potato soup.

Syd Preses, who back then was Sylvia Brook, also attended the nursery. "This is where we were brought up," she reminisced. "This is how I knew Walter, from the age of two until the age of twelve. I remember, when we went to the nursery, I thought he was adorable. Back then, he was a pretty boy. He was very, very shy. He wasn't like the other children, wild and running around. Jerry Levine would pull someone's bloomers down, you know. But not Walter. He partici-pated in some of the games, and in the holiday [activities]. One time I tried to edge next to him in the Chanukah play. I remember at the

Chanukah play he'd be singing the Chanukah songs.

"As we got older I would see these two boys, Walter and Henry, walking up and down the stairs in the nursery. They were so tall. They both stood out, at such a young age."

Years later, Matthau confided to Preses that he had a crush on a little girl named June Mellon. "I last saw her on a subway station," she recalled, "when I was about seventeen. She had a boyfriend. I never saw her after that."

She continued, "I remember Rose, the mother, coming and picking up the kids."

In future decades, a woman in Rose Matthow's situation might have depended on Social Security payments to support her children. She and her sons might have resided in one of the dozens of public housing projects that were to be built throughout New York City. However, because of Rose's inability to pay the landlord while feeding herself and her youngsters, the Matthows had to keep moving from one small Lower East Side flat to the next. Walter and Henry slept together in a single bed, or on small cots; their mother's bed was a covered bathtub, which was located in the kitchen.

"We got evicted a lot because we didn't have any money, we couldn't pay the rent," Matthau recalled. "It was high, ten dollars a month. We'd find another spot; in those days you didn't have to put up a deposit, you moved in. They saw a woman with two children, then six months would go by, and no rent, and we were out." In 1978, while ensconced in a suite at New York's tony Carlyle Hotel, Matthau continually fiddled with the radiator and declared, "Every time I smell steam heat I think someone's gonna come and evict me." On another occasion, he recalled that he lived in cold-water flats until age twenty-eight, adding, "I remember always being cold as a kid. Even now I like places that are warm." He once told Louis Zorich, his understudy in *The Odd Couple*, "When my mother bought socks, she didn't buy seconds. She bought fourths."

The Matthows resided in a host of tenements, on a host of Lower East Side streets. Those who remember them offered a laundry list of addresses: "127 Second Avenue"; "East Fifth Street, near a police station"; "303 East Fifth Street"; "61 East Seventh Street." Matthau himself recalled that they lived "on all the numbered streets from one to ten." He added, "I was always scared, always nervous. There was no point in making friends because we'd always move. I was in a state of fright and insecurity. . . ."

Rose Matthow, meanwhile, was a strict and humorless woman. As he got older, Walter did indeed establish friendships, and quite a few of his now aged Lower East Side pals recalled her as being unbalanced. Ruby Ludwin, one of Matthau's closest childhood friends, described her as "a nut." "How could I not forget Rosie!" declared Murray Juvelier, another Lower East Sider. "[She was] a nut. A short little lady. I remember how her hair used to be combed in the back. She walked very fast in the street. 'My Walter, my Walter and Hank,' she would say." Added Alex Berger, who became the Matthows' neighbor in the mid-1930s, "She had a mental problem. I'm no psychiatrist, but she always would scream and yell at the boys, and at neighbors. I would see her coming down the stairs talking to herself, and screaming and yelling. I was a little boy; I thought it was strange. Walter always would [rationalize her behavior]. He said, 'She's my mom. With all her traits, she's my mom.'"

Matthau once noted the object of Rose's anger: "My mother was always screaming that [her husband] should drop dead, that his stomach, feet, eyes, and hair should fall out." Yet when she learned that he was terminally ill, Rose brought chicken soup to his hospital bed.

Another key to understanding Matthau's propensity for fibbing directly relates to his mother. Upon describing his poverty-stricken background and his mother's dour personality, he cracked, "If she heard this, she'd say, 'Who wants to know all that? Say you're from a rich family. Your mother is the Queen of Romania.'" He also noted, not long before Rose's death in 1979, "My mother doesn't love anything. She hates everybody and everything. All she likes to do is look at the ocean and see the little ships and boats. She relaxes only at the beach; that was the only time I could talk to her, [because] she was either cleaning, scrubbing, working, or yelling. Sure, it had an effect! A sensitive young boy with one parent, an hysterical mother."

Young Walter's own playful sense of humor occasionally broke through Rose's severity. He once imitated the landlady asking for the rent, mimicking her "hyper and cockeyed" demeanor—and his mother fell down laughing. Matthau kept giving repeat performances, he noted, because "it was nice to have Rosie smiling." Rose Matthow did live long enough to see her son employ his wry humor to win show business fame. Yet her rough Lower East Side background prevented her from trusting his success.

When Rose was raising her boys, a dollar was a mini-fortune. To earn the extra pennies that were essential to his family's survival, young Walter sold newspapers and shined shoes. He traversed the Lower East Side streets with a sign that said, "Ice Cold Drinks 3 Cents." Each week, he earned between a dollar and a dollar-and-a-half; he gave his mother fifty cents, and pocketed the rest. When Matthau was six years old he organized a card game, called Bankers and Brokers, which he and his contemporaries played on tenement rooftops. With his profits as a street vendor burning a hole in his hands, he scurried up the dank tenement staircases to wager it away. This attempt to transform his pennies into nickels predated Matthau's obsession with gambling. He noted, in another irony that foretold the future, "It was almost a sure thing that I'd lose the twenty-five cents I came up to the roof with."

The poverty in which the Matthows lived was exacerbated by the coming of the Great Depression. Young Walter was just short of his ninth birthday when the stock market crashed in 1929. But this did not ease his wagering. "The boys used to play aggies [marbles] on the streets, on the curb," recalled Syd Preses. "When I was kid I used to play because I was a tomboy. But this kid [Walter], he used to bet. I would say he was about twelve years old."

During two summer vacations, Matthau left the Lower East Side for Tranquillity Camp, located in Earlton, New York, just below Albany. The camp, in existence since 1919, provided a rural respite for poor, inner-city Jewish kids, and even today bills itself as "A Children's Camp With a Heart." All campers' names are listed on a register, which serves as a permanent record of Tranquillity attendees. "Walter Matthow" is inscribed in two circa-1930 "log books," under the heading "Berry's Group," between the names Albert Aronson and Sheldon Goodman, and under "Lenny's Group," between Harry Reifowitz and Irving Staub. "Henry Matthow" is listed on one, between "Humpty" Goodman and Leon Wolf.

Burt Bloom, one Tranquillity alumnus, reported that Matthau actually visited the camp in the late 1960s. Yet Mark Stein, another ex-camper, stated that Matthau denied his Tranquillity connection. "The people who ran the camp said [Matthau] went there," Stein explained. "They'd contacted him, but he did not want to acknowledge that he went to that camp."

Meanwhile, during the school year, Walter attended Public School 25, followed by Junior High School 64. Like many youngsters coming of age in New York, he played stickball and handball, then popular street games. He shot pool at Buck Areton's poolroom on Second Avenue with Sylvan Kessler. "We'd play to a draw, I think," Kessler recalled. "One time he would beat me, and the next I would beat him. He was like any other kid on the Lower East Side." Added Sol Parker, an acquaintance from the Emanu-El Brotherhood, a neighborhood settlement house–recreation center, "As a young man of fourteen or fifteen, he was a tall, thin, lanky type who wore knickers that were constantly falling down below his knees. Otherwise, he was a pleasant, likeable young man."

Matthau was not brawny, nor was he a bully: two definite drawbacks for a lad growing up in a tough urban neighborhood. Instead, he was skinny, and unusually tall for his age. "I did a great deal of brooding about myself," he noted. He claimed that by the time he was ten—this was yet another of his exaggerations—he already was six feet tall, despite weighing ninety pounds. "When I drank cherry soda," he quipped, "I looked like a thermometer."

So at a very young age, Matthau resourcefully developed his famous snarl and glare as a way of dealing with neighborhood bullies. On several occasions he boasted that, around age nine or ten, he got into a fistfight with boxing champ-to-be Rocky Graziano. This came after he uncharacteristically smacked a kid who was lampooning an opera-singing baritone during a free concert. Graziano was called upon to exact revenge. "I was too tall for him," Matthau said. "I threw a right cross and broke his nose. Rocky walked away."

To add muscle to his frame, Matthau claimed that he began working out, which left him, as he noted, with "Popeye-like bumps on my skinny arms." When he began attending Seward Park High School, he weighed 125 pounds and already had reached his full height of six feet two inches. ("He lied about [his height]," reported his son Charlie. "He said he was six-three, but he really was only six-two.") He wrote off his thinness to a nutritional deficiency. Because he was so tall at such a young age, he was overly sensitive about his appearance and subconsciously began walking with a slouch. This habit became one of his most distinguishing physical traits, and played into his comic personality.

By then, Matthau had a coterie of neighborhood buddies. Two of his closest were Ruby Ludwin and Leon Levine. One of their favored neighborhood hangouts was the Sunshine Billiard Parlor. They and brother Henry also spent hours playing handball at courts across the city: on East First Street, just south of his various Lower East Side addresses; in the Bronx, at McCombs Dam Park; and in Brooklyn, at Brighton Beach and by Coney Island's Washington Baths. They would schlep on the subway to "Coney" and Brighton Beach, the celebrated seaside communities where the inner-city masses passed hot summer weekends breaking a different kind of sweat baking in the sun. Decades later, Matthau starred in *House Calls*, a romantic comedy in which he played a widowed doctor-turned-lothario. In one sequence, his character tries to convince a widow who hails from Coney Island not to file a malpractice lawsuit. "I used to play at the Brighton Baths," he tells her. "I used to play handball with all the champs." Matthau improvised his dialogue. While publicizing the film, he noted that his brother still played there.

Anna Berger, a neighborhood girl whom Walter would befriend when he, Rose, and Henry moved into her building on East First Street, described Ruby, Leon, and the Matthows as "handball experts," and added, "I think that Henry was the champion of them all." They made quite a quartet, well into adulthood. "When my father passed away in 1962," Berger recalled, "and everybody loved my father—he was the honorary mayor of East First Street—I was so touched because as I was leaving the funeral parlor, there was Matthau, Henry, Leon, and Ruby." Walter and Ruby Ludwin knew each other since age six. They met while roaming the Lower East Side streets. "Ruby was really Dad's closest friend from the old neighborhood," reported David Matthau.

Matthau did not confine his athletic activity to handball. With

Stanford Polonsky, Nick Gross, and Bummie Tresser, he played basketball at the Emanu-El Brotherhood. Norman Tulchin, five years Walter's junior, recalled that Walter and brother Hank were Emanu-El regulars. "They spent a lot of time there," he noted, "participating in the usual social activities." At Seward Park, Matthau made the school track team. Its captain, Leon Birns, reported that Matthau did the shot put, and ran the half-mile. Added Sylvan Kessler, "One time, he was being interviewed by Dick Cavett. Cavett asks him if he had any regrets about anything in relation to his career. He said, 'No, the only regret I have is that I couldn't beat Arnie Berger in a race in high school.'"

Other pals during Matthau's adolescence included Alex Brounstein and Ike Goldschlager. Just about all of them were big on nicknames. Brounstein was called "Much," while Goldschlager was "Ikie." Brounstein recalled that Ludwin dubbed Walter "Gvurenik"; "gvure" is the Yiddish word for courage/heroism.

"First Street and First Avenue, the middle of the block, that's where we congregated every day and night," Brounstein recalled. "We sat there every night, kidding around and having the greatest time of our lives. I'll tell you, there wasn't one night where our ribcages didn't kill us from laughing. Oy, we used to stop at the White Tower, on Fourteenth Street and Second Avenue. We'd run in there, and there'd be like thirty guys eating hamburgers. *Kinna hurra*, what appetites!"

"I hung out with Walter and his brother and Ruby and the whole bunch," added Goldschlager. "We played handball together. We ran around. We schmoozed, and all that nonsense. He was a good boy, Walter." Brounstein chimed in, "He was a lovable guy. He was the sort of guy who'd grab a hold of you, and kiss you on the cheek.

"He and his brother Henry really hustled to take care of their mother. I remember, he and Ruby would rent a pushcart, with water and ice, and sell pop. They were really hustlers."

Ludwin himself recalled being busted by one of New York's Finest for peddling without a license. When the youngster next encountered the cop, whom he described as anti-Semitic, his pal Walter was with him. "The next time you have any problem [with Ruby]," Walter brashly told the officer, "come and see me. He works for me."

Walter also gave the cop a fake name. "What chutzpah Walter had at that age," Ludwin added, "to speak to a cop like that." Then he laughingly described his old friend as a "bullshit artist."

Matthau also hawked ties. "Allen Street, which was only a couple of blocks from where we were raised, was a tie manufacturing district," recalled Barney Weiner, another neighborhood contemporary. "He and his brother used to sell ties. He would walk around with a box. If he saw you, he'd show you his wares."

He did not confine his street hustling to the Lower East Side, however. Ike Goldschlager noted, "Walter was selling ice cream in Coney Island, I remember. He was selling sodas. The cops used to chase him, and he'd run into the water because you weren't allowed to sell ice cream on the beach [without a license]. Then [once the cops were gone] he'd come back again and hustle his ice cream and soda."

CHAPTER 2

Dreaming the Dream

As millions of city boys before and after him, Matthau fantasized about one day smashing home runs and making acrobatic catches in Yankee Stadium, Ebbets Field, and the Polo Grounds. "Becoming an athlete," he observed, "was always [one] way of obscuring anonymity." Years later, he played centerfield in the Broadway Show League, which was the closest he came to being his generation's Mickey Mantle.

He also developed a fan's love for sports. One of his heroes was Jewish: Hank Greenberg, the New York–born Detroit Tigers slugger. Matthau first took notice of Greenberg when he came to play basketball at the Emanu-El Brotherhood. "He [had] arms like the cables on the Brooklyn Bridge," Matthau told Aviva Kempner, who interviewed him for her documentary *The Life and Times of Hank Greenberg.* In 1935 and 1937, Greenberg drove in 170 and 183 runs; in 1938, he smacked fifty-eight home runs. "I saw the way he was built," he continued. "I thought he could protect Jews. [They] were a group that was put upon, persecuted . . . so Hank Greenberg coming into the Emanu-El Brotherhood was quite a boost for the ego and for the psyche of a young skinny Jewish boy. . . ."

Years later, the actor befriended the ballplayer, who had settled in

Beverly Hills, where he died in 1986. Matthau even spoke at the Hall for Famer's funeral. "Greenberg gave me the notion that I didn't have to wind up a salesman in the garment center," he recalled. "I could be a ballplayer if I was good enough, or maybe I could be a guy who wrote about ballplayers, a sportswriter." Matthau admitted that he considered acting only after realizing he never could match Greenberg's ballyard exploits.

Given the realities of his childhood, it is not surprising that Matthau sought refuge in fantasy. His dreamworld extended way beyond an average American boy's illusion of athletic heroics. He became a voracious reader, and when he was as young as seven years old he began reciting Shakespeare. He may not have comprehended what he was saying, but was transfixed by the beauty and fluidity of the language and its contrast to the Lower East Side dreariness. Often, he recited out loud for hours at a stretch, in the privacy of the bathroom. "There'd be one toilet for four families," he recalled, "and I'd be in there until someone threw me out."

Decades later, he still could quote the Shakespearean monologues he learned as a child. Only then, he might jokingly recite them using Yiddish or Cockney dialects. But his love of the Bard remained with him for life. "He quoted Shakespeare *all* the time," recalled Christina Collins, an actress who worked with him in *The Marriage Fool*, a 1998 TV movie. "We had great arguments about what the last line in *Hamlet* was, and stuff like that. He would just spout out a Shakespearean line, and want you to guess what play it was from."

With his interest in Shakespeare came a love for classical music and opera. Mozart became his favorite composer; when he was a poor youngster as well as an international celebrity, he would completely lose himself in a Mozart symphony. "Walter Matthau could have been a musician. I never knew anyone who listened to music the way he did," noted his friend, the actress Marian Seldes. Added another friend, Nancy Mehta, wife of conductor Zubin Mehta, "He would often come to hear Mozart when Zubin would conduct it at the Music Center in L.A. No one was more rapt than he. He could and would hum or whistle passages that elated him. . . . He companioned with Mozart. It warmed one to see him in this intimacy."

In adulthood, Matthau's favorite music constantly emanated from the tape deck in his car or his record player at home. Yet his celebrity allowed him special access to the world of music he so loved. Little did he imagine that, one day, he would schmooze with a Zubin Mehta or guest-conduct the Los Angeles Mozart Orchestra. Given his Lower East Side background, where his closest friends and neighbors spoke broken English and Yiddish dialects and sported nicknames like "Bummie" and "Much," the impact of Shakespeare and Mozart on Matthau's life was incalculable.

The youngster also was fascinated by the stage, and the illusions created by actors reciting dialogue and building characterizations. He made his stage debut at age four, in a Daughters of Israel religious festival, and knew then that he enjoyed performing in public. In grade school, he recited poems in class assemblies. "I had a high soprano voice," he said. "When I was eight, I had a teacher, a Miss Creeden, who told me my voice was beautiful. She had her hair pulled back in a bun, and she had a sweet, soft face and wore glasses. She was always smiling at me when I recited. As I got older, my voice got louder and better."

He noted, "People always said that I didn't sound as though I was from New York, although I was brought up on New York radio speech. I used to listen to the guys on radio; [the ones] I remember were Milton Cross and David Ross, the announcers. For a long time I had a hard 'R,' a Midwestern speech [inflection], because I was mimicking announcers." Matthau once told actor Graham Jarvis of his fascination with diction: "He said that, when he was young, he'd wanted to be a radio announcer. He started paying attention to how he talked, to speaking well. When he came back from the army, he said that his old neighborhood buddies would kid him about how 'phony' and 'properly' he talked. He told them, 'You guys weren't listening. I was talking like this when I was a kid. I started on purpose. I talked like this before I left.'"

Matthau also played roles in productions at local settlement houses. He recalled that his first substantial part was The Toff, a "dilapidated gentleman," in Lord Dunsany's one-act play, *A Night at an Inn*. When he was fourteen, he played Polonius in *Hamlet* at the fabled Henry Street Settlement House.

All of this directly led to Matthau's involvement, however peripheral, with the Yiddish theater. At the time, the neighborhood's now-aging immigrants and their coming-of-age offspring constituted a ready-made audience for old country entertainment. Thus, Yiddish stage productions flourished on the Lower East Side, with Second Avenue famed as the Yiddish Great White Way. Murray Juvelier's mother, Jean, was a Yiddish stage actress, while his sister Fanny was a chorus girl. "[When] my mother [sang] *My Yiddishe Mama* and *My Shtetle Belz*," he noted, "she put tears in everyone's eyes. Jennie Goldstein would cry a song. Molly Picon and Yetta Zwerling would laugh a song. [Herman] Yablokoff and [Aaron] Lebedeff and [Boris] Thomashevsky would dramatically do a song."

Juvelier first met Matthau on the handball court. "I didn't know it at the time, but he was trying to get into acting. The reason why he liked me was that my mother and sister were in the theater. If he ever wanted a job at the theater he'd want to know if my mother would help him, which of course she would."

Only on occasion was Yiddish spoken in the Matthow household. Yet given the community in which he lived, Matthau immersed himself in Yiddish theater and Yiddishkeit, and became fluent in the language. He was fond of explaining that he had been "raised on potato soup and Yiddish theater."

Matthau often claimed that, when he was eleven years old, he began hawking candy, soda, and ice cream in the Yiddish theaters. While he did work in these venues, his doing so at such a young age is doubtful. "I don't know about that," was the response of Anna Berger, when told that Matthau supposedly had worked as a vendor as early as 1931. "He and Ruby and Henry went around selling ice cream, but they were much older than that." Indeed, Ludwin confirmed that they were older than eleven, but added that only he and Walter worked the theaters.

The boys labored for a 15 percent commission; during a busy week, they might earn upwards of $2.50. Well into adulthood, Matthau vividly remembered the ambience, noting that the Second Avenue Theatre, one of the higher-profile Yiddish houses, was located "right across the street from Moskowitz and Lupowitz's Romanian Broiler." Being a constant presence in the theater, and becoming immersed in the imaginary world created on the stage, allowed him to "be transported to a realm beyond which there was nothing but great drama and beauty and interest."

At first, Matthau had no notion that he might actually work on stage. "The only thought I gave was to selling ice cream and cherry drinks; any other thought didn't quite enter my mind," he remembered. "The three-flavor bricks I was selling cost fifteen cents, an awful lot of money for a small brick, and in order to make it sound very official, I used to holler as loud as I could, 'Get your Federal Ice Cream here!' "

Nonetheless, the richness of the theater and the talents of its actors impressed the youngster. "I got to see many of the leading Yiddish actors, like Julius Nathanson, Herman Yablokoff, and Michael Rosenberg. I watched the way they worked. The idea of becoming an actor was lurking somewhere in my head."

In a rare interview, which appeared in *TV Guide* in 1963, Rose Matthow noted that her son would "come home and imitate the actors. He'd make up at the mirror. . . . And he was always at the movies, his head filled with things." (She also described young Walter as a "loud boy," to which he asserted, "*Loud?* I thought I was a quiet boy." "First quiet, then loud," Rose retorted. She also noted, "I didn't think he'd be a success and worried and worried. Most actors come from a fairly decent home. All that Walter had was struggle.")

"I was the one that guided him to becoming an actor," claimed Alex Brounstein. "He originally wanted to go into sportscasting. I used to hear him sing the various arias from the operas, and I knew there was a talent there. He kept talking about sportscasting and I told him, 'Look, Walter, people who are qualified to do certain things should be doing them. I've always heard you sing and hum these various arias, and you have a lot of talent. Please don't let it go to waste.'"

Eventually, Matthau began playing bit parts on stage, earning fifty cents a performance and working seven shows per week. Easily his most notable appearance was in a three-and-a-half-hour-long musical comedy called *The Dish-washer* (*Der Dishvasher*), which opened at the Second Avenue Theatre on December 1, 1936. The star was Yablokoff, a Polish-born actor-singer-songwriter-playwright-director-producer and longtime president of the Hebrew Actor's Union. The plot involved a young American woman (Bella Meisel, Yablokoff's offstage wife) who vacations in Havana and falls for a cabaret singer (Yablokoff), with the setting switching between Ellis

Island and a Cuban cafe. In the cast were such familiar Yiddish stage names as Leo Fuchs, Annie Thomashefsky, Dave Lubritzky, and Yudel Dubinsky. In a review that might have been a press release, a *New York American* critic wrote that the show "packs more variety in musical entertainment into a crowded evening than many other song and dance festivals combined. Here is a colorful and melodious production that has not only the typical 'Ziegfeld' touch of beauty, but combines a thrilling melodrama and musical comedy with a symphony concert."

Matthau vividly recalled how he was cast. During the first act, some immigration officers appeared; they were supposed to smack and blind the cabaret singer. By this time, the production's powers-that-be were well aware of the young man's vocal abilities. "They said, 'Let's get those two tall kids, Matthau and Bummie Tresser, they can play the immigration police.'"

Anna Berger recalled that Matthau, his brother Henry, and Ruby Ludwin played the cops. "I remember that show very well," she said. "In one scene, Yablokoff is down and out. He is asleep on a park bench, and Matthau and Ruby and Henry are playing police officers. So they come back with their clubs, and they say 'Get off the bench, you bum.' But they did it very lightly. So after the scene, [Yablokoff] tells the boys, '*Boyis*, you're policemen. You gotta be tough. You gotta act real tough, you're policemen. You *hef* to act.' So the next time they did the scene, they went to town on poor Yablokoff. And then he said, 'It's only fa fun, *boyis*. It's only fa fun.'"

At the finale, an eighty-piece orchestra came on stage, consisting of real and pretend musicians. Matthau appeared as a make-believe cellist "because I could imitate a real cellist better than anyone else. I hammed it up like Itzhak Perlman." Berger recalled Matthau's account of the story: "He's playing the bass fiddle and—bing—one string breaks. Then, bing—the other string breaks. Meanwhile, Yablokoff is watching, and he says [in Yiddish], 'You sonofabitch bestid.' He was cursing the life out of Walter."

Matthau's other Yiddish stage credits are imprecise. "To my knowledge, the only show he did was *Dish-washer*," noted Berger. Matthau claimed to have appeared in *The Organ Grinder*, which starred Julius Nathanson, cast as an elderly woman in a shawl.

Fifteen-year-old Lillian Lux, later a Yiddish stage star, was in the chorus, and recalled that Matthau was a "candy boy" who "used to bring me back a Hershey bar. He'd walk me to the subway." But she did not recall Matthau being an extra in the show. Meanwhile, Ruby Ludwin confirmed his appearance in *Sergeant Naftula*, starring Leo Fuchs, who was heralded as the "Yiddish Ray Bolger." "In *Sergeant Naftula*, I was one of three soldiers playing pinochle in a foxhole," Matthau noted. "Fuchs bids 300, someone else bids 350, I say '400,' and then the whole trench explodes, we're all dead." According to Matthau, Fuchs may have been all tattered and bloody, but he remained ever the kibitzer as he lifted his head, looked at Matthau's cards, and exclaimed, "He wouldn't have made it."

"I was very relaxed on stage," Matthau recalled, "and not at all nervous or afraid of the audience." Meanwhile, he relished the theater ambiance. "I used to feel wonderful in the theaters—with the actors talking to each other, the girls changing costumes, the smell of stale smoke, the dampness, the upholstered chairs, the musty rugs, the buzzing in the audience, and the dead silence just before the curtain went up."

Being on hand every evening to observe the master performers of the Yiddish stage proved a special benefit for the youngster. One actor, Michael Rosenberg, became a role model. The Warsaw-born Rosenberg was a member of Maurice Schwartz's Yiddish Art Theatre and a veteran East Side stage actor who later worked as a comedian/ monologist in the Catskill Mountain resorts. It was from Rosenberg that Matthau first learned the art of comic timing. "The minute he walked onstage, he had his audience," Matthau said. "He brought a whole world out with him. He was just a little guy who wore wigs and beards—very unprepossessing off stage—but he was the most interesting actor I've ever seen. He had electricity."

During the 1970s, Matthau appeared at a benefit at the Public Theatre, a former Yiddish playhouse on Second Avenue and East Fourth Street, organized by Seymour Rexite, who had become president of the Hebrew Actors Union. He enjoyed speaking with Rexite, who noted that revisiting the Public "brought back wonderful memories to him."

While Matthau was spending his evenings and weekends immersed in the Yiddish theater, his days were consumed with his studies. His growing self-confidence allowed him to sign on as campaign manager for student candidates in Seward Park elections. Years later, he explained his success in this capacity by noting that his classmates were impressed by "the way I stood or looked or sounded." Often, when he came to the forefront in the school auditorium to promote a candidate, "the audience would start to laugh even before I opened my mouth." He also performed recitations. "Walter sometimes would appear in the 'amateur hours,' in front of the school assemblies," noted Maxie Eisenberg, a Lower East Side pal. "The only thing he did was an imitation of Maurice Chevalier. He would put on a straw hat and sing 'Mimi,' and bring the house down."

In general, Matthau was a good student, and even won a spelling championship. Outside class, he hung out with his pals, played handball, worked in the Yiddish theater, and hustled to earn nickels and quarters. He was no ladies' man; he neither dated nor attended school dances.

Yet he certainly was noticing the opposite sex. This awareness, combined with his sensitivity, was expressed in a poem he wrote that was printed in the January 1939 Seward Park High School *Folio*. It was titled "To Carolyn"; the byline was "Walter Matthow, '39." Matthau wrote:

> *My vision in the night,*
> *My thoughts throughout the day,*
> *The echo of my heart,*
> *The blessing when I pray.*
>
> *Your face, that always has*
> *A bright and hazel glance.*
> *The song upon your lips,*
> *Whose tender tones entrance.*
>
> *The spirit of my soul,*
> *The flame that never dies,*
> *The look that still remains*
> *In passion hungry eyes.*

CHAPTER 3

Building Confidence

Matthau graduated from high school in January 1939. "President of Annex 22; Seward World; *Folio* Staff; Track Team; and Class Day Committee" were listed in the Seward Park yearbook as his extracurricular activities. A quotation was printed underneath each student's name and accomplishments, the purpose of which was to capture the essence of the individual. Matthau's citation: "Ripe in wisdom is he."

Upon graduation, Matthau—whose financial situation precluded him from attending college—began accepting odd jobs. He was a floor washer in a Lower Manhattan factory, a file clerk for the National Youth Administration, a boxing coach and gym instructor for the Police Athletic League.

A couple of years earlier, Rose, Henry, and Walter settled into a Lower East Side flat that was a step up for them in that it included a private bathroom. The address was 96-98 East First Street. Yvonne Rogow (whose maiden name was Slootsky) resided several doors away, at 88-90. "Walter spent a good deal of time in my house, as well as frequently walking with my father," she recalled. "Many years later, he told me that he used my father's shuffling gait in one of his early 'old man' characters."

Maxie Eisenberg, with whom Matthau played handball, lived at 96-98. "Walter was head and shoulders above the rest of us," he recalled. "We were shrimps; he was a giant; and we used to kid him about this." Walter passed this playful needling down to the younger kids. Milton Schnur, three years his junior, also lived on First Street. "We all thought we were tough guys, you know, like Jimmy Cagney," Schnur noted. "One time, we were standing outside Hoch's candy store, where we used to hang out. I was smoking a cigar. He looked at me and said, 'Hey, kid, you got the bottom of your pants tied?' I said, 'Why?' He said, 'You're liable to shit in your pants, and it'll go all over the floor.'" For two decades, through 1978, Schnur worked at Kennedy Airport "selling tax-free cigarettes and whiskey. We'd get a list of VIPs coming in and leaving the country. When Walter would be coming in, I made it a point to run into him." Schnur joked, "He'd be walking down with some beautiful starlet and I'd say, 'Hey, Walter, you still smoking those shitty cigars, those White Owls?'"

To some in the neighborhood, Matthau was a regular guy. "He was a member of the Boy's Club of New York, as I was," recalled Herb Green. "He worked out at the gym, played a little billiards and ping-pong. He went to the Saturday night socials." But others sensed that he was separating himself from the crowd. "I hate to use the word loner, but he didn't hang out on the block like we did," noted Maxie Eisenberg. "After the Settlement [Recreation Rooms and Settlement, on First Street] closed at ten in the evening, instead of going home we would stand out on the sidewalk, shooting the breeze, you know, chit-chatting with the girls. He didn't join us. He had other exploits." Added Barney Weiner, "He was a fairly quiet guy. He was a studious guy. When we'd play stickball, he would walk around with a book. He'd sit on the curb and read." Around this time, Walter and Henry played handball in Coney Island with Frank Russo, who would become the father of actress Patty McCormack. "My dad told me that [when he was not playing] Walter used to sit in the peanut gallery reading," McCormack noted. Milton Schnur added that Walter was "determined to be an actor, and we made a lot of fun of it. But not to his face."

Also living at 96-98 was Anna Berger, then a young, artistically inclined actress wannabe who encouraged Matthau to pursue an acting career. "We knew each other when we were adolescents," she recalled, several months after his death, "and we remained friends to the very end."

Berger was one of eight children living on the building's second floor. The Matthows were on the fourth floor. Walter was in his upper teens when they met; she was a bit younger. "She was wild for him," was how Murray Juvelier described her feelings for Matthau.

"I liked Walter right away because he was more interesting than anyone else I knew before," Berger recalled. "I had to go up to his house once to deliver something my mother had made for [our] 'new neighbor,' and Walter was playing classical music on a Victrola. He knew every composer and every piece of music there was. I was fascinated, and so impressed." Added Anna's older brother, Jack, "I always would hear opera arias in the hallway. It would be Walter, singing the 'Anvil Chorus' and 'Give me those men, those stout-hearted men.'"

Most of Matthau's pals primarily were interested in dating. These immigrants' sons saw their futures in finding jobs, marrying Jewish girls, and saving enough money to leave the Lower East Side for the upward mobility of New York's outer boroughs. Matthau once observed that, had he not taken up acting, he might have become "a presser or a cutter" in the city's garment district. Perhaps he would have risen to the position of salesman. His $50 weekly salary would have allowed him to rent a $50-per-month apartment miles from the Lower East Side. "Where I grew up," he declared, "if you'd made it to the Bronx you were part of the gentry. To the Lower East Side, the Bronx was Bel Air." Population shifts eventually led many of his childhood compatriots first to Long Island, and then to retirement in Florida.

Very few of their contemporaries were drawn to music and the-ater, so it is understandable that Walter and Anna gravitated towards each other. First, however, he joined the Civilian Conservation Corps, where he found himself working as a forester in Belton, Mon-tana. He earned a dollar a day; each month, he sent $23 home to his mother. "I was an axeman," he recalled. "I chopped down trees, piled up the logs, fought fires." The physical nature of the work allowed Matthau to add muscle to his thin frame. He also started smoking cigars. Yvonne Rogow recalled that, while in the CCC, he "broke his hand in a fight with someone who made an anti-Semitic remark." Upon returning home in 1940, he had a short-lived job with the Works Project Administration as a boxing and basketball coach, earning $23 a week.

Pre-CCC, Walter and Anna merely were neighbors. "But when he came back we both got a little more courage and started talking to each other," she explained. "Then we became inseparable. Matthau and I spent practically every waking moment together. Actually, he was my first boyfriend." Despite their romantic feelings, the relationship never became sexual.

"My family loved him, and he loved my family. He spent more time in my house than in his own." Added Milt, her youngest brother, "Walter was like part of our family. He was always down in our apartment, talking art, talking theater."

Because of his sporadic income, Walter and Anna's dates were like scenes from a Depression-era movie about unemployed urban romantics. "We used to walk across the Williamsburg Bridge," Berger noted. "That was our big date. If he had some money, we'd have coffee. If not, we wouldn't. And we would recite Shakespeare—mostly, he would—and then we would both dream of being [professional] actors, which, of course, seemed like million-to-one odds at the time.

"Once in a while, when he had a bit of money, he would take me on a double decker bus, the Fifth Avenue bus. And that was romantic. When he did have some money, Walter would buy cigarillos; those were very expensive cigarettes. Even with no money, he aspired to good taste."

At the time, Berger was, as she explained, "considered the neighborhood actress." Since age six, she had been performing at the Recreation Rooms and Settlement. She knew she wanted an acting career, but felt she never could succeed because "I wasn't beautiful. I didn't look like Ginger Rogers. I thought, 'If you weren't blonde and skinny and beautiful, how could you ever be an actress?'"

Nonetheless, she and Matthau imagined themselves the stars they saw in the movies, portraying their on-screen characters. Anna became Margaret Sullavan and Greer Garson, while Walter was Gary

Cooper, John Wayne, and Walter Pidgeon. "We would spend hours going through the gestures, and then we'd schmooze, and then we'd kiss," she said. "I thought he was the best kisser in the whole world, and I think he thought the same of me. And we really loved each other, and admitted it to each other as well."

The key to their attraction, ultimately, may have been intellectual curiosity. "I was reading a lot about Freud at that time," Berger explained. "So I got him interested in that. We did a lot of reading about the subconscious, and theater, and Shakespeare, and music. He used to take me to Lewisohn Stadium. There were free concerts, and we'd sit on a hard concrete bench for the concerts and listen to *Ein kleine nacht musik*. To this day, whenever I hear this, I think of those hard concrete seats—and of Walter.

"Another thing that attracted me to Walter was that he loved poetry. What boy from the Lower East Side loved poetry? I still have a book of poetry he gave me on his twenty-first birthday. He also gave me a book on operas and composers. And he knew the opera stars. I was not into that. He introduced me to all this. We were finding out about life together."

Matthau also mixed with Berger's siblings. Her kid brother Alex recalled, "My older brother Larry was a very intelligent boy. Walter was envious of him. One day, Walter got a dictionary and studied page after page after page. Then he came down and challenged Larry to a game of 'definitions.' Larry beat him hands-down."

One of Anna's most distinctive memories of Matthau during this period involves his lack of sartorial splendor. "I think of Walter sometimes, standing on the stoop waiting for me with his pants shiny from wear," she remembered. "[He had on] a pair of pants that had been worn forever.

"Matthau was tall, and very self-conscious about his height. I was overweight, and he was very tall. So we made a fine couple! And he always had very bad skin. But I still thought he was very attractive despite everything."

Berger admitted that Walter's brother Henry was better-looking. "Henry was straightforward, honest, down-to-earth, real—and more handsome, in the commercial sense. [But] Walter had charisma, and was sexy, I thought. People would say, 'Walter, sexy?' But he was."

Berger's view was not shared by all. "He was not good-looking," maintained Grace Schneider Sealine, who lived around the block, on First Avenue. "He was not attractive at all. Look at the pictures!" Even Matthau himself commented that, as a youngster, he was discouraged from pursuing an acting career by friends and family. "They reasoned that actors were handsome, even-featured Anglo-Saxon types," he noted. "They said no one would want to see a gangling, shy, pimply Jewish boy from the ghetto. They said I should be a writer, where no one could see me."

Yet in later years others found him appealing. Anne Jackson, with whom he appeared on television in the comedy pilot *Acres and Pains* and on screen in *The Secret Life of an American Wife* during the 1960s, noted, "I was obviously very fond of Walter," and then kiddingly added, "and scared to death of him. He was bigger than life, and he intimidated me. He was taller than I was, and playing a love scene with him, well I could almost giggle. Not that he wasn't an attractive man. He was. He was extremely attractive, and Carol, his darling wife, would always say, 'He's the sexiest man I know.'" Betsy Palmer, Matthau's co-star on live television in the 1950s, declared, "He had great sex appeal, you know. The man was most, most attractive, in his wonderful, crazy way." The five-foot-seven-and-a-half Palmer appreciated Matthau's height. "By the time I got in heels I was pretty tall," she added, "so tall men were kind of comfortable for me."

Jayne Meadows, another 1950s Matthau TV co-star, had a supporting role in the 1999 feature *The Story of Us*. One day, the film's star, Bruce Willis, was "asking about the old days, and I said, 'Bruce, where men are concerned, it does not matter what a man looks like. It does not matter even if he can act in the movies.' He said, 'What does matter?' I said, 'Charm.' I was just talking to my housekeeper, and I said, 'In my first movie in Hollywood, I played opposite Robert Taylor, one of the handsomest men who ever lived. A darling man, but not a great actor, but good enough for the movies. I went down the list of all these men [with whom I'd worked]—Tyrone Power, Robert Montgomery, Gregory Peck. The ones I was most attracted to were William Powell and David Niven. Neither of these men, in my opinion, would be called handsome. But they were charming—and that was what I thought about Walter.

"Walter was the opposite of handsome, but he was a brilliant actor. And charm—oooh, such charm. He had sex appeal, and he wasn't good-looking. But he made you think he was good-looking after you got to know him. Walter was a flirt, and very appealing to women, in my opinion. It was the old charm bit."

That charm remained alive well into Matthau's old age. In 1995, Piper Laurie appeared with him in *The Grass Harp*. "When I look at his earlier movies, I thought he was a very attractive man," she noted, "and I found that when we were working together, his energy and humor and self-confidence were very attractive. I found him very sexy, even though he was not so pretty anymore. It was that energy, I think, and that self-confidence [that made him so appealing]."

Matthau still was years away from mixing with the Jacksons, Palmers, Meadowses, and Lauries—and from working as an actor. Berger, meanwhile, became affiliated with the National Youth Administration, which she described as being "the junior part of the WPA [Works Project Administration]. They would provide work for the unemployed, and I was assigned to the drama division, as an actress. I earned $25 a month. At least that was an income. And I had a chance to act." Of her boyfriend, she added, "I used to schlep him to all the community groups and theatre groups, and get him involved, get him auditions, because there was also a shyness about him. I had such confidence in his being a good actor, [so] I would push him. I would say, 'You gotta, you gotta, you gotta.'

"He would walk with a stoop, and I would tell him, 'Matthau, stand straight and tall. Whatever disadvantage you have, put it to your advantage. Do you know how great it is to be six-foot-three?' And he would try to straighten up."

Matthau attempted to join the WPA's Federal Theater Project, but was rebuffed. He was caught in a Catch-22 situation: He was turned down because of lack of experience, yet how was he to gain that experience? At Berger's urging, he tried her drama group. "You've got to audition my friend, Walter Matthow," she told the director. "No, we're not taking anybody else," was the response.

As Berger told the story, "I hocked and hocked and hocked, until he said, 'Okay, Annie, okay. Tell him to come in for an audition.' The one thing he knew he could possibly use was "Casey at the Bat." I was so excited for him. I remember he went to audition and I was outside waiting. . . . He came out with the director, and the director put his arm around Walter's shoulder and said, 'Have you ever thought of the garment district? You would make a great salesman.' Matthau always told that story whenever we got together in California. Whenever he would introduce me, he would say, 'This is Annie Berger. She's responsible for my being an actor.'"

Berger reported that, finally, her boyfriend was "hired by Miss Kilka, of the University Settlement, which was on Forsythe Street." He also found a new job, from which he earned the bulk of his meager income while continuing to bulk up his frame: cement bag hauler.

When Walter, Anna, and their generation were coming of age, jobs were scarce, the American economy was teetering on the brink, and many young intellectuals were seeking political and economic alternatives to a system they viewed as having failed. "I was shaped by the whole experience of the Depression," Matthau recalled, "the humiliation of the competition in the theater, the humiliation of poverty." He once stood in line for three hours to apply for a job as a sanitation worker. The salary: $1,700 a year. After leaving in frustration, he began walking down the street. Passing by a department store, he eavesdropped on two women conversing about the fur coats on display in the window. "I think the $12,000 one is better than the $15,000 one," noted the first. Matthau thought to himself, "Let's see, ten years of sweeping horse manure. . . . If I worked a hundred years, I could never afford that coat."

At the height of the Depression, Rose and her boys were one of thousands of New York families on Home Relief, receiving $13 a month for rent and 27 cents clothing allowance. Beyond this, Rose told Anna Berger that the only people who assisted her through the starvation period with Walter and Henry were Communist Party members. "They helped her financially; they got her some income," Berger noted. "So Rose was attracted to the Communist Party." Rose also reportedly became involved with the American Labor Party, a New York State political body organized in 1936 by labor leaders, socialists, and liberals to support the reelection of President Franklin D. Roosevelt without having to endorse the Democratic Party machine. The Party backed any candidate, Democrat or Republican, who favored progressive, social-oriented legislation. However, Rose was no card-carrying party member. Similarly, Berger described Walter as being "very progressive, and he was strongly influenced by the socialist system. But I know he never became a communist." In his old age, Matthau preferred to describe himself as "sort of pro-Roosevelt."

In the late 1940s, when Matthau and Berger were attaining their first stage roles, the United States was about to be spooked by a Red Scare. Joseph McCarthy, the junior senator from Wisconsin, claimed that communists had infiltrated the government. The House Un-American Activities Committee held hearings into alleged communist infiltration of Hollywood, resulting in the blacklisting of hundreds of industry professionals.

Had Matthau and Berger been more publicly radical, they might have had their careers snatched away from them. This did not happen because, as Berger explained, "We never signed anything, and so I was not affected and Walter was not affected."

"He was always for the workers," she added. "We'd be out until four in the morning on our walks across the bridge, and the newspapers would be out by then, and this little old newspaper vendor would be yelling 'Morning *Journal*. Morning *Journal*.' So Matthau would say, 'Never mind the *Journal*. How about the [more progressive] *Freiheit*?'" His son Charlie further explained, "My father was always oriented toward the underdog. Not just involving anti-Semitism, but also civil rights, and for everybody to be equal. In a way, maybe it was good that he wasn't more famous a few years [earlier], because he probably would have been blacklisted.

"He was not a communist, but he probably would have described himself as a socialist in the sense of his wanting a greater safety net for people who were disenfranchised."

At this early stage, his politics were tied to his dream of expressing himself through acting. Ossie Davis, who worked with Matthau on stage during the 1950s and on screen four decades later, remarked, "Back in those days when the theater was a part of the cultural richness of New York, when we actors dared to think we were important enough to be concerned about world events—before the McCarthy people had cut us down—we thought acting was a serious proposition. That sort of flavor of social importance was always a part of what Walter did.

"I would say Walter, like myself, was a bit more than a liberal. We were really left-wingers. We took an extremely radical position, in some instances."

CHAPTER 4

The Gambler

If Matthau's politics did not impact on his career, one aspect of his character did affect every phase of his life: his addiction to gambling.

"It was a terrible poison, the gambling," Rose Matthow declared in 1963. "He had that fat friend of his, who got him into it." Her son, who was present, corrected her. "Mother, I was gambling when I was six years old, only you didn't know about it." His betting also affected their relationship. "I think she may have been closer to Henry, because they were on the same wavelength," explained Charlie Matthau. "My father was a compulsive gambler, which really [upset] her because she was a money-psychotic, and it really pissed her off that he showed no respect for money with his gambling."

The little boy who, once upon a time, had organized Bankers and Brokers card games on tenement rooftops had grown into a big-stakes gambler. Jack Lemmon, his longtime friend and co-star, reported, "If you couldn't find Walter on the set, you could look in the phone booth; he'd be placing a bet."

According to his own account, Matthau began frequenting race-tracks on New Year's Day, 1950. He was in Miami, in the company of his friend, director Martin Ritt.

Matthau asked Ritt, "Who do you like?"

"Nobody," Ritt responded.

"Why are you here?" Matthau asked.

"I'm studying," Ritt answered.

Matthau joined him, and began perusing the *Racing Form*.

"I like this horse," Ritt exclaimed.

"From studying?" Matthau asked.

Ritt responded that his bookmaker liked the horse. He bet $500. Matthau bet $100. The horse lost.

"With that stunning success," Matthau recalled, "I was hooked."

After Ritt's death in 1990, Matthau recalled, "Marty was an immaculate handicapper, but he was very secretive—he'd never tell me what horse he liked." The reason: "In those days, if I got a bet down, it might influence the odds."

Matthau would not gamble merely on horseraces and ballgames. Recalled Bob Mills, with whom he played handball in the 1950s, "I used to kid him. I'd say, 'If we had a couple of cockroaches, you'd bet on which one would beat the other one to the hole.'" Matthau, in fact, did make such wagers. He might bet $1,000 on whether or not a companion knew the capital of Albania. His old friend, comic actor Howard Morris, noted, "I was with him when he would get on the phone, and he'd say, 'Well, I'll lay you ten grand on the next free shot [free throw].' It's what Shaquille doesn't do very good. And he would bet ten grand on it, from where he stood at the phone." Publicist Murray Weissman, with whom Matthau shared a three-decades-long association, reported, "They tell the story that he would bet on anything, and that he once placed a sizable bet on which of two flies would leave a wall first." Added Larry King, "Once we were at the same black-tie event in Beverly Hills. We were coming out at the same time, and he said, 'I'll bet you $20 whose limo comes first.'" King won the wager.

It is impossible to estimate Matthau's lifetime gambling losses. One rather conservative speculation is that he dropped upwards of $5 million. Late in life, he freely admitted to Roger Ebert, "I've made $50 million over the years as a movie star, if you'll pardon the expression, and I've given most of it to the bookies."

When money was low, he wagered the change in his pocket. "He would bet dollars on handball games," recalled Maxie Eisenberg, "and I don't even think he had a dollar in his pocket. If he wasn't participating in a game, he'd be on the sidelines betting on the outcome."

Added Murray Juvelier, "We had a poolroom called Solly Blacks, on Houston Street. In those days, when you came in to make a bet, you had a little piece of paper that you wrote out [the bet], and you put the money in the paper, and you handed it to somebody, and they would slide it underneath the pool table. If you hit, you came back. If you lost, you didn't. In those days [Matthau bet] small money, two, three dollars."

Matthau's career as a cement bag hauler was short-lived. "He was lost," noted Jack Berger. "He had no income. I worked for Paramount Stationery, and had the power to hire errand boys at $8 a week. One Friday afternoon I said to him, 'If you want to come in on Monday, we'll put you to work.' He said, 'It's a deal.' Monday came and went, and no Walter. I checked with his mother and she said, "Oh, he had to leave town.' It turned out that the bookies were after him."

"Frankie the Nose became very friendly with Walter," recalled Alex Brounstein. "I think he handled the bets [for] the big operators in New York. One night Walter says to me, 'Hey, Much, I made a bet with Spunky Jack [a bookmaker].' Sure enough, he hit, for $1,500. I don't think he had fifteen cents in his pocket." This win was an aberration, as his losses far outweighed his victories.

Anecdotes about Matthau's gambling followed him throughout his life. A typical—and terrifying—one was recounted by Marian Seldes. "Once when we were having lunch at the Beverly Hills Tennis Club," she reported, "he opened up the trunk of his car, and [then] opened up an attaché case. It was packed with money, the way you see in movies. [It was] because of some betting or something. There were thousands and thousands of dollars. The money was all done up the way you get it in a bank, with the band still around it." Seldes concluded, "It was very scary."

Matthau once admitted that his mother had saved $1,200, and he "forged her name on [her] bankbook and took out the money and lost it in one week, gambling. When she found out about it, she was very sad. So I always felt guilty about that. I paid her back eventually." This, arguably, was his gambling nadir.

Although the incident seems like the prank of a shameless youth, it actually happened after World War II, when Matthau was studying acting at the New School for Social Research. "We were in theater school, living on $65 a month from the GI Bill," recalled Marvin Silbersher, Matthau's fellow student and friend. "One day he calls me and says, 'Marvin, can you help me out? My mother Rosie's gonna be thrown out on the street. We can't pay the rent. $25.'" Silbersher added that Matthau made the request a second time. On both occasions, his mother loaned Rose the money.

"Walter would be behind on the baseball games, $20,000," Silbersher declared. "One night after *Twelfth Night* he said to me, 'Hey Marv, you live in New Jersey?'"

"Yes Walter, of course."

"Small town?"

"Yes, I live in Millburn."

"We have to go to Millburn tonight. We're going to Millburn tonight. The bookies are looking for me."

"This became a commute for Walter," Silbersher continued. "He was in my house a half-dozen times, hiding from the bookies. He'd be ahead $30,000 on the baseball games, then he'd be $10,000 behind. And we're living on $65 a month."

"I actually had some conversations [with him] about his gambling," noted Matthau's son, David. "Our son Willie has Attention Deficit Disorder, and I actually have been diagnosed with it, too. I had an ongoing dialogue with my father about what kinds of treatments were good ideas. We discussed the use of Ritalin, and he was always sending me articles about potential dangers, sort of a negative slant on it.

"At one point, I was talking to him about it and I said, 'Well, you know, frankly, Dad, if you had really ever been diagnosed as having Attention Deficit Disorder and taken Ritalin, I think there's a good chance that you would not have had to resort to gambling to sort of self-medicate yourself. And you probably would have saved yourself a lot of money and aggravation.

"And without even stopping to say anything or to think about it, he came right back and said, 'Yeah, you could be right.' It was like there was one real strong grain of truth in that suggestion, that he kind of responded to immediately. I always found that really interesting."

Walter told Anna Berger that he got a rush from gambling, but only after losing $40,000–$50,000. Son David noted, "I remember hearing my father talk about gambling, and putting it in terms like it's the only time he ever felt awake, alive. And that's why I kind of suspected [he had Attention Deficit Disorder]; you know, that's a very typical A.D.D. kind of thing, where you get yourself in perilous situations as a way to hyper-focus. [This is] not at all uncommon.

"And then, in the latter years, he's always making jokes, although he would tell people that he was serious, that he had stopped gambling: 'Good thing I don't have to bet on this game.' Meanwhile, I'm sure he did."

One anecdote, as told by Matthau, offers insight into his addiction. While in Florida in 1959 shooting the TV series *Tallahassee 7000*, he rented an oceanview apartment for his mother. Upon visiting her one day, he observed that her purse was stuffed with toilet paper, which she had pilfered from restaurants. After pronouncing that it was unnecessary to steal bathroom tissue, he "took out $8,000 in cash, gave it to her, and told her to buy as much toilet paper as she wanted." Rose responded by telling him, "It's not the money." Her son grabbed the toilet paper, and headed into the bathroom. Rose followed him, and soon the two were wrestling over the paper. "I won the fight, threw the toilet paper into the bowl, and walked out," he added. "I came back later that afternoon to see my mother. She was out on the balcony drying the toilet paper. Now you know why I could bet $5,000 and $10,000 on a ballgame. It gets me away."

Early on, and well into adulthood, Matthau disregarded the effect gambling had on his life. While at the New School, he debated his actor pal Dan Frazer on which was the worst addiction, drinking or gambling. Frazer recalled, "I told him once, 'With gambling, it can affect the whole family,' as if drinking didn't. Walter didn't drink, but I was a drinker, you know. It was just the idea that Walter was defending gambling, that it wasn't as bad as drinking. And I said, 'No, gambling can affect the whole family,' implying that drinking didn't."

Across the years, Matthau's views on the subject markedly changed. "I think [gambling is] worse than alcoholism," he pronounced decades later. "I think it's worse than cancer." He also stated that gambling "reduces your consciousness to a tiny dot, and takes you away from that loose-end feeling, that feeling of non-completion. The gambler, if he wins, thinks that's an omen, a sign, and he feels omnipotent—until the reality sets in, and the vigorish starts to grind you down."

Matthau often was asked point-blank why he bet. "I wish to hell I knew," was his response in 1971. "I had the gambling disease. I was addicted. I've read every book on the subject. I still don't know how it got to me. Maybe it was because my first marriage was coming apart. I got a divorce at the time I lost the $183,000. . . . That was in 1958. Maybe I was trying to escape from someone or something." While publicizing *Casey's Shadow* in 1976, in which he played a horse trainer, he noted, "Betting to win is not my objective. My objective is simply to experience some kind of apprehension that spurts blood into my coronary arteries from my adrenaline glands and constricts them. As soon as my coronary arteries get constricted, I feel terrible, which is the kind of feeling I'm comfortable with. If I'm a loser, then I don't have to feel guilty about being a success." In 1978, he chided his addiction while thumbing through a newspaper's sports pages. His hands trembled as he joked, "The fever is coming upon me—I need . . . I need . . . a fix." Then he noted, "Losing at gambling balances the inner books. I'm getting even with my psyche and my mother. I really hate it, it's so destructive. I have a name of a bookmaker right here. . . ." He peered at the paper and declared, "Oh my God. UCLA versus Arkansas." He still was pondering the question in 1990, when he said, "I'm not betting to win. I'm betting for the arousal factor, for the bigger emotion. I've been trying to figure out lately why I do it."

Matthau's friend, actor William Schallert, recalled that he once went to a psychologist to explore his gambling obsession. What did he learn? Schallert noted, "He told me, 'Oh, I'm trying to balance my inner books' and 'Well, I'm trying to demonstrate that money doesn't mean anything to me. Being that I'm Jewish, I'm trying to show that money is not important.'" Late in life, Matthau joked about gambling and psychoanalysis. One shrink he visited was a 400-pound man named Schwartz, whose presence upset him so that his betting increased. Another, Matthau wisecracked, wanted to be his bookie.

When seriously exploring the subject, Matthau reckoned that, by gambling, he may have been engaging in painful childhood games of insecurity, "the way I used to play with the idea that maybe my mother wouldn't come home from the job and feed me." He also admitted, "I think the reason gamblers habitually gamble is to lose. Because they know they have to lose, it's the law of averages. I'm not talking about bookies or gentlemen gamblers. I'm talking about the compulsive, neurotic gambler. Pain is what he's searching for. The emotion of pain. It's much greater than the emotion of pleasure. Bigger, larger, stronger. Therefore more interesting."

Over the years, Matthau paid dearly for his need to constantly reexperience that "emotion of pain." The pressure of watching horse races and basketball games, all the while knowing that he might lose or win a small fortune on a split-second knockout or last-minute basket, was a contributing factor to his suffering a heart attack at age forty-five. It also resulted in a permanent notch being worn into one of his thumbs by a fingernail on his opposite hand. "He would create stress for himself, through his gambling," noted his son Charlie. "He would not worry about the things that everyone else worries about, and then he'd create an artificial situation in which he'd be sitting there, sweating bullets over what the Kansas City Chiefs were gonna do on the next down."

Added his son David, "I think he understood the toll it was taking, but I don't think he really had the wherewithal to do anything about it, or that he really wanted to get help. I don't think that he ever *seriously* tried to seek assistance in stopping [the] habit. And I don't think he really seriously contemplated the kind of destructiveness that it had, not only on him but on the whole family, emotionally and financially.

"There was some inability or lack of desire to really ever seriously deal with it. It's a shame."

CHAPTER 5

War Stories

Like millions of Americans from Maine to New Mexico, Matthau's world was irrevocably altered on December 7, 1941, when the Japanese attacked the American naval force at Pearl Harbor and the United States was plunged into World War II. At first, he—as many Americans—did not comprehend the meaning of the attack. He learned of it while listening to the NFL Brooklyn Dodgers–New York Giants game on the radio. "I couldn't understand why they would have the audacity to interrupt a championship football game [actually, it was a regular season finale] to tell us about Pearl Harbor," Matthau recalled. "Later on, I found out why."

At the time, Matthau was unemployed. His brother Henry was working, and was the first to be drafted; he was, as Matthau explained, "the only means of support for the family, for my mother." So Walter went to the board and asked that Henry's notice be rescinded. In return, he promised to join the army immediately.

Matthau's rationale for donning a uniform: "I was reading about fascism and I thought the least I could do was to get in and try to kill a few bad guys. It was the least any Jew could do." Matthau's son Charlie revealed another incentive: "He wanted to get away from Grandma. Everybody in the army was always complaining about how bad the food was. He thought it was great; it was so much better than Grandma's cooking. Grandma was a terrible cook. [Years later] when we used to visit her in Florida, I used to put all the food in my pocket and then go to the bathroom and throw it out."

In mid-April, 1942, Matthau enlisted in the United States Army Air Corps. He never forgot his dog-tag number: 12062683. After basic training, he was sent to radio school in Savannah, Georgia. While away, Matthau maintained contact with Anna Berger. "I had a stack of letters from him, from the army. He always signed his letters 'Love and kisses.'" He also sent her a set of professionally photographed portraits of himself. All are headshots. In each, Matthau is properly posed in military uniform; in one, he even is grasping a pipe. On the back of one, it is inscribed, "Anna, Sweetest girl I ever knew. Walter."

Eventually, Matthau was shipped overseas to RAF station 144 in Old Buckenham, near Attleborough, England. As part of the Eighth Air Force, he was assigned to the 453rd Bomb Group. Al Dallmeyer, an airplane mechanic with the 735th squadron, recalled that Matthau was known on the base as "Matthews."

Matthau was a link-trainer instructor; his duties included teaching combat pilots how to fly long-range using radio signals. Countless Matthau mini-biographies list his job as radio cryptographer. "As far as I know, I never saw him do that," explained Tom Neilan, a B-24 nose-gunner-turned-link-trainer instructor who spent the better part of a year with Matthau. However, in 1980, 453rd Bomb Group historian Don Olds contacted Matthau, and asked him to provide a photo of him in uniform for a 453rd photo album/history. Matthau sent an autographed picture of himself dressed in western garb and on horseback. His inscription read, "Don, This is not the vehicle we used in the 453rd." He listed his jobs as battery maintenance man, radio operator, link-trainer instructor, and cryptographer.

While in England, Matthau sent Anna Berger's kid brothers Alex and Milt a recording he made. "We played it on our Victrola, and it was the entire 'Casey at the Bat,'" Milt recalled. "He sent it because he knew we loved baseball, and he sent my sister a book on composers, a big fat book about Beethoven and Sibelius." (Alex's wife Gloria explained, "In 1977, when our son Jon was being Bar Mitzvahed, Alex wanted to send an invitation to Walter. So we did, and a very generous check came along with a note in which he said that he couldn't come. But in it, he asked Alex, 'How can you have a son who's thirteen when you are only thirteen yourself?'")

Before Matthau went overseas, Anna Berger recollected that he, Hank, Ruby Ludwin, and Leon Levine, while home on furlough, feasted at Katz's Delicatessen, a culinary landmark located on Houston Street, across from First Street. "And I'll tell you, I still remember the amount of food those guys ate. It should have gotten into the world book of records." After he shipped out to England, Berger's mother sent Matthau packages of a Lower East Side delicacy: salami from Katz's, which became famous for the oft-quoted slogan, "Send a salami to your boy in the army."

However, this boy in the army was no spit-and-polish soldier. Matthau drank heavily, and claimed that he almost was court-martialed. Allegedly, he mouthed off to a captain, telling him, "If you didn't have that rank, sir, I wouldn't be averse to dropping you with a small left hook." Added Tom Neilan, "He couldn't get along with this major; he felt the guy was an asshole. If you didn't salute this son-of-a . . . If you walked by him, he was gonna dig you good." On one occasion, Neilan saluted him, but Matthau did not. "He chewed his ass out for about five minutes, in front of everybody standing along the road." Matthau himself was no authority figure. "I was a sergeant," he recalled. "I told the corporal what to do and he said, 'I'm not doing that.' I said, 'All right, I'll do it myself.'"

"I played on the tennis and table tennis team with the 453rd," added Neilan. "Walter was our manager. I hung around with him all the time; I'd see Ole' Matthau five days out of seven. It'd be in the evening, when we'd play. He used to say to me, 'Tom, you've got footwork like a boxer, you're pretty good on your feet.' Ole' Matthau, he got me to liking classical music, and he put on skits there at the 453rd, and plays. One was at Christmastime. But I had no idea he was going to be an actor."

When on leave, Neilan and Matthau headed for London. "We had some wild times," he recalled. "He took me all over the goddamned place. They had these Piccadilly Commandos. They all carried flashlights. They were prostitutes. We'd go into taverns and drink that crazy beer that was warm. They had this cider that would just about kill you. He could drink that pretty good.

"I had a lot of fun with him. He had a twinkle in his eye, and he had that little laugh. He was always making jokes, pulling pranks."

When asked if Matthau gambled, Neilan responded, "Oh my god yes. He and the others would carry around a cigar box filled with chips. They'd gamble in the mess hall." Five minutes after receiving his pay, Matthau would fritter it away in a crap game. "I was in a slit trench under a truck playing pinochle," he claimed, "and lost $1,500 because Schultz led with the wrong card. 'Schultz, you dumb sonuvabitch!' I said. Twenty years later, he came backstage at *The Odd Couple* and I shouted, 'Hey, Schultz, you dumb sonuvabitch.' He turns to his wife and says, 'He remembers me!'" (Another time, Matthau related a similar story, only here the game was played during a bombing raid. All the participants believed they were about to die, so they played for high stakes—and Matthau promptly lost $35,000.)

Also serving in Matthau's outfit was James Stewart, then an Oscar-winning movie-star-turned-bomber-pilot. Despite his fame, Stewart risked his life as heroically as any non-celebrity, flying missions over Germany. Matthau never claimed that he flew with Stewart, but he stated that he would sneak into Stewart's flight briefings.

After the war, when both were enrolled at the New School, Matthau became pals with actor-director Marvin Silbersher. "We both were in the Eighth [Air Force], but there was a big difference," Silbersher noted. "I was a combat flyer. I was doing thirty-five missions over Germany." With regard to Matthau attending Stewart's briefings, Silbersher noted, "He was the most incredible fantasist, shall we say. He had zero opportunity; you were not allowed into briefings if you weren't a flyer, or in the combat crew. You'd be stopped at the door." Neilan confirmed Silbersher's observation. When asked if Matthau was present during the briefings, he responded, "No. Matthau never had anything to do with Stewart, [who] was a squadron commander."

For once, Matthau was not kidding when he toasted Stewart at a 1980 American Film Institute tribute. Matthau was introduced as a "former staff sergeant"; with a period photo of himself projected behind him, he quipped, "I do look like a young Jimmy Stewart there

. . . or is it Laurence Olivier?" He added, "I know he's a brigadier general now, but I used to call him colonel when we were both in the 453rd bomb group in England during World War II." After lauding Stewart's patriotism, he concluded, "Colonel Stewart, for the men of the 453rd bomb squadron, I salute you."

Between December 1943 and May 1945, the 453rd participated in 259 missions over enemy territory. Fifty-eight aircraft were lost, along with the lives of 366 crew. It has been reported that Matthau participated in bombing runs over Germany. In his various *Playbill* biographies, it is noted that he spent "four years in the Army Air Force as a radio operator and gunner." From interviews he gave across the years, one might assume that, like any other frontline GI, Matthau witnessed death—and might have lost his life defending his country. He was never more lucid when he explained, "What was it, 60 percent killed? I had a great buddy [who was killed], and I took all his possessions home when I went back to New York, and it was very hard. I think that unconsciously there is some kind of wall that is erected by the survival instinct and that wall prevents you from falling apart and fainting and dying. What you really say is, 'Thank God it wasn't me.'"

Ruby Ludwin, Matthau's close boyhood pal, declared, "I don't think he saw any combat." Added his son Charlie, "My understanding is that he won several battle stars, but it wasn't for combat. It was for being near combat. He wasn't in foxholes, throwing grenades. He was modest about it. When I'd ask him about it, he was self-effacing. He'd say, 'Well, I took out my machine gun and started shooting at Nazis in a tree. But then I realized it was just shadows.'" When asked if Matthau was on any bombing missions, Tom Neilan responded, "No, no, no, no. He ran our table tennis team."

Matthau did not spend his entire time overseas in England. After one-too-many rows with the aforementioned major, Neilan recalled that Matthau "finally said, 'To hell with him. I'm outta here.' He pulled some strings. Paris was liberated, and he was over [there] helping the FFI, the Free French Underground, chase down collaborators." In a mini-biography that appeared in the program of one of his early New School productions, Matthau flippantly quipped that he "was arrested by the FFI in France on suspicion of being a Nazi 'because of [my] accent' and established [myself] as an American after some difficulty." Matthau remained in France until the war with Germany ended. "Then he came back to our base," reported Neilan, "and we came home on the U.S.S. *Hermitage*. He was a bunk above me on board ship."

Matthau may not have seen combat, but this is not to imply that he was fearful of battle. "They had a boxing ring on the ship," Neilan noted. "We went back there, and a lieutenant was beating the living hell out of some guy. Walter said, 'Let me take him on, Tom.' He takes off his shirt, and you can see his bony arms and black hairs all over. He was skinnier than shit. And he gets up and hits this guy with a left jab and a right cross and a left hook. Blood just splattered all over the place, and this guy's goin' down. And he walks back to me and says, 'What do you think about that?'" Neilan then described Matthau's lower-body ring moves as "the Walter Matthau shuffle."

Al Dallmeyer also witnessed the fight. He noted that the bouts were "nothing serious" and the combatants wore sixteen-ounce gloves, adding, "They just threw punches around; what damage could you do with sixteen-ounce gloves? They were like pillowcases." Yet Dallmeyer admitted that Matthau "sure knocked the hell out of him." Coincidentally, the lieutenant had been a boxing instructor with the New York City police department. It is not known whether Matthau knew this, and was recalling the various policemen who had hassled him and his pals on the Lower East Side as he bloodied the NYPD pugilist.

Upon arriving stateside, Matthau and Neilan were stationed at Fort Dix, New Jersey. After enjoying thirty-day leaves they headed west, where they met Cy Hoffman, another staff sergeant/link-trainer instructor. "Tom and Walt came to the air base at Reno, Nevada, where I was stationed. It was April 1945, and the Eighth Air Force in England was being disbanded," Hoffman explained. "He had a fair sense of humor; he was a jolly-go-lucky fellow. He wasn't serious about anything—but the gambling bug had bitten him good. He'd go into Reno and two or three days after payday he'd be flat broke." Neilan accompanied Matthau on these jaunts. "We played this blackjack," he recalled. "He could memorize two decks, but he couldn't memorize three. That's how we lost our ass, cause they had three decks in that damn Vegas."

Added Hoffman, "I do remember one time we were sitting around the barracks and talking about what we were going to do after the war. He said he was going to become an actor. One of the guys, I think he was from Georgia, said, 'Walt, you ugly bastard, who'd put out money to see you act?'"

Hoffman noted that Matthau "called his mother rather frequently. He thought the world of his mother." He added that, while in Reno, Matthau dated a WAC. He recalled her name as Barbara DiPersio. "She was a little Italian girl from Chicago," he said. "I think he had a few dates with her." Meanwhile, a more serious romance developed between Matthau and Charlotte Haverly. Anna Berger notwithstanding, Charlie Matthau reported that his father's "first real serious girlfriend was this woman Charlotte." Matthau himself described the five-foot-three, chestnut-haired, greenish-blue-eyed Haverly as "the first lady I had an *affair* with," noting that she was a "very smart lady, a little older than I."

The Barnard-educated Haverly, a divorcee seven years Matthau's senior, often has been described as a Red Cross nurse. Not so. In 1944–1945, she was the base's service club director. She was born in Northern Indiana, and grew up there as well as in Toronto and New York. She and Matthau met, and began dating.

"Walter had enough points that he was able to leave in the latter part of August," noted Cy Hoffman. "He went to a discharge center that was set up." That center was at McClellan Field in Sacramento, California. The date he was mustered out of the military was October 15, 1945. Matthau was two weeks past his twenty-fifth birthday. According to the Military Personnel Records division of the National Personnel Records Center, he had attained the rank of staff sergeant. His military decorations and awards were a Good Conduct Medal, a European-African-Middle Eastern Campaign Medal with One Silver Star and One Bronze Service Star, and a World War II Victory Medal.

Instead of heading home, Matthau returned to Reno, where he worked as a loader for Railway Express. He also was offered a job as a recreational director for the Boy Scouts in Tonopah, Nevada. Reno was attractive for two reasons: gambling and Charlotte Haverly.

Matthau often credited Haverly with pointing him in the direction of New York. He claimed she emphasized that the GI Bill of

Rights would allow him to support himself while studying. "She leaned toward acting," he said, "because she thought I was too lazy to write," and reported that Haverly eventually said to him, "Get out of Reno, because I can see that you're a little bit of a depraved gambler. Go to New York, and go to some dramatic school, or go to a writing school."

Matthau once noted, "I wonder what would have happened to me if she hadn't said that? I'd probably have stayed out West, wound up in some desk job, and been dead at the age of thirty-seven because I didn't like what I was doing." He added that he "didn't think the opportunities would ever be available to me, so I refused to dream," and concluded, "Charlotte knew me better than I knew myself."

Haverly, however, recalled that Matthau headed east on his own. "He lived in New York," she declared, fifty-six years after the fact. "That's where his mother was. That really was the best idea. New York was New York. He really wanted to study to be an actor, and I think he knew about this dramatic workshop. That's all he wanted to do. I told him it would be tough to get established, but he knew that. Being a gambler as he was, he probably thought anything was possible."

One thing on which they agreed: "He was an inveterate gambler," Haverly stated. "You can't cure them. He would have gambled no matter where he was."

So for the time being, Matthau kissed Haverly farewell, boarded a Greyhound bus, and headed home to New York.

CHAPTER 6

"Possibility, Comedy"

Of this immediate post-war period, Leon Birns noted, of the old Lower East Side gang, "We all were starting to spread out. We were getting jobs, getting married, and beginning to live our own lives." Superficially, Matthau's life did not change. He returned to First Street. He stayed around the neighborhood, and taught Milt Berger, Anna's ten-year-old brother, how to ride a bicycle.

Other Lower East Siders also were returning from the war. One was Murray Juvelier, who joined the air force and became "one of the first Jewish kids to come out of radar school in 1942." He flew "sonar-radar flights, submarine patrol" in Europe, and tested the radar on B-29s. Then he was assigned to a bomb group that flew missions over Japan. On December 18, 1944, "about ten Japanese fighters shot the shit out of us. Eventually, we flew a couple of hundred miles and ditched in the water. We got picked up by a sub." Juvelier also was on board one of the decoy planes that accompanied the Enola Gay, the B-29 that dropped the first atomic bomb on Hiroshima. "I flew forty-two times," he noted. "I wound up with twenty-three medals. Not pins, medals. But in the air force, that isn't too hard to accomplish."

Of Matthau, Juvelier noted, "I saw him in uniform on First Street. He was wearing a staff sergeant's uniform. I don't remember if he wore any cockamamie on his chest. I was really shocked to find out he was in the army in the first place. I wasn't really interested in him, or anybody else. I was interested in the boys who didn't come back, and in trying to get a memorial plaque for them."

For many a veteran, the war provided a lifetime's worth of high points that never would be repeated in civilian life. Yet for Matthau, his best years were well into his future.

For years, Matthau relished embellishing his acting credentials, telling interviewers he studied at the Moscow Art Theatre, Oxford University, and Dublin's Abbey Theatre. He also claimed to have enrolled in Columbia University's journalism school. "I think that was one of those things he made up," observed his son Charlie.

Actually, he used his GI Bill money to register at the New School for Social Research's Dramatic Workshop. "I could not have afforded to go to drama school without the GI Bill. Not in a million years," he once noted. He also observed, "There were nice people at the school, and every month there was a check from the government. It was simple."

The Dramatic Workshop was located in midtown Manhattan, at 247 West Forty-eighth Street, a block-and-a-half from Madison Square Garden. Matthau loved the location, because it allowed him to pop into the Garden for sporting events. According to classmate Louis Guss, he would bet on the basketball games at the Garden. "I remember he once said to me, 'Looie, if anybody comes around looking for me, you don't know where I am.'"

Anna Berger had been attending the Workshop since September 1945. "I was thrilled to get an acting scholarship to the [Workshop]," she said. "Walter was still in the army. When [he] came back, I told him, 'You gotta come to the Workshop.' So he finally decided that he too would go, and we were together again. We worked together in several productions."

A generation of actors and playwrights studied at the New School. Marlon Brando and Tennessee Williams predated Matthau there. (In 1967, Matthau once again stretched the truth when he declared that Brando attended the New School at the same time he did, "until they expelled him one day.") Among those who did study with Matthau were Rod Steiger, Harry Guardino, Harry Belafonte,

Elaine Stritch, Nehemiah Persoff, Tony Curtis, Bea Arthur, Judith Malina, Joseph Sargent (who later directed him onscreen in *The Taking of Pelham One Two Three* and in the television movie *The Incident*), and Gene Saks (who directed him onscreen in *The Odd Couple* and *Cactus Flower*, and acted with him onstage in *A Shot in the Dark* and onscreen in *I.Q.*). "I thought we were all great geniuses at that time," recalled Malina over a half-century later. "And some of us were."

Arthur Pollack, writing in the *Brooklyn Eagle* in 1946, noted that the students collectively "seemed to be as thick and lively as locusts" and concluded that "things are stirring in this little place. Big, fruitful things. A lot of growing is going on." "It was an inspiring place, and it was an inspiring group of people," explained Malina, the future co-founder and artistic director of The Living Theatre, the fabled avant-garde theater company. "We all were fervent about what we were doing, about acting and also expressing commitment, either personal or political." Given his Lower East Side history, Matthau fit right into the mix. "I think Walter was always good that way, politically responsible and aware," Malina added.

A Dramatic Workshop brochure from this period includes a "Notice to Veterans," in which it is stated, "The New School is authorized to accept veterans under the Serviceman's Readjustment Act of 1944. Veterans cannot be registered without their Certificates of Eligibility." As Rod Steiger once noted, admission standards were anything but stringent. "I did an audition," he said. "You got half a sentence out, [and] they said, 'Wonderful, great quality, fresh,' because they wanted the check from the government." Tony Curtis added, "We didn't know they *had* to accept us because we were veterans. You couldn't be turned down."

Still, the workshop aims were lofty: "To make the theatre that significant cultural force in the community for which it has all the potentialities—a proving ground for the problems of life—by instilling in students a feeling for the greatness of the profession." Among the courses required as part of the two-year curriculum: Acting Technique; History of American Drama; History and Sociology of the Theatre; March of Drama; March of Drama Repertory; New Plays in Work; Radio Acting; Seminar in Dramaturgy; Speech

Laboratory; and Voice and Diction. The tuition was $750 per year, with individual classes costing between $20 and $60. Productions were staged at two theaters: the President, a 280-seat house on West Forty-eighth Street; and the Roof Top, with a seating capacity of 1,000, located at Houston Street and Second Avenue, right in Matthau's old neighborhood.

One student with whom Matthau was closely linked was Tony Curtis, and not because they acted on screen together decades later in *Goodbye, Charlie* and *Little Miss Marker*. The two shared similar backgrounds. Both were native New Yorkers, and both were Jewish; Curtis, then known as Bernard Schwartz, grew up in poverty in the Bronx. Both first began acting in community settlement houses. Both saw World War II military service. Yet unlike Matthau, Curtis was a pretty boy whose looks helped lift him to movie idol status at the dawn of the 1950s.

Matthau's New School mentor was Erwin Piscator, an innovative German-born director-producer-playwright who worked on the New York stage between the mid-1920s and mid-1960s, and headed the Workshop from 1939 to 1951. Piscator was the former director of the Volksbuhne (People's Theater) and the Staatstheater (State Theater) of Berlin; producer-director of the Piscatorbuhne in the Nollendorfplatz, Lessing and Wallner theaters; and between 1936 and 1938, lecturer in dramatic art at the German University in Paris.

Rachel Rosenthal was a directing major who studied with Piscator in 1949, a couple of years after Matthau left the New School. "The funny thing about the Dramatic Workshop," she explained, "was that Piscator's style of acting was absolutely European, from the outside in. The other instructors were developing the 'Method,' and were completely from the inside, very psychological and naturalistic. When Piscator directed, he would do line readings and demonstrate exactly how to do it. He was a brilliant actor, male and female parts alike. But he would be exasperated when the students couldn't reproduce what he was demonstrating. They needed 'inner motivation,' and Piscator was 'Brechtian, Epic Theatre,' all about demo acting." Rosenthal recalled Piscator showing a student "how to play a 'stupid peasant' with 'stupid eyes.' It was brilliant, but you could see the student writhing in the pain of being quartered between the two methods. So there was a great dichotomy built into the school."

Judith Malina's take on the workshop was that it was "Piscator's school," noting his method involved acting out the meaning of an action, the "opening up of the real self and the tearing away of artifice." It also stressed a personal commitment to the political, the psychological, or the humane. "I think that Walter's commitment was always very humane," she explained. "I don't really know how Walter changed in his approach to acting. But watching him years later on the screen, I think that he continued to pursue certain principles that were taught by Piscator. And that was mostly relating yourself to the social, environmental, and political situation that you were in." Unlike Malina, Matthau never became involved in overtly political theater. Yet she noted, "I have a feeling that in all the movies he has made, he [elicited] a very personal, heartfelt, human style. He exposed the human [side of his characters] so deeply, much more than most actors in Hollywood ever get a chance to do, or try to do."

However, according to Rachel Rosenthal, the atmosphere at the workshop was rife with manipulation and gameplaying. "Piscator delegated guilt," she explained, "and the hierarchy was pyramidal. The guilt trickled down from above. The stress was so thick you could cut it with a knife. Still, the school spawned some really good artists, and I am proud to have been part of it." Matthau noted that some of the gameplaying had nothing to do with acting. He once told Leonard Maltin, "A lot of people called it The Neurotic Workshop for the New School for Sexual Research. Because that's what most people were doing there, they were looking for sex partners." Matthau then described himself as "still practically a virgin in those days. Maybe that's why I made out good in the acting field. I wasn't overwhelmed with the other activities going around."

For his part, Matthau described Piscator as "a weird, eccentric man, but he knew more about the theater than almost anybody else around at the time." He reported that Piscator told him, in clipped English, "Matthau, you say here every line wrong." "Another actor might have been destroyed," Matthau remembered. "I was destroyed for about twenty seconds." He implored the teacher to show him how to "say the line right." Piscator complied, and an actor was born. "One way or another," Matthau continued, "I began to learn how to talk, how to look, how to walk—how to act."

Later in life, Matthau downplayed the Workshop's role in

molding him as an actor. "He wasn't a big believer in acting class," noted his son Charlie. "[To him], it was like learning to be tall. He wasn't very articulate about talking about the process. It was just a gift.

"He always told a story about Mozart. A guy goes up to Mozart and says, 'Can you teach me how to write a symphony?' Mozart says, 'Why don't you start with a song? Symphonies are complicated.' The guy says, 'Yeah, but they can't be that complicated. You were writing them when you were four years old.' Mozart says, 'Yeah, but I didn't have to ask how.'"

Whatever he learned or didn't learn in acting class, one thing is certain: Matthau observed the manner in which people behaved, and developed his own personal theories that served him as he evolved as a stage actor. Even so, he was no instant master actor. "In his first performance on the stage, he played a farmer or a hick or something, with a straw hat and a straw in his mouth," recalled Alex Berger. "He was terrible. The people in the audience were laughing at him. But then he progressed." As he did so, he began honing his talent for comedy. Added sister Anna, "Matthau made a name for himself, but in a kind of crazy way. We did, he and I and Louie Guss, a play called *The Wandering Scholar from Paradise*, by Hans Sachs. It was very funny, and Walter was very funny; in fact, it was considered the funniest thing ever done at the workshop." "Anna was my wife," added Guss, "and I think Walter was the 'wandering scholar' who tries to seduce her. It was a hilarious success. He was a funny man, very New Yorkese. What made it funny was that you had three New Yorkers, with New Yorkese speech, doing a classic little play." Matthau received high praise from Piscator, who lauded his performance as the judge in *Volpone*. "He came backstage," Matthau noted, "and said, 'Possibility, comedy.'"

With Berger and Judith Malina, Matthau appeared in *The Aristocrats*. The women played inmates in a Siberian prison camp, and Matthau was a guard. He also played Shakespeare, appearing as Sir Toby Belch in *Twelfth Night*. His performance in *Lysistrata* impressed Berger. "He was such a genius in comedy. He came on stage as a senator, wearing a toga of that period, and he would be carrying a pizza! Well, he brought the house down. He would do such outrageous things. He was a courageous kind of actor. He did what the impulse dictated."

Twelfth Night was one of the productions staged at the Roof Top, which allowed for a number of Matthau's old cronies to conveniently attend. Years later, they could relate to Matthau playing Oscar Madison, but seeing him in leotards resulted in hoots and cat-calls.

While rehearsing *Twelfth Night*, Matthau met Marvin Silbersher. They became fast friends, dining twice a week at Roth's Delicatessen on Broadway between Forty-ninth and Fiftieth Streets and telling each other their life stories. Matthau and Silbersher palled around with Gene Saks; Matthau and Saks even were ushers at Silbersher's March 1952 wedding.

"One night, we were doing *Lysistrata*," Silbersher recalled. "Gene and I were onstage for a long time; we were wearing these togas, and so there was no place to put our wallets. So we left them with Walter, who was offstage. When we came offstage, Gene and I were saying, 'Now, let's have the wallets.' Walter said, 'I'm sorry, I went to the bathroom, the wallets are gone.' He then said, 'Let's search Green-berg's apartment.' Poor Irv Greenberg. We searched his apartment, turned it inside out. The end of the story is that, maybe fifteen, twenty years later, Gene Saks and I are walking down Seventh Avenue, passing the Dawn Patrol Barber Shop. Who comes out but Matthau, in a barbers' apron. Half his face is covered with lather. He said, 'Marvin, Gene, I got the money!' And he paid us back wearing the barbers' apron, with the lather on his face."

Meanwhile, Sargent remembered Matthau hanging out with Saks and Bea Arthur, who eventually married. "He was always loose and funny," Sargent noted. "It was a joy being around the three of them. They always were a cut-up."

One of Matthau's more intriguing credits was a production of Lil-lian Hellman's *The Little Foxes*, starring Elaine Stritch as Regina Gid-dens. One of the most highly publicized was Jean-Paul Sartre's *The Flies*, a retelling of the Orestes legend. The cast included Nehemiah Persoff (cast as "Tutor"), Joseph Sargent ("Cynical Man"), Judith Malina ("1st Fury"), and a pre–Tony Curtis Bernie Schwartz ("Nicias"). Matthau and Gene Saks (whose name is spelled "Jean

Saks" on the mimeographed program) played "1st Soldier" and "2nd Soldier."

Not all of the performers in *The Flies* became successful actors. One young woman became pregnant by a fellow student, and ended up in Israel. Another was working as a night clerk in a motel, and was shot to death during a robbery. Matthau himself noted, "And think of the many who had more talent than I have who went into insurance, because they couldn't stand the gaff of going up and pounding on doors. We had magnificent fellows and girls in our dramatic workshop, people with enormous talent, who couldn't take that kind of blunting. You have to be vulnerable to be an actor. But in order to succeed as an artist, you have to blunt that vulnerability; otherwise, you can't get to first base."

It was around this time that Matthau changed the spelling of his surname.

Marvin Silbersher's take was that "Matthau" was "more euphonious. It was more high-class. 'H-o-w' was too Jewish, too low-class. I remember when he mentioned to me, 'I think I'm gonna spell my name 'Matthau.' On the Broadway [marquee] and onscreen, it does look better."

Laura Winkler graduated from Seward Park High School the same year as Matthau. Well after Matthau became a celebrity, she wrote him a letter in which she asked why he changed the spelling of his name. Matthau's reply was very gracious. After exclaiming, "How nice, a blast from the past," he explained that Piscator had told him, "Now, that's supposed to be a German name and you're not spelling it the right way. You should spell it 'au' instead of 'ow.'"

In his 1980 letter to Don Olds, the 453rd Bomb Group historian, Matthau noted, "By the way, my name now ends in 'au' instead of 'ow'—that is because my teachers at dramatic school were Germans." On another occasion, he mischievously explained that the "au" appeared in several New School programs, "and I said the hell with it and left it that way."

CHAPTER 7

GERI

Matthau had lost his virginity while in the military, a fact that he revealed to Anna Berger. She recalled that before going overseas, he came home on furlough and said, "Annie, we're gonna spring for it. I'm taking you on the horse and carriage ride in Central Park." "That was really a big thing," she continued, "and that's when he told me that he finally had sex. He was very excited about telling me that he had sex. I was so happy for him." Why was she *happy* for him? Why would a woman be pleased to hear that the man she loved had not waited until the marriage night to have sex? Berger assumed that the woman in question was a prostitute; a prostitute, after all, is no competition for a hometown sweetheart. Such an experience would have taken Matthau one more step towards worldliness.

Berger commented, "Ruby Ludwin told me, 'I don't know if you knew, Annie, but when Walter was in the army, he finally had sex for the first time in his life. [Walter] described every curvature, every turn, every bit of her body. Then he stopped and said, 'What am I talking about her for, because the only girl I'm gonna marry is Annie Berger.'" However, Ludwin reported that Matthau's sex partner was a "WAC sergeant." (According to Matthau's son Charlie, his father remained a virgin until he was shipped overseas. "He went into a whorehouse in France thinking it was a restaurant, and he wanted a sandwich," Charlie explained. "That's what he [told me].")

While Matthau remained fond of Berger, now they no longer were an item. "I still loved Walter," Berger noted, "but we didn't spend that much time together anymore. He was feeling his oats, there were a lot of girls [at the New School], and I was not interested in spending any time with anybody, aside from my theater work." The two maintained contact until the end of Matthau's life. "Whenever I would call him, I would leave a message," she said. "He'd call back, and always spoke to me in Yiddish. He called me Annie or Chana, and I called him Matthau."

What Berger did not mention was that Matthau was seeing Charlotte Haverly, who had returned to New York. Her parents and brother lived there, and she took a job in the "social department" of the YWCA's central Manhattan branch. They dated "seven nights a week, much to my parents' dismay," Haverly recalled. "This went on for a year-and-a-half. I'd go and see him at the Dramatic Workshop. We went to so many basketball games—and he always had a bet on 'em." They shared what Haverly described as "tender spots" for puppies, dogs, and babies. "I hated my freckles, and he'd kid me about them. He'd tease me about going to Barnard. I'd imitate the dean for him, and he'd imitate my imitation; she wouldn't have been too happy about that. There always were funny things happening when you were with Walter."

As to why they never wed, Matthau once declared that "neither of us were ready to get married." Yet Haverly stated that he had proposed. "When he wanted me to marry him, I said, 'How can I? I can't marry a gambler.' I remembered what happened when my father lost all his money in the stock market [crash]. I had to say to myself, 'Charlotte, you just can't get into a marriage with him, you just can't, no matter how much you love him.'" Matthau was not crushed by the turndown. "He knew my attitude about [gambling]. I think he knew that's what I'd say. He said to me, 'Oh, you'll probably marry Freddie.' And I did." Haverly's husband, Alfred M. Scherz, was another GI stationed in Reno.

Just as with Anna Berger, the two maintained contact. "Walter and I remained good friends," she noted. "I'll certainly not forget him—ever!"

After breaking up with Haverly, Matthau became involved with Geraldine Grace Johnson, a fellow drama student. Five years Walter's junior, Geri was blonde, blue-eyed, and five-feet-one—a full foot shorter than Matthau. She grew up on Long Island's South Shore, in the village of Malverne. The two were married in 1948.

Those who met Geri characterized her as "a love, a lovely girl" (Murray Juvelier), "totally adorable, totally a sweetheart" (Marvin Silbersher), "gorgeous-looking, a beautiful girl [with] a face like a model" (Alex Brounstein), "very warm, very accessible" (Joseph Sargent), and, simply, "a nice woman" (Ruby Ludwin). Matthau's friend, actor-writer-newspaperman–sports commentator Heywood Hale Broun, described her as "very pretty, and she came from some family in the shoe business. And I think, probably, Walter, like me and like most funny-looking people, was attracted to pretty girls, because they show you're not as funny-looking as everyone thinks."

Sargent noted that Geri "was very much a part of the crowd that hung together. Bea [Arthur] and Gene [Saks] were [a couple]. And then there was Geri and Walter."

Marrying Geri was Matthau's passport out of the Lower East Side. The couple briefly lived on West Ninety-first Street, and then moved to 414 West Forty-fourth Street, an apartment building several blocks west of the Broadway theaters. "My wife and I were up there [in their apartment] on many occasions," Brounstein added. "We used to sit on the floor, like real thespians."

Of Geri, Matthau recalled, "While I was at the Dramatic Workshop, there was a very beautiful actress name of Geraldine Johnson." Four decades after their 1958 divorce, he described their courtship: "We took walks and had some fun, and then she said to me, 'Don't you think we should get married?' And I said, 'Sure, sure, yeah. I think so. Absolutely. No question about it.' So we got married." Louis Guss explained, "In places like dramatic schools, a lot of people fall in love, or think they're in love, for various reasons. Sometimes it's 'I think he's gonna be a star, or she's gonna be a star.' Or there might be genuine feelings—at first."

From the outset, Walter and Geri's union was far from blissful. "She seemed a very all-together kind of person, maybe a little tough for someone as sensitive as Walter," added Broun, one of the few who was not enamored of Geri. "She seemed like the kind of person who might occasionally step on Walter's toes." Charlotte Haverly also met Geri. "I know I was up at their house a few times," she stated. "It was a little apartment, in the theatrical district." Haverly's take on Geri was similar to Broun's: "She was a no-nonsense kind of person, really. She wasn't a real warm person. She was kind of practical, in her way, but the fact she married Walter showed that she wasn't too practical. She was okay, nothing outstanding."

Meanwhile, according to Anna Berger, Matthau developed an unpleasant habit of putting Geri down for small things, including her Long Island accent. "I never liked him for that character trait," she explained, "and told him so." Adding fuel to the mix was the presence of Matthau's mother. "Rose was a very difficult lady," Berger stated. "She made life miserable for Geri, and made life miserable for [Henry's wife] Ruth. And when I think about it, I think, Rose went through so much. Two boys, no money, moving from place to place to escape paying the rent. [When she moved to First Street], she finally got an apartment with a bathroom in it.

"She made life difficult for anybody who was with her, especially her daughters-in-law. And the boys would support her because she was their mother; with everything, they were tied and devoted to their mother. [Rose] used to say to me, 'Honey, I love you like a daughter.' And I would say, 'If I ever married either one of your sons, Rose, you wouldn't feel that way.'" Charlie Matthau, Walter's son with his second wife Carol, added, "Grandma would have been happiest if Henry and my father never got married, and just hung out with her and went to the whorehouse once a week. I think she actually suggested that."

Dan Frazer, who knew the Matthaus from the New School, recalled that Walter used to baby-sit his daughter. He and Geri loved children, but didn't have any at the time. The Matthaus eventually became parents: son David was born on November 2, 1953; daughter Jenny came on August 2, 1956. (Forty-eight years later, David described himself as looking like a cross between his mother and father. "Now that I'm in my mid-forties," he noted, "I'm starting to develop jowls like my father. I don't know if I'm thrilled about that.")

David recalled that, unlike his father and Anna Berger, Geri was not single-mindedly dedicated to the theater. "The story that I remember hearing was that she was not really a die-hard actress," he explained. "I mean, I'm sure in many ways she enjoyed it, but it was kind of a reaction to her upbringing, which was very typically Protestant middle-class." Of his parents' union, David explained, "Well, I think that her parents were not really thrilled with the idea, number one, that she was marrying an actor, and number two, that he was a Jew. That was a double whammy."

If a Lower East Side boy did not wed a neighborhood girl, it was expected that the outsider at least be Jewish. Yet Matthau was looking beyond the old neighborhood in every aspect of his life, which partly explains his attraction to non-Jewish women. Anna Berger provided a non-sexual, youthful relationship; she was a pre-war pal. But Geri and Charlotte Haverly were as far removed from Jewishness as a pork-loin at a Seder. In Charlotte's case, religion was a non-issue because, as she explained, "I'm not [formally] religious. But I am [faithful] in terms of treating people the way you'd like to be treated."

"I think that he was distrustful of organized religion," noted Charlie Matthau. "He said that when his father was buried, Grandma asked the rabbi to say an extra prayer. And the rabbi said, 'Sure, but you have to give me extra money.' I think that made an impression on him. The idea that you can't drive on Saturday, or you can't eat pork, that was just ritual."

Despite his choice for a wife, Matthau remained Jewish by culture. "There was always the sense that it was part of the fabric of what he was," reported David Matthau. "And it was definitely a cultural part of him, and to some extent his lifestyle." Added half-brother Charlie, "What made him proud to be Jewish was more of the cultural, the political, the social aspects of being part of a persecuted minority. He was always interested in history, and how Jews fared throughout history."

If Walter and Geri were at odds, at least they agreed on their approach to religion in relation to childrearing. David Matthau observed that, "with my mother and also with my father, we were never brought up with any organized religion, and always tended to be somewhat cynical [about religion]. I mean, my father never went to temple or anything like that. I don't think we ever seriously talked about me being Bar Mitzvahed. But he did give me a Bar Mitzvah ring. It was a gold ring, with a Jewish star. It was more of a cultural kind of thing, growing up and living in New York and so forth.

"And the kinds of characters that he played, there was a New York Jewish kind of sense about it. Definitely, it was a part of his identity. He was always extremely supportive and protective of Judaism as far as supporting Israel and pointing out anti-Semitic behavior and patterns and thoughts. He was always very outspoken, not only [with regard to] Judaism but with any other form of bigotry or prejudice." David added that he and his sister "were fortunate to have parents on both sides who were very truthful and direct about pointing out what they felt were prejudices and things that were not decent and fair."

As Matthau dated Charlotte and, then, began courting Geri, he also took his first professional acting jobs in summer stock. In 1946, he earned $35 a week at Pennsylvania's Erie County Playhouse, appearing in the John Cecil Holm–George Abbott comedy *Three Men on a Horse* and the temperence-themed melodrama *Ten Nights in a Bar-Room*. Evidence that Matthau was on the right career path came during the run of *Three Men on a Horse*. His character was Patsy, a gambler. After a performance, an audience member pulled the young actor aside and told him that he was the lone cast member whose performance he disliked. "The others looked like actors," the playgoer declared. "You just looked like a poolroom bum." Matthau considered this a great compliment, and for decades gleefully repeated the anecdote.

The following summer, Matthau worked at the Orange County Playhouse in Westtown New York, playing roles in ten productions, including Tremoille in *Joan of Lorraine*, Mr. Apoppolous in *My Sister Eileen*, and Uncle Oscar in *The Little Foxes*. He received an encouraging notice from critic Dorothea Reilly, writing in the local *Newburgh News*, who observed that he "received well-earned applause for his every appearance on the stage" in *Eileen*. Reilly added, "At Westtown you'll find a summer theater that is just as it should be—a perfect rural setting, a little old community hall up on the hill in the shadow of a church steeple, surrounded by old trees, rustling cool breezes in the light of the moon. A cow bell sounds in the night to warn of curtain time at intermission."

It was a long way from First Street.

That summer, the Playhouse brought its subscribers "both high drama and low comedy, some of it played on the stage," recalled Tom McMorrow, one of its founders. Matthau still retained the Lower East Side radicalism that was a byproduct of his youth. "One day," recalled McMorrow, "a [Westtown] resident came into the theater office to tell me that Walter Matthau was talking to the people in Dan's Lunch about the advantages of the communist form of government. Matthau laughed at me, of course, as he would always do at those who were shaken up by his conduct, when I yelled at him, 'Do you want to get us run out of town?'" The theater then was struggling to pay its bills, and its actors agreed to accept pay cuts—all except Matthau. McMorrow remembered him banging on an office door and shouting, "Give me my money, you dirty capitalist!" He was the lone performer to be paid his full salary: $46.

McMorrow described Matthau as a "long, saturnine guy, like a Jewish Abe Lincoln," adding that the young actor was both "tremendous" and "abrasive." Even at this early stage, Matthau insisted on incessantly questioning his director, to learn everything he could about his character's motivation. This was a key part of his artistic process; meanwhile, the director, who is obsessing over a dozen other production details, might find Matthau annoying.

Matthau's 1948 affiliation was the Southold Playhouse, on the north fork of Long Island. It was managed by Brett Warren, a New School faculty member, and operated out of Belmont Hall, a 350-seat community hall located on the town's main road. The initial production was *My Sister Eileen*; Matthau's role was Jensen, a plumber. "[Jensen] comes to the basement flat of Eileen and Ruth [the play's central characters] to repair a leak," recalled Ann Lewis, the theater's publicity director. "He enters and speaks this memorable line: 'I come to fix the terlet.' I shall not forget that line which marks forever my first recollection of Walter." That summer, Southold resident Verna Petty Fitzpatrick ushered at the playhouse. Her memory of him, fifty-three years later: "He acted on the street and to people the same way he [later] did in the movies. He had that same look, and same walk."

Matthau appeared in a range of productions: *Our Town*—with the setting switched from a fictional small town to Southold—*Arsenic and Old Lace, The Hasty Heart, The Late Christopher Bean, Heaven Can Wait, John Loves Mary, Dark of the Moon,* and *The Little Foxes.* Joining him at Southold were John Marley, Jack Warden, Robert Earl (father of James Earl) Jones, Vinette Carroll, Dan Frazer, and E.W. Swackhamer, who later became a noted TV director. Anne Meara was an apprentice. In mid-July, WPIX-TV, then a newly founded independent television station affiliated with the New York *Daily News,* filmed a news feature on the theater. In this apparently lost footage, actors are seen building scenery as Matthau converses with actor–stage manager Robert Brown. It was his first appearance on film.

While at Southold, Matthau's "Who's Who" biographies varied from program to program—and each was loaded with fiction. One declared that he "has had a varied career . . . in the movies," "trained for the stage . . . at Columbia University," and "played with such stars as Frederick [sic] March, Bela Lugosi & Paul Muni." Another noted that he "started his theatrical career in the settlement houses of New York, where . . . he did a two-year stint in Shakespearean Repertory." One more claimed he "played on Broadway in *The American Way* with Frederick [sic] March, *A Flag Is Born* with Paul Muni and others." Given their subjects, Matthau might have envisioned appearing in them. *The American Way,* a Moss Hart–George S. Kaufman chronicle of a German immigrant couple from their arrival at Ellis Island in 1896 through the rise of Nazism, ran in 1939. Ben Hecht's *A Flag Is Born,* a topical allegory about the need to establish a free Jewish homeland in Palestine, came to Broadway in 1946. Had he known better, Matthau might have name-dropped a star-to-be who *was* in its cast: Marlon Brando.

Despite these fibs, Matthau became a Southold favorite. In *Heaven Can Wait,* he played a fight manager. It was noted in *The Long Island Traveler–Mattituck Watchman,* "Mr. Matthau seems to have quite a large following in the audiences, by the way, to judge from the applause which greeted him on his first entrance." By mid-August, when he appeared as a preacher in *Dark of the Moon,* the paper's critic, Bob Smith, reported that Matthau "as always is wonderful." At the end of the month, *The Suffolk Times* observed, "His successive roles are looked forward to each week, with a great deal of speculation going on as to just how the unpredictable Mr. Matthau will delight the audience."

After the season, he and Geri were married. So was Will Scholz, a fellow actor. "The two couples came to our home in East Williston," added Ann Lewis, "and we all had a sort of celebration and 'old home week' talk fest. The two young actors were confident then of success and we drank champagne to their futures."

It is no wonder that the following summer Matthau returned to Southold. From July 11 to July 16, he played the lead in *Room Service*, the John Murray–Allen Boretz farce. After noting that his performances the previous year still were fondly remembered, Bob Smith—in the kind of critique that dogged Matthau after he became a star—wrote that he hoped to see Matthau playing more serious roles. This was not to be.

"We all went there because we adored [Brett Warren]," recalled Marvin Silbersher, who had joined him, "but he turned out to be a tyrant, a terrible person. So we had a revolution. I knew of a theater in Columbia County, in [upstate] New York; we could move there even at the beginning of July. It was called the Taconic Playhouse. I told this to Walter. Walter said, 'But Brett has promised me this and promised me that. I have to meet him at the tavern in a half-hour.' I drove him there, in the pouring rain. He went in to talk to Brett and when he came out he said, 'Marvin, let's go to your playhouse.'" Altogether, sixteen actors left. They immediately went into production, building the sets while they rehearsed. Two weeks later they opened, and the play was a hit. "Then Walter left," added Silbersher, "because he had gotten an agent, and was starting to get Equity work."

As he entered his late twenties, Matthau's looks were improving. He was growing into his body frame, and his face was taking on a comely quality. However, Matthau felt he was no matinee idol. His hardscrabble background and lack of formal education still fed on his insecurities. "I wasn't handsome," he recalled. "I didn't have good clothes. I used to wonder why people would hire me when they could get college graduates and Oxford scholars. Then it became apparent that when I got up on stage, people actually wanted to look at me. What did I have to offer? I was a big, rugged-looking guy, with a big, strong voice. There was that. Also, I had a way of showing enormous ease and enormous power onstage, both of which were valuable in the theater."

Matthau's son Charlie observed, "What he'd always say is that he never thought he could make a living doing that [acting]. But he was a lot more ambitious than he would admit to. Later on, when he became so successful, he would talk about it as though it were a big accident, but I strongly suspect that he was ambitious in terms of wanting to make a living at it, and wanting to be a star, and wanting to break down the boundaries of what a leading man was. The goal-posts kept changing. At one point, just making a living was a goal. Then getting a lead on Broadway, and becoming a well-known character actor. And then it was wanting to be a leading man."

At this juncture, Matthau was at the first phase of this unscripted plan. In order to succeed as an actor, he realized that he needed to change his personality and be more outgoing. "I used to be a terrific introvert," he recalled, "but I had to bust out of that, being an actor, unless I wanted to be an actor who never gave an interview, who was never on radio or television, who didn't want to have first or second billing. That's the way I started out, but you can't earn a living doing that. You've got to come out and communicate." Yet Matthau savored his anonymity, because it allowed him to travel about and observe the behavior of those around him.

By exuding confidence, Matthau was striving to mask his insecurities. And he was succeeding. In the late 1940s, he and Tige Andrews, with whom he later appeared onscreen in *Onionhead*, were pounding the New York pavement in search of work. "He was very self-assured, I remember that," Andrews recalled. "He was sharp, to the point, somebody to admire. He was not a worrywart; for his age, he was a few steps above the average. And he was ambitious. I remember him as always moving, as 'walking-hard.'

"A character face on a young guy is unusual, and he stood out [as a] great character," Andrews added. "In this business, you're either very pretty or unusual-looking. Casting people always were looking for types, and he was one.

"I thought he would do well."

CHAPTER 8

Stage Presence

"Between 1950 and 1954 I did twelve plays on Broadway," Matthau once recalled. "I liked them all. And I'm happy they all were flops, because I was able to go from one to the other and learn so much playing such different roles."

A key to an actor's connecting with an audience is his ability to milk a line or a look, and it was on the stage that Matthau honed his comic and dramatic timing. Here, through the practice of repeating and sharpening a performance, he learned how to wait an extra beat before uttering a punchline.

Plus, he savored acting before live audiences. He was, as he explained, "commercially viable": "People were willing to plunk down their two bucks to see me. They enjoyed hearing me speak. They'd laugh, applaud. It just seems that this was the way it went. That's where I was good—on the stage."

Even though he was overcoming his early insecurities, appearing on stage still was difficult. Matthau readily admitted to nervousness "especially when I was working Broadway. There were eight newspapers, and eight critics, and they sat front row center. Your life depended on what they wrote." Yet he was delighted to be a working stage actor, because "it never occurred to me that people would pay me to act."

Matthau's Broadway debut was as a candle bearer in the coronation scene in Maxwell Anderson's *Anne of the 1000 Days*, which opened at the Shubert Theatre on December 8, 1948. The show's first director was Bretaigne Windust. By the time it played Baltimore, less than two weeks before its Broadway opening, Windust and H. C. Potter were credited as co-directors and it was being completely restaged. Potter had sole credit when it came to the Shubert. The stars were Rex Harrison, playing Henry VIII, and Joyce Redman, cast as Anne Boleyn, and the show lasted a respectable 288 performances. Matthau's salary was $100 per week.

Originally, Matthau was cast as a courier who breathlessly arrived on stage, blurted out a couple of lines, and collapsed. To get into the spirit, he did knee-bends backstage just before going on. He claimed to have done 148 knee-bends prior to a performance during the show's Philadelphia tryout, and promptly "fell flat on my face" while delivering his lines. "The part was cut out," he noted, "but since they already had a suit made for me, they kept me on as a candelabra bearer." In the Shubert programme, Matthau has billing as "Servant"; along with Harold McGee, Francis Bethencourt, Terence Anderson, Charles Ellis, and Malcolm Wells, he is listed as one of the "Royal Servants."

One more Matthau story involves how he was cast in the play. He claimed that he lied to the Princeton-educated Windust, declaring that he was English and trained in Shakespearean drama. Decades later, Matthau quipped, "I'm vain enough to think I attracted attention when I did a walk-on in *Anne of the 1000 Days* in Philadelphia."

Matthau polished his character-actor credentials by understudying seven different roles. All were elderly, and all were British—quite an accomplishment for a twenty-eight-year-old Lower East Side Jew. "I was ecstatic," he remembered. "I walked up to strangers and told them about it. I was even proud that the combined ages of the seven old men came to 492."

One was an eighty-three-year-old bishop. Harry Irvine, the actor playing the role, was appearing on Broadway before Matthau was born. One time, Irvine became ill and Matthau replaced him. Upon coming on stage, a surprised Rex Harrison gave him a startled look and uttered an expletive that was heard by those seated in the front rows. Matthau heard several of them whisper, "Did he say, 'Oh, shit?'"

Anne eventually went out on tour. Matthau signed on and played the bishop in Boston in October 1949, Detroit in November, and Chicago in December. The tour ended on December 31.

Matthau was relegated to walk-on status in his next play, *The Liar*, a musical version of the Carlo Goldoni play that starred Alfred Drake. Along with the then equally obscure Edward Bryce, William Hogue, and Laurence Weber, he was one of four Venetian guards. *The Liar* opened at the Broadhurst on May 18, 1950, garnered tepid notices, and lasted twelve performances. Matthau's character was supposed to sing, yet his voice was constantly off-pitch. As a result, Lehman Engel, the exasperated musical director, requested that he mouth the songs.

Several months later, he returned to Broadway as an understudy in Wolcott Gibbs's *Season in the Sun*, which opened at the Cort The-atre on September 28. The director was Burgess Meredith, and the stars were Nancy Kelly and Richard Whorf. Before the end of the year, Matthau replaced King Calder in the role of John Colgate, a good-natured albeit dissolute journalist, and played the role for the final eight months of the run.

Although the same age as Matthau, Kelly was a veteran stage and screen performer. She was impressed with his work in *Season in the Sun*, and the two began to spend time together. Whether they were romantically or sexually involved is unclear. However, Matthau's entree into Kelly's world further explains his distancing himself from his wife. Geri may have had artistic aspirations, but she was not star material; even at Southold, she never was a part of Matthau's profes-sional life. Geri was increasingly becoming a vestige of his past, an annoying reminder of when he was a poor, struggling acting student.

Now when Matthau played handball, he no longer did so on a Lower East Side or Coney Island court. He began playing at the Gotham Health Club, on West Fifty-fourth Street off Sixth Avenue, where his opponents were anything but Lower East Side streetkids. "He used to play with Tony Randall, Dane Clark, Phil Foster, Lee J. Cobb, people like that," recalled Syd Preses. One of his Gotham companions was Bob Mills, a four-wall handball champ and pro basketball player. "I sat with Walter many times in the steam room and commiserated with him about many things," Mills stated. "We spoke about everything from the market to sports to gambling.

"There also was a roof, and in good weather we used to go up there and sunbathe in the nude," Mills added. "Walter Winchell once wrote a story about Rockefeller Center, which was a few streets away and which was a much taller building. He stated that many of the secretaries in Rockefeller Center were coming to work with binoculars. [Matthau] cracked that, had he known this, he would have gone up there and posed more often. That was his sense of humor."

Matthau wanted to learn how to play four-wall handball, and discussed the subject with Mills. Additionally, given Mills's pro-ball background, Matthau often asked his advice about certain games on which he was betting. "At the club also were some famous—or infamous—bookmakers, with whom he wagered," Mills reported.

Meanwhile, it was through Nancy Kelly that Matthau moved up in status in the theater world. His next New York production was *Twilight Walk*, a long-forgotten detective drama that opened at the Fulton Theatre on September 24, 1951. *Twilight Walk* may have closed after eight performances, but Matthau had a major role, that of a detective who joins a reporter (played by Kelly) in a search for a sex killer.

Coincidentally, Anna Berger was in the cast, but she and Matthau spent little time together during the run. "I always thought that he had a thing for Nancy Kelly, the female lead," she declared.

While rehearsing the play and nailing down the character, Matthau chose to take a naturalistic approach and play him "as a human being who just happened to be a detective. I knew about detectives, because half the friends I grew up with on the Lower East Side became either detectives or firemen or sanitation men—good, steady jobs in civil service. Most actors play detectives the way they've seen other actors play detectives. I like to watch a prize-fighter or a basketball player, not another actor, whose cliches I might automatically pick up."

In *Twilight Walk*, Matthau earned his first *New York Times* notice, and it was positive and encouraging. Despite its generally negative tone—Brooks Atkinson described *Twilight Walk* as "literate" but "not interesting"—the critic noted that Matthau "is amusing as a cynical cop; he knows how to get all the acid flavor out of his dialogue." Despite the play's short run, Matthau emerged with a coveted prize to add to his resume: a New York Drama Critics Circle Award.

Matthau's *Twilight Walk* experience established a pattern for the young actor. For the next several years, he appeared on Broadway in flop after flop, yet emerged with respectable notices. Heywood Hale Broun remarked that Matthau was the only actor he knew who established himself by playing in failures.

In his *Twilight Walk* follow-up, which came to Broadway three-and-a-half months later, Matthau was directed by George S. Kaufman, the Pulitzer Prize–winning playwright. Kaufman's co-author and star was his wife, Lueen MacGrath. Their play, *Fancy Meeting You Again*, was a comedy about reincarnation. MacGrath played a New York sculptress who has been attempting to wed the same man—played by Matthau—for 5,000 years. He played a caveman, a Roman shepherd, and a picayunish art critic.

Given the nature of the character, Matthau felt he had neither the background nor the life experience to play the critic. MacGrath suggested he separate himself from the part. When he did, he found that he was able to fit snugly into it. And when he "kissed the girl in the play and it was believed by the audience, it opened up a whole new phase of acting for me. In fact, that's when I became an actor."

Despite the pedigree of its co-author and director, *Fancy Meeting You Again*, which opened on January 14, 1952, at the Royale, only lasted eight performances. His next show, *One Bright Day*, also housed at the Royale, opened on March 19. It was a bit more successful, lasting twenty-nine performances. The plot, reminiscent of Arthur Miller's *All My Sons*, involved a pharmaceutical executive (Howard Lindsay) who learns that his plant is producing a possibly unsafe drug. Will he withdraw the product from the marketplace, which may result in financial ruin? Or will he ignore the facts, and hope that no one will suffer from the error?

Here, Matthau played a villain. Again, Brooks Atkinson lauded his work, noting, "There must be some good in the character somewhere, Mr. Matthau is so personable."

While rehearsing the show, Matthau learned a valuable lesson from Michael Gordon, the director. The actor protested that he could not say a line because he "didn't feel it." Gordon asked him, "What if you were playing Othello and you just didn't feel like killing Desdemona?" 'Nuff said.

Then in October, he appeared in *In Any Language*, a farce that opened on the seventh of the month at the Cort Theatre. He was directed by the legendary playwright-producer-director George Abbott; the leading lady was the famed stage actress Uta Hagen. Despite these luminaries, the show lasted forty-five performances.

In Any Language was a farce about a Hollywood star (Hagen) lwho heads to Rome to rejuvenate her career by starring in an art film. Matthau played her estranged, airline-pilot husband. Brooks Atkinson gave the play a mixed notice, but again cited Matthau. In an observation that might have applied to the actor's best later comic performances, the critic noted, ". . . and Walter Matthau, as the American flyer, has a dry sense of humor that suits the occasion admirably." Among those who saw Matthau in *In Any Language* was actress Georgann Johnson, then a student of Hagen's, who worked with him on television a decade later. "He looked marvelous, tall and handsome," she recalled. "I can still see him standing in his lanky glory on stage, very attractive and obviously the romantic lead."

Given his insecurity, Matthau must have been delighted when, prior to the opening, the *World Telegram and Sun*'s William Hawkins wrote that, "of all the performers, including the star, Uta Hagen, the most composed looking will be Walter Matthau, who plays opposite her. Right from the beginning of his career, Walter has managed to give people the impression that he was nerveless, and had been acting 'about 50 years.'" Yet Matthau was not around when the play closed. He had left it (and was replaced by Anthony Ross) to go into rehearsals for *The Grey-Eyed People*, his fourth Broadway appearance in 1952.

After his credits were cited in his *Playbill* biography, it was noted that "while none of these were resounding hits, they served to advance Mr. Matthau's stock to the point where he is now one of the leading men most in demand on Broadway." This was no exaggeration. Apparently, though, not all his roles were earned on merit. Matthau once told Anna Berger that he obtained one on a bet. "I don't know which show it was," she noted. "[Matthau] said, 'You know how I got it, Annie? I flipped a coin with the producer and said, "heads I get it, tails, I don't".'" Whenever Matthau won a role, the New York bookies must have celebrated. Howard Morris quipped, "On [any] opening night, the guys with the little black cases would come around and say, 'Hey, Walter, we wanna wish you well. We hope that you get a hit, here.' A hit for him was a hit for them."

Unfortunately, *The Grey-Eyed People* benefited neither Matthau nor his bookies. It opened at the Martin Beck on December 17, and folded after five performances. As a satire about a community whose members boycott a puppeteer who a decade earlier was a Communist Party member, it certainly was topical. But it was noteworthy more for its subject than its quality. Matthau's character was conflicted between fidelity to his friend, the blacklist victim, and economic survival in the wake of the Red Scare.

After beginning 1953 by playing a middle-aged salesman in Irving Ravetch's *A Certain Joy*, which closed in Philadelphia during its pre-Broadway tryout, Matthau appeared in Dorothy Parker and Arnaud d'Usseau's *The Ladies of the Corridor*, which opened at the Longacre on October 21 and lasted thirty-five performances. Matthau had the unlikely role of Paul Osgood, an erudite bookshop owner who is the romantic object of an aging widow (Edna Best). Even without a hit show, Matthau's Broadway stock certainly was rising. He merited special mention in the March 1953 issue of *Theatre Arts* magazine, which noted, in an item headlined "Misleading Man," that the plays in which he appeared the previous season had "flopped but Matthau didn't." His consistently solid *New York Times* notices segued into a one-page feature in the paper's Sunday magazine. It ran on October 18, 1953, several days before the *Ladies of the Corridor* opening. The piece, written by Barbara Dubivsky, emphasized his presence in plays that had "closed before the stage door man had time to learn everyone's name," and offered the young actor's sober analysis, over morning coffee, of how he approached each role.

Matthau almost followed *The Ladies of the Corridor* with what would have been his first hit: *Oh, Men! Oh, Women!*, an Edward Chodorov satire of psychoanalysis that opened at the Henry Miller on December 17 and settled in for a 382-performance run. The scenario involved an analyst (Franchot Tone) who learns of his fiancée's amorous past. Anne Jackson appeared as one of his patients.

Jackson, already cast, had not yet met Matthau, but almost fifty years later she noted, "I think we were both actors who respected each other. I was going to do a play called *Oh, Men, Oh, Women!* and my husband [in the story] was supposed to be a movie star. He eventually was [played by] Gig Young, but Gig wasn't in the picture at that time. Eddie Chodorov said, 'How do you feel about Walter Matthau?' I said, 'Oh, my god, he's great, he's a great actor,' and Eddie said, 'Well, I'd love to have him.' Walter came to a reading or something, and decided he didn't want to do it. He wasn't right for it, and so Gig played it."

During this period, not all of Matthau's stage appearances were in New York. During the summer of 1952, he briefly toured the straw-hat circuit as "The Gentleman Caller" in Tennessee Williams's *The Glass Menagerie*, starring Dana Andrews. He began the following summer playing Professor Tommy Turner in James Thurber and Elliot Nugent's *The Male Animal*, at Philadelphia's Playhouse in the Park. Henry T. Murdock, writing in the *Philadelphia Inquirer*, noted that the actor "has impressed Philadelphia audiences with his performances in several short-lived plays or recent issue, [and] gives the professor a performance both funny and sympathetic." As the season progressed, he toured as Patsy again in *Three Men on a Horse*, starring Wally Cox. Then in 1954, he spent part of the summer at the Ivory Tower Playhouse in Spring Lake, New Jersey, starring with Kay Medford in *Maggie Pack Your Bags*.

Matthau appeared on Broadway just once in 1954, in *The Burning Glass*, which opened at the Longacre on March 4. Here again, he was in a play that attempted to deal with the philosophical and moral issues of the era. Yet again, the play flopped; *The Burning Glass* closed after twenty-eight performances. Its scenario involved a researcher (Scott Forbes) who has constructed a machine that concentrates the sun's heat. Like the atom bomb, his invention might end up destroying the earth. Or, it could better humankind. Matthau's role, that of a misanthrope, was a supporting one. It did nothing for his career.

In his review for *The Grey-Eyed People*, Brooks Atkinson summed up Matthau's career to date when he wrote, "Mr. Matthau, a black-haired, lunging gentleman, is a good actor who is likely to find himself in a good play sometime." Echoed critic Eric Bentley, "Any producer with a sure flop on his hands should hire Mr. Matthau, for he has the ability to ignore the rubbish around him and establish on stage the fact of his own ingratiating manner and strong personality; he has become Broadway's leading stop-gap."

Matthau did not earn superlatives for every performance. Occasionally, critics ignored him, or wrote that he merely was adequate. But the actor was praised in a majority of his notices. His friend Jayne Meadows summed up his appeal when she observed, "Walter had so much charm, personality, and delivery that he could be a flop and nobody would say he was awful."

CHAPTER 9

Live from New York

As Matthau established himself on Broadway, he supplemented his income by regularly appearing on television. As he explained, when a New York stage actor was between gigs during the early 1950s, "you either [worked as a] sporting goods salesman at Macy's, or you started getting work in the television field."

This was TV's pioneering era, when many productions were broadcast live from New York. Television never was Matthau's favorite medium because, as he noted, "You have to do it fast and usually when you do something that quickly, you don't do your best work. You use tricks. You choose an interpretation and stick to it. For example, often you have to pull out, say, characterization Forty-two—the gangster with the heart of gold—and use it." While rehearsing a play, he was "tense, taut as a wire, but I'm doing what I was cut out for. TV I wasn't cut out for."

Nevertheless, live TV did prove a valuable learning experience. "If you're sitting around and doing Chekhov and the cat walks in, you must pay attention to the cat," he explained. "You cannot continue the dialogue of Chekhov without including the cat. So on live television we'd automatically go into ad-lib gear." "When we do it, you see it," observed Howard Morris, with whom Matthau appeared in a

1958 episode of *Kraft Television Theatre*. "So it'd better be right."

Throughout the 1950s, Matthau appeared on all the important live television series, including *Studio One, Armstrong Circle Theatre, Omnibus, Goodyear Theatre, Philco Television Playhouse, The United States Steel Hour*, and *Robert Montgomery Presents*. He worked with some of the medium's top directors, many of whom graduated to feature films: Arthur Penn, Delbert Mann, Sidney Lumet, Franklin J. Schaffner, Ralph Nelson, and Fielder Cook. Even after establishing himself on Broadway and onscreen, Matthau kept appearing on TV series, only stopping in 1965, when *The Odd Couple* on stage and *The Fortune Cookie* on screen made him a star—and he no longer had to supplement his income. That year, a *Time* magazine profile noted that he had 158 TV shows to his credit.

Back in 1950, Matthau made what were among his oddest and most fascinating TV appearances. For thirteen weeks, he was a regular on *Mr. I. Magination*, a daily half-hour kiddie show featuring Paul Tripp. He succeeded Richard Boone, another actor of note; his pay was $50 a week; and he was fired when the producers found someone willing to work for $35. Tripp, the show's star, director, and author of its scripts and songs, was making all of $100.

"I did 100 accents on the old *Mr. I. Magination* TV show," Matthau recalled, "six Germans, forty-two Jews, and I don't know how many others." In a typical episode, titled "Alaska Gold Rush" and broadcast on September 17, he played two roles. He wore a jacket and cap, with a fake moustache and beard covering half his face, for his role as Windy, a prospector. One might say he was typecast, because Windy was victimized by Dangerous Dan, "the craftiest, slickest card player in the Klondike." Matthau could have ad-libbed Windy's line, "Well, I swore when he took my last dollar I'd come back and someday pay him back. Cracky, I'm gonna get my money back." His other role was Barney, Dan's cohort, who appears minus the beard but with the same moustache.

"He was awfully good," recalled Tripp, "but he wasn't as funny as he turned out to be later. He just did a good acting job. But the one thing I always remembered about Walter were those El Ropos he used to smoke, those old Italian stogies. They smelled like hell, and we used to have a big laugh about it.

"Years later, we used to bump into each other on the Upper West Side, and he would ask, 'Paul, why did you fire me?' I'd say, 'What do you mean fire you? I never fired you.' He'd say, 'But you fired me,' and I'd say, 'If you were fired, which I never knew about, it was my producers, Norman and Irving Pincus.' He kept doing this for five years, and finally he said it again and I suddenly came up with the answer. I said, 'Walter, we fired you so you could go on to better things.' He started to laugh, and he said, 'You're not gonna get that question again from me.'"

After *Mr. I. Magination*, Matthau appeared on *Lux Video Theatre*, a half-hour dramatic anthology series that evolved from the popular *Lux Radio Theatre*. His roles were small: "First Coast Guardsman" (on "Shadow on the Heart," broadcast on October 16, 1950); "Cop Number One" ("Mine to Have," October 30, 1950), and "Inspector" ("Manhattan Pastorale," January 22, 1951). For "The Speech," which aired on April 30, 1951, he was an extra. He began the following season fourth-billed, playing a character who actually had a name— Craig—on "Cafe Ami" (November 15, 1951); he was listed behind school chum Rod Steiger in the credits. Yet in "For Goodness Sake" (January 28, 1952) and "Man at Bay" (April 7, 1952), he again was an extra.

One of his more interesting early TV projects was a supporting role in "The Last Cruise," broadcast on *Studio One* on November 13, 1950. The teleplay was a fact-based account of two United States Navy submarines that are ordered to conduct cold-weather operations in the Greenland sea, and what happens when a fire breaks out on board one of them. *Variety* called the result "one of television's most ambitious productions to date." Matthau was billed eleventh in the all-male cast.

During this period, Matthau occasionally acted on television using pseudonyms; for this reason, it is impossible to compile a definitive Matthau videography. One example: In 1952, he appeared in the early episodes of *Mister Peepers*, a sitcom featuring Wally Cox as a callow junior high school science teacher. The show was broadcast live from New York. In the pilot, titled *Peepers*, Cox's character comes to teach at Jefferson City Junior High. Matthau, playing Mr. Burr, the pipe-smoking, sweatshirt-garbed athletic instructor, was billed as "David Tyrell." The pilot aired on July 3, 1952; the show continued running on Thursday evenings for the rest of the summer, with "David Tyrell" listed in its *TV Guide* credits. However, when *Mister Peepers* resurfaced that October, it had an almost entirely new cast.

A year later, Matthau claimed he was offered the part of neighbor Harry Morton on *The George Burns and Gracie Allen Show*, as a replacement for the departing Fred Clark. Matthau declined, because he "didn't want to get tied down." This assertion came with a punchline. In 1965, Matthau was hospitalized with a heart attack. "I'm sick on my back," he said, "and a telegram comes from George. 'Offer still holds,' the wire said."

On April 21, 1953, Matthau appeared in "Hand Me Down," broadcast on *Danger*. His co-star was Nina Foch. Their director was Sidney Lumet. "It was a very serious show, about guns and crime and things," recalled Foch. Yet perhaps because it was being presented on TV, rather than on stage, Matthau viewed the show as a lark. "He wouldn't take it seriously at all," Foch continued. "*Life* magazine came to take pictures of us, because at that time I was hot. Walter was sitting in a chair with his hat on, and Sidney was showing Walter how he wanted him to embrace me. And there's Walter with his back to the camera, and Sidney and I are embracing . . . and Walter has his hand up my leg, up my skirt! It's a very funny picture. *Life* did print the article, but they sent me the picture and said, 'We thought you'd like to have this. We promise not to print it.' I remember this very affectionately.

"He also was always very flirty with women," Foch added. "But it didn't mean anything; it was just part of the fun of working. If anyone had taken him up on it, he would have been vastly shocked."

As Matthau's talents became recognized, the size and variety of his roles increased. Yet his name still was unfamiliar to mainstream audiences. In the *TV Guide* listing for "The Basket-Weaver," presented on *Philco Television Playhouse* on April 20, 1952, he is credited as "Walter Mattheau"; for "F.O.B. Vienna," broadcast on *Suspense* on April 28, 1953, the publication lists him as "Walter Mathau." When he was cast on "F.O.B. Vienna," his co-star, Jayne Meadows, had never heard of him, and initially was unimpressed. "I even went to the producer, Martin Manulis," she recalled, "and I said, 'This actor doesn't know his lines.' He sort of shuffled around the stage. I said to Manulis, 'This is live TV. We have to give a performance in five days.' He said, 'Don't you worry about him. He's the most brilliant actor.' Indeed, when we did the show, he knew every line and was as professional as could be."

Matthau also flirted with Meadows. "After we had been rehearsing for two days," she noted, "he turned to me in this very personal way and said, 'You know something? You're the first feminine actress I've ever played opposite.' I said, 'Really.' He said, 'Yes. All the other actresses are too dominating and masculine.'"

Despite his disdain for television, Matthau got to play one of his most satisfying roles on the small screen: Iago, in a *Philco Television Playhouse* production of *Othello*, which aired on September 6, 1953. The director was Delbert Mann, who forty years later directed Matthau in a pair of made-for-TV movies, *Against Her Will: An Incident in Baltimore* and *Incident in a Small Town*. At the time, Matthau was earning $35 for a TV appearance. "Finally rebelled," he recalled. "They wanted me to do *Othello*, and I got drunk and told them I would only play Iago and I wanted $750 to do it. You know, they agreed." (In typical skewed Matthau fashion, on another occasion he said he was earning $400 for a role, but was offered $250 for *Othello*. He upped his asking price to $1,500, and settled on $750.)

This was the only Shakespearean role of his career, and it is a special treat to see him as Iago. "[This adaptation] was so important to Walter," recalled Marian Seldes, who appeared with him. "He was so proud of it. The last time I was at [his California] house, he was talking about it. There's a place in the house where all his scripts were bound in leather, and all his favorite things were . . . and he still had that script!

"He was talking about it, and telling Garson (Seldes's late husband, director-playwright-screenwriter Garson Kanin) how important it was to him. And I'll tell you, he was brilliant. He was a wonderful Iago. He's so expressive. He's funny, of course, but he's wicked and mean, too. Anyway, I think Walter and I took it very seriously, because somehow it was as if we both know it was our one chance to do that play. And the fact that it was done in the heat of [late summer], in the boiling heat, with not enough time, and all the things that were against it. Still, it always stayed in his memory, and I think in an odd way it was the basis of my friendship with him."

According to Seldes, rehearsal lasted about ten days. "Everybody learned their parts beforehand, but still you have to accommodate the camera and go to costumes and so on. And [because of the time element] of course the play was cut. But still, to do that!

"And then of course I'd seen Walter in *Anne of the 1000 Days*. To me, he was an *actor*, not a comedian. His tremendous success came because of how funny he was, but to me, first of all he was an actor. That's why he was funny." Seldes added that, back then, "Walter wasn't known as a comic. He was then a serious actor. So [his casting] wasn't odd. It only seems odd looking backward."

Seldes was not exaggerating when she observed, "Walter could have had a completely different career as a very important 'serious' actor, and that could have been amazing, too."

A decade later, Matthau declared, "Right now, I'm studying *King Lear*, with [a] Shakespeare variorum that gives me all kinds of interpretations of the role. Maybe I'll be able to do it by 1978." He never did play *Lear*. Near the end of his life, he remarked, "Most of my work is crap, I'm waiting for something good. I did a good thing in 1952 [actually 1953], on the *Philco Playhouse*. I played Iago. That I liked."

On "Dry Run," a fact-based *Studio One* episode broadcast on December 7, 1953, Matthau played Captain Robert I. Olsen, a tough, highly principled World War II submarine commander whose ship is transformed from warrior to angel of mercy when ordered to the Philippines to evacuate survivors of the Panai massacre. At this time, Matthau had not yet appeared in a movie. He had not had a Broadway hit. But his growing reputation allowed him to not only play the lead but be the lone actor with his name in the opening credits.

Matthau's performance was not flawless. At one point, he blew a line. After declaring, "Let's see if we can get through the straits before we . . . ," he realized he has erred. He tried to correct himself, and uttered "Bef, uh" before redoing the line: "Let's see if we can get through the minefields before we worry about that." By now he had broken character, and smiled at his mistake. Such were the hazards of live television.

In "The Glorification of Al Toolum," presented on *Philco Television Playhouse* twenty days after "Dry Run," Matthau was the title character: a middle-class husband and father who wins the title "Mr. Yankee Doodle," the most average man in America. "There was one thing I remember about this show," recalled his co-star, Betsy Palmer. "[Matthau's character and his wife] were having problems with their small son. [Matthau] was supposed to suggest that [the boy] should have a Rorschach test. One day in rehearsal, instead of saying 'Rorschach,' he called it a 'roaring shock test,' which was so typical of him and his wonderful humor. It broke us all up."

The show was rehearsed for seven days. "We [did so] in interesting places," Palmer continued. "All the hour shows for NBC and CBS were rehearsed down at Central Plaza on Second Avenue. Underneath it was Ratner's [a well-known Lower East Side dairy restaurant]. When we would have a break, we'd all go down and eat kosher." Palmer added herself to the list of Matthau admirers when she noted that he was "extremely spontaneous, very, very rich in how his mind worked. This certainly was the case with [his] comedy, but he could play it very, very straight, too. He was a well-rounded actor."

On May 18, 1954, Matthau appeared in a show that is a relic of Cold War paranoia: "Atomic Attack," presented on *Motorola Television Hour*. As it opens, a narrator intones, "The play you are about to see deals with an imaginary H-bomb attack on New York City. . . . It is the prayer of every one of us that such happenings shall forever remain fictitious." The setting is a New York suburb. Matthau played a supporting role: kindly "young Doc Spinelli," who is "standing by, waiting for the first wounded from New York." At one point, he employs a geiger counter to test a child who may have been exposed to radiation. After determining she is fine, he labels her a "one-hundred-percent red-blooded American girl."

Recalled Phyllis Thaxter, the show's star, "He played a small part, and was superb. He impressed me very much, and I felt he had a great and exciting career ahead. He certainly did."

Matthau began 1955 by briefly appearing in two revivals at New York's City Center. The first was Joshua Logan's *The Wisteria Trees*, based on Chekhov's *The Cherry Orchard* and set in the post-bellum American South. The star was stage legend Helen Hayes, who also toplined the original March 1950 production. *The Wisteria Trees* was not embraced by the theater intelligentsia. Noel Coward dubbed it "A Month in the Wrong Country," while another punster labeled it "Southern Fried Chekhov." It lasted 175 performances in its original incarnation and was revived only because of Hayes's desire to play it at City Center.

The production opened on February 2, and ran for fifteen performances. Matthau played Yancy Loper, a bellicose Louisiana land speculator; the part was originated by Kent Smith. According to Ossie Davis, a fellow cast member, Matthau's approach to the character was to play him with a "Yiddish flavor." "It wasn't an outrageous kind of thing," he explained. "Walter was a redneck, alright, but there were little Yiddishisms in his redneck—and that intrigued me quite a bit." Matthau surely must have been ebullient when he spotted his billing in the headline of the New York *Daily News* review: "Helen Hayes and Walter Matthau Act 'Wisteria Trees' at Center."

During the run, he appeared in a stripped-down version of *The Lost Weekend*, which aired on *Robert Montgomery Presents* on February 7. Twelve years earlier, Billy Wilder—who was to play a pivotal role in Matthau's future fame—directed it onscreen. Ray Milland won an Academy Award as Don Birnam, a helpless alcoholic; Montgomery took the role on TV, with Matthau appearing as Nat the kindhearted bartender, played earlier by Howard Da Silva. Here, a cigar-puffing, slightly pudgy Matthau displayed a New Yawk accent while addressing Montgomery as "Mistah Boinam," giving the time as "eleven thoity," and pronouncing "person" as "poisen."

One would not associate Matthau with musical theater. Yet he was linked, however precariously, to this musical form when, beginning on April 20, he starred in the City Center Light Opera Company's presentation of the Frank Loesser–Jo Swerling–Abe Burrows musical, *Guys and Dolls*. This "musical fable of Broadway," based on Damon Runyon's stories of the district's hustlers, gamblers, and showgirls, opened on April 20 and lasted fifteen performances.

A mustachioed Matthau played Nathan Detroit, a role created by Sam Levene: a charming albeit flustered Great White Way gambler who attempts to raise the funds that will enable him to host "the oldest established permanent floating crap game in New York."

Theater critic Walter Kerr not only praised Matthau's acting in *Guys and Dolls* but complimented him on his musical performance. Writing in the *New York Herald Tribune*, Kerr observed that the actor made "a surprisingly easy transition from . . . dramatic roles. . . . [He] slouches, sneers and beats his weary breast with the confidence and energy of a trained vaudevillian." This was not Matthau's only singing gig. A decade later, he cut a recording for Columbia Records, "Bring Her Back to Me," the lyrics of which he claimed to have penned when he was fourteen. He also sang on screen while playing Yonkers businessman Horace Vandergelder, the romantic object of matchmaker Dolly Levi, in the screen version of *Hello, Dolly!*

Guys and Dolls had been a smash hit when it originally opened on Broadway, in November 1950. The screen adaptation also came out in 1955. It starred Frank Sinatra as Nathan, along with Marlon Brando, Jean Simmons, Vivian Blaine, and Stubby Kaye. A decade or so later, Matthau might have rated a role in this version; he was, after all, cast in *Hello, Dolly!* But in 1955, while he had played leading stage and TV roles, Matthau was no movie star. That year, he did appear in his first two Hollywood films. They were less-than-auspicious debuts.

Actually, Matthau had the opportunity to appear on screen even before 1955. Three years earlier, as he was set to open in *In Any Language*, it was reported in the *Boston Herald* that "Matthau's aversion for movies is evidenced by the fact that he has turned down a number of Hollywood offers in order to remain in the theater." One was as Deborah Kerr's hypocritical husband in the 1953 drama *From Here to Eternity*. "It was a lousy part, small, insignificant," Matthau recalled. "So I turned it down. Then it won the Academy Award."

Just a few years later, the practicality of bill-paying would change his thinking. His debut actually might have propelled him into the cinema stratosphere. On June 15, 1954, Billy Wilder screen-tested Matthau for his adaptation of George Axelrod's *The Seven-Year Itch*. His role would have been a wide-eyed married man who fancies his new upstairs neighbor. His co-star would have been Marilyn Monroe. In the test, Matthau appeared with the actress who understudied the part on Broadway and recently had replaced star Vanessa Brown: Gena Rowlands.

Years later, Wilder claimed to have loved the test. Matthau reported that the filmmaker exclaimed, "Walter, you were absolutely convincing. You've got the part. I'm 83 percent sure." By July, Matthau was out of the running because he was not a cinema name. Wilder wanted Gary Cooper for the part. William Holden and James Stewart also were considered. All, of course, were top stars. In the end, the role was assigned to Tom Ewell, who had played it on Broadway. "I was talked out of [selecting Matthau] by [Darryl] Zanuck," Wilder declared, "because they thought they had a pretty good actor [in Ewell]."

Instead of starring opposite Marilyn Monroe in a Billy Wilder comedy, Matthau accepted a role that embarrassed him for the rest of his life: a sideburned, whip-wielding saloonkeeper-heavy in *The Kentuckian*, starring Burt Lancaster. In the opening credits, the list of supporting players ends with the words "and introducing Walter Matthau and Donald MacDonald," the latter a long-forgotten child actor who played Lancaster's son. Critics did not receive Matthau with the same warmth they did on stage. Of his performance, *New York Times* critic Bosley Crowther noted that it was "one of the old tent-show school."

Matthau referred to Lancaster, who also directed *The Kentuckian*, as "a very, very good screen actor but as a director, I've seen better." Of his casting, Matthau figured the rugged Lancaster thought, "Well, here's a fella who's no competition in the looks department. He could play the villain." From the outset, Matthau knew it was a ridiculous part. "I did a lot of eyeball-rolling and snarled out my lines with a New York accent," he explained. He was not required to learn to handle the bullwhip with the proficiency displayed by his character. Whip Wilson, a western actor and world champion bullwhip fighter, doubled for Matthau in the more intense bullwhip scenes.

Still, for authenticity, Matthau felt compelled to master the rudiments of the whip. Prior to heading for Owensboro, Kentucky, where the film was shot, he was sent a ten-foot bullwhip. He headed up to the rooftop of his West Forty-fourth Street apartment building to practice. He threw the whip forward into the air, and the loud cracking sounds soon brought a trio of New York's Finest.

"Hello, there," they said.

"Hi," Matthau responded.

"What ya got there?"

"That's a whip."

"Aaah, ya like to play with the whip?"

"Well, I'm doing it for a movie."

"Ooooh, you're an actor?"

"Yeah."

"Who's in the movie?"

Their demeanors changed from gruff to friendly once Matthau revealed the same of its star.

Decades later, Matthau entertained Alex Berger and his wife, Gloria, at the Beverly Hills Tennis Club. "Walter was so funny," Gloria recalled. "We were talking, and he started imitating himself. Alex said, 'Oh, you're Bodine' [his *Kentuckian* character]." Alex added, "He began with some of the dialogue. He was making fun of himself, and the film."

Compared to his stage projects, *The Kentuckian* was a sham. Yet it is understandable why Matthau accepted the role. Playing opposite Helen Hayes might be artistically fulfilling, but the actor, already in his mid-thirties, felt the need for material comfort. Plus, he now was a father; in 1953, Geri had given birth to David, their first child.

At this point, Matthau viewed himself as a stage actor slumming in the movies. "I would go out to do a picture and pick up some money and then go back to New York and pay my grocery bills and pay the landlord and pay the shoemaker," he explained. "It was just a place where they gave you money so you could pay your bills and do *real* acting on the stage." Matthau's screen debut also coincided with the permanent deletion of his name from the Manhattan telephone directory. (Interestingly, as Matthau's name is missing for the first time from the 1955–1956 directory, "Mrs. Rose Matthow" initially appears. Even though she no longer resided on First Street, she was clinging to the Lower East Side. Her address: 335 East Fifth Street.)

Matthau's casting in *The Kentuckian* led to Lancaster's pal Kirk Douglas hiring him for *The Indian Fighter*, filmed on location in Bend, Oregon. Again, he played a heavy—and another bit of Matthau exaggeration appeared in the program for *Guys and Dolls*. After citing his screen debut in *The Kentuckian*, it was noted that "shooting on his next film, *The Indian Fighter*, has been delayed for Mr. Matthau's appearance as Nathan Detroit." This was as likely a tale as Matthau's presence at Jimmy Stewart's World War II bombing mission briefings. The fact was that a delay in the filming allowed Matthau to accept the two-week *Guys and Dolls* run. Two decades later, he was comically exaggerating when he recalled that Douglas "broke my jaw during a fight [in the film]. He said I leaned into the punch. I said, 'Koik, how could I lean into the punch when I was tied to a tree?'"

As a novice film actor, Matthau was unfamiliar with the assembly-line aspect of moviemaking, in which sequences are shot out of order and an actor—particularly a supporting one—may be called upon to play a scene without any buildup. According to Douglas, Matthau hesitated before reciting his lines. "Don't you want me to think?" he asked. "You want me to just say the lines?" Douglas, the more experienced film actor, responded in the affirmative. Matthau followed orders.

Ironically, it was after filming *The Indian Fighter* that Matthau enjoyed his first bona-fide stage hit: another George Axelrod satire, *Will Success Spoil Rock Hunter?*, which opened at the Belasco on October 13, 1955, and lasted 444 performances. "I wasn't much of anything until I was thirty-five, when *Rock Hunter* came along," he once declared. "Some young actors who make it—they can't take the first time they have a setback. I endured."

Axelrod fashioned a clever farce about an unsophisticated journalist (Orson Bean) who makes a deal with the devil in the form of a diabolical Hollywood agent (Martin Gabel). Matthau lent support in a role that was tailor-made for him: Michael Freeman, a playwright who assists the hero, helping him to elude the agent's grasp. The most enticing character was a Marilyn Monroe caricature (played by Monroe rival Jayne Mansfield), with whom the journalist becomes involved.

Again, Matthau received stellar reviews. Only here, he had ample time to fully understand his role, and develop a characterization. "Six months after I opened in *Will Success Spoil Rock Hunter?*" he said, "I [finally] stopped seeing the printed page, with all the commas and all the notations. The printed page can remain with you for months and months, until you are experienced enough and relaxed enough to forget it early in the run and make what happens seem to be happening spontaneously."

At one point during the run, it was announced that Matthau would be leaving the play to appear on screen in John P. Marquand's *Melville Goodwin, U.S.A.*, starring Humphrey Bogart and Lauren Bacall. Sadly, he never got to work with Bogie, as the screen legend had contracted cancer of the esophagus. Eventually, the project was filmed as *Top Secret Affair*, with Kirk Douglas and Susan Hayward. Matthau's character, a Washington journalist, was played by Paul Stewart. Ironically, *Variety* published its review of *Top Secret Affair* on January 16, 1957, two days after Bogart's death.

Still, Matthau was not yet a big screen name, and when Frank Tashlin revamped *Rock Hunter* for the movies in 1957, just about all that remained from the original was Jayne Mansfield.

Yet he was in films, and was becoming known beyond New York acting circles. Once, early in his screen career, he found himself at the track—and in desperate need of cash to continue placing bets. He recalled that "people were talking about my last picture [and] I hollered into the stands, 'Where are my fans? Can anybody cash a $75 check?' This one guy said he would. I turned around, [and] it was George Raft."

"How do you know it's any good?" Matthau asked the aging star.

"I've seen your work," was the response. "I'll take a chance."

CHAPTER 10

"To the Ends of the Universe"

On April 19, 1953, Matthau appeared on a segment of *Omnibus*, the distinguished series that offered audiences high-caliber dramas, documentaries, and musicals. Matthau's sequence was a playlet, titled "The Abracadabra Kid," in which he played Thomas Turningout, a brusque, upper-crust father who is inattentive to his son. The boy summarily loses himself in the fantasy world of "abracadabra" and, in storybook fashion, Turningout becomes sensitized to the responsibilities of parenthood.

Cast as Matthau's wife was Maria Riva, daughter of Marlene Dietrich. "One day, after playing golf, I was sitting there watching the damn TV and *Omnibus* came on," recalled Tom Neilan, Matthau's old army buddy, "and there's Walter Matthau. I said, 'Jeez, I know that guy. What the hell's he doing on TV, kissing Marlene Dietrich's daughter?' Hell, he never kissed a girl the whole time we were overseas."

The author of "The Abracadabra Kid" was William Saroyan, the esteemed playwright/novelist/short-story writer whose credits include *The Time of Your Life* and *The Human Comedy*. Little did Matthau know that, two years later, he would meet, and fall in love with, Carol Marcus Saroyan, the writer's two-time former wife.

Walter and Carol grew up on the same island. Their backgrounds were at once astonishingly alike, and as different as the Russian Tea Room and Katz's Deli. Her early years were marked by deprivation; Rasheen, her single mother, toiled in a hat factory and placed Carol and her sister in a series of foster homes. Carol did not have to wait until adulthood to escape the squalor of her early youth. She was eight years old when Rasheen married, but Carol's stepfather was no everyday working man. He was Charles Marcus, a vice president of Bendix Aviation and consultant to Howard Hughes. It seemed that, on Friday, Carol was residing in an anonymous foster home, and by the following Monday was thrust into a more permanent and stylish surrounding: an eighteen-room duplex on the tony part of Fifth Avenue. Carol's life had been transformed into a Manhattan Towers storybook. (In his notorious *Current Biography* piece, Matthau gave Carol's maiden name as Wellington-Smythe Marcus, a fiction that befitted her new pedigree.)

Young Carol became friends with eleven-year-old actress-to-be Nina Foch. "We'd stay over each other's houses at night," Foch recalled. "We were those kind of chums. Then she got very 'cafe society,' and I didn't." Carol attended the high-prestige Dalton School. Among her cronies were Gloria Vanderbilt, the heiress, and Oona (daughter of Eugene) O'Neill. She was pals with young Truman Capote, whom she met when both were thirteen, and it has been claimed that she was the inspiration for his character Holly Golightly, the heroine of *Breakfast at Tiffany's*.

"My grandmother thought [Truman] was a freak," explained Carol and Walter's son Charlie, at a Toronto Film Festival press screening of *The Grass Harp*, the 1995 adaptation of Capote's auto-biographical novel that he directed.

"She'd say to my mother, 'Why do you bring that terrible creature around?' But then, after Truman became famous, my grandmother would tell him, 'Truman, Truman, don't you remember me? I used to patronize you.'"

Another schoolmate was Marian Seldes, who appeared with Walter on television in *Othello*. "I've always known Carol, and always adored her," Seldes recalled. "When she was in school, she was William Saroyan's girlfriend. I couldn't believe it. It was so dramatic and thrilling and great."

At fifteen, Carol graduated Dalton and joined her debutante pals in enveloping herself in Manhattan glitz. She debuted in high society in 1941; her photo was published on November 6 in the *New York World Telegram*, over the caption: "Carol Marcus has two debuts this season. She'll be presented to society next month and is now gaining recognition in her first stage appearance. She appears in Saroyan's new play, *Jim Dandy*, which is having a tryout at the Princeton University playhouse." At the time, Saroyan was sufficiently celebrated that citing his first name was unnecessary. The following year, she made her Broadway debut in his short-lived play, *Across the Board on Tuesday Morning*. In the show's *Playbill*, she is described as "another Saroyan discovery . . ."

Yet Carol was no dedicated thespian. As her son Charlie noted, she acted "to support herself between husbands. It was not a passion that she had to pursue."

As her friends Oona and Gloria did, Carol married a famous, artistically inclined "older man." One of Vanderbilt's husbands was the conductor Leopold Stokowski, who was forty-two years her senior; in 1943, eighteen-year-old O'Neill wed fifty-four-year-old Charles Chaplin. Saroyan, Carol's choice for a mate, was a mere babe. He was born in 1908, and was less than two decades her senior.

Through two marriages and two divorces, Carol endured a complex and painful relationship with Saroyan, with whom she had two children, Aram and Lucy (born respectively in 1943 and 1946). Carol first wed Saroyan in February 1943, when the writer was a private in the United States Army Signal Corps, stationed in Dayton, Ohio. "I've known for a long time that I've loved Bill," eighteen-year-old Carol told the press. "We decided to get married after I came to Dayton, but had hoped to keep our marriage secret for a while."

Saroyan was no ideal husband. Womanizing was but one of his negative traits. He crossed paths with Jayne Meadows when she was a young actress in New York. "I met him at the Theater Guild," she recalled. "He leaned over the staircase railing and said, 'You with the red hair. What's your name? What's your phone number?' He called me up, took me to dinner at 21, and introduced me to George Jean Nathan. Then he took me to see his play, *The Time of Your Life*, and we went backstage. I lived at the Rehearsal Club, a place for girls who didn't have any money. He had a hotel suite on Central Park West. We were in the cab, and he said to me, 'Oh, incidentally, I wrote a little story about you. I want to get it for you. Let's go up to the apartment.' We hardly got in the front door when he pulled my coat off. The next thing I knew we were on the floor, and he was jumping on top of me. I told this story to Walter at a dinner party one night. He said, 'Talk to Carol. She can top you.'"

In 1952, after her second divorce from Saroyan, Carol attempted to forge a writing career. Her pen name was "Carol Grace," and in 1955 she published a novella, *The Secret in the Daisy*. That same year, she was cast in *Will Success Spoil Rock Hunter?* in a small role, that of "A Secretary." She also understudied the show's voluptuous star, Jayne Mansfield.

On one occasion, Carol was substituting for Jayne during a rehearsal. "I remember the first scene," Matthau noted. "I come in, [and the character is] having a massage. I pat her on the butt and say, 'Rita, baby, how's it going?' The next day, Jayne Mansfield shows up. We're rehearsing the same scene, and I say, 'Rita baby . . . ow, ooh, oooh.' Later, I said to George Axelrod, I said, 'Listen, why don't you let that other girl play the part, because I think I'm gonna break my fingers on Jayne Mansfield's butt, because she has a very hard butt?' He said, 'Well, the other girl is a good actress, but Jayne Mansfield's the one who's gonna bring the people into the theater.'"

Even though Carol never earned fame as an actress, her intelligence and outgoing personality combined with her high-society status to allow her to mingle with New York notables and international celebrities. She lunched with Merle Oberon, and was photographed by Richard Avedon. She befriended writers, including Lillian Hellman, Carson McCullers, and Karen Blixen. Some of her involvements were romantic. Post-Saroyan, she had an unconsummated yet fervent relationship with the writer-critic James Agee. Kenneth Tynan, another noted critic, reportedly was in love with her.

"When I saw her for the first time," Matthau noted, "I thought she was an old lady because she wore white makeup. I thought she was a woman in her eighties, well preserved, with a skin disease. She told me her powder was called Yak-Do." He never did approve of the makeup, which she has worn from youth. One time, he alleged that it took Carol "four hours a day to make up. She uses talcum powder and yakshit." He also observed, "She's three hours before we go to dinner, destroying her face with makeup. I told her that makeup has lead in it. It gives you narcolepsy—because she's a bit of a narcoleptic."

Of the make-up, Jayne Meadows noted, "It was something that Carol was known for." However, Matthau—one Hollywood star who, as he aged, refused to have a facelift—was not the only male who disparaged it. Howard Morris described it as "clown white, for all I know." Yet Matthau was dead-serious when he added, "And, yes, from the moment I started seeing her, I started to live. In fact, I was taken out of an abyss of primordial slime and transported on a carpet of beauty, intelligence, and spiritual generosity. And Carol and I went to the ends of the universe."

At first, Carol saw her involvement with Walter as fleeting. He was, after all, already married. Like Saroyan, he had a predilection for gambling.

She was more the party type, preferring to spend evenings out among the multitudes, whereas Walter was content to be by himself, reading or listening to classical music, or among a small group of close pals. Even so, Carol and Walter found that they were falling in love.

Marian Seldes had not seen Carol "for years." She reported that once Matthau learned that they knew each other, he brought her around for a visit. "I don't think they were married yet," Seldes explained. "He took me up to West End Avenue [at Eighty-first Street], to this big beautiful apartment with huge rooms, all decorated by Carol. It was all roses and colors and feminine and beautiful. It was just as [their future house in Pacific Palisades] finally was; it was all flowers. It wasn't a man's place, except for Walter's [space]. It was that amazing femininity."

Pretty much from the outset, Broadway insiders were aware of Walter and Carol's relationship. "Those things are whispered around the business," explained Jayne Meadows, "because we knew he was married and Carol was very well-known in New York, not so much as an actress but as an 'interesting party girl.'" Walter soon entered Carol's social circle, and began mixing with Gloria Vanderbilt.

"We were always going to her parties," he recalled, "and I was always uncomfortable. The first time I was there, she slugged me. I had to hold her wrists. She thought I was taking too much of her girlfriend's time."

Just a few years before, winning positive reviews and earning the friendship of established actresses like Nancy Kelly added a degree of separation for Matthau from the Lower East Side tenements. Now, falling for Carol Marcus Saroyan and being her escort allowed him to step further up on the social ladder. Whatever Vanderbilt's attitude, he now had entree into her and Carol's rarified world, quite an accomplishment for a Lower East Side streetboy.

Though still married, Walter eventually began freely referring to Carol as his "girlfriend." Of Geri and Carol, he once declared, "My first wife thought I looked like Wallace Beery, my second wife thinks I'm Laurence Olivier." But the bottom line, at this point in time, was that Carol's entry into Walter's life doomed his marriage. Did he ever love Geri? "Yes, yes, he did," claimed Marvin Silbersher, "but I guess he became bored. He went 'Broadway.' He became a star. He was going from one victory to the next, and was leaving [his past] life behind."

Of his parents' breakup, David Matthau declared, "What I kind of understand, from [*Among the Porcupines*, Carol's 1992 memoir], is that my father was having a relationship with her, and then basically left the marriage." Added Anna Berger, "He broke Geri's heart. She was a very unhappy lady. When she came to my engagement party [in fall 1957], she just couldn't stop crying. Matthau was out of town, and couldn't come."

A decade after their 1948 nuptials, Matthau ended his marriage. In January 1959, he went to Mexico to obtain a divorce. At the time, David was five years old and Jenny, his younger sister, was two. They were around the same ages as Walter and Henry were when their father walked out on Rose.

"I remember being at a party at Adolph Green's house with [Matthau] and his first wife," recalled Heywood Hale Broun. "They seemed a very happy couple, and the next thing I knew they had broken up and he had married Carol." Then Broun amended his rec-ollection of the evening. "[On this occasion] she was a little hard, maybe," he said. "They didn't seem very cheery and get-togethery. Usually, you can tell when a couple is throwing little darts at each other.

"Carol was the one who was married to *two* compulsive gamblers. When I saw Walter and Carol together, they seemed very happy. Carol, I think, was an insecure man's dream, because she was so anxious to make *you* happy."

In February 1959, while publicizing *The Cold Wind and the Warm*, the S. N. Behrman play in which she was appearing on Broadway, Carol gave an interview to journalist Marjorie Farnsworth in which she volunteered, "There's a rumor going around that Bill [Saroyan] and I are planning on marrying again. Say I'm going to be married. I've just this moment decided to marry the first man who asks me." That same month, she told columnist Ward Morehouse, ". . . if you write anything about me I hope you're going to say that I'm beautiful and you might also say that I'm rich. It will be good for my credit." She also told Morehouse, "I'm so single it's terrible."

But not for long. Six months later, on August 21, 1959, Carol officially became Carol Matthau. On that day, he presented her with a dimestore ring. They were wed at New York's City Hall, in a civil ceremony. Matthau recalled that the clerk read them the following "silly words": "Do you, Francis Morganbird, take Lizzy Untschuller Von Plopheimer to be your lawfully wedded wife, to have and to hold, to sing and to dance, to eat and to sleep, and to fornicate and to drink and to smoke until death do you part?"

Years later, he declared, "I think the reason I married Carol was because she was just as crazy as I was." Whatever Matthau's motives, his relationship with her was deep, lasting, and loving. "I always knew there was something about her that made me feel whole," he said. "There was something missing before her. I guess that's what love is."

Fortunately for Walter, according to Anna Berger, his ever-demanding Mama Rose made life "only slightly difficult" for Carol. "Carol was independent," Berger explained. "She had money [in her family]. Rose would say to her sons, 'You make sure that any woman you marry'—and listen to this reasoning—'has $50,000 in a bank account, before you get married. And that's security.'" Still, Rose did not give Carol a complete pass. "I remember having to get out of

New York because my mother had a fight with [Carol]," Walter recalled. "Threatened to kill her. No, she said she was going to hire an assassin to kill her. But my wife wasn't afraid, she knew my mother was too cheap. Why? She hated *anyone* I was married to."

Rose's divisive presence aside, the Carol-Walter union was not without its own fireworks. The pair would squabble, like any long-married couple. On one occasion, early in their relationship, before Walter became a movie star and they moved to Los Angeles, he and Carol attended a New York party. Walter had been gambling, and Carol was irked that he had lost who knows how much money.

"Did you gamble today?" Carol asked.

"Yes," Walter tersely responded.

"I'm never going to speak to you again," Carol retorted.

"But look what I won!" Walter declared, and promptly produced a $100 bill.

"I don't want to see it," Carol responded, unmoved.

"Okay," Walter exclaimed. He then lit a match, and burned the money right in front of her.

"I think the secret [for marital bliss] is to get rid of all your money so you have to keep on working, which my wife and I do very well," Matthau once noted. "We simply get rid of the money. She collects objects. She has 18,427,000 objects in the house. I, on the other hand, give all the money to the bookies."

Not quite. After becoming a movie star and moving West, Matthau treated himself to a Mercedes. He presented Carol with a Rolls-Royce, and a mink coat. He also established his own corporation, Walcar, Inc. (named for Walter and Carol).

Once in the 1960s, Matthau ribbed Carol about her propensity for acting moneyed and non-Jewish. "She likes the feeling of being a *shiksa* from a very wealthy old family," he joked. She cheerfully chimed in, "Is there any other way to feel?" Just short of twenty years into their marriage, he discussed her approach to sex: "Oh, she's so sweet when she wants to get laid. All 'honey' and 'darling' in this sweet little voice. Then she gets laid and [with his voice turning from sugary to spiritless] it's 'Where are we eating tonight?'"

"I heard a story about [Walter] which is so typical," recalled Howard Morris. "He and his wife went on a tour of the [concentration] camps in Europe. By that, I mean Buchenwald and places like that. On the way back, [they] were fighting in public, just fighting like mad. Somebody got him aside and said, 'Walter, what are you fighting about?' He said, 'She ruined Dachau for me.' What a perfect thing to say."

Carol was just as adept as Walter was at dishing it out. "She was the only one who could bat that ball back to him," noted Anne Jackson. "She really knew how to meet his challenges. She has a wit that is as exquisite as his was naughty. She's as dirty-mouthed as he was, but she says it with such sweetness she looks as if she's a little angel talking.

"I think that Carol Grace Matthau was the luckiest thing that happened to him, and he the luckiest thing that happened to her," Jackson continued. "They had a beautiful marriage. They were so delightful together." Added Nancy Mehta, "I've always thought that Carol's quick, mercurial mind kept him facile and highly entertained. 'Quick turns' were a form of stimulation to him." Such was the case when a leggy, bosomy starlet once began flirting with Walter, while in Carol's company. He asked her age, and Truman Capote credited Carol with the following exclamation: "For God's sake, Walter, why don't you chop off her legs and read the rings?"

In 1987, Matthau was on hand to present the "life achievement award, female" at the First Annual American Comedy Awards. The five recipients were Lucille Ball, Carol Burnett, Mary Tyler Moore, Bette Midler, and Lily Tomlin. "If anyone deserves that award," Matthau noted, "it's Carol Matthau, that's my wife, for putting up with me for all these years. Unfortunately, she did not make the cut."

While filming *The Grass Harp* in the mid-1990s, Matthau enjoyed innocently flirting with co-star Piper Laurie. They first met before the shoot, while being fitted for their costumes in Los Angeles. "I was almost finished and he was in another room," she recalled, "and the door was open and we met on the edge of the doorway. He took my face in his hands and in the most adoring way he said, 'Oh, beautiful, beautiful.' No one introduced us. We just came together, and he said that, in the dearest way."

On the set, Matthau kept teasing Laurie. "Every morning, he'd just come at me, even after I was all fixed up and made up, and give me a big, big, messy kiss. It was as if he couldn't help himself." She added, "He used to joke all the time about Carol thinking that something was going on between the two of us. I mean, I know that he was joking."

That was because Laurie was well aware of Matthau's devotion to Carol. "We were on the same plane flying to Montgomery, to the location," she continued. "And we happened to be sitting next to each other. So we had all those hours to talk, and I got to know about his life and his family. Out of that came this passion for Carol, and this complete acceptance of everything she did. He wasn't justifying it. He was just stating it. I'd never seen a man talk about his wife [that way], without any sort of judgment, and complete acceptance and admiration for everything."

For the last three-plus decades of his life, Walter and Carol lived in Pacific Palisades, where their neighbors were William Schallert and his actress-wife, Lia Waggner. "I once said to Walter," recalled Waggner, "I said, 'Walter, just give me some advice. What do you do when you're up for a part that you *really* want, more than anything?' He said, 'Well, you know, the only thing I've ever really wanted in my whole life was Carol.' I thought that was so sweet. They had a great love story."

"The Abracadabra Kid" was not the sole William Saroyan property in which Matthau appeared. On November 7, 1960, he was cast in "Two by Saroyan," presented on *Play of the Week*. The "two" in question were "My Heart's in the Highlands," an adaptation of Saroyan's 1937 play, and "Once Around the Block," from the author's 1950 play. Matthau played a starving poet and a goofy Hollywood writer. Kirk Browning, the show's director, confirmed that his casting was entirely coincidental.

When he appeared in "Two by Saroyan," Matthau already had celebrated his first anniversary wed to the twice Mrs. William Saroyan. Many more spirited, eventful—and happy—years were to follow.

CHAPTER 11

The Family

Walter and Carol Matthau were to have a long and lively marriage. But this did not negate the existence of Geri—and their two children.

After Walter left Geri, she, David, and Jenny remained in Manhattan, moving to West Eighty-sixth Street between Broadway and Amsterdam Avenue. As the children grew older they remained a part of their dad's life. Until he moved to California in the late 1960s, they came by his apartment on Saturdays and returned to Geri the following day. "We went to the ballgame," David recalled. "We went to visit Grandma Rosie. We'd go for walks. Sometimes he'd take us to the playground. Sometimes we'd just hang out at his house." Yet Walter could not conceal his gambling. "I can sort of remember that he was always peripherally watching games," David noted. "We were aware that he had a bet on a game. There was an awareness that our father was betting on games, but that was kind of like the way it was, normal and accepted."

Anna Berger recalled that, on one occasion, Matthau brought David and Jenny to the West End Avenue apartment she shared with her husband, Bob Malatzky. "They were just darling," she recalled. "He and David played basketball in our living room."

It was in such a manner that Matthau attempted to bond with his son. But his fondness for Jenny was no less evident. "Although he didn't ever mention his first wife, he did mention that daughter," noted Marian Seldes. "He must have been going to see her when he was in New York and he, Carol, Gar [Garson Kanin], and I would go out to lunch or dinner. He'd mention her, and it was with a lot of affection."

When their parents separated, David and Jenny were so little that they have no memory of Walter and Geri living under the same roof. "I don't really have any recollections [of them being together], because I was like one and two years old [when they separated]," David explained. For him and his sister, the reality that their parents once were a couple exists only in old photographs and home movies. "I have some wonderful pictures where I'm laughing and playing on a hobby horse," he said. "I have films of my mother and father in Puerto Rico. My sister is crawling around, and I'm running around on the beach and fooling around with my dad.

"Having worked through some of this stuff, I think I was devastated [when they divorced], as any small child would be. In those days, I don't think most parents had the wherewithal or understanding to really talk about what's happened much beyond 'Well, Daddy's gone away now.'"

When asked if he got to spend time with his half-brother and sister, Charlie Matthau answered, "Not really. I didn't have a chance to, because they're obviously a little bit older than I am, and they lived with their mother."

When Matthau appeared in "The Abracadabra Kid," Geri was two months pregnant with David. Matthau's role was a neglectful father who always is "in a hurry." *Omnibus* host Alistair Cooke noted, while introducing the segment, "As always in a Saroyan play where there are children, it's the adults who learn the lessons." By the finale, Matthau's character, a busy advertising executive, explains that he has forgotten what it is like to be a child, and that he does not know how to talk to his son. The story ends happily, as the character and his actress-wife realize the need to be a family, for the sake of their son.

However, there was no such storybook ending for Walter, Geri, David, and Jenny as a nuclear family. David willingly admitted that he has attempted to better understand his father, and deal with unre-solved feelings about his parents' divorce, by undergoing therapy. "I had made an effort, actually [in the mid-1990s], to work through in therapy the fact that I had really felt this loss as a little guy when my parents were divorced. And I needed to say to [Walter] that I really felt bad when he left, and I really wanted to know, 'Where was my dad?' [I wanted to say] 'I really always loved you, and missed having you as my father full-time when I was growing up.'

"And when I said that to him, it made him really uncomfortable. It was like, why was I saying this to him, or did I want something? I had to make the point, 'No, it's not that. It's just that I wanted to say that to you, that I really missed having Daddy there when I was growing up.'

"He didn't know how to react. In a way, he wasn't quite sure why I was saying this to him. I really felt determined to say that to him, because I wanted him to know that there was that part of me that missed that, and felt bad about it, and felt a loss about it, and that was really because I loved him."

Similarly, the emotional effect of her divorce reverberated for Geri. "I think my mother was pretty bitter, and really sort of felt kind of shocked and sad about what happened," noted David. "[She] never really recovered in a lot of ways. She had a fair amount of self-pity, and was angry about it at the same time and let some of that leak out onto her kids. You know, the resentment and so forth."

David commented that Walter was forthcoming when it came to financially supporting his children, but was less than generous in his treatment of Geri. "My father was a complex guy," he declared. "On the one hand, he was really extremely generous and giving and loving. He always loved his kids. My sister and I went to private schools. Any clothes that we needed, we got. We went to camp every summer, and always saw the best doctors and dentists. My father always paid for that.

"At the same time, [with regard to] the settlement that was made when my parents were divorced, my mother kind of got stiffed. She did not really have any savvy, and didn't have a very good lawyer to negotiate her settlement. So she was given a crummy, cheap deal. She got really sort of stuck. I know that my mother didn't work, and in those days very few women were in positions where they would actually go out and earn a living. When people were divorced, it was like the male was supposed to pay the alimony and child support.

"Which isn't to say that I think on the one hand my father was such a rotten person, because I don't. But he had a very sharp lawyer, whose job it was to negotiate the best deal for his client that he could get. And he got him a pretty good deal."

Geri, David, and Jenny Matthau were a closely knit trio. "Geri had two children who adored her," observed Anna Berger. But the bottom line was that she was a casualty of the pre-feminist times. Walter and Geri were married during an era when women were expected to be financially and emotionally dependent upon men. An educated woman might become a schoolteacher, librarian, or nurse: "second-income" professions that could be left upon motherhood and returned to when her children were grown. Otherwise, the center of her life was her husband and her children, her kitchen and her housekeeping.

For Geri, life was not so formulaic. Her husband had cheated on her, and then unceremoniously had dumped her. Back in the 1950s, a woman in Geri's situation had few resources, few support systems, little outside encouragement to help her define herself beyond how a woman was expected to act. In most cases, when a man walked out on a wife and two babies, he was viewed as the villain. Yet from the time of their separation, many in Matthau's circle disregarded his first family, instead focusing on his love affair with Carol.

Geri Matthau never remarried. "And then, unfortunately, she got [breast] cancer," added Berger. "Jenny was with her until she died. This was long after Walter and Geri ended their marriage."

Geri Johnson Matthau died in 1982. She was fifty-seven years old. "My father paid for the funeral completely," David recalled, "and supported his kids by coming to the funeral. He took a flower to her burial site and stood over the grave and threw it into the grave.

"I think that fundamentally he was a decent guy," David continued. "At the same time, when he had a relationship with Carol, and then started a family [Charlie, David and Jenny's stepbrother, was born in 1962], I think that, as is the case in many families, Carol really tried to keep all of his focus on his current family. She was never really very supportive of the relationship he had with us. Not that she was hostile when we came over. There was always a sense of not really feeling very welcome on some level."

In a 1968 interview given while in the company of five-and-a-half year-old Charlie, Walter offered a revealing analysis of middle-age parenthood: "The chances are that you are more settled financially and spiritually. That's the assumption, anyway, and you can enjoy the children more." Yet the defining contrast between David's and Jenny's childhoods and that of Charlie has nothing to do with economics or lifestyle, East Coast versus West Coast, Manhattan versus Southern California—or even Matthau's age when his children were born. The difference is that the first two children grew up in a broken, single-parent home, with an embittered mother and a part-time father. Charlie, meanwhile, was the beneficiary of a loving, nurturing, two-parent household.

Furthermore, in the stratified society of Hollywood, it was as if Walter and Geri's union never existed. In 1996, *The Hollywood Reporter*, an industry trade publication, feted Matthau with a special anniversary issue spotlighting his half-century-long acting career. Only Matthau's second family was represented, via a photo of him, Carol, and Charlie as a toddler. The following year, the trio was honored as a "family of artists" by the American Film Institute. In both cases, Geri, David, and Jenny were expunged from his life.

While Walter was building his career, his childhood pals were settling into jobs, entering the middle class, and forsaking the Lower East Side for the outer New York City boroughs and suburbs. Henry Matthow, for one, entered the army-and-navy store business. "His first store was on East Fourth Street between Avenue A and Avenue B. It was a little store," recalled Ike Goldschlager. "Then he opened up a store on East Broadway off Madison Street, near Chinatown. Then he wanted to expand a little bit, so he opened up another store on East Broadway between Houston and Prince [Streets]. And that's it." Henry also married, started a family, and eventually moved to Long Island.

"He was a darling fellow," recalled Anne Jackson. Henry also could kibitz as well as Walter. One rare occasion in which he was quoted in the press came in 1978, when he suggested to a female journalist that she give his brother "a good spanking. He'll like that." Henry described Walter as "*meshugener*"—Yiddish for "crazy"—and added, "He was . . . what they call slightly unconventional. *I* looked at things from a proper perspective. Say only nice things about him, only sweet things. A man like him deserves commendation—a man who was able to follow his dream."

Because of their differences, the two drifted apart in young adulthood. Charlotte Haverly reported, "They didn't see each other a lot, during the time I knew Walter." Anna Berger extended this further. "There was a time when Walter was doing a movie," she recalled, "and he wanted Henry to come out and stay with him for two weeks. So Ruth said, 'How 'bout me? I'm your wife. Shouldn't he invite me as well?'" In the end, Matthau did not extend his invitation to his sister-in-law. "Did Henry go without you?" Berger asked Ruth. "Sure," was the response. "That was callousness toward the wives, from Walter's point of view, [a vestige from life] before Carol."

That callousness could be linked to Henry and Walter's mother. David Matthau reported that, as children, he and Jenny saw their Grandma Rosie "probably two or three times a year." David described Rose as "certainly a maverick, and she was daring in many ways" in that she had left her native Lithuania and come to the United States to face an unknown future. Yet she was no stereotypically loving, nurturing grandparent. "When we went to visit her, there was never any real great warmth or sweetness or feeling of having any real relationship with a grandmother. It was strained, somewhat. Basically, we were going because we were being taken there by my dad. It was not horrible or anything. It's just that there wasn't any real sense of having a relationship with our grandmother."

After World War II, the Lower East Side demographics began changing. New immigrants moved into the community, the crime rate was increasing and, as an elderly woman, Rose was in a vulnerable position, whether going to the market or spending a couple of hours in a public park. Furthermore, Lower East Side apartments were dark and old-fashioned.

Had Walter been a cop, shopkeeper, or transit worker, he or Henry probably would have had Rose living in a spare room in their workingman's house. However, Walter's success allowed Rose to leave the Lower East Side in style. David Matthau reported that, in 1963, his father moved her into a top-floor apartment on Seventy-second Street between West End Avenue and Riverside Drive, which featured a wonderful view of the Hudson River. The relocation might have come earlier, but Rose had remained stubbornly wedded to the old neighborhood.

"I'd propagandized that move for two solid years," Matthau explained the following year, "and it took some screaming and a few suicide threats to get her going." Almost forty years later, David Matthau recalled, "I have memories of when my father moved her. I must have been real young, because I don't remember specifically when it was, or exactly what happened, or what was said. But I do remember that there was a great amount of antagonism on my grandmother's part. She was yelling and screaming at my father, and she didn't want to go."

Les Schecter, who worked as Matthau's publicist when he was filming *Plaza Suite* in 1970, recalled that the actor told him that Rose liked her new apartment, "but was unhappy because she couldn't get the chicken she liked. So every weekend he would send a car, a limousine, to pick her up and take her shopping on the Lower East Side, to the old chicken store or whatever. She just couldn't get the Lower East Side out of her blood."

On one level, noted Anne Jackson, Rose "was enormously competitive about Walter and his talent. At the time we met Walter, he was not yet a leading man. He was certainly a brilliant actor, but not a leading man. Yet Eli [Wallach, Jackson's husband] had already reached that place. He already had done *Baby Doll* [on screen] and *Camino Real* on Broadway. So Rosie would make cracks. I just got the feeling from her that there was a jealousy there, an envy."

Conversely, she could be clueless about Walter's celebrity. The story goes that she was crossing Broadway, walking near her apartment, when she spotted Walter in a cab, in the process of being filmed—and broke the thread of the filming by talking to him through the cab windows. Charlie Matthau reported that his father "would always get her tickets to Broadway shows and concerts from William Morris, and I think she would ask, 'Do you think I could just have the money instead of the tickets?' He used to have to tell her that they were free."

Years later, Rose went to live in Florida. "I remember once, in

Miami, where I got her an apartment on the beach," Matthau recalled. "I took her to a restaurant, a steak place, and there were maybe 300 people on the sidewalk, first come, first served, no reservations. I asked for [a table], they told me to walk through the mob. I did, [and] people were applauding.

"My mother pushed me, wanting to know what they were applauding for. She shoved me through the crowd, saying, 'What do those people want from you?' She didn't trust any success at all. . . . She always said, 'See if these people who are applauding you would loan you a dollar if you needed it.'"

Rose's distrust of strangers extended to those in authority. In the mid-1950s, Matthau received a phone call from her. She had been arrested and was calling from a Coney Island precinct house. "Get me out of here," she demanded. "What did you do, sock a policeman?" Walter asked. "Only afterwards," was the response. It seemed that Rose had been riding the subways and a cop apparently had looked at her "funny," thus precipitating her outburst. She could choose her sentence: three days in jail, or a $10 fine. Rose opted for jail. The judge generously reduced the sentence to one day.

Brooklynite Bea Shecter recalled that she saw Rose at Brighton Beach on several occasions during the late 1960s. "She was by herself," Shecter noted. "Somebody first pointed her out to me, saying, 'See that lady. That's Walter Matthau's mother.' She was a very frugal type, shall we say. She used to come with a double paper shopping bag, and she would look through the sand, like she was going to pick up something."

Anne Jackson also offered a vivid picture of Rose and her immigrant ways. "Do understand," she explained, "that by the time he brought his mother to see me I had been brainwashed somewhat by Walter himself and by his brother. Anyway, his mother was someone you would classify as a *balebosteh* [Yiddish for a conscientious housewife]. She was not a particularly beautiful woman, I mean physically. But she was a strong woman. Walter looked a lot like her, and Walter, as a woman, would not be your ideal girl.

"Rosie Matthow was definitely Old World," Jackson added. "She wore rolled stockings below the hemline, and conservative shoes. Big shoes, I remember. She was a kind of a mannish-type lady. But I liked her. You couldn't help liking her. I guess you liked her because she was Walter's mother. In both of them, and in his brother, too, there was a kind of no-nonsense, no airs. None, whatsoever.

"I imagine that Walter got a lot of his humor from her. She was acerbic. She was a powerful lady. I think Carol was quite devastated by her. And Walter was like a little boy when his mother was around—a good little boy. He was all sad smiles, like 'Oh, gee, Mom, would you shut your mouth?' But he never said it." While dating Matthau, Charlotte Haverly got to know her. "He'd talk to her the way he'd talk to [anybody]," she added. "He'd say, 'Well, I'll tell you, Rosie. . . .' Sometimes he called her 'Ma,' but generally it was 'Rosie.'"

Grandson David, however, perceived Rose in the same manner as many of her Lower East Side neighbors: "She was honestly and truly slightly out of her mind." He is convinced that she, too, suffered from Attention Deficit Disorder. "My theory is that there was a strong A.D.D. personality involved. [This was so] for a lot of people who are set off from their native countries."

Despite her dislike for Florida—she once told Walter, "Oh, there's nothing but old fools [there]"—Rose remained there for the rest of her life. She died in January 1979. Anna Berger, then appearing on stage in Miami, stopped by to pay her respects. "The whole family was there," she noted. "And Walter was carrying on, uncontrollably."

Yet any supposed Attention Deficit Disorder—or even Walter's gambling—were minor maladies compared to the difficulties of his and Henry's alleged half-brother, Marvin.

"I think that [Marvin] tried to make contact [with my father] a couple of times," noted David Matthau. "He was a child entertainer, a magician, among other things. I don't really know much about him beyond that. I never met him. I don't know if my father was terribly keen on meeting him."

Ruby Ludwin, Walter's boyhood pal, reported that Marvin did make contact. "Years later, he came to see Walter, after Walter became famous," Ludwin explained. "He was in show business, and wanted a helping hand. Walter was miffed because this half-brother only had come to see him, and not Henry." Syd Preses reported, "Henry told me they never discussed him. The boys didn't acknowledge [Marvin] as family." Added Charlie Matthau, "I know that someone who calls himself Marvin Matthow would write to my father and say that was the case. But I don't know if it's true or not."

In 1979, a brief item about Marvin appeared in the *New York Times*. In it, he is described as Walter's brother, and it is noted that he "appears on stages, on cruise ships and at fund-raising events, not only in his 'Bongo and Bananas the Clown' act, but also in a comedy balancing act called 'The Human Seal.'" "There's lots of talent in this family, and it's not limited to Walter," Marvin noted. "Right now, I'm getting ready to perform in an act called 'The Balancing Illusion Show,' at Manhattan Market on the Hudson. . . . My nephew, Billy Damon, who's twenty, and my daughter Marlene, fifteen, appear in the act, too." Then he added, "I told you, there's talent in this family." Marvin further explained that he also worked as a talent agent who booked "walkaround acts—jugglers, barkers, clowns," and sold insurance on the side.

Insurance was not Marvin's only sideline. In an article published in 1980 in the *Gay Community News*, headlined "Clown Nabbed in NY on Kid Porn Charge," it was reported that undercover police "entrapped" him by offering him money to procure underage models for a film. According to New York State records, he pleaded guilty to "attempted use of a child in a sexual performance, a class D felony." He was sentenced to "an indefinite [jail] term not to exceed seven years. The Parole Board set his minimum period of incarceration [MPI] at four years." In establishing the MPI, the board noted, "You are convicted of a serious crime, attempted use of a child in a sexual performance. Your record indicates a long history of sexual involvement with young boys and serious sexual problems. You require extensive psychiatric care and treatment to deal with this problem."

On March 3, 1983, three New York State Supreme Court justices ruled on Matthow's parole appeal, which had been entered on February 24, 1982. It was noted in their decision that Matthow, the Petitioner, "contends that the MPI was illegally imposed in that it exceeds the guidelines for an MPI." They determined that he "was given an opportunity to present mitigating factors to the board. Also, we find no basis in the record to support petitioner's contention that the board acted on erroneous information. Petitioner has failed to make a showing that the board's decision amounted to 'irrationality bordering on impropriety.' . . ."

Translation: Matthow's parole petition was denied.

The following year, a brief item appeared on the "People Page" of the New York *Daily News*, headlined "A new role for Matthau?" The piece, generated by a Matthow-written letter, erroneously referred to him as Walter's "big brother" and noted that Marvin "tried to carve out a career as a clown. Didn't work out. Marvin tried other work but had lots of problems. Now he has a new idea. He wants Roman Polanski to film his story." Polanski, who later directed Walter in *Pirates*, had been arrested in 1977 and charged with drugging and raping a thirteen-year-old girl. While out on bail, he fled the United States and was considered a fugitive from justice.

In his note, written from his Brentwood, Long Island, prison cell, Marvin requested information on how to contact Polanski. "Also, I would like to contact John Lindsay, the former [New York City] mayor, to be my lawyer in this movie deal." He added that his incarceration was the result of his being framed, and that he hoped brother Walter would agree to play him onscreen.

Needless to say, Matthau never did play Matthow.

CHAPTER 12

Supporting Actor

Matthau's return to the stage post–*Will Success Spoil Rock Hunter?* was yet another flop: *Maiden Voyage*, a Paul Osborne comedy in which he was cast as Odysseus. The production did not make it out of Philadelphia, opening at the Forrest Theatre on February 28, 1957, and closing on March 9.

Happily, he was reunited with George Axelrod, the director of a Harry Kurnitz–authored satire of the music world: *Once More, With Feeling*, which opened at the National on October 21, 1958, and lasted 263 performances. Matthau was featured in a supporting role. Joseph Cotten was the male lead, a moody orchestra conductor who realizes he does not wish to divorce his estranged wife (Arlene Francis). Matthau played the conductor's fretting, Sol Hurok–like manager, whose Russian accent, he explained, he "got from Mickey Richter's candy store, down on the Lower East Side." And he won his usual critical raves. Brooks Atkinson wrote, "Dressed in the sober clothes of the trade, with black hat and fierce mustache, Mr. Matthau is forever lunging at the play, the other actors and the audience, making every statement in the form of a sadistic question. Mr. Matthau's bounce and drive give a lunatic lift to the scenes in which he appears."

Paul Tripp, Matthau's old *Mr. I. Magination* colleague, saw him in the play. "He was so goddamned funny," Tripp recalled. "He created the craziest accent." Added Dan Frazer, who understudied Joseph Cotton, "Walter was hysterically funny—funny in rehearsal, funny in performance." Critic John Chapman foretold Matthau's future when he noted, "Always a good actor, Matthau is a grand comedian in *Once More, With Feeling*. . . ."

Matthau did not last the run of the play. He was succeeded by two well-known actors of the Yiddish theater: Joseph Buloff, who in turn was replaced by David Opatoshu. For his performance, he was honored with a New York Drama Critics Circle Award and a Best Supporting or Featured Actor Tony Award nomination. His competition: Marc Connelly (for *Tall Story*); George Grizzard (*The Disenchanted*); Robert Morse (*Say, Darling*); Charles Ruggles (*The Pleasure of His Company*); and George C. Scott (*Comes a Day*). Ruggles was the winner.

Matthau also remained a regular on television, playing characters ranging from a political boss ("The Big Vote," on *The Alcoa Hour*, August 19, 1956) to a business magnate's sharp, adept son-in-law ("The Legacy," *Goodyear Theatre*, June 30, 1957), a married man involved in a he-said/she-said battle of the sexes ("The Trouble with Women," *The Alcoa Hour*, August 11, 1957) to a disheveled canvassing agent suspected of terrorizing women ("To Walk the Night," *Climax!* December 19, 1957).

One of his more intriguing projects was "Code in the Corner" (*Kraft Television Theatre*, January 15, 1958), if only because it was written by Jack Klugman, who replaced Matthau on Broadway as Oscar Madison in *The Odd Couple* and redid the role in the TV sitcom. Howard Morris co-starred and the two became fast friends. Morris, who was zany in his own right, was attracted to Matthau's outrageousness. "I mean, he was so wild," Morris exclaimed. "Whenever there was a serious moment, you could count on him to razz it.

"There was always good Jewish humor involved in just about everything he did and said," Morris noted. "I remember rehearsing that *Kraft* show, and we did it in a place over on Second Avenue, over Ratner's [the same spot in which Matthau worked with Betsy Palmer]. One of the big events of the day was when we would go downstairs for lunch, and his mother would join us. She was wearing the mink that he had given her, and a babushka. And there was a lot of Yiddish that ensued. She kept calling him *boychik*." Did Matthau go by a Yiddish name when in the presence of his mother? "*Velvul-moishka*," Morris quipped.

Matthau's television visibility did not go unnoticed by his old Lower East Side contemporaries. Sometime in the 1950s, Syd Preses happened to see him on one of his shows. Afterwards, she called him at the station. She introduced herself, but was met with silence. "Then I excused myself," she recalled, "and said that he probably didn't remember me. 'Oh yes,' he said. 'I remember you as a little dark girl with a Buster Brown haircut. Your nose was always running and your bloomers were always showing.' We both laughed."

In the late 1950s and early 1960s, as the live-television era gave way almost completely to taped and filmed programming, Matthau appeared on some of the period's premier series. He guest-starred on four episodes of *Alfred Hitchcock Presents*. In "The Crooked Road," broadcast on October 26, 1958, he was a bullying, small-town Southern cop who harasses a motoring couple. Ex–New School classmate Rod Steiger might have used this characterization as a model for his redneck sheriff in the Oscar-winning *In the Heat of the Night*. "Dry Run" (November 8, 1959) featured Matthau as a sly, hard-as-nails hood, the kind who calls money "dough" and alcohol "juice" and whose conversation is peppered with words like "nuts," "bull," "snowjob," "pushover," "punk," and "kid." In "Very Moral Theft" (October 11, 1960), he was an ill-fated small-time operator who borrows $8,000 from his middle-aged, desperate-to-be-married girl-friend. In "Cop for a Day" (October 31, 1961), he was the elder of two stick-up men, a canny veteran lawbreaker who impersonates a police officer in order to kill a murder witness (played by Carol Matthau).

He guested on such high-profile hour-long dramatic series as *Naked City*, *Route 66*, and *Dr. Kildare*. He appeared on *Play of the Week*, a syndicated dramatic anthology series that depended upon Broadway actors for its casts. He narrated "Fire Rescue" and "Police Emergency," mini-documentaries presented on *DuPont Show of the Week*.

In "Footnote to Fame," a "drama of men and politics" that aired on *Westinghouse Presents* on February 3, 1962, a bespectacled Matthau played a savvy veteran politico. He might have based his character on an old Lower East Side crony. He played the role with a "Jewish intonation," sounding like Jackie Mason, only talking straight rather than telling jokes.

Matthau labeled "Big Deal in Laredo," which aired on *DuPont Show of the Week* on October 7, 1962, a "Western without guns or horses." His part: Meredith, a sweaty loser who becomes a player in a high-stakes poker game but actually is involved in an elaborate con. Matthau described Meredith as a reformed gambler, which was what *he* claimed to be while promoting the show. His old friend Ruby Ludwin might have two words for this allegation: "bullshit artist." Meanwhile, Matthau chuckled when he declared, "They say a real gambler will bet on anything. It's not true. I only used to bet on long, torturous things, like two-and-a-half-hour ballgames." His smile surely widened when he earned an Emmy nomination for this performance. He was in competition with Trevor Howard (for "The Invincible Mr. Disraeli," airing on *Hallmark Hall of Fame*); Bradford Dillman ("The Voice of Charlie Pont," *Premiere*); Joseph Schildkraut ("Hear the Mellow Wedding Bells," *Sam Benedict*); and Don Gordon ("The Madman," *The Defenders*). Howard was the victor.

Shirley Knight appeared with Matthau in "The Takers," broadcast on *DuPont Show of the Week* on October 13, 1963. She described it as "kind of a silly television thing. He played a criminal, and it was all about a kidnapping, and I played two roles. Claude Rains played my father, which was amazing. And Larry Hagman was in it. It was supposed to be a mystery, and it wasn't terribly good. About two days before we did it, everybody decided that we would play it tongue-in-cheek, as a comedy. Then it went very well. A lot of that was due to Walter, because he had a take on it. I think it was even his suggestion that we do that." Knight's other memory of the show was that, in every free moment, Matthau was off to the racetrack. He either seemed to be returning from or going to the track.

In "The Personal Touch," an episode of *The Rogues* that aired on September 13, 1964, Matthau was Aram Rudescu, a sharp, sinister Eastern European, a "poor fisherboy from a waterfront hovel" turned super-rich shipping magnate. He played the role using a thick accent; coming from Matthau, one might expect him to momentarily lapse into Yiddish. Also appearing was Dina Merrill, who described Matthau's character as "a foreign national of some kind" and added, "We never could figure out what kind of an accent he had. He just seemed to make it up along the way. Maybe Transylvania, who knew?"

Rose Matthow for one did not like seeing her son in such roles. After telling an interviewer in 1964 that she wanted Walter to have his nose "fixed into a *nice* nose so he could get leading parts, but he wouldn't listen," she observed, "I don't like him as a gangster in those TV plays, with the glasses and the cigar and the big mustache. He looks old, and he's really good-looking. You can be good-looking and still play gangsters—without all that stuff—and make a lot of money, too." When asked to cite a performer in this category, she named Edward G. Robinson.

Rose much preferred Walter's roles on *Profiles in Courage*, a series based on the book by President John F. Kennedy. On December 20, 1964, he played John M. Slaton, the Georgia governor who in 1915 commuted the death sentence of Leo Frank, a Jew who had been falsely convicted of raping and murdering a fourteen-year-old girl; two months later, he was lynched. Then on February 28, 1965, he played President Andrew Johnson.

Michael Ritchie, who would direct Matthau in *The Bad News Bears*, *The Survivors*, and *The Couch Trip*, was the show's associate producer. "The one he was most proud of was Governor Slaton," Ritchie recalled, "because of the historical importance and the quality of the writing. It was not the kind of thing you get to do on television. The fact that he wasn't playing a Damon Runyon wiseguy but a man of stature and intellectual importance meant a lot to Walter."

Despite the serious nature of the project, Matthau still was, well, Matthau during the filming. "When we were shooting it, he did something that he always did when he didn't feel a take was going well," Ritchie noted. "Many actors will say, 'Oh, can we cut? I don't like this.' Walter on the other hand would deliberately goof up the take, so that it couldn't be used. He'd do it with great seriousness, so when *you'd* say, 'Cut,' *he'd* say, 'What? Was there something I did wrong?'"

Once, Ritchie's professor father visited the set. "I invited him to [view the] dailies," he continued, "forgetting that was the day Walter had had a climactic emotional scene in which the governor realizes he's giving up his political career for principle. He's sitting with his wife on the steps of the governor's mansion and he says, 'And so that's why I've learned. . . .' You can see a look in his eye [and] you know he's lost the line. So instead he says, "And so that's why I've learned that if you eat right, you shit right.'

"Of course my father, being a raucous guy himself, let out the biggest laugh in the screening room." Then Ritchie added, "Walter never expected me to print these takes, but I always did. This was before the era of gag-reels."

Matthau's stage and TV work did not preclude his appearing onscreen. In *Bigger Than Life*, released in 1956 and directed by cult filmmaker Nicholas Ray, he played the friend of the main character (James Mason), a schoolteacher who becomes addicted to cortisone. Of Ray, Matthau recalled, "I once asked him a question. And he didn't say anything for about two minutes. Then he started walking and I started following him. And he walked for about another ten minutes, and I followed him and walked around with him. And then he turned to me and he said, 'No.' I had forgotten my question by that time, so I didn't know what the hell he was talking about."

One of his best early movie roles was Mel Miller, a savvy writer, in Elia Kazan's *A Face in the Crowd*, a 1957 drama about media manipulation, the power of television, and the cult of celebrity. Physically, Miller is an intellectual stereotype; he wears glasses, and a pipe is never far from his lips. He may be an ideal match for the story's heroine (Patricia Neal), but he is, after all, a writer, so he is in danger of losing her to charismatic, hypocritical hillbilly-turned-TV personality Lonesome Rhodes (Andy Griffith). When Piper Laurie saw the film, she noted Matthau's appearance and thought, "My God, he's trying to play Joe Mankiewicz, with the pipe and the glasses." She eventually asked him about this, and he told her, "No, I didn't do that deliberately."

Matthau's character was a functionary within the framework of the story: a definition of his on-screen presence then and for years to come. However, he is consistently fine in his few dramatic scenes, particularly as he sits at a bar with Neal and reveals that he has written a book about Rhodes, titled *Demagogue in Denim*. Neal recalled that Matthau's part was a good one, and that she enjoyed working with him. In the early 1990s, Neal's friend, Phyllis Jenkins, gave a party for her during a California visit. Matthau and Carol were present and, as Neal recalled, "They had the most magnificent flowers sent to my friend for the party and I had a small one to go with it. Walter and his dear wife were very, very generous."

Kazan, one of the founders of the Actor's Studio, was noted for eliciting naturalistic performances by having his performers focus on their own, personal feelings, rather than "acting" emotion. During the shoot, he wanted to evoke a look of fury from boxer Walter Cartier, cast in a small role. So Kazan instructed Matthau to tell the fighter, just before turning on the camera, "Hey, Cartier, I saw you fight, and you stink." Matthau told Kazan that Cartier instead would laugh, because he knew such a declaration was ludicrous. But the actor followed instructions anyway and was proven correct when Cartier broadly smiled.

Matthau recalled that Kazan "seemed exceptionally nervous" during the shoot. Previously, he was called before the House Un-American Activities Committee and chose to "name names" of Hollywood "subversives," which allowed him to avoid being blacklisted. "I don't think Mr. Kazan was quite sure whether he did the right thing in what he did," Matthau opined. "So, he seemed nervous."

During this period, most of Matthau's film roles took him away from New York, either to a Hollywood soundstage or a location that befitted the story. On *A Face in the Crowd*, he was able to remain at home. Eighty-five percent of the film was shot at the former Biograph Studios in the Bronx. Even the sequence set in the Memphis studio in which Lonesome Rhodes makes his television debut was filmed at Matthau's old stomping grounds: the Henry Street Settlement, located on the Lower East Side.

In the film *Voice in the Mirror*, released in 1958, Matthau played another sympathetic character, a no-nonsense doctor who attempts to cure a patient of alcoholism. Only here, he was not being directed by a top-flight filmmaker. "On this particular picture," Matthau recalled, "I was angry with Harry Keller, who was directing. And finally he said to me, 'Will you leave me alone? I'm really a cutter.' So I left him alone. Richard Egan [the film's star] said, 'You see, Matthau is a New York actor. He likes to argue.'

"I've never been able to get used to the fact that a group of people get together to make what is supposed to be a creative work of art, and they don't know each other. They simply 'get together.' You're rarely introduced to your fellow artists. I wanted to start some kind of a commotion, so I could get to know Julie London and Richard Egan. I got [London] angry, which was what I wanted to do, because then we spoke about it and began to look at each other and know each other."

The "New York actor" in Matthau again emerged in 1960, while being directed by Kirk Browning in "Two by Saroyan." Like Keller, Browning was an untried director, and Matthau believed in aggressively testing untried directors. Browning noted, "I remember the first time we sat down for a reading. Walter was sort of gimlet-eyed, with a dour look. I was not a very experienced drama director, and he was waiting to see what I was going to say. He sat there and glowered, and questioned everything."

At one point, Matthau and young Eddie Hodges, who played his son, were reading a scene. "It was a sentimental scene," Browning continued. "They started it, and I said, 'Walter, by now the audience knows you adore your son. Just to play the scene with all that sentiment is a bore. I think you should play it as though you are having a violent argument.' He looked at me and said, 'Now that's a very good idea.' He suddenly saw that I might occasionally have an original idea. From that moment on, he was simply wonderful."

Browning admired "the way he could get what he wanted without being nasty. That's a delicate balance. If an actor does it the wrong way, it can sour the whole process. But he did it the right way. He sat there needling me, but in a gentle way. It was a gentle needle. I realized what he was doing early enough so that I didn't let it get to me too much."

His roles in *Bigger Than Life*, *A Face in the Crowd*, and *Voice in the Mirror* aside, most of Matthau's early screen characters were more like his parts in *The Kentuckian* and *The Indian Fighter*: stock heavies. As he noted late in life, "A fellow who isn't pretty always gets cast as villains." He was appropriately menacing as a brutal New York waterfront racketeer in 1957's *Slaughter on Tenth Avenue*, and his hair was dyed red for his role as a hard-assed, alcoholic Coast Guard cook in 1958's *Onionhead*. Then, as a thuggish New Orleans nightclub owner, he harassed a misunderstood adolescent (Elvis Presley) in 1958's *King Creole*. At their initial meeting, Matthau's seasoning as an actor was contrasted to Presley's inexperience when, as he recalled, "The first thing Elvis said to me was, 'Mr. Matthau, I sure would appreciate it if you could help me out with this acting thing.'"

King Creole was the third screen credit for nineteen-year-old Dolores Hart, who five years later abandoned her promising career to enter a Bethlehem, Connecticut, convent. Today, she is known as Mother Dolores. "[Elvis] really wanted to bring his own career into something that was of the quality of James Dean," she recalled. "The ideal of his life [at that time] was to do that. He hoped that by taking on this character, he could elevate his acting career and come through to a James Dean image. Walter was willing to work with him, and I think this meant a great deal to Elvis.

"My memories of Walter were of a man who was extremely gracious, and quite contrary to the character that he played," she added. "I was a young ingenue, and he had no reason whatsoever to go out of his way to be at all courteous to me, and to open conversations with me, or to show me around the set. But he certainly did so, and he made me feel like I was [one] of the 'big guys.' He always acknowledged me as part of the team. [And so] he is part of a whole, dear memory of a time.

"I remember being on the [nightclub] set. He came in with Carolyn [Jones] and Elvis, and I remember the total authority with which Walter took over the scene."

Conversely, the actor was offered advice from Michael Curtiz, the film's Hungarian-born veteran director: "Matt-ow, you are highpriced actor. Pretend you are low-priced actor. Don't act so much." Matthau noted of Curtiz, "He was funny. He called me 'Valty.' He called Elvis Presley 'Elvy.'"

The film was shot on location in New Orleans, where Presleymania was rampant. "The kids just absolutely turned us into an island," explained Mother Dolores, "and in some situations we literally had to go to the top of the hotels because we couldn't go from street to street. They had to put planks from rooftop to rooftop; the kids just wouldn't allow us to move. They wanted to touch Elvis. As I recall, Walter was never distressed by any of the problems that any of this imposed on us."

At one point during the shoot, Matthau was called upon to bust a balsa-wood chair over Elvis's head during a fight sequence. Presley crumpled to the floor, and Matthau promptly hit him with the chair leg. The temperature on the set was warm. It was just after lunch— and Elvis promptly blew lunch. The shot was unusable. "A couple of years later," Matthau recalled, "I was doing some work down in Florida, in Tallahassee, and some girls—I remember they were fat girls—ran out of a church and ran after me and said, 'There's the guy that hit Elvis!'"

Not all of Matthau's film projects were as high-profile as *King Creole*. *Ride a Crooked Trail*, also from 1958, is an inconsequential Audie Murphy Western about a thief who is mistaken for a lawman. Yet it is made more than watchable for Matthau's zesty performance as a pompous, alcoholic judge. *Ride a Crooked Trail* is a textbook example of an unexceptional story and screenplay that is enlivened by a frequently riveting acting performance.

At this juncture, Matthau still preferred working on the stage, where he could fine-tune a characterization. "It's on the stage that I feel comfortable, relaxed, fulfilled, delighted," he declared in 1961. To the actor, working in the movies was "almost like being in the army: you set your mind to it, and you do it. On the stage, you're wide open. There are no tricks with the camera to make you look a certain way. Nobody is going to cut you out, either." Then he noted, "I love to feel I have the whole stage in the palm of my hand. It's what every actor looks for."

But of course, Matthau had not yet been lured by moviestardom. He was just a secondary actor, a character player whose purpose was to fill in the spaces and support the star. He may have developed a reputation for dependability, but he was in no position to demand starring roles and high paychecks.

Nonetheless, he was a celebrity, at least in New York. "I have no memory of it, but at maybe six or seven I began to get some awareness of it," recalled David Matthau. "People always said to me when I was growing up, and even when I was an adult, 'What was it like to grow up having Walter Matthau as your dad?' What I always [answered] was, 'Well, it was kind of like normal, because it was always like that.' I always had this sense that my dad was an actor, and was well-known and recognized wherever we went. From my earliest memories, it was like that."

In a Matthau profile published on October 7, 1962, in the *New York Herald Tribune*, Elinor Klein wrote, "Sometime recently, if you watch television at all, go to the movies, see plays or frequent Steinberg's Dairy restaurant on upper Broadway, you've seen an actor named Walter Matthau. In fact, in most any week of the year, it's possible to see him in all four places."

CHAPTER 13

Footnotes in a Filmography

Over the decades, movie actors have embellished their careers by directing. Robert Redford, Warren Beatty, and Kevin Costner won Academy Awards doing so. Burt Lancaster directed Matthau in *The Kentuckian*, his screen debut; Diane Keaton directed him in his final feature, *Hanging Up*. Jack Lemmon guided Matthau to an Academy Award nomination in *Kotch*. Actors from Lillian Gish and Lionel Barrymore to Sean Penn and Sally Field have worked behind the camera.

So did Matthau. He directed *Gangster Story*, released in 1960. But this was no glossy star-turn. The film is a cheesy, ultra-low-budget programmer—it reportedly cost a ridiculously modest $5,000 to make—in which Matthau starred as Jack Martin, a bankrobber-killer who is "one of the most wanted criminals in the files of the FBI." Wife Carol, billed as Carol Grace, co-starred as Carol Logan, a librarian with whom Martin becomes romantically involved. Matthau cast Raikin Ben-Ari, an old New School acting teacher, in the film, in a supporting role. "My father cast the movie based on whomever he ran into at the drugstore that day," quipped Charlie Matthau.

Walter did not make *Gangster Story* because he had directorial aspirations or because he wished to create a work of art. He signed on because his gambling debts had left him flat broke, and he desperately needed the $2,500 he earned as actor-director. Matthau had so little capital that he and Carol reportedly pawned their wedding gifts to afford the rent on their $220-per-month apartment. Just as it was in the worst days of her marriage to Saroyan, Carol—despite family wealth—was searching under sofa cushions for pocket money.

Gangster Story was written and shot in three weeks. "It was a poor script by a hack writer and a famous cardiovascular surgeon who produced the film with his brother who was a textile manufacturer from Philadelphia," Matthau recalled. "I made out the W-2 forms and held the boom." At one point he was instructing an actor, who told him to go to hell. Matthau's response: "Do it the way you want. . . . I have absolutely no authority." He was not kidding. Radley Metzger, the film's editor, reported that he worked with the producer, and never directly with Matthau. He added that *Gangster Story* "looked like a traditional, very low-budget film, very limited in terms of budget and time. The footage he shot was limited; it was a one-take kind of thing, very meat-and-potatoes. It was a traditional heist story, done without a lot of polish and ABC experience. I always likened it to people who speak with bad grammar. They can communicate ideas, but they'll say 'ain't' or use double-negatives."

Appalling does not begin to describe *Gangster Story*. It opens on a minor key with the song heard over the credits, titled "The Itch for Scratch." "Now my father only would listen to Mozart, and once in a while Beethoven," noted Charlie Matthau. "That song at the beginning of the film, they must have stuffed it in [during the] edit. He hated even really good popular music; he's not going to appreciate some great standard, even when it's sung by a great singer. So my father would have gotten physically ill from *that* song."

Matthau often described *Gangster Story* as the worst film ever made. Once he remarked, "Let me put it another way: it was the worst I ever made." He quipped that *Gangster Story* "premiered at Loew's in Newark, and was so bad it never crossed the Hudson."

There was a bogus report in *Current Biography* that, in 1958, Matthau authored and directed a gangster comedy that might have been an early Woody Allen effort. The title was *Chopped Herring*. "The production was not a success," *Current Biography* solemnly intoned. A variation of this story related to the manner in which *Gangster Story* was named. According to Matthau, the film's producers asked him to suggest a title. "Chopped Herring," he jokingly answered. "That's no title for a story about gangsters," was the response. "You have to let them know that there are gangsters in the story." "You mean like 'Gangster Story,'" Matthau declared. "Great title!" the producers exclaimed.

Despite its poor quality, *Gangster Story* remains a visual record of Walter and Carol Matthau acting together, and playing a couple of romantic scenes. Beyond the fact that Martin is an unrepentant hood, there are aspects of his character that are semi-autobiographical. In one sequence, he is at the races, betting on the ponies and cheering on a favored horse—which gave Matthau an excuse to get in a couple days at the track! In another, he tells the librarian that the only beaches he has ever visited are at Normandy and Coney Island.

Had he made the effort, Matthau's son Charlie believes that he "would have made a great director. But he would not have been good at certain aspects of the process of directing. He wouldn't have had the patience for all of it. But certainly, the working with the actors part, there would have been no better director."

Gangster Story was not the only project Matthau accepted out of financial desperation. Dan Frazer reported that Matthau left *Once More, With Feeling* "way before he should have" to take a job "in something called *Sheriff of Dade County.*" Actually, Frazer was referring to another Matthau career nadir: *Tallahassee 7000*, a mercifully short-lived television series in which he starred. *Tallahassee 7000* was thirty minutes long; it was syndicated; and it was partially shot on location in Polk County, Florida. Lia Waggner, the wife of William Schallert, appeared in one episode, in a small role. "I don't know how many people would admit to being on the show," joked her husband.

Matthau's role was the polar opposite of Jack Martin: a special agent for the Florida Sheriff's Bureau. His character name arguably was the unlikeliest of his entire career: Lex Rogers. He once admitted that he accepted the role "primarily for the minor convenience of making a living."

Twenty-six episodes were produced. The first, titled "Coldball," debuted on January 17, 1961; the names of subsequent ones had a pulp-fiction ring, from "The Alibi" and "Best Laid Plans" to "Vendetta" and "The Violent Road." The premiere began with Matthau narrating, Jack Webb/*Dragnet*-style, and setting the scene. After an opening sequence came the credits: "Walter Matthau in *Tallahassee 7000*," with a telephone dial surrounding the lettering. What followed was a third-rate meller in which Rogers is summoned by a local sheriff when a police informant is murdered. He goes undercover to gain the villain's confidence.

The first take is the last in this low-budget production, even if an actor blows a line or loses concentration. The fight scenes are awkwardly staged, and the pounding music on the soundtrack telegraphs the action. Matthau, meanwhile, looks grim and determined as he puffs on a cigarette and spews out his staccato narration about law and order, and the difficulty of his assignment. Even Matthau's line readings are inconsistent. Some are read straight; others are recited with a slightly exaggerated southern-fried accent.

At the finale, Matthau/Rogers sits behind a desk, stares somberly into the camera, and declares that "crime and criminals seldom recognize boundaries. But when their activities cross over into the state of Florida, they become the business of the Sheriff's Bureau. Next week, join me and other Florida law enforcement officers in our never-ending war to protect those citizens who would abide by the law. Good night." The *Variety* critic, reviewing a future episode, noted that the show "runs along familiar lines," adding that Matthau "came off as sturdy, steady, and brave. . . . He may be shot at, choked, or trapped, but like all good leads do, in 'based on the files of' series, he'll survive."

At this juncture, Matthau's gambling problem had been building for years, and had become so out-of-hand that he accepted the series to earn a steady paycheck—and ensure his *own* survival. "When I first met Walter, sometime in the early 1950s," recalled Heywood Hale Broun, "he was betting heavily on baseball. I took him to task, because I'd been a baseball writer. I said, 'I can't make any money on baseball games,' and I'm in the dugout and clubhouse. He said, 'Oh, I have a system,' and right away, I knew here was the compulsive gambler of all time.

"Years later, when I met him in the Eighty-first Street post office, he was wearing army surplus clothes. I said, 'Walter, stars don't dress like that.' He said, 'You know how much I have to make every month before I pay the shylocks!' Apparently, he had to give them $12,000 a month or something like that, just to stay even."

During the 1958 baseball season, Matthau had lost a wad betting on the second game of a long-obscure doubleheader. On another occasion, he lost $48,000 betting on a New York Yankees–Baltimore Orioles doubleheader. He had $12,000 down on the first game and $36,000 on the second. Like a good New Yorker, Matthau bet on the Bronx Bombers. Inexplicably, they lost the twin bill.

Now, Matthau was extending his wagering to spring training games. During the Broadway run of *The Odd Couple*, Louis Zorich, his understudy, asked him, "Is it true you did [*Tallahassee 7000*] only to pay off a gambling debt?" Matthau responded in the affirmative. Zorich asked, "Is it also true that you owed the gamblers something like $250,000?" "He admitted it," Zorich noted. Yet during a two-week period while in Florida shooting the series, he forfeited $183,000 betting on games. Of this figure, $38,000 was lost on a single game. It took him six years to pay off the debt. The cost: just about every extra dollar he earned. "I did pay off my bookie with some of the money I made," Matthau admitted, "but I accrued the gambling debts while I was doing the TV show." Then he chuckled, and added, "The series was so boring, I had to do something." To keep his creditors happy, he even requested salary advances; he did just that after agreeing to appear onscreen in *Lonely Are the Brave*, released in 1962.

Gangster Story and *Tallahassee 7000* aside, Matthau kept on appearing in character/supporting roles in A-budget features well into the 1960s. In *Strangers When We Meet*, released in 1960, he was a snoopy, slimy, self-described "observer of the human scene" who spies on his adulterous neighbor (Kirk Douglas). Another supporting player was Nancy Mehta, then known as Nancy Kovack. She confused Matthau's billing when she recalled, "Over forty years ago my studio put me in a film in which Walter starred with Kirk Douglas," but her feeling for her friend was unquestionable as she added, "Always whenever in public Walter would say, 'I was in a film that Nancy starred in.' Was this not love?"

In 1962's *Who's Got the Action?* Matthau played a character he might have known in real life: a high-powered bookie. At this stage, he still prided himself on being a New York actor. In a statement that would make even the most experienced studio publicist weep, he described Lana Turner, the female lead, as "a professional movie star with an elementary grasp of acting. But she's a very good movie star. Next to her, I'm an amateur at moviemaking. She knows all about camera angles and how to turn her body just the right way. She knows when to blow a line so she can get a retake. She's very expert at being a movie star."

One of Matthau's best films during this period featured him in one of his favorite supporting roles: a sympathetic modern-day Western sheriff who observes the wanted man he is tracking in *Lonely Are the Brave*, starring Kirk Douglas. For his performance, Matthau won a Film Daily Award.

Lonely Are the Brave is a portrait of a loner who values his individuality and recoils at the idea of sacrificing his freedom to what he views as the blandness and conformity of modern civilization. "The picture was received very warmly by the critics," Matthau recalled, "but it never really was a moneymaker, which are two different things. In Hollywood, there are moneymakers and there are good pictures. Once in a while, you get a good picture that's a moneymaker." He correctly noted that it should have been marketed as an art film and allowed the opportunity to build an audience.

Of the film's star, Matthau observed, "The only guy that was ever affected by climactic conditions in his acting was Kirk Douglas. He did a superb job in *Lonely Are the Brave* because we were shooting that picture up at about 12,000 feet and the rarified atmosphere sapped him of any energy or strength that he had. That was his best performance." He also described Douglas as an "intellectual actor" and explained, with some amount of cynicism, "When an actor gets intellectual about his craft, he can no longer act. He's got to do it instinctively. Actors should be doers, not thinkers."

It was while shooting *Lonely Are the Brave* in New Mexico that Matthau became friends with William Schallert, cast as the sheriff's dimwitted deputy. The two remained pals for almost forty years, sharing a love of Mozart. Professionally, they were fated to travel in different worlds within the Hollywood community, but as Schallert noted, "He never stood on ceremony as an actor with me. He was a major star, and I was basically a supporting player. But there was a mutual respect."

Some of Matthau's films were wholly forgettable. During a 1983 interview, Robert Preston had nothing to say about *Island of Love*, a tepid comedy, other than that he disliked the film. *Island of Love*, released in 1963, featured Matthau as a vengeance-seeking hood hustled by Preston's conman into financing a movie. "Sometimes, with some of the older stuff, he'd say, 'Oh my god, that was such bad acting,'" noted Charlie Matthau. "He would laugh about what a ham he was [in films like] *Island of Love*." At least Matthau got a free trip to Athens and the Greek islands of Hydra and Spetsai, where the film was shot on location. The following year, he appeared in a forgettable film that was an indirect link to his future: *Ensign Pulver*, a comedy-drama charting the antics of the title character (Robert Walker Jr.) on board a United States Navy cargo ship during World War II. The film was a sequel to 1955's *Mister Roberts*, one of the early successes of Jack Lemmon, Matthau's soon-to-be co-star and friend. In *Ensign Pulver*, Matthau was Doc, the ship's medical officer, a role played in *Mister Roberts* by William Powell.

Matthau fared better in the 1964 comedy *Goodbye, Charlie*, in which he supported Tony Curtis, his old friend and New School classmate. Matthau played Sir Leopold Sartori, a Hungarian film producer—a character reportedly modeled after Sir Alexander Korda. The scenario has Sartori killing a screenwriter after discovering him in a compromising position with his wife. As Matthau cavorted through the role, he kept changing accents, sometimes aping Bela Lugosi, other times imitating Peter Sellers. He might have ad-libbed the following line: "My dear, you are exquisite, like the fragile beauty of an early Mozart quartet. . . ."

Matthau's playfulness resulted in his possibly initiating a prank on straightlaced co-star Pat Boone. "I've always suspected that he put [director Vincente] Minnelli up to having me rehearse a champagne scene all afternoon one day, causing me to open a fresh bottle . . . and drink from it in every rehearsal, and countless takes," Boone recalled. "I could never figure why Walter Matthau, the great comic, was waiting around behind camera watching me rehearse with Debbie Reynolds, when he wasn't in the scene. Thinking back, I believe he and Vincente and perhaps Tony Curtis had a ball watching me get looped, the only time in my life that ever happened. I was very, very lucky to get home alive."

The title *Goodbye, Charlie* was ironic, given the personal events unfolding off-camera. This period of Matthau's life might have been called "Hello, Charlie." On December 10, 1962, two years before the film's release, wife Carol gave birth to their only offspring, a son who reportedly was named Charles after Carol's stepfather, Charles Marcus; Charles DeGaulle; and Charlie Chaplin, the husband of Oona O'Neill. Richard Widmark was Charlie's godfather; *New Yorker* writer Lillian Ross was his godmother.

"I remember one time [when I was a kid] we were having dinner with Chaplin," Charlie Matthau recalled, "and he said, 'You know, you were named after me.' I said, 'I was named after my grandfather, Charlie Marcus.' And my mother was kicking me under the table. I was named mostly for my grandfather, and a little for Charlie Chaplin, but I don't know about Charles DeGaulle."

During the advanced stages of Carol's pregnancy, she and Walter were in Paris where he was filming *Charade*, a chic mystery-comedy-melodrama that came to movie houses in 1963. "They wanted the baby to be born in the United States—and become president, God help us," Charlie continued. "My mother flew back; she thought she might have the baby on the plane."

For the rest of Walter's life, Charlie Matthau was his pride. In *Charade*, the elder Matthau's role was a villain masquerading as a CIA honcho. "He got a big charge out of playing with [the film's stars] Cary Grant and Audrey Hepburn—especially Cary Grant," noted Charlie. "They liked each other a lot; my father admired his style of acting, and considered him underrated." Yet in 1997, all Walter could recall about the film was that "Charlie was born the day after *Charade* finished [shooting]."

In *Fail-Safe*, a dark 1964 Cold War–era drama, Matthau played a hawkish political scientist/civilian Pentagon advisor who coolly rationalizes the horror of nuclear war. "Some of his very best [performances] were when he played evil," noted Larry King. "In *Fail-Safe*, he was so detestable." In 1965's *Mirage*, a psychological thriller, he was a refrigerator-repairman-turned-private-detective who is killed off part-way through the story. "My part is the film's only comedy relief," Matthau noted, and I told [director] Edward Dmytryk not to cut me out too soon. I should be on the screen longer. Disagreeing with me, he wouldn't change it. My opinion was substantiated by a friend in California. He called me, said he saw *Mirage* at a sneak preview in San Diego, and was disappointed because they get rid of me too soon. The 'opinion cards' said the same. Made my day, friend and fans agreeing with me. It was a lovely thing for my friend to do, call me all the way from California to give my morale a boost." Such is the plight of the supporting player. Yet despite Matthau's lack of screen-time, Dmytryk admired him because, as he developed his character, "he did things that I hadn't even realized were in the script." Whether this would have improved the film or not, Matthau had to acknowledge that he still had almost no clout as a film actor. Audiences bought tickets to *Mirage* to see star Gregory Peck—not character player Walter Matthau.

Most of these pre-star credits are footnotes in Matthau's filmography, yet they remained ingrained within the actor for the rest of his life. Carlos Lopez, a Beverly Hills Tennis Club employee whom Matthau fondly nicknamed "Jerry Lewis," recalled, "One day in the dining room, he turned on the TV and started to watch an old black-and-white movie. He said, 'Hey, Jerry, come over here. Do you know who that is on the TV?'" Lopez responded, "Oh my god, it's you." Matthau began relating all that happened next in the story, and even recited his dialogue. "It was incredible," Lopez concluded.

One film in which Matthau did not appear was *The Thrill of It All*, a 1963 Doris Day–James Garner comedy. The role he was offered, a middle-aged expectant father, eventually was played by Edward Andrews. Matthau requested a $100,000 salary from producer Ross Hunter, who publicly chastised the actor. "I felt that with the part inconsequential to the core of the story—which I thought was strictly featherweight material anyway—it was an insult," Matthau explained, while filming *Ensign Pulver*. "I know I wasn't worth $100,000. But if you are offered a weak part you ask for a hike in salary to compensate for it. If somebody asked me to carry a spear in *Last Days of Pompeii* I'd say sure—for $150,000."

His old political radicalism resurfaced as he added, "That's always the dream of the boss—to set his own limit on what his workers can make. They think that $150 a week for an actor would be just fine. Fortunately, the system of free enterprise is still in effect. There is still competitive bidding for talent. For 5,000 years the actor has been relegated to the stable, cellar, or kitchen. It's fitting that he has finally escaped that tainted triumvirate of actor, vagabond, and rogue."

Matthau revealed that, for the previous five years, his average salary for a film was "at least" $150,000. Even so, if he were unemployed for two months, he had to borrow money. In addition to taxes, he listed his expenses as: 10 percent agent commission; 10 percent business manager commission; $60,000 annually for alimony and child support; plus "the time, energy, and money which must be spent in convincing everybody how much in demand you are." An actor must dress well, look good, and get invited to the right social events where "a producer is apt to see an actor and yell, 'Holy jumping Jehosaphat—you're just the man I wanted for the part of Oscar Wilde in *Tomorrow the Oven*'—or something to that effect."

Matthau neglected to list another expense: Gambling debts.

Of the spottiness of his screen career at this juncture, he observed, "On Mondays, Wednesdays, and Fridays, I feel like the greatest guy in the world, and I'm outraged that they're not paying me $18 million. On Tuesdays and Thursdays, I wonder why they pay me more than $150 a week."

CHAPTER 14

Back to the Boards

Matthau's increased film work kept him off the stage from 1958's *Once More, With Feeling* until 1961, when he and Carol appeared in *Once There Was a Russian*, a one-performance bomb that opened and closed at the Music Box on February 18. This Sam Spewack farce purported to tell the story of Catherine the Great (Francoise Rosay) and her trip to the Crimea. Matthau played a humorously manipulative Prince Potemkin, who is out of Catherine's favor and schemes to manipulate his way back into her graces.

The actor meticulously researched the part, reading books and articles about Russian history and the temperament of the Russian people. He even studied pictures of Catherine the Great and Potemkin, whom he described as "a fascinating scoundrel." In order to tower over his fellow actors, he was fitted with a pair of Adler lift shoes that added three inches to his already imposing height. But it was all for naught. Matthau recently had starred in and directed the atrocious *Gangster Story* on the big screen, and appeared in the ho-hum *Tallahassee 7000* on the small one. So any gambler would lay odds that his return to the stage in *Once There Was a Russian* would be a fiasco.

Louis Guss and Marvin Silbersher, Matthau's New School classmates, joined him in the cast. "Terrible play" was how Guss described it. Yet Silbersher recollected that it was "the funniest, most delicious, most commercial, most attractive play that Sam Spewack ever wrote." Among his other credits, co-authored with his wife Bella: *Boy Meets Girl* and the book for *Kiss Me Kate*. When Silbersher initially read the play with Matthau, the two were "convulsed [with laughter]. There were six producers, and they too were convulsed. The cast was fantastic. You remember Sig Rumann? Julie Newmar? Francoise Rosay?"

Yet the play was doomed from the first rehearsal. "Ten minutes before we started to read this wonderful play," Silbersher continued, "who walks in but Bella Spewack. She's about three-feet-one, and total poison. She looks at Sam across the room, [gives a Bronx cheer, and says] 'Fuck you, Sam, you can't write a play by yourself. Fuck you.' Then when we started to read, Sam—who's been affected by Bella—yells out to us, 'No accents!' Now how is Sig Rumann going to lose his accent? That's what he was hired for. It's part of why he is funny. How is Madame Francoise Rosay going to lose her accent? We're all funny in this venue. And right then and there, the play died.

"We had a great director, Douglas Seale, and they fired him." Officially, Seale withdrew from the production during tryouts in Wilmington, Delaware. His replacement, Gene Frankel, began "beating us all to death," according to Silbersher. "Every day we had new pages. The script was changing further as we got the pages. We didn't know what we were going to get at rehearsal the next day. The [New York] previews went on forever, trying to breathe life back into this play that Bella Spewack had killed.

"The night before we opened, at the last preview, we all were in a good mood. Then came opening night. Everybody's terrified. The critics were all there. Madame Rosay had the runs. It was a disaster. And so our joke was, 'Only once, there was a Russian.' Walter came to the cast party wearing a tracksuit. He was ready to run, but not in the play. He said, 'Marvin, get your things out of the dressing room before they pull the switch.'"

Michael Ritchie was in the audience during that single performance. "It was weird, because the cast [collectively] acted like rabbits in car headlights," he recalled. "On the one hand, they didn't know what was about to hit them. You had Julie Newmar acting like she was about to get hit by a truck. On the other hand, the old pros like Walter, who had been there before, were just having a great time. [Walter was] behaving like he was going to dare [the truck] to hit him again."

The production's problems were not limited to onstage chaos. "There was some difficulty between Julie Newmar and [Carol], who complained about her to Walter," Guss recalled. "He got very upset, and had a bit of a brouhaha with Julie."

Four days after *Once There Was a Russian* opened—and three days after it closed—the curtain at the Brooks Atkinson Theatre went up on a new comedy by a promising young playwright. It was titled *Come Blow Your Horn*, and it was the initial hit for this writer, who was fated to play a dominant part in Matthau's professional life. That author was Neil Simon.

Later that year, Matthau's string of bad luck changed, albeit at the misfortune of another actor. Donald Cook, twenty years Matthau's senior, was cast in *A Shot in the Dark*, a Marcel Achard farce that originally was titled *L'Idiote* and was adapted by Harry Kurnitz. *A Shot in the Dark* told the story of Josefa (Julie Harris), a peasant girl, and her experiences while toiling as a parlor maid in the household of the rich, aristocratic Beaurevers clan. Along the way, she is suspected of murdering her lover, the family chauffeur. Cook's role was Benjamin Beaurevers, the debonair family patriarch. It was a part that required an actor who exuded culture and elegance, and Cook had been perfectly cast.

During the pre-Broadway tryout, Cook suddenly died. Director Harold Clurman asked Harris to suggest a replacement. She came up with Brian Aherne, George Sanders, and Claude Rains. "What about Walter Matthau?" Clurman asked. "Walter Matthau!" Harris responded. "He's so rough and funny and uncultured-looking. I don't see him in that part at all." But Matthau was cast; one of those in his corner was Harry Kurnitz, who noted that the actor "really can do anything." The events unfolded rapidly. Cook suffered the fatal heart attack in New Haven on a Saturday and died Sunday. On Monday, Matthau saw the play when it opened in Philadelphia; Joel Thomas, Cook's understudy, played Beaurevers. Matthau signed the next day, rehearsed for two days, and replaced Thomas on Friday.

Beaurevers was one of Matthau's favorite stage roles. "It's a vignette, really," he explained. "I don't have to take on the job of building the plot, making the expositions, getting the audience involved in the story line. The story line is all set up for me, and all I have to do is to sit down facing the audience for twenty minutes and say funny lines in a funny way."

Despite his brief time with the company, Matthau quickly understood the essence of the character. During rehearsals, Clurman handed him a watch. He knew immediately that this prop did not jibe with the character, and refused to wear it. "No," he told Clurman, "this man makes his *own* time, he's so rich and so elegant."

Also during rehearsals, Clurman told Matthau, "I don't like the way you walk. I want you to walk as though you were walking to music."

"Rock 'n' roll or Mozart?" Matthau asked.

"Anything that makes you feel like an aristocrat," was the response.

With this in mind, Matthau chose to disregard music and recall the manner in which his mother walked after washing the floor in their tenement. She placed newspapers on it and, with the utmost care, stepped on the paper. This was the image Matthau conjured up as he perfected his character's stride. Noted Clurman (who remained convinced that Matthau had taken his "musical" advice), "Well, the audience opening night, I'll never forget: he stepped on the stage, took two paces, and the audience was in an uproar of laughter." Another time, Matthau joked, "I spoke in an exaggerated English accent, and I walked like a combination of Charles DeGaulle and my mother having desperately to go to the bathroom."

Louis Zorich was one who saw the performance. "He was hysterical," Matthau's future Oscar Madison understudy recalled. "I didn't even know who he was [at the time]. He had a funny walk, which almost made the character. I can't even describe it." Shirley Knight was another. "He did this extraordinary, bizarre movement, the way he walked and moved his hands," she noted. "It was as if his hands were pushing a wheelchair. I thought, 'What a strange thing he's doing.'" For Knight, Matthau's performance was an acting lesson. "By watching him, I saw that if an actor is absolutely committed to doing something, it doesn't really matter how bizarre it is. If it's his characterization, and he's fully committed to it, it will work, even if it seems odd."

A Shot in the Dark opened at the Booth on October 18, 1961, and became a hit. One of Matthau's co-stars was William Shatner, who five years later began playing Captain Kirk on *Star Trek*. During the run, the two became good friends. They did not see each other too often in later years, but Shatner reported, "when I did see him, either in person or on the screen, I welled up with laughter because we shared a very funny moment.

"One night [on stage], something happened. I'm still not quite sure what. One of us went up, probably me, and we stared at each other in that blind, horrified, hysterically funny moment when actors lose it. Not only can they not remember their lines, they can't remember their names. Welling between us was the potential for gales of laughter, but each secretly thinking that *we* were the superior professional. We choked on our bile, our spleen, and that valve inside your stomach that won't open and close and gives you heartburn. We choked on all that and our laughter."

Long seconds passed. A full house looked on in silence as Shatner and Matthau stared at each other. Then, a singular laugh rang out, which quickly was followed by guffaws. "It welled up," Shatner continued. "It shook the roof of the theater. . . . And then, as laughter does, it started to die out.

"And still, we held the look. And still, our appearance imperceptibly changed. And the laughter began again—2,000 people, laughing at nothing, and yet, at everything. They were laughing at the two characters created on stage; they were laughing at a situation in which a young attorney was interrogating a cuckolded husband. . . . They were also laughing at the imperceptive discomfiture of two actors on Broadway determined not to break."

The laughter died out, only to return once again. "It could have been, it might very well be, the funniest thing that has ever happened to me. I stared into those hangdog eyes for what seemed like centuries, neither one of us giving way to any sort of an amused glint. And yet we both knew that deep inside the comedic soul of both of us, we were hysterical."

A Shot in the Dark played on Broadway for 389 performances. For his performance, Matthau won the Tony Award as Best Actor, Featured or Supporting. His fellow nominees were Godfrey Cambridge (for *Purlie Victorious*), Joseph Campanella (*A Gift of Time*), and Paul Sparer *(Ross)*.

The ceremony was held on the evening of April 29, 1962, in the Waldorf Astoria Hotel's Grand Ballroom. Host Ray Bolger introduced Olivia de Havilland, the presenter for Matthau's category. She carefully enunciated the nominee names and then announced, "The winner is, Walter Matthau." Matthau arose from Table #10, kissed Carol, who was at his side, and strode to the stage while the band played an appropriate tune, "Luck Be a Lady," from *Guys and Dolls.*

After de Havilland handed him the award, Matthau began, rather formally, "Uh, when one is nominated for an achievement award in any field of endeavor, I suppose it's natural that one immediately starts thinking of an acceptance speech in the event that one wins. I must confess that I've given the matter some thought, but I haven't been able to come up with anything." After a burst of audience laughter, he continued, "However, my wife"—and he paused right here, for added emphasis—"wrote something for me." He removed a piece of paper from his breast pocket, which he began reading: "This award, which I have won tonight, is due in no small part to the constant inspiration and selfless devotion of one beautiful, wise, witty, charming, and rich girl whose being is a monument to pure love. Carol Matthau, thank you." As he read the note, he paused after each phrase. Then he strode off the stage to the strains of "Luck Be a Lady."

Later on, Margaret Leighton, upon being named Best Dramatic Actress for *Night of the Iguana*, lampooned Matthau's speech by exclaiming, "My wife said that she thought if I thought of anything to say or if she thought of it for me, I might not have a chance to say it. . . ."

In 1963, Matthau was set to appear in the play's screen adaptation. A United Artists press release announced his signing; the scheduled stars were Sophia Loren and Peter Sellers. However, the project was reworked into what became the second Sellers–Inspector Clouseau comedy, and was filmed without Loren or Matthau.

That same year, he made one, next-to-last Broadway appearance.

Again, it was in a failure: *My Mother, My Father, and Me*, which opened at the Plymouth on March 23. Despite working with a top director (Gower Champion) and co-star (Ruth Gordon), in a play authored by a fabled writer (Lillian Hellman), this cynical satire of middle-class Jewish-American life lasted only seventeen performances. Matthau, forty-two years old, was cast as the deferential husband of sixty-six-year-old Gordon.

Heywood Hale Broun was one of the supporting players. "This anecdote illustrates Walter's clumsiness and sensitivity," he recalled. "I had a very small part in the second act, and he of course was the star. At one point during rehearsals, he suggested to the director a piece of business for me. I tried it, and hated it. When we came off [the stage], I said, 'Walter, you unprofessional bastard. You don't do that. You suggest it to me.' He said, 'I thought it would be amusing.' I said, 'I don't think it's amusing. It's not fair. You [should] talk to the actor.'

"Well, in a couple of days, it was dropped. At the end of the week, Walter said, 'Come into my dressing room.' I said, 'What do you want?' He said, 'You're a wonderful actor.' After a lot of schmoozing back and forth he said, 'Oh, just one thing. *Like* me!' I said, 'Walter, I like you.' He said, 'No you don't. You're mad at me.' I said, 'Anyway, what difference does it make if I'm mad at you? I'm playing a small part in the second act.' He said, 'I don't want you to be mad at me,' and I thought, 'How unlike him that was. If he got upset, he could run over you like a tank, but beneath all that rumbling and grumbling, here was this really shy, sensitive person.'"

Matthau concluded the conversation with a promise: "When this play is over, I'm gonna get you a job." That time came sooner than anyone anticipated. The following week, Matthau got Broun a part in a reading at the Ethical Culture Society. Matthau played Baruch Spinoza; Broun earned $100 for playing a court clerk. "He kept his word," Broun concluded.

Broun blamed Hellman for the failure of *My Mother, My Father, and Me*. "Miss Hellman was rather like the Wizard of Oz: a big noise, but really a timid, uncertain woman. She let that play be destroyed because she wouldn't make any big decisions. She just liked to snarl ineffectually." Marian Seldes was in the audience for one of its few performances. She would marry Gordon's husband, Garson Kanin, after Gordon passed away. "The last time I saw [Walter] on the stage was in *My Mother, My Father, and Me,* which of course I went to see because of Ruth Gordon," Seldes recalled. "She adored Walter. If you could talk to her now, she would tell you how she loved working with him. The play didn't exactly work, but they *were* wonderful."

As much as he disliked appearing on television, Matthau agreed to shoot *Acres and Pains,* a pilot for a CBS comedy series that aired on May 13, 1962, as an episode of *General Electric Theater. Acres and Pains,* which had a literary pedigree—it was based on stories by S. J. Perelman—was not developed into a series.

Matthau starred as Tom Dutton, a Greenwich Village writer who has tired of city living and who forsakes New York for a broken-down farmhouse in Bucks County, Pennsylvania. Anne Jackson played Dutton's wife. "We were the sophisticated couple going to the country," she recalled. "We just looked like Mutt and Jeff. I came up to his tit, or right under his tit, to his heartline, and he really had to bend over to give me a peck.

"We were both happy to be working together, but the network decided that they wanted Eva Gabor and Eddie Albert." While *Acres and Pains* failed to stick, it inspired *Green Acres,* the hit sitcom about a New York lawyer and his chic wife who relocate to the sticks. *Acres and Pains* remains a fascinating curio, if only because it offers evidence that Matthau already had mastered the whiny voice and comic mannerisms he employed onstage in *The Odd Couple.*

Then in November 1964, a three-character comedy opened on Broadway, at the Booth Theatre. It was titled *Luv,* and was written by Murray Schisgal. The stars were Alan Arkin, Eli Wallach, and Jackson, and it became a smash hit. Arkin's role was despondent, suicidal Harry Berlin. Milt Manville (Wallach), Harry's old, married friend, is in love with another woman, whom he wishes to wed. Only trouble is, his wife Ellen (Jackson) refuses to divorce him. So Milt schemes to pawn Harry off on her. Then the plot thickens.

"Eli [Jackson's husband] and I were going to do *Luv,*" Jackson reported. "Mike Nichols was directing it, and we wanted Walter to be in the play. And Mike, who also was going to direct *The Odd Couple*, said, 'He's going to do Doc Simon's *Odd Couple* for me. I'd rather have him in that.'"

So Matthau missed out on co-starring in a hit comedy, just as he missed out on obtaining the financial security of a hit TV series. Yet these disappointments made him available to create the role that would define his career and make him a star.

CHAPTER 15

Oscar

On March 10, 1965, Walter Matthau was not considered a genius—comic or otherwise. He was a forty-four-year-old character actor who had enjoyed a degree of success on the stage, screen, and television, and who worked to maintain a certain lifestyle while supporting a wife, an ex-wife, and three children, the youngest of whom he was determined to raise as a prince.

More than most actors, he had been earning a steady paycheck for almost two decades. Occasionally, he obtained good billing. In *Fail-Safe*, he was second in the credits, although the film was an ensemble piece. In *Mirage*, the stars were Gregory Peck and Diane Baker, and Matthau received special billing after the supporting player credits. He was respected within his profession and had amassed a scrap-book-full of laudatory reviews. Audiences might recognize his face, and enjoy his performances, but few could match his face and name.

"It happens over and over again," he explained in a 1963 interview from a table in Sardi's, the fabled Broadway eatery. "I get into a taxi and the guy looks at me and says, 'Hey, I know you—what's your name again? I seen you on TV the other night, right?' Or I go outside in the street, right outside here, and I'll bet you that four people will turn around and look at me, and they'll say to each other, 'There's . . .

oh, you know who! We saw him in that picture with Dean Martin last week. Now what *is* his name anyway?'"

The situation changed after Matthau became a star. Publicist Murray Weissman once accompanied him to Miami, for the Orange Bowl Parade, and reported that a woman in an elevator asked Matthau, "Are you who I think you are?" Matthau's response: "Absolutely not."

But for now, Matthau exclaimed that he would "like to get my name out so that people will know who I am, so that I'll be able to pick and choose the kind of things I want to do—and get the kind of money that other actors get. The ones whose names are already known."

While shooting *Mirage*, Edward Dmytryk admiringly declared, "Walter, you're going to become the greatest character actor in the business." Matthau responded, "Character actor! I'm gonna be a leading man." Yet he had no reason to believe that this would come to pass. His less-than-matinee-idol looks were not improving with age. He was known mostly for character work. So more than likely, Matthau could look forward only to supporting roles for the rest of his career.

All that changed on March 10. That night at the Plymouth Theatre, *The Odd Couple*, the now-legendary Neil Simon comedy, bowed on Broadway with Matthau as a star.

In the future, Matthau appeared in other Simon properties: *Plaza Suite, California Suite, The Sunshine Boys, I Ought to Be in Pictures*, and *The Odd Couple II*. Yet *The Odd Couple* is their most enduring collaboration. When one thinks *Odd Couple*, one thinks Walter Matthau. He forever will be associated with the character he originated: Oscar Madison, New York sportswriter and slob extraordinaire.

New Yawker Oscar's world is one in which New Yawker Matthau could relate.

He lives and works within an all-male bastion of athletics and Friday-night poker games. He carouses with his pals while reeking of stale beer and cigars amid the unkempt grandeur of his eight-room, twelfth-floor Riverside Drive apartment. The entire play unfolds here; in the first scene, in which Oscar and his cronies play poker on a steamy summer night, filthy dishes, worn clothes, aging newspapers, empty bottles, and half-used glasses are scattered throughout his living room. Given Oscar's slobby maleness, he would be as much at home living in a press box, with an occasional trip to a locker room for a shower and shave, oblivious to the fact that his shirts are awash in ketchup and mustard stains.

Oscar is contrasted to his new roommate: fastidious Felix Ungar (Art Carney), a compulsive neatnik who is obsessed with cooking, decontaminating the air, and removing every speck of dust from his realm. To Felix, ring around the collar is a catastrophe of epic proportion. He is a man consumed with neuroses; it is no wonder that he has just been booted out by his wife.

Simon reportedly had Matthau in mind while creating the character of Oscar. A decade earlier, he had seen Matthau as Nathan Detroit in *Guys and Dolls*: a performance that, in Simon's mind, served to link the actor and Oscar Madison. Simon has noted that, upon seeing Matthau in this performance, he felt the actor was destined for major stardom.

In an anecdote that has been repeated often, Matthau initially met Simon at a 1964 party at the Westchester home of Hal and Candy March. Their conversation was brief and to the point. "You ought to be in my next play," the writer told the actor. "Who are you?" was Matthau's response.

Matthau first read the play while filming *Goodbye, Charlie* in California, near Malibu. "Going through this Neil Simon play I laughed so loud and hard that [wife] Carol came into the room and asked, 'What on earth is so funny?'" he recalled a couple of months into the show's run. "The first two acts were hilarious, but in the third act the playwright got serious. I told Saint-Subber [the show's producer] that I would take the part, but he and Simon should change the last act. Keep the laughs coming, keep it funny all the way, and you will have yourself a three-and-a-half-year run. They took my advice and made the last act as amusing as the first two."

Walter told Carol that *The Odd Couple* even might enjoy a ten-year run. He backed up his belief by investing $10,000 in it, on a guarantee of 7.5 percent of the weekly gross against a $2,000 minimum. For once, Matthau's gambling instinct served him well. He eventually earned $80,000 from the venture. Other investors included Danny and May Simon, the author's brother and mother ($15,000), and Mike Nichols ($8,000). Matthau's gambling instinct again worked for him after he became a movie star, when he accepted percentages of profits from his films rather than flat salaries. When those films were successful, he emerged with additional millions.

Ironically, Matthau initially wanted to play Felix. He discussed this with his friend, the actor Martin Gabel, who agreed that he could play Oscar with little effort. "I was being rather arrogant," Matthau recalled. "I said to Neil, 'Anybody can play Oscar. I'd like the challenge of playing the other role. That's real acting.'" Noted Carole Shelley, cast as one of the Pigeon sisters, Oscar and Felix's giddy British neighbors, "Walter wanted desperately to play Felix, but Neil wouldn't hear of it."

Matthau was not the only actor who understood the appeal of playing Felix. Noted Larry King, "I told Walter that Jackie Gleason told me before he died that he wanted to do *Odd Couple*. I said, 'Jackie, you'd be great as Oscar.' He said, 'I don't want to play Oscar. I want to play Felix.' Walter then told me, 'Felix was a much better character. You could play off Oscar, and get laughs off laughs.'"

As rehearsals began, Matthau and Carney transformed themselves into Oscar and Felix. Eventually, they became so adept at playing together that they might have been a veteran comedy team—a designation that Matthau resented. "Listen, don't give me the bit about we're a comedy team," he protested. "Hell, Art and I, we don't shoot gags. We don't push the laughs. We play it as a story of two guys in a whacked-out situation. If the audience decides something is funny—let them laugh. If they don't laugh, the hell with them." Matthau had long ago learned that an actor must take a sober approach to playing comedy. "When I was doing *The Odd Couple* with Art Carney," he recalled, "in the scene where I come out to kill him, I really was determined to kill him. And the audience screamed with laughter because I wasn't trying to be funny." He added, "The straighter you play comedy, the better chance it will be funny. It takes discipline. A guy who does comedy well should be a good actor."

For years, Matthau steadfastly defended the sanctity of the

written word, seeing the actor's role as an interpreter of those words. Yet as he perfected his characterization in out-of-town tryouts, he became increasingly aware that Oscar was the role that would make him a star. He would do anything to ensure that this would be his breakout performance, including ad-libbing and adding shtick.

"One day in rehearsal," recalled Louis Zorich, his understudy, "Walter and Art were doing the top of the third act, in which [Felix and Oscar] fight, and Mike was in the house, directing. And he said, 'Walter, what's going on? You're not playing the scene.' Walter would do [it] again, and again Mike said, 'Look, Walter, it's a fight. You and Art have a fight here.'" Matthau looked at Nichols and made a declaration that would bridge the first and final phase of his career: "Listen, for twenty-five years I've been a serious actor. Now, I want to be a popular actor." "He wanted to do it his way," Zorich added. "I think he sensed that his character was likable, and didn't want to be mean."

Added Carole Shelley, "There were times when he just sat there and howled, along with the audience, during a performance." Yet he was not breaking character because his behavior "was perfectly Oscarish." More to the point, at one juncture Oscar, referring to Felix, rhetorically asks, "Why doesn't he hear me?" While speaking this line, Matthau was supposed to look at the ceiling. While performing in Wilmington, Delaware, he began looking at an audience member. He liked the effect and kept using it, despite Nichols's protestations. (After the play opened, one bit of Matthau improvisation came out of necessity. "One night, Carney had a cold," he recalled. "It was difficult for him to speak, so I turned my back to the audience. I did the whole play with my back to the audience. . . . I didn't get his laughs, but I was able to get mine, yeah. And he was able to get more laughs because he had full-front.")

For the rest of his career, Matthau ad-libbed whenever he felt it was appropriate. He did so thirty-three years later, while filming *The Marriage Fool*, a TV movie. Arlene Mazerolle, who appeared in the film, reported that Matthau would tinker with the script to hone his characterization. "In one scene, Matthau was supposed to answer a telephone," she said. "He was just supposed to quickly say, 'I'm sorry, I'm busy, bye.' But he embellished it. He said the word 'yes' about twenty times, and went with that. It was totally improvised. And that was kept; that's in the film." During one scene, Mazerolle's character was supposed to "freak out, but it was a contained freak-out. Walter whispered in my ear, 'Why don't you just totally lose it? Just go for it.' We did another take, and he just broke up laughing. The producers told me, 'Don't worry, we won't use that take.' But I thought it was the best one."

Thirty-six years after *The Odd Couple* premiered, Larry King reported, "Mike Nichols told me that, when he rehearsed, he always wanted input from actors, and Walter gave him a lot of help." However, while mounting the production, creative differences existed between the two. One issue involved an entirely different kind of improvisation, one that was more conceptual and less grounded in the development of a specific character.

Carole Shelley recalled that, during one rehearsal, Nichols requested that she, Matthau, and Monica Evans (who played the other Pigeon sister) improvise.

"Pretend you're stuck in the elevator," Nichols declared.

"Uh, come on, let's rehearse," Matthau responded.

"No, no, no, come on, this is very important," was Nichols's retort.

Shelley added, "Well, the three of us stood there like pieces of herring, absolutely unable to improvise. And here was the king of improvisation directing." Matthau eventually began rubbing his eyes with his thumb and first finger. What started as a low, soft chuckle became louder and louder, as if to say, "Do me a favor. Let's get on with the rehearsal. Nothing is going to come of this." "I don't think it was his style of acting," Shelley explained. "He just liked to do it. He did his homework in his head."

On another occasion, as Nichols was deriding Matthau's approach to a particular scene, Matthau reportedly quipped, "Okay, Mike, can I have my balls back?" "Certainly," Nichols responded. Then he gestured offstage and yelled out, "Props."

Speaking of which, Matthau went to his personal wardrobe to outfit his character. At the beginning of the run, he wore his own dungarees on stage, a pair he supposedly purchased in Chinatown for twelve cents. Shelley believed the sneakers he wore in the film version were his. "They were so disgusting," she noted, and then quickly added, "The irony was that he seemed to be this slob of the world, playing Oscar, but he wasn't. He was this natty, Beau Brummell kind of man, who loved dressing up." Matthau also designed one of his patented walks and postures for the character. "If you looked at him," Shelley noted, "with his head jutting forward and the lanky, loose body, he looked like a cartoon. He really looked like a walking Hirshfeld."

While Matthau loved the play, he felt that one of the lines fell flat. Referring to their date with the Pigeon sisters, Felix dares Oscar, telling him, "What's the matter, afraid of a double-header?" Matthau believed the line was out of character. He told this to Simon, who ignored him. The story goes that a mischievous Matthau composed a letter to Simon, which was signed with various fictitious names from the credible ("Dr. Irving Blane," "Morton Cantrow") to the ridiculous ("Sigmund von Schmeerfartz, professor of psychology from Berlin University," "Professor von Steinmetz from Hanover, Germany"). In the note, Blane/Cantrow/Schmeerfartz/Steinmetz explained why the line should be eliminated, and Simon deleted it. Matthau reported that Simon always claimed to have known that the letter-writer was Matthau, and was planning to excise it anyway.

This deletion was not the only alteration in Act III. From the outset, Acts I and II were riotous but the finale was flat. Louis Zorich recalled that, while the company was in pre-Broadway tryout, Simon rewrote the last half of Act III "about eight or ten times." Just after opening night, Matthau noted, "There were so many changes that at any given time with the wrong cue I would have been in *Macbeth*."

Despite these problems, *The Odd Couple* built up momentum as it played Wilmington, Boston, and Washington. When the show opened on Broadway, Matthau, Carney, Simon, and Nichols won sterling notices. Typical was the one penned by Richard Watts Jr., of the *New York Post*, who called *The Odd Couple* "one of the happiest collaborations in the American theater in many years . . ." Critics and audiences alike agreed that the first sequence—the one featuring Oscar and his card-playing cronies—was an instant classic. Larry King recalled, "That just blew me away, that opening scene. It was hysterical."

Of all the reviews, the most telling one in relation to Matthau was written by the British critic Philip French. "I remember the excitement of seeing this production on Broadway, and experiencing the confident arrival of a star," wrote French, who added that Matthau "combined the bull-like ferocity of Wallace Beery with the rebarbative humor of W. C. Fields." With regard to his supporting-player anonymity, *Time* magazine noted that Matthau's name "may sound familiar, but . . . is mostly just something dimly recalled from the grey of the co-credits. But no more . . . he is so bellyachingly funny . . . that no one will ever forget him again."

After their opening-night triumph, Saint-Subber hosted a party at Trude Heller's nightclub, where Nichols, upon hearing some of the reviews, merrily danced the hully gully. Soon afterward, with their rehearsal squabbles in mind, Matthau reported that the director had told him, "You're a good actor, but a bad man."

Unsurprisingly, the show quickly became an audience favorite. By 10 A.M. on the morning after opening night, 200 persons were lined up outside the theater clamoring for tickets. Simon stopped by to pick up some congratulatory telegrams and was met with spontaneous applause. By late afternoon, over $20,000 in tickets had been sold; the advance sale had been approximately $500,000, and Paramount Pictures already had purchased the film rights, for $400,000.

Ten days after the opening, one might have expected to find Matthau floating on a cloud. Instead, he was feeling anxiety, which he attributed to his religion. "Jews are supposed to worry when things are going good," he explained. "That's always when the Cossacks come." As his interview concluded, he exclaimed, "Do you know what I'm going to do now? Buy a bottle of cleanser and scrub down my dressing room."

Matthau need not have fretted. *The Odd Couple* enjoyed an extraordinarily long Broadway run of 964 performances. Sports journalists came backstage to ask if he ever covered baseball or boxing on a newspaper. "[The *New York Post*'s] Jimmy Cannon, in his column, even wrote a kind of open letter to me," Matthau noted. "He said, 'How do you know so much about my life?'"

During his run in the show, Matthau was involved in plenty of off-stage shenanigans. "He used to mooch cigarettes off me," recalled Carole Shelley, "and I was being paid maybe 10 percent of what he was being paid. He would pass me by and say, 'Gimme a cigarette, Pussycat.' One day I sort of hissed, 'Walter, I'm on a very restricted amount of money. I cannot keep you in cigarettes.' The next thing I knew, he had gone out and bought me something like twelve cartons of cigarettes, and put them in my dressing room. I was so embarrassed. I took them back and said, 'Mr. Matthau, I have this dreadful sense of humor. I don't smoke.'" Shelley summarily obtained the equivalent price of the cigarettes in quarters. "I knocked on his door and I said, 'Walter, it's Carole, I've come to say thank you.' He said, 'Go away, Pussycat.' I opened the door and threw however many dollars worth of quarters into his dressing room. He shrieked with laughter. He loved it. He just thought that was hilarious."

Matthau presented the cast with wristwatches featuring Hebrew numerals. "There were nice little ladies' ones, and great big chunky men's ones," Shelley explained. "He gave me mine and I was thrilled, and I wound it up and set it. Then on Friday it died. It just wouldn't move. I went in that night and said, 'Walter, should I have this repaired? It's obviously a Jewish watch. It stops on Friday night.' And he laughed. He liked the idea that it was a Jewish watch. And it never worked. But I've still got it."

At one point in the play, Oscar asks the Pigeons if they would like drinks. Shelley noted, "My sister says, 'I'd like a large double vodka,' and I say, 'Oh, please darling, not before dinner,' and she says, 'Oh my sister, the mother hen. Okay, make it a small double vodka.' Then [Oscar] turns to me and says, 'And for the beautiful mother hen?' One night Walter said this, and we heard in the beat pause after the line a woman in the front row say, 'She looks like a chicken.' And he howled. He just crawled off the stage. He didn't finish the scene. I must say I sat there and laughed, until tears ran down my face."

Publicly, Matthau billed and cooed about his co-star. Just after the show opened, he described Carney as "the most considerate of actors, a gentleman from the old school. Lord Byron can take a back seat to him as far as I'm concerned." Even to insiders, the actors were simpatico. "During the show, they got along very well," recalled Louis Zorich. Yet beginning with rehearsals and continuing into the run, their opposing acting styles clashed. Carney memorized his lines and repeated them as written, while Matthau constantly added distracting bits to his performance. Carney then was suffering a host of offstage problems; he was drinking heavily and immersed in marital woes. This quiet man never challenged Matthau, keeping his complaints to himself. A couple of weeks after the show opened, Matthau—still yearning to play Felix—claimed that he and Carney had agreed to exchange roles one year into the run.

Matthau merrily admitted to embellishing his role. "When I did *The Odd Couple*," he claimed, "I would do it a different way each night. On Monday, I'd be Jewish; Tuesday, Italian; Wednesday, Irish-German—and I would mix them up. I did them to amuse myself, and it always worked." Once, early in the run, he opened a can of beer onstage and accidentally sprayed its contents. The bit immediately was made into a nightly ritual. When he was in what he described as a "pixyish mood," he might let a pickle—a prop during the play's eating scenes—fly off the stage and into the audience. "Well, a couple of people have come back and complained to the management that their clothes have been soiled," he admitted during the run. "They say they don't think it was a very wise idea to send a real pickle into the audience, but mostly the people throw it back. . . . Naturally we don't want any lawsuits, but the flying pickle does get a bigger laugh when it goes out into the audience."

Additionally, Matthau kept altering Simon's dialog. "When we were running the show," recalled Louis Zorich, "Mike [Nichols] would give [the actors] notes. At one point he gave Walter several, [which advised], 'Walter, before a line you're adding an 'and' or a 'but' or something that's not in the script. You've got to say every line the way that Neil Simon wrote it, because there's a certain comic rhythm.' And Mike was right. You've really got to adhere to Neil's words."

Despite all the acclaim and tumult surrounding *The Odd Couple*, Matthau was well aware of his good fortune. One day, he and Zorich were walking along Broadway, heading to the theater for a matinee. They joined each other and began chatting. Zorich recalled that Matthau was "grousing about something," and said, "Walter, what are you grumbling about? You're in a hit show. You're the lead in one of the funniest shows on Broadway." Matthau's response revealed that he was feeling like a stranger in paradise: "I've never been in a show that they were knocking down the doors to see, for Christ sake."

Upon signing for the play, Matthau agreed to stay with it for a year, and potentially longer, depending upon the availability of quality film roles. Nevertheless, Zorich recalled that, during previews, Matthau told him he would be leaving in the fall to shoot *The Fortune Cookie*—the film that made him a movie star. On November 8, 1965, just under nine months into the run, Matthau was replaced by Jack Klugman, who in turn was succeeded by Pat Hingle and Dan Dailey.

Matthau earned the New York Drama Critics Circle Award and Best Actor Tony for *The Odd Couple*. For the latter, his fellow nominees were John Gielgud (for *Tiny Alice*), Donald Pleasence *(Poor Bitos)*, and Jason Robards (*Hughie*). Neil Simon joined Matthau in the winner's circle, as Best Author (Dramatic); so did Mike Nichols, for directing *The Odd Couple* and *Luv*. *The Odd Couple* was nominated for Best Play, but lost to Frank Gilroy's *The Subject Was Roses*.

The ceremony was held on June 13, 1965, in front of 1,200 persons seated in the Astor Hotel's Grand Ballroom. Just as he did in his earlier Tony Award acceptance speech, Matthau declared that his words were composed by Carol. In what *Variety* described as a "poker-faced reading," he managed to cleverly work in the names of his children, mother-in-law, and wife.

During his *Odd Couple* run, quite a few of Matthau's Lower East Side pals came by to enjoy his performance and cheer on their old friend. By now, they all were married, middle-aged workingfolk. Yet here was one of their own, who had been appearing on stage and television for fifteen years and in the movies for a decade, and who now was headlining in a hit Broadway comedy.

Matthau's roots and present-day celebrity met head-on when Leon Birns and his wife attended the show. "We went backstage and were visiting with him," Birns recalled. "My wife had not yet met him. We sat and chatted, and he began to talk Yiddish to my wife. Friends of his came and greeted him. Then he said, 'Leon and Naomi Birns, I'd like you to meet Marge and Gower Champion.' We were a little taken aback. He said, 'Would you care to have dinner with us?' I felt a little out of place. As nice as they were, it wasn't my circle, as they say. I thanked them and said we'd get together some other time."

Birns was in the advertising-printing business. "He used to call my office, and he'd say, 'This is Mr. Matthau.' The receptionist would say, 'Mr. Matthau who?' And he'd say 'Walter Matthau,' and everyone got excited."

Another of his visitors was Syd Preses, his old Daughters of Israel nursery-mate. "Remember, he hadn't seen me since I was twelve years old," she explained. "When I did come backstage, he did a double take. Then when he approached me he picked me up and twirled me around the room and yelled out loud, 'Sylvia.' We had lots to talk about. He asked me about all the kids in the nursery."

Because *The Odd Couple* was a hot commodity, Preses left a note at the box office asking for Matthau's help in purchasing tickets. He wrote her on May 20, 1965, explaining that even he could not secure tickets until August 20. "My mother hasn't seen the show yet," he added in a P.S., "and she called yesterday. I told her I could get her a ticket for August 19 and she hung up on me. That's life." Added Preses, thirty-six years later, "I got a kick out of the P.S. about his mother. I remember her like it was yesterday."

Barney Weiner, another Lower East Sider, recalled that his wife, who had never met Matthau, played mah jongg with her friends; they all would pool their dollars, and purchase Broadway show tickets. After selecting *The Odd Couple*, Weiner noted that his wife "told the girls that her husband knew Walter very well. A couple of them were skeptical; they thought she was bragging. One girl said, 'If your husband knows him, why don't you send him a note back-stage?' Which is just what she did. So my wife goes backstage. People are running around, all over the place. Then a door opens, and Walter comes out. He's wearing a bathrobe and a pair of house slippers. And he yells out, 'Who here is married to somebody from First Street?' So my wife says, 'Me.' He says, 'Who are you married to?' She says, 'Barney.' He says, 'Barney Weiner, where is that son-of-a-gun?' He invited her out to the Russian Tea Room, but she was with her girl-friends so she didn't go."

During the show's run, Matthau had an unusual dresser: his twenty-year-old stepdaughter, Lucy Saroyan, then studying with fabled acting teacher Sanford Meisner. "Lucy also went to Dalton," recalled Marian Seldes, "and Lucy was always my friend because I'd go back to Dalton and speak, as a graduate. I just fell in love with

Lucy. When I went backstage to see Walter in *The Odd Couple*, there was Lucy. She was his dresser. It was so enchanting. I'd never seen a woman dress a man before backstage. It was so Walter. It was so off-the-wall."

"It's hard to explain to anyone who doesn't know anything about the stage," Lucy declared during the show's run. She explained that, upon coming to Broadway, her stepfather observed his four-by-seven foot dressing quarters and exclaimed, "You're the only one I know small enough to fit in this hole-in-the-wall with me. Wanna be my dresser?" She remained on the job even after Matthau left the show.

Most significant of all, Matthau's *Odd Couple* stage success permanently catapulted him to the upper echelons of the show business stratosphere. When he played Oscar Madison on stage, and then onscreen, an eruption of humor spewed forth and his days as a supporting player were permanently in his past. It was as if all his years playing supporting roles, all his years appearing on television, were erased from memory. From here on in, he would be the star, the drawing card.

And he never again returned to Broadway. He had worked diligently in theater for almost two decades; excluding his time in the military, he had lived in flats until he was nearing age thirty. So he no longer was thrilled just to be paid to act. He could not afford to be. Now, he was a star, who commanded a star's salary. It was time to savor the economic fruits of his labor.

"For twelve weeks of easier work I can make more than in two years on Broadway," he casually observed in 1967, while shooting the screen version of *The Odd Couple*. Eight years later, he complained, "I don't know why actors should have to work [in theater] under 'Lower Depth' conditions, and catch tuberculosis in a rat-infested, dank apartment, bombarded by the slings and arrows of outrageous fortune. Besides, it's a great deal of work, you have to fight with cab drivers, and you may close on Saturday night."

In 1989, Matthau presented Simon with a prize at the Third Annual American Comedy Awards. "Neil, I just want to thank you very much for saving me from a life of anonymity, crime, and squalor," he noted while concluding his introduction. "Thank you for allowing me and my family the opportunity to pursue and capture the universal goal of freedom and happiness. I am eternally grateful to you." Simon reciprocated with, "If Walter Matthau and I didn't have each other, we both would have starved to death."

Matthau went on to play other Simon characters, yet he understood the impact that Oscar Madison had on his career—and his life. "That was the plutonium I needed," he observed six years after playing Oscar on Broadway. "It all started happening after that."

CHAPTER 16

"Whiplash Willie"

The Odd Couple finally made Matthau a Broadway star, but he had not yet found comparable success on the screen. A big movie role still eluded him: a showcase role that would win him above-the-title billing. For this reason, he could not count on reprising Oscar Madison when Neil Simon's play was transferred to film.

Fortunately for Matthau, he followed the play with a screen role that blasted him into movie stardom, allowing him to become, in his own words, "a big-time schmuck superstar." The film was a dark comedy, *The Fortune Cookie*. The director was the legendary Billy Wilder, whose credits included *Some Like It Hot* and *The Apartment*, two classic comedies headlining Jack Lemmon, Matthau's *Fortune Cookie* co-star and lifelong friend-to-be. Wilder directed the pair twice more, in *The Front Page* and *Buddy Buddy*.

Over a five-decade-long career, Wilder worked with an all-star roster of Hollywood luminaries. He directed Ray Milland to an Oscar in *The Lost Weekend*, and William Holden to one in *Stalag 17*. So when Wilder described Matthau as "a genius" and "one of the handful of great actors," it was no small compliment.

During *The Odd Couple* Broadway run, Matthau—despite his fib to Syd Preses that he could not secure a ticket for Rose—had house seats for every performance. He gave them all to sibling Henry for distribution among the latter's friends and clients. He did so with one proviso: On occasion, he might need them back.

"So once I called and asked for my tickets and Henry says he's sorry, he's given them out for tonight. My friends will have to come some other time," Matthau recalled. "So okay, I switched." In contrast to Louis Zorich's recollection that Matthau secured his *Fortune Cookie* role during previews, Matthau continued, "But then I hear from Billy Wilder. He's coming to town and he wants to see the play because maybe he has a movie for me, and he's only going to be in town *one* night, the 29th."

"You're out of luck," Henry said. "I've already given out the 29th."

"But Henry, *Billy Wilder!*" retorted Walter. "He's a very big director. He's here for only *one night*, and it may mean a good movie for me, and the movies I've done so far are insignificant. Please get those tickets back and give your friends any other night." Henry acquiesced and, as Walter continued, "Billy Wilder saw *The Odd Couple* and that's how I got *The Fortune Cookie*."

Oscar Madison aside, Matthau had the role of a lifetime: William H. "Whiplash Willie" Gingrich, a shyster lawyer who is the brother-in-law of Harry Hinkle (Lemmon), a CBS-TV cameraman who is knocked over while working a Cleveland Browns–Minnesota Vikings football game. Harry is not seriously injured, but Willie sees the mishap as a chance to fake the extent of Harry's pain and suffering and sue for a bundle. "It's a story about greed," Wilder noted as he began filming, "but there are plenty of laughs in it."

Like Matthau, Lemmon was a veteran of live television. "We both did so many *Playhouse 90s* and *Studio Ones* and all the rest that you'd think we'd have co-starred a full decade before we did," Lemmon recalled. Actually, he and Matthau almost did appear together, in a television production of *Room Service*, but Matthau withdrew from the project prior to rehearsal.

By 1965, Lemmon was a ten-year veteran movie star. Five years before, when Matthau was in the show biz basement, working on *Gangster Story* and *Tallahassee 7000*, Lemmon was earning accolades for *Some Like It Hot* and *The Apartment*. (While shooting *The Odd Couple* with Lemmon in 1967, a woman allegedly asked Matthau for his autograph. After signing, he quipped, "You know, she said she liked *Gangster Story* . . . better than she liked Lemmon's *The Apartment*. She's got good taste.")

In *The Fortune Cookie*, Lemmon was the star and Matthau the supporting player. But Hinkle spends most of the film confined to a wheelchair—and "Whiplash Willie" is the plum comic part. In an oft-quoted anecdote, Matthau told Lemmon, "You know, you don't have the best part in this picture. I have it." "Well, it's about time, slick," was Lemmon's comeback. "It's about time somebody saw you in a good picture."

After the film was released and became a hit, Matthau contemplated Lemmon's comment and noted, "I thought that was a pretty damn fine thing to say." He generously added, "Lemmon was the really great performer in *The Fortune Cookie*. Remember, he has to play the whole film in a wheelchair. He was not allowed to use his body. He was totally throttled."

Not only did *The Fortune Cookie* win Matthau movie-star status, but it is just as memorable for pairing him with Lemmon. They would go on to be one of the cinema's great comedy teams. Previously, when appearing with such stars as Gregory Peck, Burt Lancaster, Cary Grant, and Kirk Douglas, Matthau only could play a villain, a sidekick, a secondary role within the framework of the story. While his acting was effective, he never developed a charismatic relationship to the star. But in Lemmon, he found someone with whom he could share the fantasy world created in the script. These two were just a little bit offbeat, a little zany. Their personalities complemented each other. Both could show warmth and vulnerability, as well as play broad physical comedy.

Additionally, Matthau and Lemmon shared the same professional roots. Ossie Davis, who worked with both of them, observed that they "were solidly anchored in the theatrical tradition—a professionalism that could only have occurred by an exposure to the stage. They were not Hollywood creations. They were brought to Hollywood with a well-developed sense of craft."

Matthau and Lemmon had met prior to their *Fortune Cookie* pairing, but each offered a different story regarding the circumstances. Matthau claimed it was in a Kosher-style delicatessen in

As a youngster, Matthau attended the Daughters of Israel nursery while his mother toiled in sweatshops. He appears in the top row, three heads to the right of Herb Port, a nursery supervisor. Childhood friend Syd Preses is at bottom right. A partially obscured June Mellon, on whom Walter had a crush, is third on the right, in the second row from the top; right below her is Milton Brown, another Lower East Side contemporary. *(Syd Preses)*

In 1936–1937, Matthau worked as an extra in the Yiddish-language musical *The Dish-washer,* starring Herman Yablokoff. He appeared briefly as an immigration officer and cellist, and hawked refreshments during intermissions. *(Authors' Collection)*

For years, Matthau claimed that he had listed his middle name as "Foghorn" on his Social Security card application. This was one of his many youth-related fabrications.
(Social Security Administration)

Matthau, a newly minted GI, towers over Lower East Side mates Eddie and Syd Green, at left, in 1942. The soldiers on the right are unidentified. *(Herb Green)*

While studying at the New School for Social Research Dramatic Workshop, Matthau—who recently had changed his name from Matthow—appeared as the "1st Soldier" in a 1947 production of Jean-Paul Sartre's *The Flies*. "Bernie Schwartz"—later Tony Curtis—was cast as "Nicias." *(Authors' Collection)*

Matthau co-starred with Nancy Kelly and Walter Brooke in *Twilight Walk*, which ran eight performances on Broadway in 1951. Despite the play's failure, Matthau emerged with solid reviews—and a New York Drama Critics Circle Award. *(Billy Rose Theatre Collection, The New York Public Library for the Performing Arts, Astor, Lenox and Tilden Foundations)*

Appearing on live TV series during the 1950s proved a valuable learning experience for Matthau, who had supporting and starring roles on dozens of dramas and comedies. Here he is, all properly domesticated, in one of his countless early roles, opposite Neva Patterson. *(Lana Morgan)*

Matthau, around the time he was appearing on Broadway and playing character roles in films and on television. *(Archive Photos)*

Matthau slugs it out with James Mason in *Bigger Than Life*, released in 1956, one of the early films in which he was featured in a supporting role. *(Authors' Collection)*

In 1957's *Slaughter on Tenth Avenue*, Matthau is appropriately menacing as a brutal New York City waterfront racketeer. *(John Cocchi)*

A sultry Carol Matthau, billed as Carol Grace, co-starred with Matthau in the 1959 potboiler *Gangster Story*. This was Matthau's only film as director; he called it "one of the worst films ever made." *(John Cocchi)*

On *Tallahassee 7000*, a mercifully short-lived syndicated TV series that aired in the early 1960s, Matthau played Lex Rogers, two-fisted special agent for the Florida Sheriff's Bureau. *(Lana Morgan)*

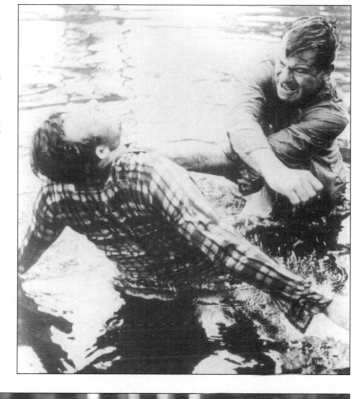

Matthau, cast as a villain masquerading as a CIA honcho, eyes Audrey Hepburn in 1963's *Charade*, a stylish mystery-comedy-melodrama. *(Charles Matthau)*

A cigarillo-puffing Matthau and Art Carney relax backstage at the Plymouth Theatre on
March 9, 1965, the day before the opening of *The Odd Couple*.
(New York Times Company/Sam Falk/Archive Photos)

A baseball cap-clad
Matthau on stage as Oscar
Madison.
(Walter Daran/Archive Photos)

In 1966, Matthau was an eleven-year-veteran of movies when he became a star—and won a Best Supporting Actor Academy Award—for his role as "Whiplash" Willie Gingrich in Billy Wilder's *The Fortune Cookie*. Here, he poses with co-stars Jack Lemmon and Judi West. *(Authors' Collection)*

Matthau as "Whiplash" Willie, in *The Fortune Cookie*. *(Authors' Collection)*

Matthau counsels his young son Charlie in the 1960s. Jack Lemmon described the connection between the two as "one of the great father–son relationships."
(Charles Matthau)

Matthau poses with David and Jenny, his children with first wife Geri, at a screening of the 1970 Julie Andrews–Rock Hudson musical comedy *Darling Lili*.
(Frank Edwards/Fotos International/Archive Photos)

Matthau and Jack Lemmon flank columnist Army Archerd at the Hollywood premiere of *Fiddler on the Roof* in 1971. *(Murray Garrett/Archive Photos)*

Matthau, then in his early fifties, was cast in 1971's *Kotch* as seventy-something Joseph P. Kotcher and emerged with a Best Actor Oscar nomination. His director: Jack Lemmon. *(Authors' Collection)*

Matthau and son Charlie on the field at Dodger Stadium during a 1973 celebrity baseball game.
(Archive Photos)

Matthau, director Billy Wilder, and co-star Jack Lemmon pose while rehearsing *The Front Page*, which came to movie theaters in 1974. *(Keystone/Archive Photos)*

A mischievous Matthau and a smiling Carol in January 1976. *(Evening Standard/Archive Photos)*

Glenda Jackson was one of Matthau's favorite screen co-stars. Here they are in *Hopscotch*, released in 1980. *(Authors' Collection)*

In 1973, Matthau starred in Don Siegel's *Charley Varrick*, playing a stunt pilot-turned-bankrobber. Two years earlier, Clint Eastwood played another of Siegel's iconoclastic anti-heroes in *Dirty Harry*. Here, Matthau and Eastwood mingle at a Hollywood event in the early 1990s.
(Darlene Hammond/Archive Photos)

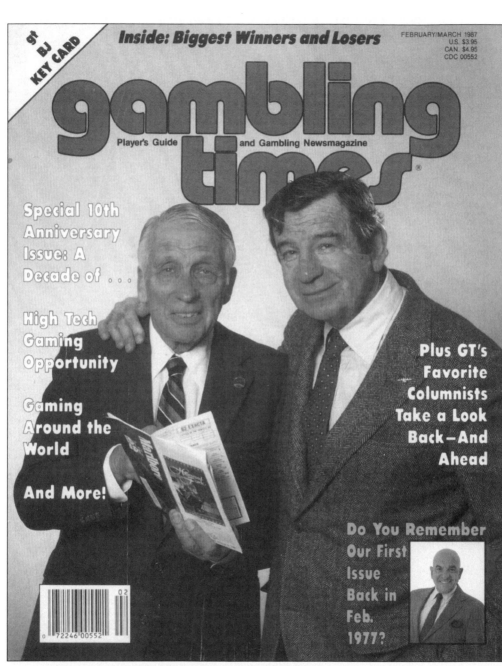

Given Matthau's lifelong obsession with gambling, it was appropriate for him to be a cover boy for *Gambling Times* magazine. He, Howard Koch, and Telly Savalas graced the periodical's premiere issue—and, here, Matthau and Koch, along with a Hollywood Park racing form, make a return appearance on the cover of the tenth anniversary issue, dated February/March 1987. *(Stanley Sludikoff, Gambling Times magazine)*

Father and son: Walter and Charlie in the 1990s. *(Charles Matthau)*

Matthau—who created the role of Oscar Madison in *The Odd Couple*—jests with Jack Klugman, who played the part on the TV series, at the 11th Annual American Comedy Awards in 1997. Matthau was honored with a Lifetime Achievement Award.
(Darlene Hammond/Archive Photos)

In September 1997, the Matthau clan—Walter, Charlie, and Carol—was honored with the First American Film Institute Platinum Circle Award.
(Darlene Hammond/Archive Photos)

Matthau and director/co-star Diane Keaton publicize *Hanging Up*, in which Matthau made his final screen appearance, on *Larry King Live*. The date: February 10, 2000. Matthau passed away on July 1. *(Reuters/Archive Photos)*

Matthau is buried in the Memorial Gardens section of Pierce Brothers Westwood Memorial Park, a small cemetery located behind the high-rises of Wilshire Boulevard. *(Audrey Kupferberg)*

Brentwood, where Lemmon ordered a very un-Kosher meal: fried shrimp and a chocolate frappe. "I figured he was nuts," Matthau concluded, "and I fell madly in love with him." (This is a continuing motif for Matthau, who also repeatedly declared that he loved Carol because she was "nuts.")

Lemmon remembered the circumstances differently. He recalled they met at the bar in Sardi's during the run of *Will Success Spoil Rock Hunter?* Matthau's backside was so sore that he was unable to sit. Lemmon asked, "Are you feeling all right?" "Hell, no," Matthau responded, adding that, the previous evening, he and Carol had attended a party at Gloria Vanderbilt's Long Island beach house that was packed with guests. He could not find an empty chair, so he took the only available space: a glass coffee table. His weight shattered the table, resulting in a cut groin and a bloody mess. Vanderbilt's alleged response to Matthau was, "You broke my table!"

Matthau recalled the incident, but discounted Lemmon's story because, as he remembered it, he was out of commission for two weeks. "They rushed me to a hospital on [Long Island's] North Shore to remove the pieces of glass and sew me up. The surgeon said the glass just missed an artery which would have ended my career right there." He added, "Gloria in her inimitable way kept calling Carol and saying, 'Is he really all right, darling, I mean really, I mean really?'"

Of this version, Matthau cracked, "Maybe I should leave Jack's story alone. It's more dramatic," and "[Lemmon] doesn't remember his name on the best of days, so how can he remember what happened thirty-odd years ago?" Charlie Matthau explained, "Jack's version is the true version, but my dad's story [also is] true. After they had been friends for years, they went to a deli and Jack ordered fried shrimp and a chocolate frappe."

What goes without debate is that Lemmon and Matthau struck gold together in *The Fortune Cookie*. In the first scene they shot together, Willie visits Hinkle in a hospital room and aggressively exhorts him to fake the injury. "Boom, from that first scene on," Lemmon recalled, "it was like silk working with him." That day, Lemmon arrived on set at 9 A.M. Matthau was sitting on the steps of a trailer. Lemmon greeted him. Matthau looked up and asked, "Do you know how a Japanese rabbi gives a circumcision?" After Lemmon responded negatively, Matthau shouted a loud nonsense word and slammed his arm down in a cutting motion. "I knew it was gonna be fun," Lemmon concluded.

Lemmon reported that later in the day, "Billy starts explaining to Walter in his thick German accent, 'OK, here's what you have to do. Now you go here and there, do this and that.' And he went on for what seemed like five minutes. Walter just gaped at him and waited. Billy said, 'Walter, you got that?' And Walter stared at him and replied, 'You speak kinda funny, Billy, you from out of town?'"

Over three decades later, while hyping their comedy *Out to Sea* on *Larry King Live*, Matthau and Lemmon discussed the longevity of their kinship. "How could you not be friendly with him?" Matthau asked. "This man is amenable, delightful, generous. . . ." Lemmon's fondness for Matthau began with "his sense of humor, his appreciation of humor, and in working with him it just seemed to be like butter melting from the beginning. It was so easy and fluid."

What was not so delightful was the health scare Matthau suffered during the production, a crisis that made the glass table incident seem like a hangnail. With ten days left on the shoot, Matthau, then in his mid-forties, suffered a serious heart attack. Fearing that he would be tossed off the picture, Carol hid the news from the studio suits and Walter's co-stars. First she explained that he was suffering from indigestion. United Press International reported that he was "under treatment for hepatitis at Midway Hospital . . ." Upon admitting the heart attack, Carol downplayed its severity. It was uncertain when Matthau would return to work, and so the powers-that-be wanted to replace him and reshoot the entire film. Carol's lies helped prevent this from occurring. Furthermore, the notion was unacceptable to Billy Wilder, whose response was, "Absolutely not. Under [no] condition can we replace him. There isn't anybody who could play the part like that. We'll wait, no matter how long it [takes]." Wilder's admiration for Matthau had become boundless. "As far as I'm concerned," he noted, "Walter can play anything from Rhett Butler to Scarlett O'Hara."

Filming was suspended for five months, until Matthau could continue.

While recuperating, he lost approximately thirty pounds, which played havoc with the film's continuity. He recalled, "People said to me, 'How did you do that? You were 195 pounds at the bottom of the stairs. You walked up the stairs and, at the top, you were 165.' I said, 'I just acted lighter.'"

The Fortune Cookie opened in October 1966—and it was Matthau's show. The *Variety* critic spoke for reviewers and audiences alike when noting that Matthau "delivers the standout performance." He emerged not only with movie-star status but with a Best Supporting Actor Academy Award. His co-nominees were Mako (for *The Sand Pebbles*), James Mason (*Georgy Girl*), George Segal (*Who's Afraid of Virginia Woolf?*), and Robert Shaw (*A Man for All Seasons*). The ceremony was held on April 10, 1967, at the Santa Monica Civic Auditorium. Matthau showed up with his face bruised, and his left arm in a cast. Two days earlier, he had been riding a bicycle near the Pacific Coast Highway. The front wheel hit a block of wood, and he was hurtled over the handlebars. His arm was broken in sixteen places. His face and legs were scratched. His chin required six stitches. He noted that "about three pounds of gravel [ended up going] into my eyes, nose, and throat."

Walter and Carol, garbed in a pastel gown and shawl, were sitting in their seats, in front of Steve McQueen and behind Mike Nichols. Shelley Winters took the stage, announcing that she was to "give the award to the talented man who gave the best performance by an actor in a supporting role." As she cited the nominees, the television camera caught Matthau scratching his nose. Then she spoke the words, "And the winner is Walter Matthau for *The Fortune Cookie*." McQueen applauded, and whispered several words in Matthau's ear. After kissing Carol, a dapper, bespectacled Matthau, garbed in a tuxedo and bowtie, strode to the stage. As she handed him the statue, Winters quipped, "You had a hard time getting here!" He was interrupted by laughter after declaring, "The other day, as I was falling off my bicycle . . ." Then he continued, "I had the following thoughts. I was given a very juicy part. I was allowed to work with talented, exhilarating, and beautiful people. I was given a good deal of money and a great deal of joy. And, now, really, don't you think this is going a little too far?" Then he smiled, and graciously added, "Thank you anyway." Winters gently grasped his broken arm, and the two exited the stage. He partied well into the night, with a bottle of champagne at his lips.

The Lower East Side streetboy now was an Oscar-winner! The following morning, Matthau was in a deep sleep when the phone rang. It was his seventy-year-old mother, whose bellowing voice jarred him out of his reverie. "Strangers are calling me," she exclaimed. "It must be important." A month later, Matthau declared, "I take her to the opening nights of my plays, but she has never seen one of my movies. She doesn't like to go to movies."

Matthau's Oscar signaled his arrival as a movie star. When he left *The Odd Couple* to play "Whiplash Willie," it was announced that he would rejoin the show in three to four months. He never did. Nor did he ever return to Broadway.

Matthau told conflicting jokes about his Oscar victory. "The Academy Award? Yeah, I wasn't surprised. I thought I'd get it. I looked at the competition and thought I'd get it." He kidded that the only reason he won was because of the heart attack. "People thought I was going to die," he quipped, "so they gave me the award to take to my great reward." Also, he attributed his health problems to playing comedy: "That's why I got a heart attack when I was making *Fortune Cookie*. Comedic work is hard work." His son Charlie noted that he "said the first Tony [award] meant the most to him. But I'm sure the Oscar meant a lot to him."

Despite the Oscar, this period of Matthau's life remained just as inexorably linked to his heart attack. While watching *The Thorn Birds*, a 1983 TV mini-series starring Richard Chamberlain (which he jokingly renamed *The Thornbergs*), he kidded, "Oh, now I remember, Richard Chamberlain. Doctor Kildare. I once did an opening segment on his show, in which I had a heart attack. A year later, I had a real heart attack because I wanted to see if I had done it correctly." In the episode, Matthau played Franklin Gaer, a hard-working salesman who is felled by heart disease. Decades later, Matthau wisecracked, "It's a fighting word, heartattack. It's one word, you know. A Jewish word. Heartattack. He had a heartattack."

In retrospect, Matthau could kid about the calamity. But at the time, it was no jest. Lana Wood—the kid sister of Natalie—had appeared on the *Doctor Kildare* episode as Matthau's daughter. It was titled "Man Is a Rock," it aired on September 24, 1964, and it was one of Matthau's final TV-series roles. "I don't know what was going on with him personally during that period of his life," Wood recalled, "but he really did not have anything to do with me whatsoever. We would say good morning, and that was it. He seemed very distracted. He was very intense in what he was doing, but he would just do his work, and then retreat." (Georgann Johnson, who played his wife, had an explanation for Matthau's diversion: "I mostly recall his concern about the *Odd Couple* [stage] negotiations. [He was] on the phone to New York a lot—it was a big break for him.")

A year or so later, Wood was under contract at Fox. "I had gone into a portion of the commissary which was not open to the public," she continued. "It was just for people working on shows. I had a little toy cap gun that was actually given to me by Bobby Darin, which I thought was fun and silly. I was a very silly young girl, and I'd been shooting people all morning, and I thought that the caps were gone. I took it out, and was showing it to the person with whom I was having lunch. I pulled the trigger, it went off, and the next thing I knew Walter Matthau was towering over my back. He was tapping me on the shoulder [and] saying, 'Yoouuungg laaddy,' in that voice of his, 'I have just come out of the hospital from having a coronary and I don't appreciate your thoughtlessness.' I mean, he reamed me from one side to the next, and I sat there shaking and praying that he wouldn't remember that he had worked with me."

Did Matthau recollect her from *Doctor Kildare*? "Nope, nothing," Wood explained, "and I was very pleased. I was so devastated. I didn't mean to do it."

The story goes that Matthau's cardiologist, Dr. Clarence Agress, attributed the attack to three bad habits: smoking several packs of cigarettes and assorted pipes and cigars each day; lack of exercise; and worry over his incessant gambling. Matthau's handball-playing days were long gone; the doctor implored him to be more physically active, and to give up smoking and gambling. While Matthau did not return to the handball courts, he did become an enthusiastic walker, starting with short, daily strolls and eventually averaging fifteen miles per week; occasionally, he jogged ten miles per day. Not that he was grossly overweight before the heart attack, but his exercise regimen did slim him down. Still, this was no simple task. "I wish it were as easy to lose weight as it is to lose money," he quipped two years later. Added his son Charlie, after his death, "He was really good about the walking for a long time."

Matthau tried not to overwork. "There was a standard rule: Walter didn't work after 5 P.M.," explained Graham Jarvis, who appeared with him several years later in *A New Leaf.* The reason: "He'd had the heart attack." Added Robert Carradine, who acted with Matthau in *The Incident*, a 1989 television movie, "When you worked with Walter, you knew what time you'd be done every day. He never worked after five. Our director, Joe Sargent, was really adamant about getting Walter out of there by five." This slowing down also was one reason that Matthau never returned to Broadway. In 1996, he told Leonard Maltin that he did not miss working in the theater "because it gave me a heart attack. It's too nerve-racking. Your whole life is in front of eight critics, and they're gonna tell the whole world whether you're good or bad."

Matthau also stopped smoking. "For years, I was half alive," he admitted, "waking up every morning with a cigarette hangover and smoker's hack. Now, having survived the heart attack, I feel as though I've been given a second life. And better than my old one, too." Nonetheless, wife Carol kept on smoking—often when his back was turned. But he knew, and he cracked that she "would be a great actress if she'd stop smoking."

Anne Jackson related a story involving Matthau and cigarettes. "I was staying at the Chateau [Marmont], and I think Walter was there, too. It was such a lonely place to be. If you weren't working on a day, you just didn't know what to do with yourself. I don't think I drove at the time. The studio would come and pick me up."

One afternoon, Matthau invited Jackson to lunch. In their company was his doctor. "I smoked at the time," Jackson continued, "and Walter did not approve of smoking. So he said to the doctor, 'Now this is a great actress,' which made me feel terrific. Then he said, 'Now she shouldn't be smoking. Should she be smoking, doctor?' And [the doctor] said, 'Well, no, I guess not.' [Matthau] said, 'Well, can you hypnotize her out of it?' The doctor said, 'I don't know if she'd like that.' I said, 'Oh, yes I would. I'd love to stop smoking.' So Walter says [to the doctor], 'Hypnotize her.' So I'm sitting in a restaurant with Walter and this doctor, and I'm put under. I remember thinking, 'This is ridiculous,' but I went along with it. Do you know that, when I finished, I didn't smoke for about seven months?"

Another culprit was Matthau's temper. "Until [he had the heart attack], there was like a streak in him where he'd go into fits of anger and kind of fly off the handle," recalled David Matthau. "In one way, my sister and I were terrified of him. He was prone to just fly into a rage, and kind of go crazy. Everybody would sort of freeze with fear. After his heart attack, that changed. He started to really mellow, in a way."

Those fits occasionally resurfaced. While filming *The Marriage Fool*, his 1998 television movie, he was conferring with his son Charlie, the film's director. Arlene Mazerolle, one of the supporting players, joined them. "I don't remember what I said," she noted. "It was something about the scene [we were shooting]. Walter snapped at me; he said, 'You, shut up!' My heart was torn. I was angry, and thought, 'How rude.' I walked away, and about a half-hour later I was in my trailer getting my makeup redone and he came over and kissed my neck and said, 'How're ya doin'?' He rubbed my shoulders, as if to say, 'Sorry about that.' I thought that was [nice], because he acknowledged that he'd been an asshole—as we all can be."

Marian Seldes believed that Matthau's gambling was the primary cause of the heart attack. Bookies were phoning him on the set. "I guess Billy told [this] to Gar [Garson Kanin] or something, that he nearly had a heart attack because they were coming to get him for some money or something."

Following his illness, many of Matthau's friends assumed that he had forsaken gambling, at least temporarily. But his heart problem did not cure his addiction. "He still bet on games but for a while he really did back off in terms of the size of the bets that were being made," observed David Matthau. "But he still gambled.

"I think that when he was younger he was furiously gambling . . . but when he became very successful, he never really got in that kind of predicament again, even though very large amounts of money were still being gambled away. He made enough so that he wasn't in a life-and-death kind of situation."

Three years post–heart attack, Matthau commented that his race-track bets now were limited to $20 before adding, with a twinkle, "Yeah, I'll only bet about $20." Once he joked, "But of course, you can get a heart attack from the strain of standing in line at a $2 window." And he kiddingly noted, "I like to think of myself as a non-drinking, non-smoking, non-cursing violinist who quietly has his gefilte fish and goes to bed and reads a book—which I do. I like to listen to a little Isaac Stern in a Mendelssohn violin concerto. I could listen day and night. I'd like to project an image of a clean-cut American fellow who never had a heart attack and never gambled."

Of course, Matthau did have the heart attack. And he did gamble.

In the early 1980s, on the set of *Buddy Buddy*, Roger Ebert asked him if he still was betting. "Hardly at all," Matthau responded. "For big stakes, that is. Of course I gamble, to make the games interesting. But $500 a game, tops. Or sometimes a thousand. No heart attack bets." (The actor did some of his wagering with Ebert's partner, Gene Siskel. They used to play poker in a Gardena, California, card parlor. Siskel's widow Marlene Iglitzen recalled sitting in their car while her husband and Matthau were inside. "It was just like an ATM," she said. "Gene won and Walter lost every time, and Gene would come out with the money." She added that, as they drove off with their booty, "We felt like Bonnie and Clyde." Of his father's cardplaying capabilities, Charlie Matthau noted, "[He] was brilliant in terms of strategy, but he was not great at patience . . . and also he didn't have a killer instinct.")

Syd Preses once sent Matthau a lottery ticket. "He wrote to me right away," she explained, "and said, 'DO NOT GAMBLE!' I wrote him back and said, 'I'm a very conservative gambler. Don't worry about it.' He said if I win, I should keep the money. The next week I get a letter from him, and he says, 'I've changed my mind. If you win, I want the money.' I was hysterical."

Added Larry King, "Once he said to me, 'I stopped betting. I stopped all betting.' I said, 'When?' He said, 'Ten minutes ago. I'll start again in twenty minutes.'"

CHAPTER 17

Odd Couple Redux

Matthau's first post–heart attack feature was a comedy, *A Guide for the Married Man*, released in 1967. *Guide* may not be the actor's best film, but it allowed him his initial starring role in a major Hollywood movie. Meanwhile, the increasing number of Matthau newspaper profiles trumpeted his success, featuring such headlines as "Walter Matthau is odds-on favorite for super-stardom" and "Fame Held Off, But Walter Matthau Has Made It."

During the filming, Matthau exuded the self-confidence of a newly minted movie star who knew he was no flavor of the month, because he had worked too long and hard to attain his success. He merrily joked with his co-workers, throwing off such quips as "Have no fear, this is a scene I've been studying intensively for about ten seconds" (to director Gene Kelly) and "This $3 million picture should cost $80,000" (to a studio suit).

In *Guide*, Matthau played Paul Manning, a Los Angelino undergoing a seven-year itch after twelve happy years of marriage (to gorgeous Inger Stevens). His philandering pal (Robert Morse) offers to teach him about adultery, but tender thoughts of his wife and family prevent him from consummating a relationship with an alluring divorcee. Initially, Matthau was offered Morse's role, but refused it.

"It didn't seem very funny for the older fellow to corrupt the morals of the younger," he explained during the shoot. "Besides, I didn't want to play another con man."

Linda Harrison, who appeared in the film, recalled decades later, "What I remember about *Guide* was that it really [helped to bring] Walter out as a comedian. Walter had this uncanny knack for making a *look* that would make you laugh."

The following year, Matthau starred in a comedy that is linked to *Guide* . . . by its parallel title: *The Secret Life of an American Wife*, in which he was reunited with George Axelrod. The scenario involves a suburban housewife (Anne Jackson) whose press agent husband tells her she never could be a call girl. Eventually, she poses as a hooker and attempts to seduce her mate's movie star client (Matthau).

Both films are comic fantasies that acknowledge the then-broadening sexual revolution, but deal with the subject in terms of their target audiences: the tradition-minded, middle-aged middle class. The characters ponder sexual experimentation, but the audiences are assured that sexual permissiveness, in the form of extra-marital flings, leads to comical chaos, emotional disquietude, and public embarrassment.

After the film's release, Matthau declared that, because of its subject, it should not be "exploited like an underground picture of perverse practices. [Besides], nobody wants to see the nude torso of a six-foot-three Jew."

During the shoot, Matthau had moments of mischief with Jackson. "We had a bedroom scene together," she recalled, "and I was uncomfortable with these sex scenes. I hated them, because they were all so phonily written in the movies in those days. He'd come on the set and he'd say, 'Now, you're looking at a man who just had a heart attack. So there's to be no hanky-panky.' Then I'd have to get under the covers with him, and he'd put his finger under the covers and lift it, as if he had an erection. I guess he did this to try to make me feel comfortable, but I'd think, 'Oh, my god, what am I getting into?' He was a terror!"

Matthau's second 1968 release was the screen version of *The Odd Couple*. Given his status as a hot Hollywood commodity, odds were that he would be chosen to play Oscar Madison. Matthau knew this, and was a take-no-prisoners negotiator during contract talks. Initially, he was offered $150,000 for the film, but wanted twice as much. When the powers at Paramount Pictures threatened to hire Frank Sinatra or Jackie Gleason, Matthau up and left for the racetrack. The studio eventually raised its offer to $220,000, then agreed on $300,000.

Such was not the case with Art Carney. Despite his Emmy Awards and familiarity to audiences as Ed Norton, Ralph Kramden's beloved sewer worker foil on TV's *The Honeymooners*, Carney was no movie name. So when it came time to cast the film, he was not considered for Felix Ungar. Replacing him was Jack Lemmon, who accepted on condition that Matthau play Oscar. The director was Gene Saks, Matthau's old New School classmate.

The Odd Couple is memorable for its classic comic bits, from an irate Oscar hurling a plate of linguine against a wall and informing Felix that his dinner now is "gaahbage" to Felix's fabled "fpnawwwwwww," a sound that could not be replicated by anyone except Lemmon himself. He repeated the sound three decades later in the sequel, *The Odd Couple II*. "I can never do that too much," he noted. "Audiences love it." What they also loved was the Matthau-Lemmon chemistry. "I think Jack and Walter had an incredible working relationship," observed Carole Shelley, who reprised her Pigeon Sister role. "They made it very safe for each other to be dangerous." For example, in one sequence, as Shelley explained, "Walter breaks down, he's really crying like a kid. It could have been a big man with a funny face pretending to cry. And it isn't. It's a big, strong, sloppy man crying. That's quite dangerous."

"Chemistry is just something that you have," Lemmon once explained, "like the color of your hair. It's just when the two of you are on the same wavelength. I can tell where Walter is going with something before he gets there in a scene." He also noted, "Matthau drives me crazy. He can be saying something, and then [excuse himself] and walk out and, bang, in the middle of a sentence, he can pick it up. And, son of a gun, you believe him. I don't know how he does it. He's a closet Method actor."

Unsurprisingly, *The Odd Couple* was just as much of a hit on screen as on stage. It was hailed by the critics, and played a record fourteen consecutive weeks at New York's Radio City Music Hall. In November 1968, several months after its opening, Lemmon and Matthau made a gag appearance on *Jack Benny's Bag*, a TV special. At the start, Eddie "Rochester" Anderson converses on the telephone with Benny, his boss. After the discussion is completed, it becomes clear that Rochester has been playing cards with four men, one of whom is cigar-puffing Oscar Madison/Matthau. Then Felix/Lemmon enters, and begins spraying air freshener and swatting a chair with a towel.

Walter Matthau and Jack Lemmon never were billed as a comedy team. Nonetheless, their *Fortune Cookie* and *Odd Couple* performances propelled them into screen history as among the elite mirth-making duos, ranking alongside Laurel and Hardy, Abbott and Costello, Martin and Lewis, and Hope and Crosby. As actors who played off each other with consummate professionalism and an almost intuitive sense of timing, they rate alongside Katharine Hepburn and Spencer Tracy, Hepburn and Cary Grant, and William Powell and Myrna Loy.

Over the course of the next three-plus decades, Matthau and Lemmon appeared together in ten films: *The Fortune Cookie* and *The Odd Couple* were followed by *The Front Page*; *Buddy Buddy*; *JFK*; *Grumpy Old Men*; *The Grass Harp*; *Grumpier Old Men*; *Out to Sea*; and *The Odd Couple II*. Lemmon directed Matthau once, in *Kotch*, and they appeared on stage in 1974, in Sean O'Casey's *Juno and the Paycock*, presented at the Mark Taper Forum in Los Angeles.

Often, Matthau and Lemmon played Oscar and Felix–like adversaries. Yet off-camera, they were the greatest of friends, buddies for life. The fact that they shared the same values and politics—both were liberal Democrats—added to their fellowship. Plus, their wives—Lemmon's longtime mate was actress Felicia Farr—became close friends. Felicia and Carol Matthau have been known to spend hours dining together, or talking on the telephone.

Over the course of a long marriage, a couple will endure everyday disagreements. Certainly, Walter and Carol had their share of squabbles. Yet in 1993, Matthau declared that he and Lemmon never had a falling-out. "I swear to God, never," he said. Matthau once kidded about the secret of their friendship. "The main thing I like about

Jack," he explained, "is that he bathes every day, so I don't have to worry about being assaulted odoriferously."

Almost three decades after *The Odd Couple*, Piper Laurie appeared with them in *The Grass Harp*. The film was shot on location in the small town of Wetumpka, Alabama. "We all thought that there was one really fabulous restaurant [in the area]," Laurie recalled. "So when we had a late call, or when it was Friday or Saturday night, we individually would book that restaurant. Often I would see just Walter and Jack eating [at a table] by themselves. It struck me that they were like an old married couple, who didn't need to talk. They were just there, and comfortable, and enjoying their dinner. [There was] not much conversation at all. I thought that was interesting, these two funny men just very quiet with each other, and comfortable."

"There was a kind of unspoken sweetness that went on between Jack and Walter," added Lana Morgan, director of creative affairs for The Matthau Company, his son Charlie's production company. "On the surface, they would often be poking fun at each other, growly or gruff, but you could see right through the kidding. There was this sort of gentle looking-after-each-other between them. I think they would treat each other like the other one was a younger brother."

In 1993, the duo filmed *Grumpy Old Men* in icy-cold Minnesota. By then, Matthau had experienced a myriad of illnesses. "The conditions were terrible [during the shoot]," Morgan noted. "There was a tremendous amount of snow, and [what seemed like] a record low wind-chill. Jack and Walter were constantly going up to each other, and checking on each other. Walter was probably the one who did it more. Yet he was the one with all the health problems. He was the one who had to make sure he didn't get sick.

"There was a scene where Walter was supposed to get into this big old ugly sedan. He was supposed to open the door and get in the front seat, and continue having this conversation with Jack where they're yelling at each other. There's this huge snow bank between the door and where Walter was standing. Plus, it's icy. And he's trying to figure out how he can climb over [the bank] while doing the scene. The director was telling him, 'You've got big, long legs. Reach up there.' Jack was watching this, and [is being] protective of Walter.

Now Walter was saying, 'I'm fine, I'm fine, I'll do it.' And so Jack said to Walter, 'No you won't, you big dummy!' He was worried, but he was picking on Walter.

"Now one of them was not going to come out and say, 'Oh, I'm worried about you' or 'You have to do this for safety.' Instead, they would just sort of bully and growl at each other. They would do this all the time with each other. Finally Jack said to the director, 'Can't we just shovel away some snow to the edge of the car door?' And [the director] said, 'I can't. We already shot the master shot.' Well, Walter has been around a long time; he knows [that], with all the weather problems on this shoot, the studio is leaning on the director. So Walter doesn't want to be the cause of any further delays, or give the director a hard time—and of course, I'm sure Jack knows this is what Walter is thinking. So Walter said, 'Don't worry about it, I'll do it.' Instead of yelling at the director, Jack is yelling at Walter . . . as if this is all Walter's idea. And Jack starts kicking the snow away. He didn't care about the master shot. He was not going to let his friend fall."

Three years later, while promoting *Out to Sea*, one of the final Lemmon-Matthau comedies, Lemmon referred to his pal as a "brother." "Working with him is not work, and it's not rehearsal," he explained. "It's more like a conversation, like sitting down to break-fast and just chatting." He added, with the utmost sincerity, "I've never found any actor that was easier for me to work with than Walter."

And when Matthau passed away, the very public tears shed by Lemmon were real, rather than show-business phony.

CHAPTER 18

Character Actor/Star

Jack Lemmon might have been talking about Walter Matthau as well as himself when he observed, in the mid-1990s, "I'm one of the lucky ones—and there's always an element of luck to this profession, especially when it comes to getting your career launched. Plenty of fine actors are not working. Acting is the highest-risk profession I know of, and that includes professional athletics."

Three decades earlier, Matthau considered himself fortunate to have a career that was solidly launched. Now, he no longer was a mere working actor. He was an Academy Award winner. He was a headliner. He might share the camaraderie of William Schallert, his longtime friend, but on the Hollywood food chain Matthau was A-list and Schallert, while a busy and respected supporting player, strictly was B-list. Schallert never hosted a major awards ceremony; Matthau, on the other hand, became an Academy Awards semi-regular. On April 14, 1969, he and Ingrid Bergman, Rosalind Russell, Frank Sinatra, Burt Lancaster, Jane Fonda, Natalie Wood, Diahann Carroll, Tony Curtis, and Sidney Poitier were the "Friends of Oscar" who hosted the show. On April 15, 1971, he was one of thirty-two "Friends" handling the duties. On April 1, 1983, he hosted with Liza

Minnelli, Dudley Moore, and Richard Pryor. Over the years, he was a frequent awards presenter.

Nor would Schallert be lumped with A-listers in film credits. Matthau's star status is reflected in his cameo appearance, along with heavyweights Marlon Brando, Richard Burton, and John Huston, in *Candy*, a 1968 sex satire. His role: right-wing General Smight.

Fortuitously for Matthau, his *Fortune Cookie* and *Odd Couple* successes came at a point in time in which the definition of celluloid stardom and the rules of the fame game were rapidly changing.

Matthau was thinking about Hollywood's Golden Age when he commented, "Hollywood has been known, in my youth anyway, as a place where the beautiful people are the leaders. If you weren't beautiful or handsome, you were asexual. No sex! Your only worth is that of a helper to the beautiful person who's in the leading role."

In the late 1960s, Hollywood was undergoing a revolution. Such youth-oriented movies as *The Graduate*, *Bonnie and Clyde*, and *Easy Rider* were changing the industry. Hollywood filmmakers were thinking young, thinking Baby Boomer, and Baby Boomers wanted realism on screen. Granted that, decades earlier, non-pretty-boy character actors like Edward G. Robinson, Humphrey Bogart, and Paul Muni had become stars. But they were in the minority. Most male movie stars, from Cary to Gary to Clark, were pretty boys, macho men—and leading men. Now, the traditionally handsome star was being replaced by a more unconventional type. Many were, at heart, character players: Dustin Hoffman, who earned stardom as *The Graduate*; and Gene Hackman, a supporting actor in *Bonnie and Clyde*, who won a Best Actor Oscar for starring in *The French Connection*. In a few short years, the De Niros and Pacinos would be the reigning celluloid anti-heroes—and the Robert Redfords were in the minority.

"Today," Matthau happily noted in 1967, "they're looking for actors instead of sticks of wood"—and so unlikely, traditionally unhandsome middle-aged character actors/master craftsmen like Matthau, Hackman, and George C. Scott became leading men. This trio, in fact, had much in common. Prior to their acting careers, they were in the military. They worked in summer stock, on the New York stage, and on television, and became supporting screen actors.

Matthau's son Charlie declared that his father "really broke down a lot of barriers for the kind of leading man who became popular in the '60s and '70s." So it is appropriate that, in 1966, as Matthau was on the cusp of super-stardom, he mockingly described himself as the "Ukrainian Cary Grant."

Yet unlike De Niro and Pacino (and Brando and James Dean a generation earlier), Matthau was no die-hard Method actor. Nor would he expound for hours on the "craft of acting." Sure, he had trained in a program that turned out a generation's worth of Method actors. But as Charlie noted, "He didn't believe in the Method. He said that he tried it, and was so busy trying to remember his 'sense memory' that he couldn't remember his lines." When asked to name Walter's favorite actors, Charlie cited Al Pacino—but the first two names he uttered were Robert Donat and Ralph Richardson, performers of a more classical mold.

In spite of Matthau's often flippant attitude toward Method acting, during the early part of his career he was attracted enough to its theories to want to learn more about it. "He tried to get into the Actor's Studio, and they wouldn't let him in," Charlie admitted. "He auditioned for it a few times. Then when he became a Broadway star, after he won his first Tony Award, they wanted him to join and be an honored member and lecture and teach. So he thought they were star-fuckers."

Once, when questioned about The Method, Matthau quipped, "I'm a lifetime member of the Actors' Studio. I do a lot of sleeping there." While filming *Who's Got the Action?* he was required to cry. He did so flawlessly, but director Daniel Mann, in order to see if Matthau could continuously shed tears, requested twenty takes. Matthau elicited his rejection of Method acting by declaring, "I wasn't thinking of the sadness, of my mother dying, of my child being run over by a car. I just did it! You gotta just do it, and it either comes or it doesn't." Decades later, he noted, "I have no 'method.' I read the script. I think about the character. I read the script again . . . and then I'm ready."

In *House Calls*, their 1978 comedy, Matthau and Richard Benjamin played doctors who perform on-screen surgery. "We have to go see an operation," Benjamin declared.

"What for?" Matthau asked.

"We have to know how to do this," Benjamin answered. "People are going to hand us scalpels and things."

The response: "You know, I'm Walter Matthau. Are people going to think that in two months I became a doctor? I don't think anyone's going to think for one minute that I'm really a surgeon."

Yet Benjamin insisted they see one. "So we went," he continued, "but he didn't go in. I did. I saw the beginning, and the next thing I knew I was looking at the linoleum on the floor. I was out. . . . I had no idea what I was going to see."

Afterwards, Matthau had a broad smile on his face. "So," he said, "What did you learn?"

Matthau and "The Method" may have been oil and water—and Matthau never would have offered a treatise on acting theory—but as Ossie Davis stressed, "Walter is not only an actor, but a practitioner and honorer of the craft of acting. He always was—and always remained—solidly grounded in theater. Even when he went to Hollywood, there was, underneath everything he did, a kind of substantive resting on his experiences in theater. I don't want to be snobbish about it, but Walter was never one of those who had been chosen because of his personality, and developed in Hollywood to become one of those stereotypical stars. Underneath everything he did, even the wildest comedy, was that sense of the tradition of theater.

"Walter understood, as I understood, how people in the past had used theater and performing and humor as a way of surviving as a minority in an oppressive culture. And so [his acting] had all of this rich subtext under it. It's hard to explain what it was, but you know it when you see it. You look at two actors and say, 'This man was grown in a hothouse, but that man was grown in real soil.' Walter was one of those real-soil actors."

When Matthau was building his career, Brando and Dean were, acting credentials aside, youthful hunks and wild ones whose surly sexuality had much to do with their winning stardom. Back in the 1950s, Matthau strictly was a character type. But he knew his pal Tony Curtis, the former Bernie Schwartz, had the right Hollywood look. While at the New School, Bernie/Tony could not comprehend the meaning of some of the dialogue in *Twelfth Night*, and asked

Walter for assistance. Matthau told him not to worry about such triv-
ialities, because he was destined for movie stardom. Both had roles in
the production and, as Matthau recalled, "His costume was so tight
everyone was whistling at him."

In 1949, Curtis went Hollywood. His first film was *Criss Cross*, a
film noir that, coincidentally, starred Burt Lancaster, who also
toplined Matthau's debut. Curtis—then billed "Anthony Curtis"—
appeared briefly in a dance sequence, paired with the female lead,
Yvonne De Carlo. "He was waiting in Shubert Alley when I came out
of a stage door," Matthau recalled, of a Curtis trip back home. He was
"jumping up and down and shouting about how he had made it with
Yvonne de Carlo." (Curtis's version of the story differs. In his autobiography, he noted that, upon his return from Hollywood to promote
one of his early films, *City Across the River*, he instructed his limousine driver to take him to the President Theatre. Matthau was
standing out front, garbed in a long coat with a *Racing Form* pro-
truding from one of its pockets. Curtis instructed the driver to stop in
front of Matthau, at which point Curtis rolled down the window and
exclaimed, "I fucked Yvonne De Carlo!" Then he rolled up the
window, and told the driver to skedaddle.)

Within a couple of years, Curtis's pretty-boy looks made him a
star. Matthau would not appear onscreen for another five years. Back
then, when teen girls were swooning over Curtis and his sleek
physique and black curly hair, Matthau never would have been cast
as the lead in *Cactus Flower*, an Abe Burrows–penned romantic
comedy which had been a Broadway hit in 1965, four years before it
arrived on screen. The character was a Fifth Avenue dentist whose
young mistress thinks he is married. To maintain the sham and avoid
wedding her, he convinces his nurse, who for years has secretly been
in love with him, to pose as his mate. Originally, the real (rather than
Ukrainian!) Cary Grant was sought for the film, but the actor chose
to make his final feature, *Walk Don't Run*, in 1966. Leonard Hirshan,
Matthau's agent, suggested him to the film's director, Gene Saks—
and Matthau was hired. Goldie Hawn was cast as the mistress, while
Ingrid Bergman played the nurse. In the film, Matthau had romantic
scenes with both.

"It was very good for my ego," he recalled, "to think that Ingrid

Bergman is crazy about me and trying to jump on me, and Goldie Hawn is nuts about me." Such feelings remained with Matthau for the rest of his life. In the 1990s, while in his seventies, Sophia Loren played his romantic interest in *Grumpier Old Men*. "I just love the idea of *me* fooling around with Sophia Loren," he said.

At the same time, Matthau was aware of the precariousness of his position. "A lot of parts I want they give to Robert Redford," he noted in the late 1970s. "But I have a little more choice than I used to have. I can say 'thank you' now—and I do until things start looking a little shaky."

Many of Matthau's starring roles might well have been designed for another rough-and-tumble-looking master actor: Spencer Tracy. As a Tracy character entered into a male-female sparring match with a Katharine Hepburn–like counterpart, he played out the pressures facing a male awkwardly attempting to coexist with a modern-era woman. Matthau played this character several times, notably opposite Glenda Jackson in *House Calls* and *Hopscotch*.

The one comic actor with whom Matthau compared himself was Woody Allen. Both were New York Jewish natives who were funny on screen, "though of course I'm better looking than he is," Matthau wisecracked. After a pregnant pause, he added, "Well, taller anyway."

Actually, the relation between Matthau and Allen is superficial at best. Matthau's characters are diverse and well-rounded human beings who sometimes happen to be Jewish, whereas the stock Woody Allen character wallows in his Jewishness, and his New York Jewish angst and neuroses. A Woody Allen character frets about love, sex, and death, and spends thousands on psychoanalysis. Ask a Matthau character to expound on the problems of the world or the problems of the psyche, and he shrugs his shoulders and heads off to the kitchen to fix a corned beef sandwich.

Allen's New York Jewish sensibility doesn't play in Peoria. But Matthau was beloved by audiences everywhere, who saw within themselves the characters he played. He once noted, "I don't look like an actor. I could be anyone from a toilet attendant to a business executive. Most people look at me on the street and say, 'Who the hell is that guy? Was I in the army with him?'" While admitting that he might be recognized as an actor, he noted, "People either ask me,

'Are you a television actor?' or else, 'Are you from Erie, Pennsylvania?'"

Matthau might remind one of a friendly next-door neighbor, a picturesque pal who might spill mustard on his shirt at a ballgame, a crotchety but lovable uncle who would try passing off his fictional exploits as fact—or a toilet attendant, business executive, or old military buddy from Erie, Pennsylvania.

Hence, his universal appeal.

In 1968, Matthau was queried as to how he handled his fame. In typically sardonic fashion, he wisecracked, "Oh, yeah, it's easy, it's a snap. I don't allow myself to be treated like a movie star. I wash my own car. I went to Coney Island and a fellow said, 'What are you doing in Coney Island?' I said, 'What do you do for a living?' 'I'm a plumber,' he said. 'Is Coney Island only for plumbers?' I asked."

In the end, Matthau simply was a working actor, playing a range of roles. "My father really wasn't like Oscar Madison," confirmed Charlie Matthau. "But in certain ways he was, to the extent of being happy-go-lucky." Off-camera, he was no slob, and he became piqued when strangers assumed he was an Oscar clone. One day he entered a drugstore to purchase razor blades and shaving cream. "What do you think you're doing?" the woman behind the counter asked in a huff. "We know you. You're that guy from *The Odd Couple*." Matthau admitted as much. "Then what are you acting like this for?" she retorted.

"Preconceived notions," was how Matthau explained her behavior. "They get a set image of you. They say, 'We know his personality.' Based on one role that you've played, the public expects you to be that guy, and the producers, if they are paying you a great deal of money, don't want you to change that image. They even put in the contract, 'The man we are hiring must be recognizable.'"

The real Walter Matthau would show up for an interview dressed not in a ketchup-stained sweatshirt but in a natty crew-neck sweater and tweed slacks, or a pin-striped suit with polished English loafers. Once he noted, "Sometimes I'm gross just to prove I'm real. I think Brando started that." Then he segued into a comical Marlon Brando impersonation.

Not all of Matthau's future screen characters were as memorable as Oscar Madison. Not all his future films were as successful as *The Fortune Cookie* and *The Odd Couple*. But rarely if ever was Matthau blamed for their deficiencies. Why? Because viewers related to him, and loved him.

He freely admitted that he was fortunate to come to stardom at a time when anti-heroes—or, as he might say, "the funny-looking guy"—were increasingly appearing on screen. "I've been hollering for twenty years to play the leading man," he noted. "I was always told I didn't have a chance, my features weren't even enough. Now suddenly they've decided that I'm a leading man after all—they figure with my looks the common man may identify with me."

CHAPTER 19

West Coast Life

In November 1965, just before exiting *The Odd Couple* Broadway cast and heading for the West Coast to shoot *The Fortune Cookie*, Matthau bemoaned leaving his hometown. "In New York there is more of a reality than the cardboard reality of Los Angeles. And certainly, the climate is better here than out there. The climate in Los Angeles will turn you into a noodle, a soft, warm noodle"

Spoken like a true-blue New Yorker.

Except the climate in New York had changed drastically from those sweltering summers in the tenements. The Matthaus did not have to pass July and August evenings taking fresh air on apartment stoops, or sleeping on fire escapes. Instead, if he wished a quick respite from "The City," he and his family could head north, to the small lakefront house they had built in the town of Day, in upstate New York.

Yet within a few years, the Matthaus abandoned the isle of Manhattan for sunny, smoggy Southern California. The reason was practical: Matthau's ascension to movie stardom required a West Coast presence. While he returned to New York on occasion, to shoot a film or complete a publicity tour, he became a bona-fide Southern Californian who found irresistible the lure of the Hollywood A-list lifestyle. Once, a few years after settling in California, he compared the two coasts: "In New York if you behave civilly they take it as a sign of weakness. You can get stepped on. I could think of another word for it—pusillanimity. They think in New York that you're being pusillanimous if you're not rude." Then he added, "Maybe that's why I find it's possible to say 'Good morning, nice day, isn't it?' in Los Angeles, without somebody wanting to call a cop."

By leaving New York City, Matthau in essence was severing all his East Coast connections. He had to play his cards carefully in Hollywood because he was making his commitment to his livelihood there. He needed to keep his professional reputation high and his private life unsullied. After all, he wasn't a James Dean or a Sinatra or a Brando. He was another breed of actor, one more easily replaced—one more quickly forgotten.

Not long after leaving New York, Matthau labeled himself a California resident "politically, socially, morally, and spiritually." In 1971, he cut his final New York ties by relinquishing his apartment. "I suppose it's good for young people, New York," he stated at the time. "Young people and other assorted maniacs." He neglected to mention that one of the young people he left behind was Jenny Matthau, then fifteen. Her eighteen-year-old brother David eventually followed his father west, when he attended the University of Southern California cinema school.

Matthau's view of the theater also was changing. Once he was a die-hard New York stage actor who only made movies to embellish his bank account. However, during a 1968 interview, he extolled the virtues of the medium that was bringing him international renown when he noted, "[The movies are] less pretentious. The theater is very pretentious. It only pretends to be cultural. Almost everybody is trying to get a role in the movies, although some people like the purity of the theater." This view deepened as the years passed. In the late 1990s, when asked if he felt nostalgic for working in live TV and theater, he firmly responded, "My answer is no. It's a good experience, but I have no nostalgia about it . . . because you had a dressing room on the third floor, full of mice and cockroaches. And they said, 'This is for the theatah. You're doing it for the theatah.' You go out to Hollywood, and they give you fifty times more money than you made on the stage, which means you can at least pay the grocer. I'm skeptical about it. I'm cynical about 'the glory of the American theatah.'"

Who could blame Matthau for luxuriating in his hard-earned comforts? He was not exaggerating when he declared, in the same 1968 interview, "I was shaped by the whole process of war and depression, through one humiliating experience after another, Home Relief and charity camps, humiliating behavior in charity clinics, the humiliation of auditioning for a role against 3,500 other young people, the humiliation of the competition in the theater, the humiliation of insensitive people, the humiliation of poverty."

Switching coasts in 1968, the Matthaus first sublet Paul Newman and Joanne Woodward's Beverly Hills house. The cost: $3,700 per month, which was more than his family had spent on Lower East Side rent over a twenty-year period. Of Beverly Hills, Matthau sardonically noted, "Everything runs by itself. Nobody dies here. There is no poverty. The vegetables are ripe and clean and fresh. You never see the landlord. If you're lucky, your family leaves a million [and] you convert that into a half-million of income a year."

His stay in the 90210 zip code was brief. For one thing, the Beverly Hills roadways were not conducive to his post–heart attack walks. While strolling the community's usually empty streets, he noted that he had "the feeling that a clean bomb fell and everyone is dead and a real estate man is going to clean up as soon as some people come around." Furthermore, Charlie Matthau recalled that young girls came to the door at 3 or 4 A.M. in search of Newman. Carol was not pleased, and the Matthaus quickly moved to the suburbs.

Their new digs were on Toyopa Drive, a quiet street off Sunset Boulevard in Pacific Palisades, an upscale community located between Beverly Hills and Malibu. Matthau purchased a large two-story brick structure with wrought-iron trim. Built in 1934, the five-bedroom home took up two lots, covering 9,800 square feet. Matthau noted, "We're overlooking the ocean on a mountain that looks like a little Swiss canton, with 20,000 flowers around." The elegant interior exuded a comfortable, moneyed Southern California lifestyle. Its lavish albeit tasteful design, from wallpaper to pillows to upholstered chairs, was Carol's doing. "We put most of the stuff into this house ourselves," Matthau noted, soon after moving in. They had a new kitchen installed, and put in a swimming pool and a large brick patio.

Flowers—a favorite of Carol's—were omnipresent. On her first visit to the house, Jayne Meadows noticed that flowers were printed on towels, washcloths, curtains, and wallpaper. Lana Morgan observed that the house was decorated in "roses, ribbons, and ruffles, from top to bottom." To Morgan, Matthau's presence amid the ultra-feminine decor made him seem like "an out-of-place hound dog—and I always had this feeling I should tell him to get off the furniture or send him out to the doghouse. But after I got to know them better I realized Walter was the true heart and soul of this home.

"Carol told me an interesting story about their first apartment," Morgan continued. "Walter was in a Broadway play working night and day. She decided it would be best to just take care of the deco-rating details and surprise him with it. She wanted Walter to feel at home so she picked out masculine colors and muted tones for every room except for her little girl Lucy's bedroom. The first time Walter saw the apartment she took him around to each room. He didn't say much but when he got to Lucy's room he just stood there staring at the floral wallpaper and canopy bed.

"When Carol asked Walter if he liked everything he was polite and said the apartment looked nice but later he blurted out, 'Why can't we have a room like Lucy's?' He loved the femininity and refinement of Carol's taste and missed the way she decorated her previous apartment. From then on she stuck to her favored décor. The more feminine and elegant Carol made their home, the happier Walter was."

The Pacific Palisades move came at the urging of Walter's friend, William Schallert, who became their neighbor. It was Schallert who told Matthau that, because the neighborhood was closer to the ocean, the air was fresher than in Beverly Hills. There was more room to roam, and little Charlie even could play in the street. "I doubt that he ever let Charlie play outside," Schallert added, "but Walter and Carol loved the neighborhood. For Walter, it really became home."

Here, he could stroll about to his heart's pleasure, and he claimed that he rarely was recognized. His attire usually was shorts, a beach cap, and an old sweatshirt; "Most people think I'm a dirty old bum," he quipped. But of course, the neighbors knew their local beach-comber was Walter Matthau. "Matthau actually was the friendliest neighbor," noted Schallert. "He knew everyone by name. In this regard, he was a regular guy." Schallert reported that Matthau especially enjoyed shooting hoops in the backyard with one of his neighbors, a high school athlete, and loved the fresh produce that could be found in the Pacific Palisades markets.

"Driving down Chautauqua Boulevard, to get to the Pacific Coast Highway, I'd see him walking his big, shaggy dog," recalled Betsy Palmer. "There was a wonderful shag and shamble about both of them. [The pet] was like a sheepdog, with long hair over the eyes. Really, the two of them looked quite a bit alike. I'd always put my window down and say, 'Hi, Walter. It's Betsy.' He'd say, 'Oh my god, how are you?' Then of course the traffic made us move on." Paula Prentiss, a longtime friend who appeared with Matthau in *Buddy Buddy*, added, "He had this great big dog, which only he could have had because it was so much like him. It was this wonderful big dog, a sheepdog of some kind. It was the size of a table."

Not all of Matthau's pets were humongous. While driving down Santa Monica Boulevard, Jerry Cutler, his rabbi and friend, once spotted him walking a small dog. Cutler promptly parked his car, and ran across the street to say hello. He was out of breath when he arrived, and Matthau promptly asked, "What took you so long?" Charlie Matthau reported that, through the years, his father had three dogs: Puff'n Stuff, an English sheepdog; Dumpsy, a Father's Day present from Charlie, which Walter named after what Charlie described as the dog's "favorite activity"; and Aunt Bea, a mutt.

In the mid-1980s, the Matthaus remodeled their home and took up temporary residence in Coldwater Canyon. William Schallert explained that Carol spent most of her time supervising the overhaul; when not working, Walter came down for his walks. Over the years, he and Schallert were frequent walking companions through the neighborhood.

With Dr. Clarence Agress, his cardiologist, Matthau purchased a forty-five-foot custom-built cruiser, the Miss Pam. He also bought a beach house in Trancas, north of Malibu. Among his neighbors were Jack and Felicia Lemmon, and Billy and Audrey Wilder. He passed hours strolling along the nearby beach. He might walk for up to ten miles at a time, accompanied by a small radio on which he listened to ballgames.

Given Matthau's predilection for betting the ponies, it should be no surprise that he became involved in breeding racehorses. In 1970, he and his friend, producer Howard Koch, purchased a fifty-acre ranch in San Jacinto. They became part of a sixteen-person syndicate that owned a stable of racehorses. "I accompanied Howard to the track the day the first horse born on the ranch was running its first race," recalled director Arthur Hiller. The horse was named Sweet Ott, after New York Giants' Hall of Famer Mel Ott. "A group of their friends gathered nervously and excitedly in the club, waiting for the big moment. All except Walter, that is. He wouldn't watch from the club. He would watch from the ground level, standing right up against the fence. When I went down to say hello, I couldn't believe what I saw. Walter was almost knee deep in torn and trashed betting receipts.

"Well, at least we won *that* race. Sweet Ott came through."

In 1971, during a New York visit, Matthau alluded to his quote of six years earlier when he acknowledged, "Living in California, your brain can admittedly turn into a large soft noodle." Then he quickly added, "when I breathe the air in New York I know that I'm never going to live in this place again. As a matter of fact, if I do another Broadway play, which I'd very much like to do, I'm going to live somewhere far out in the country and have a clause in my contract that says I have to be driven in and out of the city in a closed, air-conditioned limousine. In New York, when I see all of these gray faces, everyone looking as though he'd just been told that he has terminal cancer, I realize that this town has become unfit for human life. When in New York, I'm always eager to get back to California." Yet he refused to acknowledge that the world now knew him as a Hollywood name. "If I thought I was a Hollywood actor, I'd kill myself," he observed in 1974. "A Hollywood actor is an actor who can't act, a robot. A New York actor is intelligent; he understands what he's saying, he thinks."

While Matthau did live out his life in California, he never returned to Broadway. "No, it's much too difficult," he explained in the mid-1980s. "Working in films, you establish a certain way of life, and treading the boards is far less comfortable. And since I'm a normal human being with a very strong laziness factor in my bones, I don't want to go back." Around this time, he seriously considered starring in *A Month of Sundays*, cast as a mentally sharp but physically debilitated elderly man who resides in a rest home. "I might do it," he explained, "but I have a lotta mixed feelings about it. You see, it's such an easy life here." Matthau never did appear in *A Month of Sundays*.

Garson Kanin wrote a play for Matthau, titled *Autumn in the Air*. "It was a wonderful play about a rich older man and his children," explained Marian Seldes, Kanin's widow. "He'd been ill, and they wanted his fortune. And he had this wonderful black nurse who took care of him, and he realized that she was the most important person in his life." Kanin wanted to stage the play in Los Angeles, at the Mark Taper Forum, so Matthau would not have to leave the West Coast. "But by then Walter was sort of, well, he told Gar he just didn't want to do theater anymore," added Seldes. "Reading between the lines, I thought it was health as much as anything else. I didn't think Walter wanted to put it into those words.

"When Gar and I would talk about it, we [agreed] that the part was perfect for him. If he doesn't want to do it, we felt it should have been a movie." But the project never came to pass.

Howard Morris authored a play, called *King of the Hill*, which he sent to Matthau. It was a take-off on *Your Show of Shows*, the groundbreaking variety series in which Morris appeared with Sid Caesar, Imogene Coca, and Carl Reiner. Matthau would play the Caesar character; after reading it, Morris reported that Matthau told him, "Howie, I gotta do this." Once more, the project remained unproduced.

Back in 1960, Matthau appeared as Joxer Daly in a TV version of *Juno and the Paycock* that aired on *Play of the Week*, a New York–produced syndicated television series. Hume Cronyn starred as Captain Boyle. A *New York Times* critique prompted him to send the paper a lengthy letter-to-the-editor. "When an actor of [Cronyn's] stature undertakes a classic role in a classic play," Matthau wrote, "and exposes himself to comparison with Barry Fitzgerald and F. J. McCormick, the great players of the Abbey Theatre, and receives the minimum wage rate for his labors in an arduous two-week rehearsal period, he should be highly commended. The *New York Times* critic, Jack Gould, says, 'He was ill-advised to undertake the role.' Why? Broadway and Hollywood are artistically emaciated because of this kind of thinking. Too many actors reaching a level of prominence are 'playing it safe,' guarding meticulously their professional appearances, encasing themselves in a protective shell of what has succeeded for them in the past. This kind of thinking is for banks and insurance companies. This kind of thinking stifles and chokes artistic endeavor. It leaves the theatre thin, sterile, robbed of its life's blood, depleted of the richness and quality that comes only with the trial and error of experimentation. If an actor hasn't the 'guts' to try something different, be he good or bad, he's in the wrong field."

As he aged, Matthau himself became less the firebrand purist and more the play-it-safe Hollywood star. Nonetheless, he refused to play the Hollywood game and become immersed in the rigmarole of stardom. He kept the same agent, Leonard Hirshan, for the rest of his life, and was not obsessed with his films' box-office receipts. As his son Charlie observed, "He [didn't] worry about whose motor home is bigger." Observed Carole Shelley, "Walter lived in his own little world with Carol and Charlie. I think the three of them just went out there and played together."

Matthau did not socialize solely to be seen; "I don't go out in the jungle where I can get bitten," he once explained. Instead, he preferred partying in the company of close friends. Linda Harrison recalled that Walter and Carol enjoyed attending parties at the home of screenwriter-producer-director Ernest Lehman and his wife Jackie. They were intimate affairs, the kind in which someone might get behind a piano and play and sing. "At [them]," Harrison explained, "Walter had that same dry humor and comic timing he had on screen. The thing that I remember most about him was his personality, which was exactly as it was on film."

The Matthaus also hosted get-togethers of their own. "At other [Hollywood] parties, you would expect to find mostly an A-list of

Hollywood people," explained Marian Seldes. "But when you went to Walter's house, nobody was better than anybody else. Everybody was just having a wonderful time.

"He had a genius for friendship. People just wanted to be with him. I can't tell you how I looked forward to being with him. And he always surprised you. There'd always be a subject you wouldn't expect him to talk about, whether it was what was happening in politics or some hilarious joke. And he was an amazing host. It was sheer pleasure, being with the man."

Richard Benjamin echoed Seldes's sentiments: "The great thing about Walter was that he treated everyone the same way. It didn't matter who came into the room. There are people whose heads snap around when a bigger star comes in, or a more important executive. That wasn't Walter. When you were with Walter, you were with him and he was with you. You saw great people [at his parties], people you'd want to be with. But there was such a kind of relaxed warmth there, [because] he just saw everybody as people."

Unlike Jack Lemmon, who never ceased loving to act and discuss the nuances of his craft, Matthau came to favor relaxation over work. He was satisfied to play his part, collect his paycheck, and enjoy his hard-earned leisure time. In fact, he lived a very middle-class lifestyle, within a very un-middle-class milieu. Between projects, he headed off to the track. "Most people don't recognize me [there]," he explained, "[because] I don't look like an actor." Woodstock, New York, residents Dr. Norman and Sandra Burg were ones who did, one time in the clubhouse at Saratoga. "He looked like a perennial gambler," recalled Norman. "He was alone. He was unshaven. He was not wearing a tie. He seemed totally preoccupied with the *Racing Form*, working over it diligently." Sandra added, "He was checking out the horses, and was not at all concerned with people recognizing him."

When not at the track, he attended Lakers and Dodgers games. Roger Ebert once asked him how closely he followed basketball. "Pretty closely," was the response. "How many games did Indiana lose during the regular season?" Ebert inquired. "Nine," Matthau answered, adding, "What scores do you want to know?" If the Lakers were in a playoff series, as they were in June 1982, against the arch-rival Boston Celtics, Matthau would be at courtside, with his presence almost as conspicuous as that of Jack Nicholson. If the Lakers battled the Celtics in a key regular-season series, as they did in February 1984, Matthau was among the throngs of rooters.

Or, he relaxed with his pals. In the 1970s Matthau, Jack Lemmon, Billy Wilder, and producer Armand Deutsch converged at Wilder's beach house to watch—and bet on—Monday Night Football. Each usually wagered $100, which was a pittance for Matthau, who bet four figures via his bookmaker. Matthau also regularly played cards. "We met at least once or twice a week for probably fifteen years," explained Asher Dann, a Beverly Hills Realtor. "I spent more time with him than my wife." Their main card-playing group included Martin Ritt; Dr. Robert Kerlan, the sports medicine pioneer; attorney Neil Papiano; restaurateur Michael Chow; lumber dealer Jimmy Raskin; and film executive David Begelman. They convened at Chow's restaurant, or at Matthau's or Begelman's house. "We played poker, Texas Hold-em, what they play in Vegas in those million-dollar tournaments," Dann noted. "In general, we played a pot-limit game. Whatever was in the pot, you could bet. Thousands [were in the pot]."

"We just had a good time. Matthau was a good card player, and a great sport. We used to have fun and kibitz. Matthau used to tell jokes; sometimes, he'd burst out singing an aria, from one of the operas. Winning or losing, he always had a good sense of humor. He would listen to the ballgame sometimes when playing cards—whatever game he was betting on. Marty Ritt used to read the *Racing Form*."

Matthau, additionally, savored an altogether different kind of company. Most opera or classical music lovers pass through life content to listen to their favorite compositions on recordings, or from a seat in a concert hall. Matthau's celebrity allowed him not only to establish friendships with the top classical performers but to appear with them onstage. In 1990, he joined the Los Angeles Mozart Orchestra at the Wilshire Ebell Theatre, introducing a piano concerto with an illustrative monologue and then taking over the conductor's baton. "I don't really conduct," he explained. "I move my arms. The orchestra is a little ahead of me." Six years later, he was the joke-cracking master of ceremonies at a benefit concert at the

Dorothy Chandler Pavilion celebrating the one-time-only return of Zubin Mehta to the Los Angeles Philharmonic, which he had conducted between 1962 and 1978. The event raised funds for the Los Angeles Philharmonic and Israel Philharmonic.

While Matthau's fame enabled him to schmooze with the elite, he claimed that Lemmon was his only close movie-star pal. "Most of my friends are doctors," he explained. "Actors are the nicest people in the world, but very boring. That's why I'm boring."

He remained cordial to his old Lower East Side friends. Back in 1955, after filming *The Kentuckian*, Matthau visited Yvonne Rogow and her husband Melvin, who were living in Los Angeles. Yvonne recalled that his wrist was swollen, from his bullwhip-wielding. "We walked over to visit my parents for an affectionate welcome, but our lives went in different directions. I did, however, run into him several times in Westwood and the Pacific Palisades. He always asked about my father, and told me about his mother."

Anna Berger and her brothers paid him visits. Numerous old pals reported that they saw him when in Southern California, and enjoyed his hospitality—but not at his home, only at the Beverly Hills Tennis Club. Norman Tulchin, a Lower East Side acquaintance, recalled that he "ran into Walter out here on the West Coast in the late 1970s. It was at the Ahmundsen Theatre, and we briefly reminisced about the old days. He was with his wife, and his friend Jack Lemmon. He was very friendly. He even took the time to introduce me to Jack Lemmon."

Only rarely was there conflict. "Every time Murray [Juvelier] went out to California, Walter was very nice to him," noted Berger. "But Walter kind of resented Murray, because one time Murray said something that Walter never forgot. Instead of [acknowledging] that Walter had the talent, Murray would ask, 'Who did you know? How did you get up there? What happened?'"

Matthau found a second home at the Beverly Hills Tennis Club, where he entertained his old friends and conducted interviews. He savored lounging around its outdoor cafe, located right near a swimming pool surrounded by attractive, bikini-clad women. He tanned himself under the California sky. To protect himself from the sun's rays, he donned a baseball cap. One of his favorites was emblazoned not with a New York Mets or Los Angeles Dodgers logo, but with the name "Mozart." "It irks me that people sometimes ask about my hat," he once noted from his chair at the club. "They figure a guy with a face like mine who plays the sort of roles I do in movies wouldn't be the Mozart type. Can you beat that?"

Matthau did not know how to play tennis, nor did he desire to learn. "I joined," he told Aviva Kempner, "because Hank Greenberg was a member. It's the only reason I joined." Often, he dined there with Greenberg, his boyhood idol. However, while lunching there with him, Leon Birns asked, "Hey, Walter, how come you belong to a tennis club and you don't play tennis?" Matthau's response: "They serve good borscht here."

Otherwise, Matthau relished the comforts of home while listening to Mozart, playing board games and card games with family and friends, and watching sports and quiz shows on TV. Often, several sets were on at once, tuned to different ballgames. Among his favorite non-sports diversions were Scrabble, Jeopardy, Mensa (a high-IQ game), poker, rummy, and pinochle. "If we've got girls, we play spin the bottle," he once joked.

Matthau described himself as a "forced social animal," adding, "I'd rather hang out at home with my wife." And his son Charlie. With them and his record players around, he explained, "it is *very* hard to get bored." Noted Charlie, "We had all the same interests. We liked the same music. We liked the same movies, betting on sports, going to the racetrack, going to Dodger games. We loved to watch the news, and talk about politics. Every night, we played Jeopardy. Even if I was going to go out later, I would have two dinners so we could hang out."

Added Lana Morgan, "I always would know that it was time to wrap things up at the [Matthau Company] without even looking at the clock because Charlie would start getting distracted. Then he would shoot out the door, because he was going to watch *Jeopardy!* with his dad. That was their routine. They would compete against the television contestants. I was surprised how they always seemed to know every answer. What really stands out to me is how it was so like Walter to associate learning and challenging your mind with having a good time."

Morgan recalled that Charlie was desperate to become a *Jeopardy!* contestant. He applied, and passed all the exams, but "then they realized he was Walter's son and said, 'Oh, we can't let you be on the show. It wouldn't look right.' Charlie was so disappointed. Walter and Charlie would both have been more thrilled if he won a tough round of *Jeopardy!* then if he had won an Oscar."

Of the difference between his parents, Charlie observed that Carol was more of a stay-up-late/sleep-late person, while Walter preferred daytime activity. He was fascinated by astronomy, animals, and nature. He read a lot: history books, World War II books, books about Mozart. He did crossword puzzles. He liked to cook. He was very low-maintenance. The Matthaus had a housekeeper, but Walter preferred doing his own cooking. Of his house, Morgan observed, "The bookshelves were overflowing every room. Wherever [Walter and Carol] ran out of shelf space there were stacks of books on the floor, around every chair and bed. I always enjoyed looking at the titles on their bookshelves to see what each of them was reading."

Another obsession was spelling. "He would give people spelling tests all the time on the set," Morgan added. "He tried to give Brent Spiner (his *Out to Sea* co-star) the 'Mensa' test. He wasn't making fun of him or anything. It was a show of validation, of support.

"Walter was very encouraging of knowledge and learning. He also would correct people's grammar all the time. That was one of the things that set Jack [Lemmon] off. That was a Felix Ungar thing for Walter to do, to correct his grammar all the time."

Seeing the world was not one of Matthau's priorities. "I'm not much of a tourist," he once noted.

Matthau had, indeed, entered a comfortable middle-age. But unlike so many others who turn conservative with age, Matthau remained solidly, unfailingly liberal. Unlike actors from anti–Vietnam War Jane Fonda to gun-toting Charlton Heston, he kept his opinions to himself. "I think it's bad for an actor to paint himself into a corner—i.e., left-winger, right-winger," he explained. "So I always say I'm an independent thinker, a centrist."

Even so, he was not averse to becoming involved in controversies. "Many years ago," recalled Graham Jarvis, "Armand Hammer wanted to drill an oil well right at the foot of the bluffs in Pacific Palisades.

People were up in arms. Walter came to a meeting. Somebody said, 'You wanna say something, Mr. Matthau?' and I was impressed with how articulate he was. He told a story that had to do with advertising one thing and giving you something else. Essentially, it was not about oil, or resisting the wealthy or the bastards who were trying to take over the town. But he made it fit."

Matthau was politically active in relation to Judaism. Rabbi Jerry Cutler observed, "Years ago, one of the oil companies had stopped [sending] shipments to Israel. I know that Walter took his credit card and cut it in half and sent it to the [company's] chairman of the board, and said 'I will never buy your oil again.' He was there for us when we participated in a boycott of French goods, when [the French government] let go an [Arab] terrorist they had in custody. We staged a boycott, throwing out French perfume and champagne in the middle of Beverly Hills. He was part of that, too. He also got into a tiff with Vanessa Redgrave [with regard to her support of the Palestine Liberation Organization]. He told me about that. He thought she was a brilliant talent, but that she had been led astray emotionally, that she was a little emotionally off-balance."

Jewishness also remained a key component of his humor. In relation to overzealous fans, he once joked, "I'd rather not be badgered and overcome by hoards of fans, but if someone comes up to me in a civilized manner and says, 'Loved you in *The Last Jew from Trinidad*,' I'd say, 'Thanks very much.'"

CHAPTER 20

L'affaire Streisand

Across the years, Matthau co-starred opposite dozens of alluring actresses. Yet he did not parlay his movie star-status into love affairs with any of them. Matthau was a dyed-in-the-wool married man. He may have been a bookie's best customer, but he knew enough not to gamble on a happy marriage.

Matthau's primary interest in his co-stars was their professionalism. While shooting *The Fortune Cookie*, he growled, "If you want a good young actress for a role today you're in trouble. They are all ridiculous, spoiled, incompetent, slovenly, lazy, and self-indulgent. They are waiting to be attended to like queens, and they don't deserve it. They don't know how to move or speak. They figure it's good enough if they can brood a little." Of one unnamed actress who appeared in the film, he declared, "Her, an actress? They've got to be kidding. She's so bad, I don't know if I can stand it. If she's an actress then so is every other dame in the country." He cited Anne Jackson, Maureen Stapleton, Kim Stanley, and Dame Edith Evans as breaking this mold.

While filming two of his 1969 releases, Matthau had incendiary relationships with two female co-stars. One was minor; it involved *Cactus Flower*, and Goldie Hawn. In her autobiography, *Ingrid*

Bergman: My Story, Bergman, their co-star, quoted Mike Frankovich, the film's producer, as declaring, "Walter Matthau is notoriously unimpressionable. But just before Ingrid arrived [on the set], he looked very worried and kept nagging me, 'How do you think we will get on? Will she like me?' Ingrid loved him. The three of them, Ingrid, Goldie [Hawn], and Walter, got on like a house on fire."

Well, not quite. In 1973, Hawn recalled her time working with Matthau by noting, "Walter? Oh, he was OK. He tends to needle people. I have this uncle like him, who used to needle me constantly. He would always call me 'Goldele,' knowing I didn't like it." Almost two decades later, Heywood Hale Broun appeared in *Housesitter*, a Goldie Hawn-Steve Martin comedy. One day on the set, he and Hawn were talking about Matthau. "I said how much I liked him," Broun reported. "She said she didn't like him at all. I said, 'Well, I mean, nobody dislikes Walter.' She said, 'He was in my first [major] movie.' At some point early on, he said, 'You wanna run lines at lunchtime? You wanna do a little something?' She said, 'Oh, I'm supposed to have lunch with a Hollywood reporter.' He took great offense, and felt she didn't want to work with him. So he set out to destroy her timing, by changing *his* all the time. That was a side of Walter. If you made him mad, he could be extremely difficult."

Over the years, Hawn and Matthau apparently patched up their differences. In 1997, she was honorary co-chairwoman of an American Film Institute Associates Platinum Circle Award tribute to Walter, Carol, and Charlie.

Matthau's other tiff with an actress became the source of Hollywood legend. It was with Barbra Streisand, his co-star in *Hello, Dolly!* Matthau played Horace Vandergelder in the screen version of the hit Broadway musical, opposite Streisand's matchmaker Dolly Levi. Streisand's much-anticipated screen debut as Fanny Brice in *Funny Girl* was in the can, but the film had not yet opened when she and Matthau began filming.

Carol Channing won accolades playing Dolly on Broadway. Ernest Lehman, the film's producer-screenwriter, considered casting her, but declined because he allegedly felt that she was not moviestar material. Streisand was signed because she would be more of a box office draw.

Ironically, Matthau guest-starred on a Channing television spe-cial, *Carol Channing: One Hundred and One Men*, which aired in November 1967, several months before filming began. After being introduced, Matthau jokingly informed Channing that he neither sang nor danced, adding, "Carol, I have trouble walking." The two appeared in several skits in which they sang and clowned and, as the show progressed, Matthau told the audience, "I was very apprehen-sive about doing this kind of a show, but I'm having a wonderful time." After a commercial, he confided, "You may not believe this after that last song, but I've never had any formal musical education. In poker, I had a little schooling. I got a doctorate in horses—a very expensive degree, I might add."

George Burns, with whom Matthau co-starred six years later in *The Sunshine Boys*, was an unannounced guest, and the two joined Channing in a skit. Matthau's presence with them was further evi-dence that he no longer was a supporting actor. From hereon in, instead of random TV guest gigs, his small-tube appearances were star spots, in which he cavorted with—and was on par with—the show-business elite.

Most intriguing of all, at the finale Matthau introduced Channing, who performed the *Hello, Dolly!* title song in different languages. Halfway into the number, he joined her, grasped her hand, and sang the first verse in English. One might have thought that Channing was auditioning for the screen version, opposite Matthau.

Horace Vandergelder was, for Matthau, a challenging role. "[It] isn't much of a part," he noted. "I took it because I wanted to work in a musical. A lot of things about it were rather painful. There is a tremendous amount of work one must do to become proficient in song and dance. Acting is easier for me. I always enjoy working with Gene Kelly, who also directed me in *A Guide for the Married Man*, because he is charming, intelligent, and has an inordinate amount of patience."

However, dancing and singing were kid stuff for Matthau com-pared to co-existing with his co-star. Matthau allegedly came to *Hello, Dolly!* with a pre-formed negative opinion of Streisand. He had been given an earful by Sydney Chaplin, her *Funny Girl* stage co-star; Chaplin was the son of Charlie, whose wife Oona was Carol

Matthau's girlhood chum. Sydney's few degrees of separation from Walter made whatever gossip he put forth appear credible.

Matthau and Streisand first met in 1965 at the Brooks Atkinson Theatre, which housed a revival of Tennessee Williams's *The Glass Menagerie* that featured Maureen Stapleton, his and Carol's close friend. By then, Matthau was firmly anti-Streisand. Legend has it that he approached her and quipped, "Oh, you're Barbara Harris. I see you've had your nose done." The cruel barb left Streisand speechless. It was the type of insult humor that cropped up every so often from Matthau, which is surprising for someone who usually was sensitive to his fellow human beings.

Piper Laurie also was in the cast. "Walter and Carol came to see the show, to see Maureen," she recalled. "They were sort of pacing in and out of her dressing room after the performance. Now my neighbor, who lived in my building, was Barbra Streisand. [She and Matthau] had never met, until that night. And [it just so happened that] Barbra had come to see me. They sort of encountered each other in the hallway, and I could hear [their conversation]. My husband heard it as well."

According to Laurie, Streisand politely said, "How do you do?"

Matthau's response was abrupt: "Why don't you get something done about that nose?"

"All these years, I thought that he was just so insensitive and horrible," Laurie continued. Then, three decades later, while co-starring in *The Grass Harp*, she asked Matthau about the encounter. "He said, 'The reason I did that was because. . . .' I don't want to repeat what it was, but apparently Barbra had offended a very close friend of his, and hurt that person, and he was just getting back [at Streisand] for his friend."

Despite this incendiary encounter, Matthau and Streisand agreed to appear together in *Hello, Dolly!*—and, from the outset, they acted like Hatfields and McCoys. Matthau claimed he tried to be courteous to Streisand, but resented her attempts to overstep her role as actor and usurp the authority of Gene Kelly. He was miffed when she laughed at him while recording the title tune. For her part, Streisand maintained that she was chortling over the humor inherent in the Vandergelder character, not the actor who played him.

Then, on April 15, 1968, Streisand attended the Academy Awards ceremony, where she handed out the Best Song prize. Her hair was made up in an elevated, curled, stylized manner. The following day, upon her return to the set, Matthau asked her if she wore her hair that way as a joke.

As rehearsals ended and filming began, their barbs escalated—and their feud was anything but private. During the shoot, Matthau admitted, "I'm simply not on the same wavelength as her. She's not my kind of dame." He called her "Madame Ptomaine," while Streisand labeled him "Old Sewermouth" and quipped that the film might be retitled *Hello, Walter!* Matthau retorted, "I would like to work with Barbra again on something more suited to her talents— like *Macbeth*."

The lights were hot and tempers were short on the film's Garrison, New York, location on June 6, just after the assassination of Senator Robert Kennedy. The actors were filming a scene in which they sit and converse in a wagon. Streisand proposed to Kelly that she alter her dialogue, to make it funnier. Matthau breathed fire at her, not so much asking as pronouncing, "Why don't you let [Kelly] direct?" He suggested that she focus on learning her dialogue, that she was jealous of his acting talent, and that the crew and her fellow actors despised her. He added that she didn't have "the talent of a butterfly's fart." Streisand, taken aback by Matthau's outburst, fled the set in tears. Shooting did not resume for three hours.

Matthau expressed his regret over this incident—but not without a tinge of sarcasm. "It was a hot day on location," he explained. "Bobby Kennedy had just been shot, and I was in a mean, foul mood—so I took it all out on Barbra, poor girl." He also noted, "We had a fight, but I have worse fights every night with my mother." Decades later, Matthau observed that the *Hello, Dolly!* shoot was made "bearable" only by Kelly. "He knew his camerawork," he said, "and he didn't give you instructions on acting. And he always had a joke or two." He reported that the daily stresses during the shoot resulted in his suffering from headaches, abdominal pains, and other physical discomforts.

From the completion of the filming and thereafter, the tension between the two only intensified. "I found it a most unpleasant picture to work on and, as most of my scenes were with her, extremely distasteful," Matthau recalled. He did commiserate with Streisand, noting "Barbra has moments of likability," "she has a great deal of potential and she should become an enormous star," and "it's very difficult for anybody, let alone a young person, to become a star." Yet he could not refrain from being catty. While noting his status as a top-ten box office star, he observed, "I'm number ten. Right under Streisand. Can you imagine being under Barbra Streisand? Get me a bag, I may throw up."

Several years later, he further expressed his anti-Streisand feelings upon running into director Sydney Pollack in a restaurant. "I just finished working with your favorite actress," Pollack sardonically noted. "Does she hate me as much as I hate her?" Matthau asked. "She didn't say," Pollack responded. After he left, Matthau declared, "I took the part to build up my salary. There was a strange kind of attraction to the fact that I was going to work with Streisand. I almost knew that I was going to blow up at her. I tried very hard, very hard to be civil, but it's extraordinarily difficult to be civil to her. See, she's a soloist, and she likes to tell the conductor when the flutes come in, when the violins come in."

Regarding salary, not in his youthful fantasies could Matthau imagine what he would earn for *Hello, Dolly!* In 1978, he jokingly told a reporter, "I have come back to the old capitalist theory of never divulging your sexual or fiduciary exploits." This was not the case a decade earlier. "One day I was at home preparing dinner, and the phone rings," recalled Anna Berger. "It was Matthau. He says, 'Annie, I'm in New York. I'm doing a movie. I'm doing *Hello, Dolly!* with Barbra Streisand. Guess how much money I'm making?' I said, 'I have no idea, Matthau. How much are you making?' He said, 'A million dollars.' That was coming from a guy who couldn't afford to buy me coffee. I was so happy for him. He said, 'Can you imagine. I'm getting more money than the President of the United States!'"

Matthau's mother was far less impressed. "The first time he got $1 million for a movie," reported his son Charlie, "[Rose told him] 'Yeah, but I still want you to become a lawyer. I still want you to become a doctor.' Her stand on abortion was that you're a fetus until you graduate from medical school." Charlie maintained that Rose was proud of Walter's successes, "but she would never let him see that. He was always wanting to make her proud, and seeking her approval."

(It was during this period that, when signing contracts, Matthau began accepting profit percentages instead of straight salaries. He had done so for *Cactus Flower*, a decision that netted him over $1 million. Nonetheless, Rabbi Jerry Cutler reported, "Once I was sitting with him in the MGM commissary. He had just been offered $1 million for a film; this was before the megabuck [contracts]. He said 'Nobody's worth that kind of money.' I'll never forget that.")

Not all of *Hello, Dolly!* was shot in New York. "He was doing *Dolly!* on the [West] Coast, and he asked me to visit him," recalled Marvin Silbersher. "And there's Gene Kelly, who's directing, and Barbra Streisand, who's directing *everybody*." Silbersher claimed that Matthau introduced him as "Arthur Von Silbersher, the famous Austrian film director," and further alleged, "All day, Gene Kelly, Barbra Streisand, and Michael Crawford are coming to me one at a time demanding to see my films. Barbra Streisand comes into the trailer and says, 'Mr. Von Silbersher, I must see your films. Will you send them to my office as soon as possible?' This is the power that Matthau had with his fantasies, the way he could con people. He was the master of the con. Nobody could tell a tale like Walter."

During this trip, Silbersher first joined Matthau at the track. "Out of eight races, he won five," Silbersher reported. "He had the *Racing Form* in front of him like a Bible. He had this stubby pencil, and was just going through the *Racing Form*. He was quite a student of what he was doing. Then [on another occasion] he comes to New York and calls me and tells me, 'Marvin, we're going to the track.' In his party were [restaurateur] P. J. Clarke and Howard Koch. A horse owned by Clarke's daughter was going to be in the fourth race. These three men bet something like $35,000 to win on her horse—and the horse lost. So without skipping a beat, they went on to the next subject, whatever it was."

Not long after working with Streisand, Matthau found himself in the professional company of another famously difficult female show-business personality: Elaine May, the author, director, and co-star of *A New Leaf*, his 1971 screwball comedy. The film also brought Matthau back to the New York area. During the summer of 1969, the company spent ten weeks shooting in Glen Cove, Long Island, on the forty-room estate of Harold R. Pratt, a deceased oil tycoon. While filming, he frequented Roosevelt Raceway in Westbury, where he watched the races on a closed-circuit TV monitor. A stranger recognized him and asked, "What are you doing here?" Matthau countered with a question: "What do people come here for?" The man responded with another query: "Do you wager on these things?" Matthau replied, "I didn't come here to eat hot dogs."

Of May's script, Matthau declared, "It's fast, fresh, and on a kind of literary plane which may or may not work. I think it will." In the film, he played Henry Graham, a millionaire-gone-broke who is reluctant to abandon his upper-crust lifestyle. Till then, he has avoided matrimony, but decides to wed wealthy Henrietta Lowell (May), a dizzy, plain-jane botanist. At first, Henry plans to murder Henrietta, but changes his thinking by the finale.

May, the former sketch-comedy partner of *Odd Couple* stage director Mike Nichols, was making her feature directorial debut. "I had doubts about Elaine directing and acting, too, and from her own script," Matthau noted during the shoot. "The first six or seven weeks of work were rough, but we've straightened things out. She's a tough little lady, that one. You suggest one thing, OK. Then a minute later, if you deviate by one single comma, you find out who's in supreme authority." Richard Benjamin noted, "The story goes that Matthau and Elaine May would disagree, often vociferously, yet Matthau respected her."

Years later, Matthau wisecracked, "Have you ever worked with Attila the Hun? *A New Leaf* was two months late, two million bucks over budget, and when Paramount asked her why, she said, 'It's all on account of Matthau. He keeps trying to grab me, and by the time he finally succeeds it's four o'clock and too late to do any work.'" Matthau summed up his feelings for her in a remark he often made about his mother and wife Carol: "There's only one thing wrong with Elaine—she's completely crazy."

May, a perfectionist, was notorious for ignoring shooting schedules and devoting the time she felt necessary to complete her films. Unsurprisingly, *A New Leaf* quickly fell behind schedule. Yet the slowdowns were not all her fault. "One afternoon," recalled Graham

Jarvis, who appeared in the film, "there suddenly was a lot of noise out on the lawn [where we were filming]. It was a helicopter. In it was Robert Evans, coming from Paramount Los Angeles. Walter said, 'Oh, god, the 'producer' is here. Now nothing will get done for the next two hours.' He was absolutely right."

In May's original script, according to Jarvis, Matthau's character killed two people. "Howard Koch and others involved with the picture said, 'No,' but Elaine wouldn't give up on this idea. These scenes were actually filmed, and Elaine fought like crazy to keep them in the picture. But Paramount released the film without them.

"When you read the original script, you got the sense of a person who starts off with no regard for humanity. Then a relationship with the rest of the world gradually begins to develop within him—and he turns over 'a new leaf.'" May reportedly presented Paramount with a three-hour-long final cut that was darker than the 102-minute version that went into commercial release. She took unsuccessful legal action to have her name removed as director.

Of Matthau, Jarvis noted, "He was a very decent person, not nicey-nice, just Walter Matthau, his sharp-witted self. You couldn't pull the wool over Walter's eyes. You couldn't tell Walter a joke. I mean you could; he would listen, but he'd heard it before. Elaine was the same way."

Both Matthau and wife Carol worked with May in the future. Walter co-starred with her in the screen version of Neil Simon's *California Suite*, while Carol had a rare acting role in *Mikey and Nicky*, May's 1976 film about small-time hoods. Carol played the girlfriend of one of the thugs; the *Variety* critic wrote that she gave a "beautiful performance."

In 1996, May interviewed Matthau in a short, funny article published in *The New Yorker*. In the piece, the actor joked about him and Jack Lemmon being compared to Spencer Tracy and Katharine Hepburn: "I am Hepburn and Lemmon is Tracy. Although when I asked Jack he told me he always thought I was Tracy and he was Hepburn. Oddly enough, I'm told that Tracy had the same problem." Regarding his ethnicity, he cracked, "Many years ago my mother told me that we were actually Irish, and that the family surname really was McMatthau."

CHAPTER 21

Building on Success

Matthau was in his early fifties when he starred in *Kotch*, a humanistic comedy in which he played a seventy-something widower named Joseph P. Kotcher. The film arrived in movie houses several months after *A New Leaf*, and it gave the actor one of his most rewarding screen roles.

Unlike the comedies in which he starred a quarter-century later, *Kotch* is no lighthearted entertainment featuring sprightly seniors who still savor sex lives. Instead, it offers a poignant portrait of a man who had reached old age in a throwaway society, where seniors no longer are valued. At his most charming, Kotcher is friendly in an innocent, old-fashioned way; at his worst, his desire to be familiar with those he does not know causes him to ramble. His personality puts him at odds with his coldly suspicious suburban Californian environment and his mild-mannered son and callous daughter-in-law, who wish to dispatch him to a "retirement village." His usefulness is reestablished as he befriends an adolescent, unwed mother-to-be (Deborah Winters).

Kotch was directed by Jack Lemmon. It was his sole directorial credit. Surprisingly, Matthau was not his first choice as star. "I tried to get Freddie March, but he was ill and uninsurable," Lemmon recalled. "I thought Walter was too young for the part. One night I was talking about it with Carol and Felicia. Carol didn't say anything but evidently went home and told Walter about it. Walter called me and said, 'Ya got anybody for it yet?' I said no. He said, 'Well, if you think it's right, I'd love to play it.'"

When Lemmon told Matthau he had the part, Matthau responded, "Hell, now I'll have to read the damned thing." "He hadn't read one word," Lemmon added. "He was just going on what Carol said, and she hadn't read one word, either."

On the first day of the shoot, Matthau arrived and asked Lemmon the $64 question: "You're not gonna tell me how to act, are you?" "Every now and then," Lemmon claimed after the film's completion, "we'd be shooting a scene or rehearsing, and I'd say, 'Walter, I've got an idea.' And he'd say, 'I gotcha.' And he'd do it! It became a joke. We just communicated to each other without the need for words." A decade later, Lemmon revised this a bit by noting, "I directed Walter once. Well, I *tried* to direct Walter. He did what he wanted to do, and it was his best performance."

Furthermore, *Kotch* was a family reunion. Not only did Matthau work with Lemmon, but Lucy Saroyan had a small role and Felicia played Kotcher's daughter-in-law. Back in 1958, more than a half-decade before *The Fortune Cookie*, Farr played Matthau's wife in *Onionhead*. Then in 1973's *Charley Varrick*, they were unmarried sex partners.

Two decades later, Matthau noted, "I think my best movie acting was in *Kotch*. Like everything else, there was some comedy in it. All of life is part tragedy, part comedy. You just have to know the difference."

Ellen Geer, daughter of actor Will, who appeared with Matthau sixteen years earlier on stage in *The Wisteria Trees*, acted in several intimate flashback scenes as Kotcher's young wife. "That was kind of scary for me," Geer noted. "But Walter was polite. He made jokes. He made me feel comfortable, and I was deeply appreciative of that. When a new actor meets a star, it can be scary, and you don't function as well as you should. But he was a professional beyond a professional. He'd say to me, 'If you turn a little that way, you'll get a better shot for yourself.'"

Geer worked with Matthau and Lemmon once more, a quarter century later in *The Odd Couple II*. "I adored their relationship," she added. "It was one of those things you don't often get in life. There was a deep respect that they had for each other, a playful, deep respect. They just threw the ball back and forth at each other. Their friendship went beyond acting, and into their acting. You've heard of stage couples, like the Lunts or the Cronyns. They to me were like them, only it was two males. It was amazing. In every department, they were a team."

An initial indication that *Kotch* was a success came when it received an enthusiastic ovation during a sneak preview in San Diego. Several months before its release, Matthau was the Best Actress presenter at the Academy Awards. He came onstage following Goldie Hawn's announcement of George C. Scott as Best Actor for *Patton*. Scott declined the award, decrying the forced competition inherent in such contests. Upon reaching the podium, Matthau deadpanned, "Next year, I'm gonna try that George C. Scott routine." After the laughter and applause, he quickly added, "I'm only kidding." Indeed, Matthau had the opportunity to pull a George C. Scott upon earning a Best Actor Oscar nomination for *Kotch*. His competition was strong: Peter Finch (for *Sunday Bloody Sunday*); Gene Hackman (*The French Connection*); Scott (*The Hospital*); and Topol (*Fiddler on the Roof*). Hackman was the winner.

Any excitement surrounding Matthau's or any other nomination paled beside an event that made this Oscar ceremony memorable. After a two-decade-long absence from the United States, Charlie Chaplin returned to Los Angeles to accept an honorary Oscar. His feet had not touched American soil since 1952, when his passport was revoked by the United States government, which suspected him of having leftist political views. On the Sunday before the ceremony, the Matthaus hosted a luncheon in honor of the husband of Carol's old friend. Crowding their home were ninety-three invited guests, including Greer Garson, Lewis Milestone, Oscar Levant, Martha Raye, Frances Goldwyn, Danny Kaye, and Groucho Marx. Walter and Carol sat with Charlie and Oona during the Oscar ceremony, and later accompanied them to the Governor's Ball.

Nineteen-seventy-two also featured Matthau in his first film opposite one of his all-time-favorite co-stars, Carol Burnett. The film was *Pete 'n' Tillie*, a comedy-drama; they later appeared in *The Front Page*, the TV movie *The Marriage Fool*, and on *Insight*, a religious program, cast as Adam and Eve. In *Pete 'n' Tillie*, Matthau and Burnett played the title characters, solitary middle-agers who court, wed, struggle with their emotions upon the death of their only child, separate, and reunite. During the shoot, the two became fast friends. While flying from New York to Boston for a sneak preview of the film, they noticed that Jackie Onassis was a fellow passenger. "Aaaah, if this plane goes down I get third billing," Burnett whispered to Matthau. To which he promptly responded, "Yes, and she gets second."

Pete 'n' Tillie was directed by Martin Ritt, Matthau's old gambling pal. That same year, Ritt joined with Matthau for a rare on-camera appearance in *Awake and Sing!* by Clifford Odets, which aired on PBS's *Hollywood Television Theatre* on March 6. Matthau now rarely acted on television; his stardom allowed him to select his projects. He chose *Awake and Sing!* because of its theme: the struggle for survival of a Depression-era lower-middle-class Bronx family. Matthau played Moe Axelrod, a bitter World War I amputee. Six years later, he had a cameo in one of the final *Hollywood Television Theatre* productions: *Actor*, an original musical about Paul Muni and his performer-father. Matthau played the legendary Yiddish stage star Boris Thomashevsky, and got to perform, albeit briefly, a scene from *The Yeshiva Bucher*, a loose adaptation of *Hamlet*. The part called for Matthau to wear a moustache, beard, and sidecurls, a floor-length black coat, and various religious accoutrements. Leo Postrel, an actor and baritone with the New York City Opera, appeared as Yiddish actor David Kessler. "Postrel had to teach Matthau that his role necessitated a very confidant, toreador-like sweep of the 'tallis' [prayer shawl] as he put it on," recalled Sam Kweskin, Postrel's friend. "Up to that point, Matthau was all thumbs throwing it over his shoulders."

Shakespeare brought him back to TV in the mid-1980s, when he hosted *The Shakespeare Hour*, a PBS series in which he offered knowing insights into the Bard. "[Matthau's] presence signals a reminder to viewers that Shakespeare's works were written for all of us and not just an elite few," wrote television critic Kay Gardella.

"Picking him was a stroke of genius." Matthau joked that he was the second choice for the job. The first: Sylvester Stallone. He made this declaration with a certain defensiveness. Matthau *was* a cultured man, an actor who had the verbal skills and intellect required to play major Shakespeare roles; he always harkened back to his television role of Iago as an early milestone part. What made his involvement seem so populist a casting decision was that Matthau had boxed himself into mainstream Hollywood movie roles.

At this point, beyond appearances on awards shows and late-night gab fests, most of Matthau's TV work consisted of guest shots, in the company of fellow Hollywood royalty. For example, in 1981, he guested on *Magic of the Stars*, a special in which stars performed magic tricks; he clowned with Jack Lemmon, Milton Berle, and Ruth Buzzi, and humorously tried to solve the "suspenseful double trunk mystery." The following year, he was one in an all-star line-up in *I Love Liberty*, a special consisting of patriotic skits and musical numbers. It is unfortunate that Matthau did not accept additional assignments similar to *Awake and Sing!* and *Actor*: ambitious productions that for economic reasons were unsuited to the big screen. But his sparse TV acting was his choice. "Reminds me of [the old] days," he declared, while glancing about the crumbling old KCET studio, where *Awake and Sing!* was rehearsed. "Not that I'd like to go back. It's too easy being a movie actor. Spoils you for other things."

Being a movie star, rather than a mere movie actor, allowed Matthau the choicest seats at sporting events. The end of 1972 found him in Chicago, at courtside with critic Gene Siskel at a Chicago Bulls–New York Knicks game. In his right vest pocket, he had written his projection for the final score: Bulls, 132; Knicks, 127. Yet he bet $200 on the Knicks. The score was close, and Matthau was intensely rubbing his thumbs, as if he was aching to pull his skin off; then, he began picking at the skin. To avoid the inevitable crush of autograph-seekers, Matthau and Siskel left before the end. The final score: 90-86, Bulls. Despite being $200 poorer, he was consoled by the fact that he "was only off by one point. The Bulls won by four points, and I said it would be five."

Afterwards, in the Pump Room of the Ambassador Hotel, Matthau ordered Fernet Branca, an Italian liquor that, according to

Siskel, tasted "as if it was made from the essence of a radial tire." "It's so bitter only Jews can enjoy it," Matthau explained. Matthau then was fifty-two years old, and noted why he recently had been giving his age as forty-eight. "You see, I have to be forty-eight years old for the next twenty years if I am going to get leading man parts. I can't be older than forty-eight and still get the girls."

Matthau was paired with several "girls" in the screen versions of two Neil Simon plays in which he starred during the 1970s: *Plaza Suite*, released in 1971; and 1978's *California Suite*. In between, in 1975, he was partnered with George Burns in *The Sunshine Boys*.

Plaza Suite, which came to Broadway in 1968, consisted of three comic one-act playlets: "Visitor from Mamaroneck"; "Visitor from Hollywood"; and "Visitor from Forest Hills." George C. Scott starred in each, playing a trio of guests who, one after the other, are housed in the same suite at the venerable New York hotel: a jaded suburban husband whose marriage is failing; a slick, aging Hollywood producer who entices an old girlfriend; and a flustered father-of-the-bride dealing with a flipped-out daughter. In each, Scott's co-star, playing his wife, girlfriend, and wife, was Maureen Stapleton.

Prior to signing for *Plaza Suite*, Matthau expressed his desire to play all three roles, opposite different actresses. Simon reportedly was against the idea, even though one actor had played them all on stage. During pre-production, Peter Falk and Kirk Douglas cropped up as possible Matthau co-stars. But Matthau was a major box office draw, so Simon acquiesced. His co-stars were Stapleton, Barbara Harris, and Lee Grant.

Stapleton, in fact, was one of Matthau's closest friends. They, along with Carol, shared an unabashed sense of the absurd. "I remember Maureen once sent him a carload of kasha," recalled Anne Jackson. "Maureen could handle Walter. Maureen could handle any-body, because she would escape into a bottle of wine. She could match him, wit for wit.

"Maureen was someone who could stay close friends with someone like Walter, I think," Jackson added. "In my case, I would be thrown by some of his humor. He would [pepper his conversation] with toilet humor, and so would Maureen. A lot of four-letter words would be [tossed about when they were together]. I know I envied them their talent and freedom of expression. I loved them, but was intimidated by them. My fear was that I couldn't come up to [Walter's] standards. He just awed me. He was terribly funny."

From a table in the Plaza Hotel's Edwardian Room, where he was shooting the film on location, Matthau declared, "It really isn't fair that I should play all three parts and Maureen Stapleton play only one." Then he mischievously added, "In Hollywood they think if a girl is seduced she must be pretty. Apparently they didn't think Maureen was pretty enough to be seduced. I've tried to seduce 3,423 girls and none of them were pretty. I was telling Maureen about it when I was sleeping with her the other night."

"A suicide schedule" was how Matthau described the film's promotional tour. Howard Koch, his producer friend, asked him to undertake it. Matthau reported that he had asked Koch, "Do I have a percentage of that picture?" After learning he did, he responded, "I'll be delighted to do it."

While giving an interview in a Manhattan eatery, Matthau was greeted by a surprise visitor: step-daughter and aspiring actress Lucy Saroyan, who noticed his limousine outside and dropped in to say hello. Matthau played the role of Jewish mother when he told her, "If you don't order any food I'm going to be really angry. Have some *latkes*. Have some *r-r-r-oti de l'agneau*." After ordering eggs benedict, Matthau switched into kidding, dirty-old-man mode and declared, "See what happens to girls. They walk around the streets of New York. . . . I can see how you become prostitutes." To which Lucy replied, "Oh, Walter."

The Sunshine Boys, which came to Broadway in 1972, starred Sam Levene and Jack Albertson as Al Lewis and Willie Clark, veteran vaudeville partners whose offstage relationship is as sunny as a film noir thriller. They have not seen each other for eleven years. Now, a television special on the history of comedy is in pre-production. Who better to appear than Lewis and Clark, the beloved "Sunshine Boys"? Clark's theatrical agent nephew attempts to broker the deal, and reunite the warring parties.

Matthau was in his mid-fifties when he played Clark. With appropriate age makeup, he was believable as the elderly vaudevillian, just as he had been as Joseph Kotcher. Initially, he was reluctant to accept the role because he did not like the play; he saw only gloom in the relationship between Lewis and Clark. Then he read the script to his twelve-year-old son Charlie. "He got a terrific charge out of listening to me say the lines," Walter noted. "He went into gales of laughter. And I thought, hmmm, maybe I ought to do this role." Over a quarter-century later, Charlie vividly recalled "laughing and laughing" at the lines. "Of course I was very young," he added. "It wasn't as if I had talked him into doing it. That was more of a father-to-son—really father-to-kid—kind of thing."

Another inducement was the chance to play opposite a radio-television comedy legend: Jack Benny, then approaching eighty, who had not had a major screen role in three decades. However, in December 1974, before production began, Benny died of cancer. The initial replacement suggestion reportedly was Red Skelton, who declined the part. Eventually, Benny's close friend, seventy-nine-year-old George Burns, was cast as Lewis. Although Burns had had a full career in radio, television and nightclubs over the past decades, this was his first screen role in thirty-six years, since 1939's *Honolulu*.

Richard Benjamin joined Matthau and Burns in the cast, playing the nephew. "During the first read-through of the script," he recalled, "Walter and I were at [director] Herb Ross's house and we were turning the pages. George was sitting there, but he didn't open his script; it was just shut on his lap. So we thought, 'Well, sooner or later someone's gonna have to tell him what page we're on. Does he realize what we're doing here?' I think I had the line before [his first one]. I said it, and of course he picked up his cue right away and said his line. We did the whole [reading], and he didn't touch the script. And Walter said, 'Have you learned all this? Are you just trying to make us look bad?'"

Then and there, Matthau and Benjamin realized they were working with "a pretty sharp guy."

Benjamin added, "George was always funny. My father had passed away long before this, but he always loved Burns and Allen, and would have been thrilled to know that I was talking to George Burns, let alone working with him. [Burns] would say, 'Hey, kid, you wanna have lunch?' and I couldn't believe this was happening. Walter usually stayed in his dressing room, listening to classical music. So

George and I went. As we walked between these sound stages at MGM, he would tell me the same joke every day. And it would make me laugh, every single day. He said, 'You know, Gracie and I made a picture here thirty-five years ago.' I said, 'Really.' He said, 'They liked it so well, they asked me back.' It wasn't like he'd forgotten that he told me, but he told me every day.

"Then we'd go to the commissary. There were waitresses who'd been there for a long time—and he knew them from thirty-five years ago. And they'd heard *this* joke thirty-five years ago. He'd say, 'I want some soup, and I want it hot. You know how hot I want it? If you can carry it, it's not hot enough.' That was everyday."

"I was crazy about George Burns," Matthau recalled two decades later, "and the picture seemed to work." Of Matthau, Burns declared, "Walter doesn't need to be funny. He's fearless—no inhibitions. If you want him to play soprano, or be a dancer, he'd do it."

In developing his characterization, Matthau did not soften Clark. He made the character exasperatingly spiteful and cranky, and unmerciful in his disdain: a thoroughly miserable human being. Furthermore, to play Clark, the actor drew upon his past—despite his scorn for The Method. "It's a very interesting question in acting," Matthau recalled. "If you didn't have such a naysayer, such a dour, sullen, bitter, disappointed person in your life as your mother, do you think you could have played *The Sunshine Boys*? The answer would be no, not the same way." The previous decade, just as he was at the cusp of superstardom, he noted that "acting is a form of self-expression, and social adversity frustrates you. So you need to express yourself. Had I grown up in a palace, I doubt I would have made much of an actor."

"Many times I would recognize that he would use his mother Rose in developing his character," observed Anna Berger. "I always saw Rose in his playing—especially in *Sunshine Boys*."

Matthau, in fact, was not the only comic actor who experienced a harsh childhood, and who used laughter to separate himself from his pain. Charlie Chaplin spent part of his youth as a London street urchin; his mother had suffered a mental breakdown, and he ended up in an orphanage for indigent children. W. C. Fields was abused by a violent father, and ran away from home at age eleven. He thieved in order to survive, and often was whipped in street fights. Matthau might have been thinking of his own miserable childhood when he observed, "There must be an enormous tragic button in the head of an actor in order for him to do comedy, because if you examine the lives of most comedians you'll find their lives have been swamped with ill fortune of the worst kind."

Matthau and Burns won raves for their *Sunshine Boys* performances, and Matthau earned a second, and final, Best Actor Academy Award nomination. His competition: Jack Nicholson, the eventual winner (for *One Flew Over the Cuckoo's Nest*); Al Pacino (*Dog Day Afternoon*); Maximilian Schell (*The Man in the Glass Booth*); and James Whitmore (*Give 'em Hell, Harry!*). Burns won the Oscar as Best Supporting Actor.

Of the anticipation involved in awaiting the "And the winner is . . . ," Matthau once noted, "I jog a mile a day. Actually, it would be a good idea if they had all of the Oscar contenders jogging up and down the aisles. They could call it 'Jog for Oscars.'"

In April 1975, five months before the film was released, Matthau and Burns were saluted by the Friars Club in a black-tie event at New York's Americana Hotel. Alan King was the emcee; on hand were Milton Berle, Henny Youngman, George Jessel, Phil Foster, Norm Crosby, and other names that one might associate with such events. While addressing the attendees, Abraham Beame, the New York City mayor, kept calling Matthau "Mathoo" and "Mathoos." After the politician departed, others purposefully botched the pronunciation, leading to gales of guffaws. Matthau pal Maureen Stapleton joked that he was enjoying good health "because every bookmaker in American is praying for him to stay well."

Prior to its release, Matthau and Burns embarked on a publicity tour to hype *The Sunshine Boys*. Together, the pair ad-libbed their way through some hilarious interviews. Roger Ebert published what he described as a dialog between Matthau and Burns that is one of his favorite pieces. Among Matthau's queries and observations: "Those are modern pants you're wearing, George"; "When does sex stop for you, George?"; "Merle Oberon, she has silicone in her face, her behind. . . . She looks like she's been dead for nineteen, twenty-two years . . ."; and "Our ad is right next to the ad for *The Story of* O. They'll go to the wrong movie, they'll be sitting there looking at all the ass on the screen, they'll be saying, which one is supposed to be Smith and which one is Dale?" Among Burns's quips: "I've got a coat for Altoona"; "How much do you think a good toupee costs?"; and "Gracie married me for laughs. I got more laughs in bed than when I played Vegas."

A decade later, Matthau was a guest on TV's *George Burns' 90th Birthday: A Very Special Special*. After the showing of a *Sunshine Boys* clip, Matthau strode onstage and began, "For his performance in that picture, George Burns got a Best Supporting Oscar and I got laryngitis from hollering, 'Entaaaah.'" He told a brief anecdote relating to how Burns got younger and he got older during the shoot, ending it by explaining, "My wife Carol said to me, 'Send George Burns over. You're getting too old for me.'"

California Suite, the third 1970s Matthau-Simon film, opened on Broadway in 1976. On stage, it consisted of four individual playlets. For the movies, Simon dispensed with this structure and fashioned a screenplay in which all the characters intermingled while guests at the Beverly Hills Hotel. Matthau's role was Marvin Michaels, a straying husband who must explain his unintentional infidelity to his wife (Elaine May). The *Variety* reviewer noted that the pair "seem to be doing an encore of their work in *A New Leaf*."

By this time, Matthau admitted that he occasionally phoned in a performance. He was prepared to do so in *California Suite*, but noted that "the director got angry. Herbie Ross. Started picking on me. I bawled him out. He bawled me out. We had a terrific fight for a week. He was right. I've grown lazy being a successful actor and a movie star. I've grown very lazy so I come in with an absolute *surface* performance and the guy's gotta really rile me up.

"When you become successful you lose what it is that made you successful. You start going to exclusive clubs. You see the most *boring* people—they're successful just like you. They have no need to use their bodies and their brains and their charm and don't need to be generous emotionally. They become large buckets of goatshit."

CHAPTER 22

Return to Roots

When Matthau won stardom as Oscar Madison, he declared that he favored comic over dramatic roles, because they were far more challenging. A decade later, he observed, "To be a comedian in France, for instance, is the highest honor you could pay an actor. The national theater is called the Comedie Francaise. The feeling is that straight drama could be done by the average actor, but it would take an extraordinary actor to do comedy. I'll go along with that." Two decades after that, he noted, "Comedy, that's the serious stuff. People say, 'When are ya gonna do serious stuff?' I look at them as though they were crazy. My serious stuff is my comedy."

Yet Matthau still opted to play drama, which he did in three 1970s features: *Charley Varrick* and *The Laughing Policeman*, both from 1973, and *The Taking of Pelham One Two Three*, released the following year. His roles were a stunt-pilot-turned-bank-robber; a homicide detective sniffing out a killer; and a transit detective investigating a hijacked subway car. "I haven't been playing different sorts of roles lately," he noted, while filming *Pelham*. "I've been playing different sorts of roles all my life. It's just that I fell into seven years of comedies and I began to resent the fact that's all I was sent." After a brief pause, he continued, "Of course, I didn't get really successful until I did good comedy . . . but it was time for a change."

All three films were shot on location, in New Mexico (*Charley Varrick*), San Francisco (*The Laughing Policeman*), and New York (*The Taking of Pelham . . .*). Matthau especially liked shooting in San Francisco. Between takes, he enjoyed walking the streets of the hilly city.

In *Charley Varrick*, a taut Don Siegel crime drama that has developed a well-earned cult reputation, he played the title character, who is chased by the law and the mob after masterminding the robbery of a small-town bank that actually is a front for laundered money. Varrick is a classic anti-hero. He may be a lawbreaker, but he is kinder and gentler than the gangland thug (Joe Don Baker) who is out to kill him. And sexier: Varrick even has a bedroom scene with an attractive woman, a bank secretary (Felicia Farr).

Initially, Matthau did not want to play Varrick. He claimed, "[Siegel] said to me, 'I see that you're a pretty good ping-pong player. I'll play you a game of ping-pong. If you beat me, you don't have to do the movie and I'll give you your salary.' I said, 'OK, it's fair enough.'" Given his background in table tennis, Matthau was confident that he would win—but Siegel, a champion-caliber player, beat him 21-2. Matthau attributed the film's success to the fact that "Siegel was directing it, and he knew what to do with the camera."

Back in 1967, Matthau declared, "I am afraid when I ride the [New York] subway. I usually try to project the image of the detective, and often it works." He then was unaware that he would play just such a role in *Pelham*. Matthau's character, savvy lieutenant Zachary Garber, originally was written as a thirty-two-year-old African American. "I read the script and told them I loved the role," he explained. "'But that's the role of the black policeman,' they said. So I said, 'Tell you what. I'll play the role, and we won't tell the people I'm black.'"

The film was directed by Joseph Sargent, Matthau's old New School pal. "He was a surprise for me," Sargent said. "I got the script from UA. I thought it was fun and interesting, but it was a caper picture, so I wasn't that excited about it. Gabe Katzka, who was the producer, walked in one day and said, 'Guess who we have to play the lead?' It was Walter, and I just fell down. I didn't expect someone of his magnitude to be interested in a picture like this.

"But then Walter opened up the whole thing. His casting made the picture work, because there had to be that element of humor, that slightly, 5 percent off center that he brings to everything he does. That droll quality that he brings made the picture work."

That offbeat humor highlights the film's final sequence, in which Garber is on to the identity of the one surviving villain, a sneezing ex-subway conductor (Martin Balsam). The cop remains speechless yet, by his raised eyebrow, you know he is aware that he has found the culprit. Two Charlies, Chaplin and Matthau, provided inspiration for the sequence. "I met [Chaplin] first in Switzerland," the younger Charlie recalled. "He thought I was a cute kid. I would always imitate the expression on his face, and my father used it for the last scene."

During the shoot, Matthau befriended British actor Robert Shaw, cast as the chief hijacker. Initially, Shaw was unaware that Matthau was a Grade A kidder. "When we started rehearsing, Walter came in with a tight, curled, kinky wig," recalled Sargent. "He said that, because the part was now Jewish, he had to wear a wig. I said, 'Walter, you're Jewish, and you don't have tight curly hair. Enough already.' Bob Shaw especially took umbrage with this. He said, 'Well, if he's gonna wear a wig, I'm gonna limp.' And Shaw, who was very competitive, was serious. He didn't realize that Walter was a great put-on artist." He soon did, and the two spent the rest of the shoot trading quips.

For Matthau, *Pelham* was a reunion of friends and family. In addition to Sargent, Anna Berger and Lucy Saroyan played terrorized passengers; Marvin Silbersher was the New York City comptroller; and Michelle Matthow, brother Henry's daughter, was a Transit Authority receptionist.

Matthau's next film also was a reunion, but of another sort. With Billy Wilder directing and Jack Lemmon co-starring, he made *The Front Page*, Ben Hecht and Charles MacArthur's satire. Here again, the pair played adversaries. Matthau was Walter Burns, a sharp, manipulative Chicago newspaper editor who schemes to prevent Hildy Johnson (Lemmon), his best reporter, from quitting the newspaper racket and retiring to marriage.

Austin Pendleton, who appeared in the film, confirmed that Matthau adhered to the script. "It was, after all, a Billy Wilder picture," he noted. "As always, everybody was pretty strict about the script. That was just the way that [Wilder] made pictures."

Matthau ended 1974 by making one final stage appearance, albeit not on Broadway. Along with Lemmon and Maureen Stapleton, he starred in *Juno and the Paycock*, presented at Los Angeles' Mark Taper Forum from November 7 through December 22. Matthau accepted the part because he wanted his son Charlie to see him act on stage. He admitted that he was nervous about the enterprise, but agreed to it for Charlie's sake, and because Carol felt it would be good for him to return to his professional roots.

Matthau played "Captain" Jack Doyle, the egotistical "peacock" of the title, while Stapleton was Juno Doyle, Jack's long-tormented wife, and Lemmon was Joxer Daly, Jack's deceitful drinking buddy; fourteen years earlier, Matthau had played Daly in a TV version. This restaging was not universally acclaimed. Dan Sullivan, theater critic of the *Los Angeles Times*, wrote, "The fear in this corner was that Jack Lemmon, Walter Matthau, and Maureen Stapleton would make a vulgar Hollywood star-trip out of *Juno and the Paycock*. In fact, the production at the Taper sees them so determined to do right by Sean O'Casey that the effect is just a bit inhibited. Wednesday night's press opening was a lovely display of acting craft but not, as *Juno* should be, an experience to take home with you." Sullivan's piece so annoyed Carol Matthau and Felicia Farr Lemmon that they co-authored a letter to the *Times* editor. In it, they chastised Sullivan, using such adjectives as obscure, uneducated, empty, arid, and sterile to describe his criticism. They concluded, "We hope you will print this letter despite our love affairs with Messrs Matthau and Lemmon."

Occasionally, Matthau considered leaving "retirement acting"—his phrase for screen acting—to return to the stage, even though theater work was physically demanding and the pay was wanting. "The movies are bits and pieces," he said. "You do a scene, and two months later you continue the scene. It's really a different game. Right now, I like acting in movies better because it's much easier, more fun, though not as satisfying. Doing a play is like having a seven-course meal, but a movie is like eating a lot of hors d'oeuvres. You get filled up, but you're never quite satisfied."

Matthau never again opted for the feast, but he had some of his tastiest hors d'oeuvres in *The Bad News Bears*, released in 1976, playing Morris Buttermaker, a beer-guzzling, broken-down swimming pool cleaner-turned-Little-League-coach.

Many of the scenes were shot on a sandlot baseball field in Chatsworth, California, in the San Fernando Valley, and Matthau relished working with the young actors playing the Bears. "He was wonderful [with them], because he loved kids and loved the kind of scoutmaster role that he can take on when he works with kids," recalled Michael Ritchie, the film's director. "He never left the dugout. I would say to him, 'Walter, we finished that take. It's gonna be a while setting up the next one, so you can go back and read the trades or do whatever stars do in their trailers.' He'd say, 'No, I'll hang in here with the kids.' One reason the kids had rapport is that they viewed him as an equal, not as a star who would retire [to his trailer].

"He would tell them riddles, and slightly off-color jokes. When I say [this], I don't want to give the impression that Walter was corrupting minors. It's just that the nature of the script encouraged that kind of raucous thinking and behavior. So this helped me a lot; it loosened [the kids] up.

"So Walter became a beloved teacher of raunchy jokes. He was on their team, in every way." Added Joyce Van Patten, who played a supporting role, "[Ritchie] would lose his temper with the children," resulting from "the combination of [the] heat and responsibility and kids that were kids and could not help it. Walter remained their friend 'til the end."

Matthau's co-star was Tatum O'Neal, cast as the Bears' ace pitcher. Pre–*Bad News Bears*, twelve-year-old O'Neal had one film to her credit: *Paper Moon*, for which she had won a Best Supporting Actress Oscar. During the shoot, she acquired a nickname: *Tantrum* O'Neal. "Tatum on the other hand would go back to her motor home, and was much less interested in fraternizing," Ritchie recalled. "That was fine, as far as I was concerned, because that was the nature of her character." Yet the youngster still needed to be "handled," and Matthau did an expert job. "Tatum viewed herself as a big star," Ritchie stated, "so Walter, by becoming an equal [with the boys], set a pattern that she had to fall into. It becomes important when she thinks she has a really good relationship with him, and then he plays the scene where he throws beer in her face and yells at her and says he won't be her father-figure or anything like that. The shock on Tatum's face is absolutely genuine, because that is Walter the consummate actor scaring the shit out of a twelve-year-old."

During the shoot, Matthau heaped over-exaggerated praise on his difficult leading lady by describing her as "a natural actress. She's like Greta Garbo. Whatever she does, you suddenly see it in the rushes the next day. She has her way of acting . . . she flubs the first two or three takes, maybe four or five takes, but then when she finally does it, it's astonishing." A quarter-century later, Ritchie explained, "He knew that she wasn't proficient enough as an actress. She'd only done one film, and that was largely by rote, which is to say that Peter Bogdanovich gave her line readings. So he had to use an actor's trick, the kind of trick that Kazan and other great directors have used, which is to suddenly make the scene so real, so intense, that that actor you're playing against shows true emotion, true fear. At that point in the movie, Walter is bringing a tremendous amount of knowledge as an old pro to bring a performance out of a terrified amateur."

By this time, Matthau had long been signing profit percentage deals on his projects, rather than working for straight salary. For *The Bad News Bears*, he received $750,000 against 10 percent of the first $8 million of gross box office receipts; between twelve and 12.5 percent of the next $5 million; and 15 percent of all earnings over $13 million. Three years after the film's release, he sued Paramount Pictures for selling it and its two inferior, Matthau-less sequels to television for approximately the same price—$6.75 million for the original and $6.25 million and $5.5 million for the sequels—even though the original earned far more than the follow-ups. In 1979, *The Bad News Bears* had taken in $24.8 million in domestic box office alone, while the follow-ups earned $14.5 million and $6.4 million. Matthau asserted the studio did so in order to decrease the money owed him.

The case was settled out of court in 1981. While the terms were kept secret, Matthau attorney Louis Blau noted, "We deserved more and we got more."

CHAPTER 23

"...He Thought He Was Going to Die"

In the mid-1970s Matthau was at the zenith of his powers as a Hollywood commodity. He had his choice of movie roles. During the first half of the decade, he won two Best Actor Academy Award nominations. He was beloved by audiences. Whether acting in a comedy or drama, he was adept at playing what he described as "older leading [characters] with a kind of sincere and roguish charm." It was, he noted, "a category that doesn't have too much competition."

Then, in April 1976, reality came crashing in on him. A decade after suffering his first, near-fatal heart attack, the fifty-six-year-old actor underwent coronary bypass surgery. After experiencing a bit of angina during a four-mile uphill walk, Matthau went to see his doctor, who promptly ordered a coronary angiogram. "It showed a definite occlusion in the left anterior descending," Matthau reported. "I knew that that's the artery that can't be clogged, so I said, 'How soon can you do it?' They said, 'Tomorrow morning.' I wore my baseball cap during the angiogram. I never took it off. I guess I took it off for the operation."

Then he cut the clowning and added, "I really didn't even have time to be scared." Yet William Schallert recalled an entirely different Matthau. "I know that when he had the open heart surgery for the first time, he was really scared," Schallert noted. "He told me that he thought he was going to die."

After the operation, he resumed his good humor. His old friend Leon Birns read about the operation, and wrote Matthau. "He wrote me back to thank me," Birns recalled, "and he ended by writing, 'From the bottom of my new heart.' That was Walter."

While recuperating, Matthau received a blood transfusion that carried hepatitis, leading to impairment of his liver enzymes. His post–heart attack therapy included exercise, while his post-hepatitis therapy involved rest. Matthau's solution: "I compromise," he joked. "I do my push-ups in bed." Despite these setbacks, Matthau kept on working. While publicizing his next film, *Casey's Shadow*, he observed, "I wasn't ready [to die]. I had a couple more things to do on this planet." Pointing his finger upward, he added, "I just hope God is not naughty and doesn't do anything untoward." Two years later, he told a reporter that he felt great, and hoped to maintain a two-picture-a-year schedule.

As soon as he was able, he re-started his walking routine. Three-and-a-half months after the operation, he began shooting *Casey's Shadow*, cast as a character he was born to play: an insolvent but determined quarter-horse trainer (albeit a Louisiana Cajun, rather than a Lower East Side Jew). Matthau nailed down his character's accent by listening to Cajun records. "I'm doing [it] in what I call Brooklyn Jewish Southern, with a bit of 'Merci' thrown in," he explained during the shoot. "Marty Ritt [the film's director] said we'll need English subtitles." Yet prior to the shoot, he quipped that he did not have to research any aspect of the role because he'd "*lived*" everything. I've been a waiter, a gambler, a pimp, a murderer. I'm from the ghetto, and the only time I do any research is when I play aristocracy." He described the film's moral as "Don't worry if you compromise your principles, because everything is going to turn out OK in the end," adding, "You might say I play a character like Richard Nixon." He also savored working with Alexis Smith, his veteran co-star. "I always thought Alexis Smith was a very sexy-looking woman," he added. "I recently met her, and she looked even sexier than before. Alexis is sexy because she has no pomposity."

Filming began in the Sierra Blanca Mountains, 7,200 feet above sea level. Matthau enjoyed this outdoor setting. He also relished being on hand for the $1 million All-American Futurity, held on a mini-track in Ruidoso, New Mexico, in which two-year-old quarter-horses race 440 yards; the event also played a role in the *Casey's Shadow* scenario. On the day of the real (as opposed to reel) Futurity, thirteen races ran. At their conclusion, Matthau was $10,000 poorer.

During the shoot, Matthau frequently tired. He looked ashen and was noticeably thin, and often had to be excused after a couple of takes. Yet his sense of humor was thriving. "I did two takes yesterday, called my doctor, and said I was dying," he exclaimed, "He said, 'What are you doing all day?' I said, 'Rooting for horses at the top of my lungs!' He said, 'Schmuck, you're just hyperventilating.'"

While publicizing *Casey's Shadow*, he noted that it "was the first horse script I ever liked." To Matthau's way of thinking, most were penned by writers who knew nothing about horseracing; this one was written by Carol Sobieski. In one, he explained, a character says to his wife, "Look up the results from Saratoga and Tropical." "I closed that one right away because Saratoga and Tropical are different times of the year. [In] a second one, a guy walks over to the $20 window. There are no $20 windows [at racetracks]. I've read about ten dozen horse pictures. This was the only picture I ever liked. So did Marty Ritt, who directed it, and who's also a brilliant handicapper."

Matthau expounded on his non-betting interest in horses—and revealed his own thirst for knowledge—when he noted, "Horses are very interesting. I've been reading about them. You know, millions of years ago they were the size of a fox. They were called eohippus. Now they weigh thousands of pounds. I guess they grew big running away from saber-toothed tigers. They exercised a lot and ate a lot and today they are enormous beasts; and still, a leaf, a shadow, a butterfly can spook a horse."

All this knowledge did little to improve his betting odds. During a press junket to Santa Anita, he lost $3,500.

In 1986, Matthau was asked to cite actresses with whom he would like to work but never had. He listed Meryl Streep, Jessica Lange, and Debra Winger, and added, "I'm crazy about Glenda Jackson." Actually, Matthau already had twice acted opposite Jackson. In 1978, they co-starred in *House Calls*; two years later, they appeared in *Hopscotch*. In *House Calls*, Matthau played a widowed surgeon; Jackson was the divorcee with whom he becomes romantically involved. Their union is inevitable, if only because Charlie Matthau played Jackson's teen-age son. In *Hopscotch*, Matthau was a comically rebellious CIA agent who writes an expose of international espionage; Jackson was cast as his mistress.

"The first time I saw her on the set I thought she was an assistant grip," Matthau said of Jackson while promoting *House Calls*. "She's got that kind of bantamweight swagger." It was just such comments that led Rex Reed, who interviewed Matthau during this period, to observe, "From all reports, no love was lost between Matthau and Glenda Jackson on the current *House Calls*."

Yet Matthau continued his description of Jackson by noting that, "when she starts talking, you realize she's a very great talent." Jackson, for her part, publicly gushed over Matthau. In 1979, she guested on *The Mike Douglas Show* to plug *Lost and Found*, her latest film. Douglas remarked that she and Matthau had a "mutual respect thing going" and Jackson quickly broke in, declaring, "In my case it's love. It's out-and-out love. If I could steal him from Carol, I would. I adore him."

The previous year, Matthau appeared on *The Today Show* to plug *House Calls* and *Casey's Shadow*. During the broadcast, he clowned with Gene Shalit and Tom Brokaw. Brokaw described Matthau and Shalit as "two young men who will try to overcome their inhibitions and talk to you about the lighter side of life. It is a struggle for the two of them." Shalit referred to Matthau's horsetrainer role in *Casey's Shadow* as "sort of typecasting 'cause Walter Matthau loves horses, so long as they're not from France." Matthau protested, "Why is Tom Brokaw picking on me all the time? I watch *The Today Show* regularly. Yesterday, he said, 'That international statesman, Walter Matthau.' I mean, what makes Tom think that the clowns we have who are international statesmen in what is known laughingly as real life know what the hell they're doing?"

He continued his questioning: "Why does he pick on my nose? I notice people with small noses pick on people with big noses. I used to have a small nose, but I had a lot of fistfights on the Lower East Side, in defense of justice, in defense of decency and goodness. I wear this [nose] as a badge of honor. I was punched in the nose twice, three times a week." Then he launched into one of his long, tall tales. It involved his lone professional fight, against a five-foot two-inch homosexual, held at the "Coney Island Velodrome" when he was in the Civilian Conservation Corps.

Then he added, to a laughing Brokaw, "Why are you picking on me? You didn't think I was romantic enough for Glenda Jackson in *House Calls?*" Next, he offered a joke: "This director who looked like me is sleeping with the leading lady. And so is the leading man. The leading man comes over to the director and says, 'Hey, the only reason she's sleeping with you is because you're the director.' And the director says, 'The only reason she's sleeping with you is because you're good-looking.'"

In December 1978, Matthau was even more outlandish while guest-hosting *Saturday Night Live*. During his opening monologue, he placed a tissue in his right nostril and quipped, "I just bet $5 I'd get a laugh on the opening." In the skits that followed, he played a camp counselor in a *Bad News Bears* parody; a pushy, cigar-puffing Coca-Cola distributor in a Greek diner; Gilda Radner's nostalgic, possessive dad, who intrudes on her and her husband (Bill Murray) while in bed; Ernie, "the only one who didn't get caught," opposite Dan Aykroyd's ex-President Richard Nixon; and Hank, a brusque schlock shop proprietor. At one point, Matthau professed to be unable to understand the type of music usually presented on the show. He favored Mozart, he exclaimed, and then introduced Garrett Morris, "a fine operatic tenor," who sang a solo from *Don Giovanni*. After Morris's performance, Matthau applauded and declared, "We'll be right back with the regular crap."

Earlier that year, the Matthaus were present at the final appearance of conductor Zubin Mehta with the Los Angeles Philharmonic. Barbra Streisand also attended. Matthau had just completed *House Calls*, and had been flustered by director Howard Zieff's propensity for on-set indecision. While publicizing the film, he noted that he was "angry at the inexperience of the director. . . . His experience was limited mainly to photography." Streisand then was considering working with Zieff on a new project, a comedy titled *The Main Event*. At one point, Matthau's and Streisand's paths crossed, and the story goes that she asked him for a report on Zieff. "He's the greatest director in the world," he told her. "You *can't* use anybody else. He knows every shot he's going to take a week before he's on the set." Streisand was unaware that Matthau was yanking her chain, and Zieff was hired for her film.

Hopscotch, a comedy–spy thriller that was one of Matthau's favorite films, was shot across the globe, on locations from Marseilles to Bermuda to Atlanta. "I had artistic, creative control, and the result agrees with everything I had in mind," explained Brian Garfield, the film's co-author/co-associate producer. That control resulted in the casting of Matthau. "I had seen nearly all his films, dating back to *The Indian Fighter*," Garfield noted. "The book is not a comedy, yet the film is, even though they're both the same story. The movie is funny because the character's prime motivation is his sense of humor. He's thumbing his nose at all the self-important secret agents. It's a good-natured kind of revenge. There's a comic potential here, and Walter's ideal for the part."

Matthau liked the screenplay because his character did not depend upon guns and firepower, but uses his wits and his savvy. Furthermore, the filmmakers agreed to his suggestion that they include Mozart on the soundtrack.

David Matthau, Walter's son, and Lucy Saroyan, Carol's daughter, have featured roles in *Hopscotch*. Previously, Lucy appeared in *Kotch* and *The Taking of Pelham One Two Three*, while David was in *California Suite*. Yet according to Marvin Silbersher, Matthau was not so generous with all his relatives. Once during the 1970s, Silbersher was "walking down Lower Broadway, and I see [a sign that read] 'H. Matthow, Army & Navy.' So I thought I'd go in and buy a shirt. I walk in and there's Hank and he says, 'Marvin!' I buy a shirt and we talk and talk. Then Hank takes me aside and says, 'Marvin, can you do something for me? You're one of Walter's best buddies. Can you get my daughter an audition with Walter?' That's the truth. That's the part of Walter we don't want to know about."

Perhaps this conversation culminated in Michelle Matthow being cast in *The Taking of Pelham One Two Three*.

While attracted to show business, David did not set out to become an actor. He studied film history and criticism at USC. "I gravitated toward acting, though, and then never really thought about doing anything other than acting," he explained. "It was sort of a given."

After graduation, he took acting jobs, worked for film companies as a production assistant, and became a Universal Pictures contract player. "But I never really kind of enjoyed the whole lifestyle of being an actor. It was sort of a real conflict for me, having a very famous father as an actor." One benefit of the Matthau surname was that it singled him out from the hoard of movie actor wannabes: Columbia Pictures went so far as to announce in a press release his casting as a bellhop in *California Suite*. Conversely, a debit for David was his lack of identity and individuality within the Hollywood culture.

"In a way, my dad had always been very supportive, and had helped me in terms of contacts and introducing me to people and setting up interviews," he observed. "But there was kind of a real conflict in me about that, because part of me hated the fact that I had this famous father. I don't know that I was conscious of it at the time, but I felt that I didn't want to be in anybody's shadow—and certainly not my dad's.

"Some people have been able to deal with that in a healthy way, and use it to their advantage. Ultimately, I always believed, and still do, that you make it on your own talent and ability. I never really felt comfortable having that kind of shadow. And being in that shadow, I wasn't really able to stand up and be my own person.

"You look at other acting families"—and, here, David cited Michael Douglas and his father, Kirk—"where those kids were really able to use [their name] to whatever advantage it was able to give them, and at the same time succeed because they have wonderful talent. I never felt comfortable in that lifestyle. I never felt comfortable in California, in Los Angeles, in that whole atmosphere, and so I was never really able to celebrate that in a great way. Frankly, I'm almost surprised that I had the modest—and very modest—success that I had, because I was never really committed to it.

"When my wife became pregnant [in the mid-1980s], my feeling in my life was, well, now, what am I really gonna do? It's time for me to go out and get a real job. Because when you're acting, even when you have a job it was like you're almost unemployed. Some people tend to thrive in that kind of lifestyle. I didn't. Acting is hard because it's so hard to get a part. It's so competitive. And even if you do, so many times the kind of show or film you're in is not terrific. You're completely at the mercy of whatever the director and writer want. Unless you're a big, big star, you're just one little element in the grand scheme of things. So it was always difficult, and I never really was thrilled with it."

David eventually studied broadcast journalism and worked in various jobs on radio and cable television. He then settled in at New Jersey 101.5 FM radio, where he works as a field reporter and anchor. "It's the biggest station by far in the state of New Jersey," he noted, "and a real fun one to work for."

At this point in his life, David freely admitted, "Reality has always been more fascinating to me than film or theater. . . . I've always been fascinated by news and sports and so forth. So I kind of gravitated toward that. That career change for me was a real, huge benefit. It gives me a satisfaction that I don't think I ever got in acting."

Back in 1965, Matthau observed that daughter Jenny, who then was nine, "looks like me, has the makings of a fine soprano, [and] her goal is grand opera. And we will help her make it." Instead of show business, Jenny opted for another kind of creative career, becoming a co-president, director, and instructor at New York's National Gourmet Cookery School, affiliated with the Natural Gourmet Institute for Food and Health. She is a 1985 graduate of the school's double apprentice/teacher's training programs. She also worked as a private chef, and had several featured recipes published in cookbooks.

"I was a wholesale carpet person," recalled Murray Juvelier. "One day I was in my store, and a guy comes over to me and says, 'Hey, Murray, see that girl over there, that pretty girl? Her father's a very famous actor.' I said, 'Really, who is that?' He says, 'She says her father is Walter Matthau.' I walked over to [Jenny], and almost fell on the floor. I hadn't seen her since she was three years old. She was building a cooking school. She had the most beautiful little girl I'd ever seen in my life, an adopted child. And Walter wasn't very close to them.

"She was very nice. And she called Walter in California in front of me to verify [who I was]. She put me on the phone with him, and he said, 'Give her the best. Give her the best.' I was dying to say to him, 'Are you gonna pay for it?'"

To this day, Ruby Ludwin and his wife Ethel are friends with David and Jenny. Ruby described the now-middle-aged offspring as "nice kids," adding that Jenny is "a wonderful cook. She owns her own cooking school."

Indeed, David and Jenny Matthau have become their own persons.

CHAPTER 24

Aging Star

Matthau's New York background, combined with his crapshooter mentality, made him ideal for playing in Damon Runyon vehicles. Back in 1955, he was quite a hit as Nathan Detroit on stage in *Guys and Dolls*, based on a series of Runyon short stories. A quarter century later, he starred in the comedy *Little Miss Marker*, adapted from another Runyon tale. His role was Sorrowful Jones, a miserly bookie who finds himself looking after a little girl who has been left as collateral and then abandoned by her gambler-father. The results were not as successful.

The property had been filmed three times before: in 1934, as *Little Miss Marker*; in 1949, as *Sorrowful Jones*; and in 1962, as *Forty Pounds of Trouble*. Tony Curtis starred in the latter. By 1980, Curtis no longer was a heartthrob. He was middle-aged. He had put on weight. Now, he was another working actor—and Matthau was the star. In *Little Miss Marker*, Curtis supports Matthau, playing a villain.

Little Miss Marker was a fiasco, earning poor reviews and dying at the box office. The *Variety* critic concluded his review by noting, "Incidentally, if Matthau gets one more script calling for him to be stranded outdoors in undies or women's clothes, he should take that as a hint and junk it."

The film's reception was an omen for the 1980s. While Matthau still was a star, he was an aging one. While he still had the clout to be cast alongside a new generation of comic actors, from Dan Aykroyd to Robin Williams, none of his films from this period rank with his earlier hits.

In addition to starring in *Little Miss Marker*, Matthau was the film's executive producer. Two years earlier, he had signed a three-picture deal with Universal; he was set to executive produce the films, but this was to be his lone credit in this capacity. One of the primary pre-production chores was finding the right little girl for the title role. Newspaper ads were placed in venues across the country, seeking "a six-year-old girl with outstanding personality to star with Walter Matthau and Julie Andrews in *Little Miss Marker*." In March 1979, ninety-two Miss Marker wannabes came to a casting call, held in a Manhattan moviehouse. Among the girls' names were Missy, Venus, Tara, Desiree, Calliope, Juno, Peggeen, and Alexis. "I want to be a movie star," one little girl declared, as she was prodded by her mother. "I think I could be another Olivia Newton-John."

Ultimately, more than 5,000 girls were interviewed, and the cream of the candidates—a total of eight youngsters—made screen tests with Matthau. The chosen child was Sara Stimson, a first-grader from Helotes, Texas. Her mother had taken her to meet with a casting director at a Holiday Inn in San Antonio.

Little Miss Marker was the directorial debut of Walter Bernstein, a veteran screenwriter. It was Matthau's job to pick a director. While on the phone with Bernstein, Matthau—ever the gambling man—whistled a Beethoven violin concerto. If Bernstein guessed its name, he would be hired as director. He knew the correct answer.

The following year, Matthau starred in *First Monday in October*, based on the Jerome Lawrence–Robert E. Lee stage hit. It was one of his more literate films. Matthau played a liberal Supreme Court Justice contending with a new, conservative colleague (Jill Clayburgh), who also is the court's first woman member. The film's premiere was moved up to August, to tie in with Judge Sandra Day O'Connor's Supreme Court nomination. Only in Hollywood could a movie team think their production was so significant as to be made a commercial tie-in to an appointment to the Supreme Court!

While researching the role, Matthau read a couple of books by William O. Douglas, the justice his character resembled. He patterned the character's outward manner on Democratic Party power-broker Robert Strauss, throwing in bits of Walter Huston and Henry Fonda, who played the role on stage.

In the scenario, Matthau's judge notes that he is in favor of freedom of expression when a case involving pornography comes before the court. It was a point-of-view with which the actor concurred. Matthau revealed that years before, when he worked in the Second Avenue Yiddish theaters, ushers screened "dirty" movies in the basements between shows. "I went once," he said, "and stayed for less that five minutes. I got frightened and sick. Then when I was nineteen, I had another opportunity to see one and I begged off." The only pornographic film he claimed to have seen was in the mid-1970s, when XXX-rated movies were coming aboveground. An unnamed producer friend invited him to see one, and Matthau went out of curiosity. "I sat through the entire film, but it again made me sick," he explained. "It disturbed me. It defiled what I think is a really beautiful relationship between a man and a woman."

It might have been Matthau speaking when his character says, "I agree that porno is crap, but that isn't the point. It has a right to be crap." Matthau, in his own words, further expressed his liberalism by adding, "I feel that if a person is qualified [for the court] it doesn't matter if the person is a woman, a dwarf, six-foot-nine, Jew, or freckle-faced black. The only thing that matters is whether the person meets the high standards of the court."

Writer Max Wilk attended the film's wrap party. "[It] was a jolly reception," he reported, "at which the gang presented Matthau with the complete Oxford Dictionary in nine or ten volumes. It was such a literature scene—or shall I say literate? He was absolutely delighted." Despite the timeliness of *First Monday in October*, the film broke no box office records.

Matthau's follow-up was highly anticipated, because it reunited him with Jack Lemmon and Billy Wilder. The film was *Buddy Buddy*. Released in 1981, it is the story of another sort of odd couple: a suicidal schnook (Lemmon) who is too oblivious to what is occurring around him to realize that his new "best friend" (Matthau) is a hit man. Given the course of Matthau's career, it fits that *Buddy Buddy* was the trio's least successful outing.

Previously, Matthau never dared fiddle with the dialogue on a Wilder film; now, he constantly changed the words, and he and Wilder argued over his line readings. "For all the trouble and aggravation he puts me through," Wilder noted, "I wish I could have him for my next fifty pictures." *Buddy Buddy* was Matthau's celluloid swan song with Wilder.

The film is as memorable for what occurred off-screen as on. At one point in the story, the schnook and the killer slide down a hotel laundry chute. The sequence, filmed on the MGM lot in Culver City in April 1981, was designed so that the actors would drop from the chute and fall onto a mattress-cushioned platform. They were returning from lunch; no one was around, and they did not realize that the chute was not ready to be used. In their ignorance, they began to rehearse. The sixty-year-old Matthau was the first to go down the chute. He missed the platform and fell backwards, his head jerking up in the air and his body landing with a frightful thud on the cement floor twenty feet below. In an oft-told anecdote, Lemmon—who even repeated it at Matthau's memorial service—was the first to reach him. Matthau was barely conscious and in excruciating pain, but he was awake enough to clutch his chest and keep repeating, "This is it, I'm gonna go." A frantic Lemmon carefully placed his coat under Matthau's head and asked, "Walter, are you comfortable?" To which his pal responded, "I make a living."

Actually, Matthau was in too much pain to crack jokes; the "I make a living" quip made for a clever punchline. "What I really said was, 'Jack, it's curtains,'" Matthau revealed while promoting the film. "I never expected to live more than another ten minutes after that. I was in the most vile pain." Initially, it was feared that he had broken his neck, but Matthau suffered bruises and a busted shoulder—serious injuries, to be sure, but a light sentence considering the alternative. He continued filming after a brief respite.

In 1993, Matthau repeated this story and its "I make a living" punchline to Roger Ebert. Only, here, the accident occurred while filming *Grumpy Old Men* on a frozen lake in Minnesota. This time, Matthau fell and hit his head and shoulders. Before the punchline, he claimed that he yelled at Lemmon, "Get the prop man. He's got a gun. Shoot me, will you? I can't take this pain!" Lemmon once remarked, "Walter thinks I'm the reason for everything that's ever ailed him, because something does happen every damned picture we do. Heart attack, an ulcer, duodenal hernia, all kinds of stuff, and it's always me. I swear I'm innocent."

In December 1981, Matthau and Lemmon plugged *Buddy Buddy* on *The Tonight Show*, and the duo had a blast kibitzing and clowning. Prior to Matthau's entrance, Lemmon joked that the film spotlighted the schnook. Every other character, including Matthau's hit man, was incidental. Upon his introduction, Matthau announced, "My wife said, 'Don't tell any toilet jokes on the Johnny Carson show,'" but he had just heard one, which he related.

As they chatted away, the affection between Matthau and Lemmon oozed off the screen. At one point, Matthau noted, in describing his friend's talent, "This kid can do anything he wants." He then turned to Lemmon, who was sitting to his right, exclaimed the actor's surname, and patted him on the head. Larry King reported that he interviewed Matthau "about ten times" on his CNN talk-show. His favorite "was just sitting with him and Lemmon. Two screen idols, two real giants who were loved even by the young."

One of Matthau's more noteworthy early-1980s projects was *I Ought to Be In Pictures*, if only because it was his final film based on a Neil Simon play. The 1982 comedy was the least-distinguished Simon adaptation in which Matthau appeared. He starred as a screenwriter who favors gambling and drinking, and who links up with his estranged, nineteen-year-old daughter. Simon had created the character with Matthau in mind, and wanted him to play it on Broadway. He did not wish to return to New York, so Ron Leibman was given the role. Yet the play world-premiered in Los Angeles, at the Mark Taper Forum. Matthau's choice to pass on it—his old pal Tony Curtis starred—reflected his aversion to appearing on any stage, regardless of its location.

Then he took roles in three ambitious but unexceptional satires which lampooned America's obsession with guns (1983's *The Survivors*), the movie industry (1985's *Movers and Shakers*), and psychiatry/self-help talk radio shows/Los Angeles superficiality (1988's *The*

Couch Trip). He played a gas station owner who loses his business, a studio executive, and a kleptomaniacal misfit. In *The Couch Trip*, the sixty-eight-year-old Matthau is not the star. He is billed after the title, with an "and Walter Matthau as 'Becker.'"

The Survivors and *The Couch Trip* were directed by Michael Ritchie, and featured Matthau with Williams and then Aykroyd. "In both instances, you had co-stars who had tremendous admiration for Walter, and recognition of his formidable comedic talents," Ritchie explained. With regard to these pairings, the director cited the delicate and constantly shifting balance between straight man and comic. So, while shooting *The Survivors*, "Walter becomes straight man to Robin, and then Robin is straight man to him. That doesn't happen in great comedy teams, where they form a pattern; Dean Martin is always in a certain relationship with Jerry Lewis, or Abbott is with Costello. Instead, with Walter and Danny or Walter and Robin, you have this balance constantly shifting."

Matthau's pairing with Williams resulted in a stark contrast in comedy styles. "You put those two together," Ritchie noted, "and you have a real dervish effect, with Robin the dervish and Walter the maypole that Robin was spinning around. But Walter didn't move. Walter wasn't intimidated by the dervish. This baffled Robin. He wasn't used to this. He was used to having people back off."

In the past, Matthau might improvise, but not when working with Williams. "I think he was smart, great poker player that he was, in knowing where is strong cards were," Ritchie added. "His strong cards weren't in improv against Robin Williams. His strong cards were in relying on the script, and his knowledge of the character. The danger for the great improviser is to slip out of character. The good movie actor knows that, if it's out of character, unless it's a Bob Hope movie, it'll be on the cutting room floor. So Walter is always playing for the final cut. He's saving for the close-up."

Matthau was not the studio's first choice to play opposite Williams. An actor who was closer to middle-age was preferred and Joe Bologna, sixteen years Matthau's junior, was hired. After a week's shooting, the dailies were terrible and Ritchie exclaimed, "We've gotta have Walter." Matthau was hired virtually overnight, and completely reshaped the character.

Easily Matthau's 1980s nadir was *Pirates*, directed by Roman Polanski. In this dead-on-arrival 1986 swashbuckler, Matthau at least has a jolly good time as he chomps the scenery, offering a Wallace Beery imitation in one of his most unusual roles: Captain Thomas Bartholomew Red, a glowering, peg-legged, Cockney-accented pirate. In one of his all-time cinematic low points, his character even eats a rat.

The casting of Matthau came about in the wake of a Beverly Hills dinner party he attended, hosted by Gregory Peck. He was seated next to Tarak Ben Ammar, the film's Tunisian-born producer. Matthau, as always, was telling jokes, using French, British, and Yiddish accents. Ammar envisioned Matthau as Captain Red and passed the suggestion on to Polanski, who offered him the part. Initially, Matthau was disinclined to accept, because of the location shooting in Tunisia, Malta, and the Seychelles; unlike other actors, who might savor a free trip to an exotic locale, he preferred his creature comforts. Then there was the physical effort required for the role, what with Red's peg leg and weighty costumes, and all the fencing, fighting, and climbing into and out of ships. Matthau only accepted upon the intervention of his son Charlie, who liked the idea of his dad working with Polanski.

Polanski initially wanted Matthau to play Red using a Bristol accent. In order to nail it, he watched tapes of BBC programming. Eventually, he concluded that "an authentic Bristol accent is going to sound like a bad Irish accent coming from a poor American actor." They settled on a Cockney accent.

"Anyway, I'm pretty good with accents," Matthau added, "and I've been doing Cockney jokes for forty years. Wanna hear one?" He then related a story about a cursing Cockney who is mistaken for the Archbishop of Canterbury.

Of the controversial, enigmatic Polanski, Matthau declared, "I actually enjoyed him with a ferocity that I didn't expect, and I especially enjoyed listening to him. He spoke five languages on the set—and threw tantrums in four. Of course we had disagreements. He called me names, I called him names. I think that overall the general feeling was like a meteoric love affair—wonderful, but you knew it'll never last." Matthau then paid Polanski a high compliment by adding, "I must admit I spent a great deal more time listening to him than I usually do to a director."

Matthau endured what turned out to be a ten-month-long shooting schedule by shipping over cans of salmon and peanut butter and boxes of crackers and cereal, along with "Trivial Pursuit and an assortment of baseball hats—all the essentials of life." For several days during the 1985 Christmas holiday, Jack and Felicia Lemmon visited Walter and Carol on location. Four months later, Lemmon was guest at a Museum of Broadcasting (later the Museum of Television & Radio) seminar. Invariably, he was asked to recount some "Walter Matthau stories." "If I told you what Walter was doing the last time I saw him, you wouldn't believe me," Lemmon responded. "Walter is now in his sixth month [on location]. He is two hours out of Tunis, Africa, surrounded on three sides by dirty, flat sand, and the ocean on the other. There is nothing to do there. I went there for four days, and I might as well have been put in Leavenworth." Lemmon then recounted a lengthy story involving a stir-crazy Matthau becoming fixated on scaling flat, brown rocks into the ocean. After two hours of this, his wife Carol informed him that his new toy was dried camel shit. "He hasn't been out on the beach since," Lemmon concluded. "I never saw a man so crestfallen in my life."

During the shoot, Matthau squared off against an especially nosy rat. "There was one scene where this rat was supposed to be gnawing away at my peg leg," Matthau recalled, "and they hired a rat-man from Paris who looked much like a large rat himself. Anyway, he put cheese in the leg to entice the rat, but it didn't work—the rat was far more interested in something else, and it kept crawling up my pants. At first I tried to ignore it, but in the end it just got to be too much, so I hauled it out by its tail and said in my best Jimmy Cagney voice, 'You dirty rat.' Of course, no one understood the joke, 'cause I was surrounded by Tunisians, Frenchmen, Poles, and Italians. Only Polanski laughed."

Pirates fell short of everyone's expectations, which Matthau freely admitted. "I could be more pleased than I am," he declared, of the end result. "I think the story lacks clarity, and I found that a little disconcerting."

In July 1986, Matthau appeared on *The Tonight Show* to plug

Pirates, which already was in release. "I have to remember to sit up straight, and I'm not supposed to twiddle my thumbs," he told host Johnny Carson. "And no toilet stories. . . . Toilet stories are out. . . . So shall I leave now?" Whether he realized it or not, it was virtually the same toilet-story line he had made four-and-a-half years earlier on the Carson show, while plugging *Buddy Buddy*.

Carson asked him if he ever wanted to be a pirate when he was a kid. "No. Never had any desire to be a pirate whatsoever," he responded. "Uh, maybe a St. Louis Cardinal." He described Tunisia as "maybe what Fresno was in 1283." He added, "I once asked for a chicken sandwich. They gave me a whole chicken between two pieces of bread. I mean, the gristle was there, the skin, the bones, everything. They didn't know about taking it out. It's a cultural shock, is what it is."

He reported that working with Polanski was "a snap, because he's much shorter than I am." However, unlike many a Hollywood star who proclaims his latest film is a diamond, even if it is only chipped glass, Matthau could not convince himself to extol the merits of *Pirates*. "Every frame is a piece of cinematic Rembrantian art," he mocked, "and the great notices we've gotten were all deserved." After Carson showed a clip, Matthau laid it on the line: "Did you ever see such rotten acting!"

Matthau followed *Pirates* with another foreign-made feature. He worked with Roberto Benigni, in what is his all-time least-known screen role: Father Maurice, a priest who exorcises the title character (played by Benigni) from the body of an overweight woman, in *Il piccolo diavolo* (*The Little Devil*).

Matthau accepted the part after Benigni flew in from Rome and acted out the script. The end result, released in 1988, was shot in Rome and environs. It was made in Italian and English, the latter in deference to Matthau and to benefit from the success Benigni had enjoyed speaking his brand of fractured English in Jim Jarmusch's arthouse hit, *Down By Law*. Matthau noted that he was speaking his dialogue in both languages, but was botching the Italian: "Today I was about to say my line, 'Finally we have enough time together,' but I goofed. It came out, 'Finally we have enough wind together.' The woman I was acting with couldn't stop laughing."

Despite his aversion to travel, Matthau loved being in Rome. "I just had this great dinner," he declared late one evening. "This is the best place in the world to eat. Any restaurant in Rome is a great place to eat. It's so hard to find a decent place to eat in America, especially in L.A. It's so hard to find a restaurant that cooks stuff you like. Last night, I had dinner on the street, and it was fantastic. They had fruit and cheese and cappoline and God almighty."

Matthau gave the name of his co-star as "Robert Bernini," whom he described as "quite a decent man, and a very good actor." He added, "I'm having a lot of fun. Is it a comedy? I think so. It's a morality play. But I find everything that's good to be funny. If it's good, it's funny. I laugh my head off when I see a good production of *Hamlet*."

Il piccolo diavolo became the highest-grossing film in Italian cinema history, due in part to Benigni's popularity in his homeland. However, in a commentary on Matthau's declining status as a big-money movie star, it never was released in the United States.

Around this time, Matthau was asked what he looked for in a potential role. "New challenges," he responded. "There has to be something about an offer that's appealing—either the script or the director or the location. Right now, I'm considering doing a part in a very ordinary script, but the role is appealing—it's an incompetent doctor." He jokingly added, "I've never seen one on the screen . . . but lots in real life." Matthau never did play the part.

He also passed on other, more celebrated films. "One may surprise you," noted Charlie Matthau. "It was *Dirty Harry*. That was not his kind of movie. It was not his cup of borscht, as he would say. Another was *10*, which he thought was too dirty." Matthau's take on these decisions: "I turned down a few roles that were big hits, but I never regretted it because what I said to myself was, 'There's something about this that you don't like, that you don't think you can handle, that you won't lend anything to.'" Borscht or matzoh balls aside, Matthau proved that he would have made a terrific Dirty Harry Callahan a year after the film was released, when he starred in another Don Siegel film, *Charley Varrick*. The characters were mirror images: a lawman capable of bending the rules, and a criminal with a moral code.

Then there were the roles he coveted, but failed to get. One was Salieri, in *Amadeus*. "That's the role that got away; that's the role that Walter wanted more than anything," explained Lana Morgan. Another desired part was the title role in *The Scout*. "He loved that script," added Charlie.

On a less serious note, if Kevin Spacey, who was mentored by Jack Lemmon, had any say, another Matthau-Lemmon co-starring effort might have been *Star Wars*. While appearing on *Saturday Night Live*, Spacey enacted Matthau screen-testing for the role of Obi Wan Kenobi, and Lemmon testing for Chewbacca.

Back in 1966, after the success of *The Fortune Cookie*, Matthau was Billy Wilder's first choice to star in an adaptation of Franz Lehar's *The Count of Luxembourg*, but the project fell through. So did what Matthau called an "offbeat, still-untitled comedy" by Bernard Gordon and Arnaud d'Usseau, to have been directed by Norman Lloyd, about a Madison Avenue advertising executive who backs a retired Air Force general for the United States presidency. So did *The Whitewash Conspiracy*, a presidential assassination drama. Matthau's role: a television commentator who becomes involved in the story.

In the late 1980s, he was set to star in a revised version of Garson Kanin's *Born Yesterday*, opposite Whoopi Goldberg. Matthau would have played Harry Brock, a bullying, up-by-his-bootstraps tycoon; Goldberg would have been Billie Dawn, Brock's uncouth mistress, a role made famous by comedienne Judy Holiday. "Gar had written another script for Walter and Whoopi to do," declared Marian Seldes. "It was a wonderful script, and [the project] even got so far as to have a full-page ad in *Variety*." Seldes recalled that "a pair of Israeli brothers" had purchased the rights. They were director-producer Menahem Golan and his cousin, Yoram Globus, the powers behind Cannon Films during the 1980s. In the trade ad, the now long-defunct Cannon is heralded as "The Company of the Future." "They didn't have the money for the picture," Seldes noted. "It was all talk, just talk. Eventually, they sold it to the people who [did] that dreadful remake of it." The 1993 redo featured John Goodman and Melanie Griffith. "There also was a plan for Walter and Bernadette Peters to do the [original] version, before Gar rewrote it," Seldes added.

Matthau was set to star in *Thanks Dad*, a Walter Bernstein–directed drama about a father-son relationship. However, the project was scuttled by a July 21–October 23 1980 Screen Actors Guild strike, during which SAG attempted to establish royalty payments for performers in the then-burgeoning video and cable TV industries. This issue might have little impact on a star like Matthau, but it was fundamental for working actors—and Matthau's liberal Democratic politics had him firmly on the side of the performers. He even joined them on the picket line outside the Warner Bros. studio.

Another failed project, to have been directed by Michael Ritchie, was titled *Mudshow*. It was set in the world of travelling tent shows. "The idea was for Walter to be this circus manager," Ritchie recalled, "but it never happened. There were so many [other projects]. Inevitably, when you write the history of the films that you made, you have to write four volumes on the ones that didn't get made."

CHAPTER 25

Personality

In their public personas, show business folks are notorious for being kissy-face. When they guest on talk shows or sit for interviews, their latest co-stars always are brilliant, wonderful, generous, kind: exemplary human beings.

Many who knew Matthau described him in such a manner. Yet the fact was that he could be just as ornery as sweet, just as crude as witty.

Matthau's wiseacre wit was a byproduct of his streetboy youth. If he did not like someone or something, he employed sarcasm and exaggeration. When he spoke of Tatum O'Neal, his "difficult" *Bad News Bears* co-star, he compared her acting style to that of Greta Garbo. While publicizing the film fiasco *Pirates*, he likened its images to those of Rembrandt. At the same time, when he described someone he truly admired, such as Jack Lemmon, Billy Wilder, or Carol Burnett, he also laid on the sarcasm, as if to parody the innate phoniness of show-biz puffery.

Of all his fans, Matthau's greatest is his son Charlie. "You know, my father is the nicest guy in the world," he once declared. "I know a lot of actors who, the moment the camera is turned off, become horrible human beings. Not my father. He's nice to everyone all the time."

In April and May 1954, Patty McCormack appeared on two live TV shows with Walter, "Atomic Attack" and "Last Date." That December, she opened on Broadway in *The Bad Seed*, cast as a murderous child. The show won raves, and ran for 334 performances. McCormack replayed the part in the 1956 screen version, and earned a Best Supporting Actress Oscar nomination. But the Matthau-McCormack connection transcends their working together. Years before, Walter and Henry played handball in Coney Island with McCormack's father, Frank Russo, who became a Brooklyn fireman.

By the 1960s, McCormack, like countless ex-child stars, could not find work. "I needed an agent," she noted. "I didn't realize the connection I had with Walter, but he always remembered that my dad was Frank Russo. Anyway, I was at a terrible age, very insecure. He set me up with his agent, Lenny Hirshan, who didn't want me. But he did set that up. It was very sweet of Walter. He was an excellent human being. And I learned from that. No matter where I'm at, if someone's in need, I turn him on to my guy."

In fall 1964, Matthau guested on the TV series *Dr. Kildare*. He then was preoccupied with negotiations for *The Odd Couple* on stage. "In the midst of all the turmoil," recalled Georgann Johnson, who played his wife on the show, "he was very good at his job and very thoughtful of me, offering to drive me from the hotel to the plane I was taking back to New York and my family when we were finished. I have always remembered how special and dear that was to me—a quality actors often lack. I was alone and probably taking the Red Eye after a long shoot. It was kind and caring, and a gesture I never forgot. He was the best."

Added Shirley Knight, who also worked with Matthau on television, "I remember seeing him once with Jack Lemmon at some event. I was very moved by the fact that he came straight over to me to say hello. I hadn't seen him for twelve years, but it was like I'd seen him yesterday. He was so effusive and loving and friendly. I introduced him to my children, who were with me, and he was equally charming."

After Matthau's death, his son Charlie received a letter from Susan Sarandon, in which she said that she lost her wallet while making *The Front Page*. "My father just peeled off a bunch of hundreds, gave them to her, and said, 'Here, you can pay me back when you become a famous star.' Yes, she paid him back." Yet Matthau was just as generous before becoming a million-dollar movie star. Back in 1952, Jane Lloyd-Jones, the wife of Heywood Hale Broun, was an understudy in *The Grey-Eyed People*. "She lost her bag on the way from New Haven to Philadelphia [during the show's out-of-town try-out]," Broun recalled. "Walter came over to us during rehearsal and said, 'I heard you lost your baggage.' He shook hands with her, and when she took her hand away, there was a $100 bill in it. I said 'It's all right, Walter,' and he said, 'No, no, come on, you'll need it for the little necessities.'

"I thought it was strange, generous, and rather like Walter."

In 1993, during a sub-zero Minnesota winter, Matthau filmed *Grumpy Old Men*. During the shooting of an outdoor wedding sequence, the crew was bundled up but the actors were in costume—and freezing. One was a tuxedo-clad Burgess Meredith, who was shaking from the cold. "Walter took his coat, and put it around Burgess," recalled Lana Morgan. "And Don [director Donald Petrie] said, 'Walter, no, we're about to shoot.' Well, Walter realizes that 'right away' is probably going to turn into fifteen or thirty minutes, maybe longer. But even if it's only two minutes, Walter is not going to let Burgess, who's like eighty years old, stand there and shiver. Never mind that Walter himself gets pneumonia easier than a cat gets fleas.

"So Walter keeps buttoning the coat, and the whole time he's bundling Burgess up all nice and snug he's growling and deflecting Donald with his grumpy humor. He was watching over Burgess, Jack [Lemmon] was watching over him, [and] they were all just growling and taking care of each other. It was so sweet."

Matthau's compassion extended beyond his peers. He noted, in the early 1960s, "I have a tremendous emotional reaction to social injustice and stupid behavior. I'm fascinated by the way a businessman, for example, will speak condescendingly to an elevator operator, or the way, if I walk into the grocery wearing shabby clothes, the clerk says to me, 'Whaddya want, Mac?' and if I wear a suit and tie, he says, 'Yes, sir?'"

"In a general sense," reported his son David, "I think that my father was a very wonderful person in many ways, very kind, very giving, very generous. And he always really cared about people who were less fortunate. He was aware of the fact that there was a great deal of inequity and lack of decency in society, and in many ways went out of his way to support causes to help people, to help different minority groups, [to help those] who needed help." In 1986, Matthau was one of the many guests on the first *Comic Relief* special, which raised money for the homeless. In his brief bit, he spoke about supporting the cause "in a world in which compassion is in short supply."

David added the following anecdote: "I remember once he was working [on location] on a film . . . and some hobo had wandered onto the set. Everybody was getting on line [at the catering truck] for food, and this homeless guy just sort of got into the line figuring, oh, this was a chow line or something. I don't remember if it was the security guy or not, but somebody came over to the guy and took his arm and said, 'Okay, let's go, Pop.' And my dad went over and said, 'Nah, it's okay, let's let him get some food.'

"If we were going down a street in New York and if anybody ever said he was hungry, [my dad] always gave him money. It was his pet peeve to not be disturbed in the middle of eating, but he'd very graciously give an autograph or say hello or shake hands or whatever. He was never nasty to people. He was always extremely kind and good-natured."

Anna Berger recalled that Walter's driver on a film shoot was a "young boy [who] was new on his job. He didn't know his way around so well, and the poor kid was nervous, so nervous picking up Matthau, this big star. So they got into the car, and Matthau must have sensed this guy was nervous. So Matthau said, 'I'll tell you what. Let's change seats.' And Matthau took the wheel.

"He could be very generous in his way, and also very kind in his way."

Matthau may have conjured up countless fibs about his background, but he never denied his roots. Throughout the years, he maintained contact with his Lower East Side pals. Surely, Murray Juvelier was speaking for many when he declared, "He was a wonderful host. Whoever came out to California, he treated them like they were people he'd just seen yesterday."

Unlike celebrities who treat "hired help" inconsiderately, Matthau respected the working person who served him. He was downright adored by the employees of the Beverly Hills Tennis Club. "He always knew the staff [member] names," noted Jean Longacre, the club's manager. "He never failed to greet whoever was in the office or dining room by name. Everyone just loved him dearly. I don't think there was a time he didn't walk through the dining room and fail to pick up and kiss a baby. I don't think there was a baby he didn't love. Also, one time he invited the staff to see one of his new movies." The film in question was *Pirates*. "I thought it would be in a theater, with a lot of people, but it was in a private viewing room. Only his family was present."

Longacre's workers echoed her adulation. "He was one of the best men in the club," noted Artoro Alfaro, who reported that Matthau often provided him with Lakers tickets. Each time Matthau came to the club, Alfaro greeted him by calling him "Mr. Dennis."

"Why do you call me Dennis?" Matthau asked. "You know my name is Walter."

"My son, he told me to call you Dennis because he really loved your movie *Dennis the Menace* [released in 1993]," Alfaro responded.

"Artoro, are you sure your son liked the movie?"

"Sure, I took him twice already to the theater."

A couple of days later, Matthau sent Alfaro an autographed picture, signed to the boy. "As soon as my son saw the picture," Alfaro added, "he almost cried because he couldn't believe it. I didn't ask him to do it. Believe me, he's one of the sweetest."

Added Beryl Richmond, "On two different occasions, I had relatives over from England who loved his movies. He came over to take photographs with them. He was laughing and joking with them. They couldn't believe it. Whenever I served him, he'd put an English accent on, a Yorkshire accent like mine. Every time he was in, no matter who was with him, you could bet that his table was always the one with the most laughs on."

Matthau's own hardscrabble youth left him with an affinity for children. He became fond of two child actors cast in *The Marriage Fool*, his 1998 television movie. "They didn't have any lines, but Walter was enthralled by them," explained Arlene Mazerolle, who played their mother. "He was teaching them jokes. He told me he loved working with kids. He loved doing *Dennis the Menace* because it allowed him to be around kids." Matthau also bonded with Maze-rolle's real-life son. "He was in a baby carrier, and it was at lunch. I wanted Walter to meet him and my husband. He hardly acknowl-edged my husband. He went right to Bobby and said something like, 'Didn't I meet you in the subway three weeks ago? I lent ya thirty-three cents.' What Walter said wasn't very funny. It was just the way he said it." Decades earlier, Matthau responded in a similar manner when Louis Guss brought his infant child to the set of *The Laughing Policeman*. "He held it in his arms," Guss recalled. "He was very nice."

Matthau was acutely aware of, and sympathetic to, young people who were outsiders. Joyce Van Patten, who played a supporting role in *The Bad News Bears*, recalled that he cultivated a relationship with one of the pint-sized cast members. "He seemed to have a special feeling for a little Mexican boy, George Gonzalez," she noted. "He was chubby and unsure of himself and Walter seemed to know this—a good guy's radar."

Matthau established a two-decades-long friendship with Kevin Day, a young man from Jackson, Mississippi, who is 90 percent deaf and mentally handicapped. In the late 1970s, Day, then in his late teens, sent Matthau a fan letter and received what his mother, Vir-ginia Adams, described as a nice little note written by a secretary. However, Day kept writing Matthau, who soon began sending back personal letters.

The two never met face-to-face. However, they almost did when Matthau was shooting *The Grass Harp* with his son Charlie in Wetumpka, Alabama, a six- to seven-hour drive from Kevin's home. Adams called Charlie's office to arrange for Kevin to meet Walter. The arrangements were made, but the date had to be cancelled because Carol's mother suffered a heart attack and the Matthau clan returned to New York. On the next-to-last day of filming, Adams received a call from the Matthau camp, asking if she and Kevin could show up the following day. "As it turned out, Walter was ill and was not on the set," she recalled. "But we did get to go and spend the day, and had a wonderful time.

"The point is that Walter didn't forget. And it made Kevin feel so special."

Adams has no idea why Matthau maintained the correspondence.

"To me, this was an extraordinarily compassionate man. This is not something you find a lot in the show business community. Kevin wrote fan letters to other [stars], and got curt replies from them. I don't know. All I can say is that Walter must have picked up on the fact that, being handicapped, this meant so much to Kevin.

"He was so kind to Kevin. He wrote wonderful, wonderful letters. Walter picked up on every little thought in every one of Kevin's letters, and would comment on them. He'd send many wonderful little items, and memorabilia from the places he filmed. We treasure them."

Matthau's letters are friendly and chatty. They comment on the content of Kevin's previous missives, acknowledge a birthday, or note a film project. Many are adorned with happy faces drawn by Matthau, which he often added to correspondence. (In February 1992, he was one of a roster of celebrities who donated their own original artwork for a Massachusetts College of Art fundraiser. His contribution was one of his happy faces, only with a frown instead of a smile. Beneath the scribble, he scrawled the words, "Can't Draw!")

If Matthau was kind to Kevin Day, he could be downright disagreeable to those who were not as vulnerable. As Charlie Matthau admitted, "He liked to embarrass people."

Of his propensity for telling tall tales, one who was fond of Matthau might react with a smiling, "Oh, that's Walter," or acknowledge that he was a "bullshit artist"—the words of his friend Ruby Ludwin—and still be his pal. Or, if one disliked Matthau, for whatever reason, one might harshly condemn the man as a fraud.

Back in 1971, journalist Joseph Gelmis offered a cogent analysis of Matthau when he wrote that the actor's humor "consists of equal parts bluster, abrasive insult, ineffectual villainy, and disarming candor. He is not a wit. He is blunt. In a business full of double-talk his straight talk is refreshing, if not really humorous. He makes up for his directness, however, by taking refuge in the put-on. That way he can have it both ways—be everything he can claim he is mocking." Gelmis also noted, "He can be crude and rude and sensitive at the same time."

As the years passed, a level of crustiness overtook him, a personality trait that enveloped him during the 1990s, the final decade of his life. Tact was not in his vocabulary. If he felt like acting impolite, or allowing his mind to drift while in conversation, he did just that. "Walter tackles people verbally when he first meets them," declared Jack Lemmon. "Often, he is insulting. It's almost as if he doesn't want people to like him." Observed Billy Wilder, "There are two Matthaus. One minute he can be Saint Francis of Assisi, and the next, very, very cantankerous and tough to work with."

In 1996, filmmaker Aviva Kempner interviewed Matthau for her documentary, *The Life and Times of Hank Greenberg*. "It was the funniest hour of my life interviewing him," Kempner recalled. While she was entertained, she also was subjected to Matthau's caustic wit. "He had his agent present," added Kempner, "and he kept on looking to him. I said, very meekly because this was, after all, Walter Matthau, 'Walter, do you mind looking at me?' Without missing a beat, he looked at me and said, 'Your husband has to look at you. I don't have to look at you.'"

To his credit, such cracks were not just reserved for non-celebrities. His son Charlie might be included in the joke. While on *The Tonight Show*, Matthau told guest-host Bob Newhart that he had to make an early exit because the young woman Charlie was dating had been raped. "She's in the hospital," he noted, "and she keeps calling my name." The audience hadn't stopped laughing when Matthau arose, and left the set. "If we were somewhere and there was a pretty girl," Charlie reported, "he would yell, 'Hey, you, would you like to sleep with my son?'

"[One time] we were at a party, and Marlon Brando, whom he admired, was there. And he said to Marlon, 'Hey, Marlon, how come you got so fat?' Marlon gave him a bewildered look, and walked away." While filming *Twilight Zone—The Movie*, released in 1983, director John Landis presided over an accidental helicopter crash that killed actor Vic Morrow and two Vietnamese child actors, for which Landis was admonished for "reckless endangerment." "One time we were at a dinner party," recalled Charlie, "and we were sitting next to Landis, and all of a sudden [my father] said, 'So, why'd you kill those kids with that helicopter?' He didn't do it to be mean. He did it to be shocking.

"One time my mother took him to see her friend Claire Bloom, and she told him, 'Whatever you say, don't say anything about her moustache. She's really self-conscious about it.' So of course as soon as they sat down, my father started staring at her upper lip. She said, 'Why are you staring at me?' And he turned to my mother and said, 'Carol, she doesn't have a moustache. What are you talking about?'"

With typical wit, Matthau once acknowledged his irascibility and generosity by noting, "I am not a humble man. I am occasionally lovable and always totally impossible. Not psychologically speaking but figuratively speaking. I have a good heart. In my house we serve large portions. . . . I like people, even schmucks. When they become too terrible or boring, I make up stories which amuse me.

"I don't want very much in life. I have everything that I ever wanted: a washer-dryer, a transistor cassette recorder."

CHAPTER 26

A Star Is Reborn

In the 1980s, Matthau did not have a critical or commercial success that ranked with *The Fortune Cookie*, *The Odd Couple*, or *The Sunshine Boys*. By the early 1990s, he was an aging, fading star, in a fast-changing world that was reflected on screen. The kinds of substantive characters he played in films as diverse as *Pete 'n' Tillie*, *Charley Varrick*, and *The Sunshine Boys* were becoming increasingly rare in mainstream movies.

A decade earlier, while publicizing *House Calls* and *Casey's Shadow*, Matthau observed that, "as an actor, you can enlighten the human mind." Then he smiled, and added, "Although not with most of the stuff produced today." He also squeezed humor out of the situation, noting, "I don't shy away from violence and explicit sex if the part calls for it. Hell, I would do Macbeth stark naked if it was necessary. I think we'd have a little trouble with some of the Shakespeare soliloquies, like 'Is this a dagger which I see before me?'"

Matthau's pragmatic side surfaced when he explained, "As much as I like to do stuff that is literate and bright and worthwhile and has some merit to it, I like the fact that the pictures make money. That appeals to me. We are living in a society in which we count our blessings with how much we have made." Yet this did not prevent him from complaining about the state of current cinema. In 1989, he declared, "My taste is to do stories about people, interpersonal relationships, [but] they are considered too dull at the studios today. They want squealing tires, gunshots, or extra-terrestrials." Then he hit on another truism: "It's hard to find a decent part for a fellow like myself, a craggy American with a face like a melting bullfrog." This situation presented Matthau with an additional dilemma. As his son Charlie admitted, "He was having trouble getting his price in movies."

The dearth of quality scenarios was never more apparent than when, in the late 1980s, Richard Benjamin came to him with a script he wished to direct. He wanted Matthau as his star. After reading it, the two met for lunch at the Beverly Hills Tennis Club. "Now the script I'd sent him was pretty clean," Benjamin recalled. "What I saw was something that looked like it had been dragged through the Hundred Years War. It had every kind of bend and turn and hand-fingering; you couldn't get a prop to look like this. And he had gone through that script with underlines. He had corrected everything, including the English. He said, 'Now I'm not going to be doing this, but here's what's wrong with it.' By the end, I thought, 'I don't think I better do this.'" The film was never made.

Matthau's cynicism regarding the "art" of moviemaking was summed up, in his own inimitable way, when he and Jack Lemmon co-presented the Best Director Academy Award in 1982. Before listing the nominees, Matthau explained, "Some directors are short and some are tall. Some are old and some are young. There are American directors, French, Czechoslovakian, and English directors, et cetera. There are directors who know everything about human behavior and nothing about the camera. There are directors who know camera angles, camera lenses, camera sprockets, and depth of focus, but who are totally ignorant of the human condition."

So, like many an aging movie star, Matthau began appearing in television movies. He starred in a trio—*The Incident*, *Against Her Will: An Incident in Baltimore*, and *Incident in a Small Town*, which aired in 1991, 1992, and 1994—in which he played Harmon Cobb, a small-time, small-town lawyer whose best pals are Jim Beam and Jack Daniels.

Matthau had high hopes for the first, which was directed by Joseph Sargent and originally titled *Incident at Lincoln Bluff*. The year is 1944, the setting Lincoln Bluff, Colorado. German prisoners-of-war are camped nearby and Cobb, a World War I veteran, is reluctantly recruited by a federal judge (Harry Morgan) to defend a POW who has been charged with murdering Old Doc Hansen (Barnard Hughes). Cobb discovers the POW was framed, realizes the trial is a charade, and uncovers a conspiracy to conceal the murder of at least one prisoner.

"The theme of the piece is that Americans believe in justice and will follow through regardless of prejudice or the consequences," Matthau explained during the filming. "The lawyer isn't noble. He's simply doing his job as an American." He added that such a serious-minded scenario would not cut it on the big screen. "They seem to be doing more quality movies about the human condition for TV," he said. "I'd rather sit in front of a TV and watch drama than go to a theater and see most of the stuff that passes for drama. And comedy isn't what it was. Today, the main objective is to make the audience laugh. I don't agree with that. The real objective of any project is to tell a story. The laughter is gravy if it's a comedy. Don't go for the laugh. Go for the story."

Years later, Joseph Sargent reported that Matthau was genuinely taken by the story. "He saw its importance," the director explained, "and it was a chance for him to remind the world that he was more than just a comic. A lot of people had forgotten that. And I think he was tickled by the fact that he was being paid $1 million for it. So it was a triple whammy for him."

Robert Carradine appeared in *The Incident* as Cobb's courtroom adversary. "I remember we had one pretty good-sized scene," Carradine noted. "I'm dressing him down about how I'm going to kick his ass in the courtroom. I'll never forget the way he looked at me. Especially during my close-up, he was really good off-camera; he looked like he was looking right through me. His intensity and professionalism were awesome.

"When we were on location in Colorado Springs," Carradine added, "I once was getting my makeup done and he was chatting up my wife, who is a beautiful blonde. He was telling her how I reminded him of himself when he was my age. She was like, 'Really,' and he said, 'Yeah. He's an arrogant prick.' I said, 'Well, thank you, Walter.' That one really stuck. I never considered myself an arrogant prick, but I think Walter was finding an excuse to talk to my wife Edie. I was playing an arrogant prick in the show, a know-it-all lawyer."

As was often the case, Carol joined Walter on the set. They and the Carradines dined together, during which, as Carradine recalled, Matthau regaled them with stories. Meanwhile, Sargent described an unusual Walter-Carol pact: "If Walter spent $10,000 on a bet and lost, then Carol would go out and buy $10,000 worth of merchandise. This one Saturday, he lost $18,000 on a couple of games. Carol and my wife went shopping, and Carol just pulled out sweaters and skirts that she liked, and some antiques. She went from shop to shop, until she spent $18,000.

"And they were even. It was like a scene out of *Breakfast at Tiffanys*."

The Incident was a critical and ratings hit, and won an Emmy Award as Outstanding Drama/Comedy Special. However, Matthau was not nominated, and Sargent reported that "it was a disappointment for him. We assumed that if the picture was going to get nominated, and I was nominated, then Walter would be too. But for some reason, he wasn't."

The sequels, both directed by Delbert Mann, featured the further exploits of Cobb. While publicizing the second with Harry Morgan, he was asked what made Morgan such a great actor. Matthau's response was a left-handed compliment at best: "I kept thinking he's Jack Lemmon, and then I look up and he's Harry Morgan." If Matthau was proud of *The Incident*, he was unimpressed with the last, describing it as "a good way to kill a couple of hours."

At this point, with regard to starring in feature films, age was Matthau's greatest handicap. Who in Hollywood over the age of seventy could call himself a star? Sure, there were dozens of elderly Hollywood icons who were the focal points of tributes and awards ceremonies, but were they working? Not often, and not in starring roles. If they were headlining a production, it likely would be at a dinner theater. Imagine, Gloria Stuart, the aged 1930s movie queen who made a brief splash in 1997 in *Titanic*, believably playing a 101-year-old woman, was only a scant ten years older than Matthau!

In any case, it was important to Matthau to continue working. Like many immigrant offspring, he developed a work ethic early on in his life. As a child, he hawked refreshments in Second Avenue theaters; as a senior citizen, he was determined to keep appearing in movies—and refused to ease his schedule. He reflected his ghetto roots, and the fears of many who grow up in poverty and attain a modicum of material success, by noting, "I get tired of not working and scared of not working—so I work."

In the early 1990s, it was suggested to him that he consider retirement. "That word is alien to my vocabulary," Matthau retorted. "Retire to what? I'm doing the work I like." On another occasion, he bellowed, "I like the idea of working. I don't like the idea of getting up at six in the morning, but I like working." Money was another motivation for keeping employed. "What I make," he noted, "my wife can spend in a week." He reported that his salary for *Grumpy Old Men*, one of his biggest 1990s hits, was a cool $3 million: "You know how long that lasts? Six months. Money is flowing like Niagara Falls into the shithouse. And if I get lucky, I'll die before I go broke."

Before the decade was out—and despite his face being more hangdog than ever—Matthau resurfaced as a hot box-office commodity. He appeared in a string of comedies that appealed to viewers of his own generation while making his kisser familiar to those who were young enough to be his grandchildren.

Matthau's first 1990s hit strictly appealed to youngsters: *Dennis the Menace*, a 1993 adaptation of the Hank Ketcham comic strip. Matthau played Mr. Wilson, the grumpy old nemesis of the tiny title character. "When they offered me the part," Matthau recalled, "I said 'I thought Mr. Wilson was fat, short and bald.' It didn't matter. They also wanted to make it a musical, even though I can't sing. People laugh when I sing. So they dropped that idea."

Despite his occasional singing role—Nathan Detroit in *Guys and Dolls* and Horace Vandergelder in *Hello, Dolly!*—Matthau was not exaggerating when he chided his singing voice. In 1986, at the American Film Institute Life Achievement Award ceremony, he sang a portion of his tribute to honoree Billy Wilder. The *Boston Globe's*

Michael Blowen dubbed the actor's warbling "what may be the worst vocal performance in the history of television."

Singing or no singing, Matthau initially was reluctant to play Mr. Wilson. He felt the script was silly and cartoonish, but accepted the role on the advice of his son Charlie. During the shoot, he was visited on the set by his older son David and six-year-old grandson, Willie. "[Willie] never really talked about Grandpa being famous, or Grandpa being in the movies," David recalled. "Coming back on the plane, the stewardess came by to see, you know, what we would like to drink. And my son said to the stewardess, 'My grandpa's Walter Matthau!' She said, 'Oh, really, isn't that wonderful!' She was very sweet."

After the film's release, Matthau and Charlie were accosted by a young boy who had recognized "Mr. Wilson." The child ecstatically began repeating the character's name, and asked the actor for an autograph. Matthau complied. Then the boy blurted out, "You were really good. Was that your first movie?"

A sequel to *Dennis* was contemplated. "They made me sign for it before the first one," Matthau noted. "That's to prevent me from becoming another Macaulay Culkin, asking for $8 million." However, the actor was so irked by the lack of quality of the script that he pulled out. "The script I saw for *Dennis II* was junk," he bellowed. "The first film wasn't much to start with, but the second one was like lemon meringue pie with so much meringue that it was sickening." That film, titled *Dennis the Menace Rides Again*, eventually was made as a direct-to-video feature. Don Rickles played Mr. Wilson.

The following year, Matthau had one of his most unusual roles in *I.Q.*, a romantic comedy. He played Albert Einstein and, in makeup, his resemblance to the theoretical physicist was uncanny. The scenario had Einstein acting as matchmaker for his fictional niece (Meg Ryan), a brilliant mathematician, and a garage mechanic (Tim Robbins). Matthau towered over Einstein by six inches and, during the shoot, fellow cast member Joseph Maher asked him, "Can you play Einstein a little shorter?" "Played him shorter," Matthau reported. "Somehow Einstein being six-foot-two is not right." While filming on location in Princeton, New Jersey, where Einstein lived for over two decades, Matthau was besieged by hoards of youngsters clamoring for his autograph—and calling him "Mr. Wiiiiiiilson."

Gene Saks appeared in a supporting role. Decades before, the two ate lunch while sitting on a curb on West 48th Street, outside the New School Dramatic Workshop. Now, while shooting in Princeton, they dined in a similar manner and Matthau joked, "Well, here we are fifty years later, still out on the street."

Matthau presented a photo of himself as Einstein to Howard Morris, who described it as "something else." He also sent one to his penpal Kevin Day. He autographed it "To my pal Kevin from Professor Albert Einstein, sometimes known as Walter Matthau." He also wrote Day, "Everything went well with *I.Q.* except the temperature was too high, the humidity was too high—Every day we got a new script. It was very exciting!!!"

For years, Matthau's Pacific Palisades residence housed all the antiques and career memorabilia he and Carol collected. "I used to visit him once in a while up in his museum of a house," noted Morris. Sadly, in January 1995, most of their possessions were destroyed in the Los Angeles–Northridge earthquake. "Forty years of collecting, smashed to pieces," Matthau exclaimed. He added, "I got an award once, the Jack Oakie Award. And Mrs. Jack Oakie said to me, 'You know, that award cost $5,000 to make, Walter, so take good care of it.' [The award was] smashed to smithereens. [My] Oscar survived. Those cost about $7."

Matthau's final serio-comic role came in 1996. In Herb Gardner's adaptation of his play, *I'm Not Rappaport*, he played a character who might have been modeled after himself: Nat Moyer, a Jewish philosopher, radical, and cranky codger who recoils at the idea of relinquishing his independence and tells tall tales about his past.

Gardner was an old friend, and he originally hoped Matthau would play Moyer on stage. "Are you crazy?" was the actor's reaction. "I'm not going to learn all those lines. You got me talking for ten to fifteen minutes without a stop. You do it as a movie, I'll do it." Matthau had the play on his mind early in 1994, while being interviewed with Harry Morgan. Responding to a comment that he and Morgan enjoyed a great rapport, Matthau declared, "That word is not *rapport*. It is *rappaport*. We have a great rappaport together."

His co-star, playing a partially blind apartment house super, was Ossie Davis, with whom Matthau had appeared in the 1955 City

Center revival of *The Wisteria Trees*. "They didn't want Ossie Davis, he was my choice," Matthau explained. "They had gotten Lou Gossett, and he was much too young." Matthau then obliquely referred to Herb Gardner when he noted, "The director, who was also the writer, the fool . . . I told him not to direct his own picture that he wrote. He saw Ossie do it on the road and thought he was too bland, but that was ridiculous.

"He wanted electrical sparks like Cleavon Little had on Broadway. It depends on who plays the other part. Ossie was perfect for me because I liked him, and it was believable that I would sit on a park bench and spend the whole day arguing with him. It was a believable possibility." Because Matthau was Matthau—without him and his star power, there likely would have been no screen version of *I'm Not Rappaport*—his casting wish was granted. Added to the mix was his willingness to act in the film for what his son Charlie described as very little money.

During the decade, Davis also supported Matthau and Jack Lemmon in their comedy, *Grumpy Old Men*. He described working with Matthau after so many years as being "like old home week, like getting together with an [old friend]." During the *Rappaport* shoot, the two retired to Matthau's trailer where they listened to Paul Robeson records and recalled the old days. Davis noted, "We talked about what had happened to him over the years, and what had happened to me, and what had become of some of the people and institutions we had known—how things had changed. We were two people looking back at life, and laughing at what we saw, and laughing at our own behavior."

The film was partially shot on location in New York's Central Park. "Walter was pissed one day in the park, because the planes were flying overhead," Davis added. "He had these nice, long speeches, you know, set pieces that he had to do, and in the very middle of it these planes would fly overhead. After a while, he began to take it personally."

Publicist Murray Weissman recalled that, during a press conference prior to the film's release, Matthau "questioned his agent on why he [didn't] get more Oscar-winning parts, like the one given Geoffrey Rush for *Shine*, and then demonstrated how he could perform the same kind of part by stuttering and mumbling and making guttural sounds." Nevertheless, *I'm Not Rappaport* was something different: an ambitious and thoughtful film that allowed Matthau to play a offbeat character.

Matthau's most memorable films of the decade, however—the ones that secured his late-career popularity—reunited him with Jack Lemmon. They co-starred in a series of light, broad comedies, playing comically bickering senior citizens, seventy-something versions of Oscar and Felix. The first was *Grumpy Old Men*, released six months after *Dennis the Menace*.

Actually, the initial 1990s film featuring Matthau and Lemmon was *JFK*, Oliver Stone's high-profile, star-laden 1991 Kennedy assassination fantasy, but the actors did not share scenes. Toplining was Kevin Costner, playing New Orleans District Attorney Jim Garrison, who becomes obsessed with uncovering the truth about the assassination. Matthau played Louisiana senator Russell Long, who briefly chats about the assassination with Garrison on board a plane. "The most interesting part about making that picture was, I had never seen Kevin Costner before, because I'm not a movie-goer," Matthau recalled. "So we were shooting the scene on the airplane, and they had him sitting next to me, but I thought he was a stand-in. So, I said to him, trying to be pleasant, 'Do you live in New Orleans?' He looked at me and said, 'No, I live in L.A.' He was so indignant that I realized it had to be Kevin Costner. [So] I turned around and said, 'KEVIN, how are you? Are you happy?'—hitting his name very hard, to let him know I knew who he was.

"I had enough on my mind during that scene," he continued. "I had twelve speech teachers watching me. All the other passengers on the airplane were speech teachers and every time I got [the Louisiana accent] wrong, one of the speech teachers would jump up and correct it. Finally, it came out okay. But I think I sounded like Andy Griffith."

Grumpy Old Men was Matthau and Lemmon's first co-starring comedy in twelve years, since *Buddy Buddy*. Initially, Lemmon wanted to do the film, but Matthau balked. His son Charlie, who by now was a trusted adviser, talked him into doing it. "In the last ten years of his life, he relied more on me," Charlie reported. "I think he always felt he was better at judging a play; he'd go by the dialogue. He was not as comfortable reading a script, or visualizing something on the screen. [With him], it was 'What's the script? When is it starting? How much?' That kind of thing. He didn't like the development process."

Regarding *Grumpy Old Men*, Charlie felt it a perfect vehicle for his father and Lemmon. He began hyping its virtues to Walter on a Friday evening. Matthau's response: "Stop it, Charlie. I read that script, and it's a piece of shit. And you have the worst taste. I can't believe I raised such a schmuck." Finally, on Sunday at about 4 P.M., he relented, declaring, "Alright, I'll do it, but leave me alone." "Dad was definitely shocked when it became a hit," Charlie concluded.

Matthau and Lemmon played Max Goldman and John Gustafson, Minnesota neighbors who have been feuding for five decades, yet cannot even recall why. Perhaps it is because both are ferociously competitive ice fishermen. In any case, their bickering reaches a crescendo when a beautiful woman (Ann-Margret) moves into their community. At first, Matthau claimed that he wanted to play Gustafson, allowing Lemmon to "be the Jewish guy, 'cause I figured . . . the Christians get the girl and the Jews are funny so I thought it would be a good idea if we switched parts. But they refused. It was like when we were first doing *The Odd Couple* on Broadway."

Of the success of *Grumpy Old Men*—it took in more than $70 million in domestic box office, plus $50 million outside the United States—Matthau observed that "it made me, if you'll pardon the expression, hot. I'm now a hot old actor. I had no idea it would be grabbed by the public with such voracity." He then noted, with characteristic sarcasm, "You'd think if they had any guts or class, they'd give me some of that money." In explaining the film's success, he added, "Maybe they got tired of all the dinosaurs screwing. You get a couple of dinosaurs screwing, it should be good for $100 million." Matthau also reported that he received twenty times more fan letters about *Grumpy Old Men* than on any other film. Their content: "My father was just like you." "My grandfather was just like you." "My uncle Willie is just like you."

Grumpy Old Men was followed by a 1995 sequel, *Grumpier Old*

Men. Matthau and Lemmon's co-star was Sophia Loren, playing a five-times-wed seductress who wishes to transform a bait shop into an Italian restaurant. Of Loren, Matthau remarked, "I met her about twenty years ago. This was the first time I worked with her. She was so talented. Not badly built, either."

Like its predecessor, *Grumpier Old Men* was a box-office smash. "I think without any question the two *Grumpys* were a tremendous shot in the arm for both Walter and me," Lemmon noted. "Not that we had to make ourselves felt as actors, but just the fact that at this point in our lives people would give us romantic leads—even though they are character parts, thank God. But it also is a shot in the arm for the industry, because it made the industry wake up and realize that there is a vast market for these kinds of films. In which older people are romantically involved."

For a while, a second sequel was planned, to be set in Italy and pair Matthau and Lemmon with Loren and Ann-Margret. The budget spiraled out of control, a suitable script never was completed—Matthau declared that he would not appear in the likes of *Grumpy Old Men Work for the CIA*—and the film never was made. Instead, they co-starred in *Out to Sea*, a 1997 comedy featuring Matthau as Charlie Gordon, a gambler who becomes a luxury liner dance host. Lemmon played Herb, his widowed brother-in-law. During the course of the story, both characters dally romantically, Charlie with sexy Liz (Dyan Cannon) and Herb with forlorn Vivian (Gloria DeHaven).

In one sequence, Charlie bets the ponies at the Santa Anita racetrack while attempting to dodge his bookie, to whom he is $4,000 in debt. Milt Berger, Matthau's Lower East Side neighbor, who works in films as an extra, was hired as background for this sequence. He did not want to make a show of knowing Matthau, but eventually was placed up front, by the betting window. "Walter turned around and saw me," Berger explained, "and he said, 'Stop the cameras.' The director was stunned, and asked, 'What is it?' Walter said, 'See the guy over there. That's Milton Berger. I haven't seen him since he was six years old.' The joke is that, ever since I'd been living in California, which was about ten years, I'd see Walter every couple of months. He'd invite me and my sister Anna and my niece to join him at the

Beverly Hills Tennis Club. We'd have four-hour lunches, and talk about old times. He'd seen me just two weeks earlier."

As originally written, Charlie Gordon was a dance host. "I'm a lousy dancer, always have been. It's impossible for me to learn, never could," Matthau declared. He reported that, sixty odd years before, "some girl" attempted to teach him. "She was well-proportioned and very animated. She disturbed me physically, so I ran away and threw up. Ever since then, your honor, I cannot dance." So the character was switched to a gambler who fakes his way into becoming a dance host.

While shooting the film, Matthau's character was called upon to refer to an off-camera no-goodnik named "No-Neck." To spice up the dialogue, he ad-libbed "No-Neck O'Brien." Director Martha Coolidge delicately attempted to guide Matthau back to the original dialogue. Perhaps there was a real-life "No-Neck O'Brien" who would dislike being cited in such a disparaging manner and sue the moviemakers. This resulted in a discussion among cast and crew of the world's most common surnames.

"You know what the most common name in the world is?" Matthau stated. "Chang. There's 1.2 million Changs in the world."

"What about Jones?" one of the crew queried. "That's a common name."

"Only in the National Football League," Matthau responded. Then he segued into a discourse on a subject he knew well: Immigrants in America, and their unconventional application of the English language. He ended with a quip about a man who has romantic relations with a virgin midget.

Upon returning to the set, Coolidge elicited assurance that Matthau would desist from uttering "No-Neck O'Brien." The cameras began rolling, and Matthau called the character "No-Neck Chang."

Matthau was not finished with his naughtiness. He looked towards Coolidge and declared, "Jeez, was that me [messing] up all the dialogue?" with all the innocence of an eight-year-old caught with his hand in a cookie jar.

Twentieth Century-Fox, which released *Out to Sea*, had on its docket another ocean-going film scheduled for summer 1997: *Titanic*, projected as a blockbuster. Meanwhile, *Out to Sea* would be a nice little comedy for the aging parents of Baby Boomers. When the *Titanic* postproduction took longer than expected, the studio repositioned *Out to Sea* from a late-May release to June 27, the advantageous, upcoming holiday-weekend date for which *Titanic* was scheduled.

Once again, Matthau was thinking of special effects–laden films like *Titanic* when he quipped, "I suggested that, in this picture, they add a scene of two dinosaurs playing poker with us, then making love. [The studio] thought it was a good idea, but they didn't think they could really fit it into the picture.

"I saw *Out to Sea* the other day with a small audience, and it seemed rather dull to me. But I can understand that it could be a success at the box office because it has music in it and jokes in it. It's not too believable: it's a nice film to fall asleep in. And it has some interpersonal relationships, instead of dinosaurs and explosions and hot sex with Julia Moore and Demi Roberts.

"We'd probably make more money, though, if we had two dinosaurs in *Out to Sea*."

To Hollywood's way of thinking, they had just that!

CHAPTER 27

The Return of Oscar and Felix

In 1991, Matthau and Neil Simon discussed making an *Odd Couple* follow-up. The pair met over lunch at the Beverly Hills Tennis Club, and the actor queried the writer about the sequel. Apparently, Simon already had been pondering the idea. At the core of the story would be a reunion between Oscar and Felix when the former's son marries the latter's daughter.

"There may be an *Odd Couple II*," Matthau declared in the early 1990s. "We all sat around and Simon was throwing out ideas and I was throwing out ideas and Simon said, 'If you would just shut up I would have the first act written already.' Actually, I think he's got fifty pages written already."

Simon, in fact, began penning the sequel in 1988. He wrote thirty-eight pages, to see if the premise would work, and then moved on to other projects. His conversation with Matthau revived it, yet *The Odd Couple II* did not go into production until 1997. It had been delayed because Simon and Paramount Pictures, the film's producer, could not agree on a deal. In the meantime, the success of *Grumpy Old Men* reestablished Matthau and Lemmon as a box-office force.

In *The Odd Couple II*, Oscar has left New York and his beloved Mets for Sarasota, Florida, where he covers minor league baseball and plays poker, albeit with a cadre of widows. Felix has gone through three more marriages, with his neat-freak habits and sinus condition having driven three more women batty. They meet at a California airport and set out on a road trip to their childrens' wedding. (Matthau conjured up an intriguing plot twist: Oscar dies at the beginning of the film, and returns as a ghost to torment Felix.) Before filming began, Matthau expressed apprehension about replaying Oscar, and wondered if all the effort that would go into the production would result in a funny film.

If Matthau disliked working in icy Minnesota while making *Grumpy Old Men*, he was as equally against filming *The Odd Couple II* in scorching Central California. "I told the director I won't work in the heat," he declared, "and when we got there, it was ninety-seven degrees—with a hot wind." But not all the filming was unpleasant. "I remember one moment, which was wonderful," recalled Ellen Geer, who had a supporting role. "We were sitting around a table with a bunch of extras, while we were filming the wedding scene. We all were playing a game; someone would sing a lyric from an opera, and all the players would have to guess the source. Walter of course won all the time."

Another cast member was Joanna Sanchez, the daughter of Anna Berger. "We had so much fun [during the shoot]," she recalled. "We always were kidding around. I'd call him up and say, 'This is Senorita Sanchez.' He'd call me 'Senorita,' or '*Tchotchkeleh*.' He was very sweet to me. I loved him a lot."

Prior to the film's release, Lemmon put forth the appropriate spin, asserting that Simon's screenplay was "funnier and more touching than the first, and how often can you say that about a sequel?" He labeled it the second best comic script he ever read, after Billy Wilder and I. A. L. Diamond's *Some Like It Hot*.

"Oh, he's full of shit," Matthau retorted. But he did get into the spirit of hype when he noted, "The writing on this one is much funnier [than the original]" and, with regard to Simon, "I talk the way he writes, and he writes the way I talk."

Unfortunately, those anticipating the magic of the original were disappointed. Many of the reviews were scathing. Among the more colorful comments: ". . . the script is so lousy it seems as if it were slapped together by no-talent Pauly Shore" and ". . . [it's] a dispiriting, flavorless travesty, the equivalent of moldy tofu mystery meat and rancid skim milk." Box office–wise, *Odd Couple II* was the least successful of the 1990s Matthau-Lemmon comedies.

While publicizing the film, Lemmon suggested that a second sequel might be in the works. "He says we're doing number three," Matthau barked. "That's as true as me telling you I had an affair with Marilyn Monroe."

Matthau was right. *The Odd Couple II* was his and Lemmon's final film together. It was an uninspired swan song to the great Matthau-Lemmon collaboration.

After all the decades, the duo had not tired of working with each other. "Walter says that it's gene makeup, that he has X-42 and I have X-41, and that combination is terrific," Lemmon declared in 1996. "Whatever it is, there's a chemistry there, but I don't think anybody knows how to define it, frankly. Except that we are on the same wavelength, obviously. And we think the same, usually, which helps."

Matthau's explanation for his being in sync with Lemmon was typically tongue-in-cheek: "Well, we're both gay, you know." One could imagine the tabloids feasting on this "admission." "It's easy to work with Lemmon," Matthau added, "because he's bright, he's perceptive. . . . It's nice, it's pleasant to go to work and know you're not going to run into a stone wall. He's a short, ugly fellow and I'm tall and handsome, so [we're] a good counterpoint for each other."

During the *Grumpy Old Men* filming in Minnesota, rumor had it that the pair had had a falling out. "All lies," Matthau declared. "We were roommates. We had five rooms on the top floor of the Whitney Hotel. It was the penthouse, overlooking the Mississippi River and some abandoned buildings. Actually, the place looked a little bit like I imagined what Auschwitz would have looked like. But we loved it. Sometimes we insulted each other a little, just for fun. That's what the guys do in this picture. They insult each other because they love each other. They don't know how to express love, so they call each other obscenities and profanities."

The Matthau and Lemmon suite was the site of an unusual Oscar party. "Right after the picture started, the [1992] nominations came out," recalled Lana Morgan. "Jack had done *Glengarry Glen Ross* that year. He loved that role, and really put himself into it, and felt it was one of the best pieces of work he had ever done. Of course, it feels good if your peers acknowledge you for the stuff that you feel you did well. So I think he was kind of disappointed that he did not win a nomination. Walter was worrying about Jack, and wanted to cheer him up. So he just made a few indirect smart-ass comments about the awards. Like the whole thing wasn't important."

Matthau and Lemmon invited a small group to the suite to watch the show on television. "When I walked in there," Morgan continued, "it totally felt like the *Odd Couple* apartment. There was something about the energy, the whole layout. But what really got me was how Walter and Jack were in reality behaving in the reverse of the characters they played. Sitting right in front of the TV was Jack, in this big ugly chair. It was such an 'Oscar Madison' sort of chair. And Jack was sitting there and watching the pre-arrival [coverage] as if it were a sporting event. His reactions were boisterous."

Morgan made her way into what she described as an adjoining kitchenette area. "And there was Walter, fussing over the buffet. It was really just casual deli food, but beautifully presented. It looked ready, but Walter was still tweaking and adjusting to make sure it was 'just right.' Everything was color-coordinated, with matching plates and cups, and a flower arrangement that was an extension of the colors. The napkins were arranged all symmetrically.

"The funniest part was that Walter was having this big 'pickle drama.' Apparently the deli put the wrong ones in his orders. He was calling around trying to find the 'right' pickles. It reminded me of the line in *The Odd Couple* where Jack as Felix is mortified that Oscar can't make the distinction between spaghetti and linguini. Well, Walter just had to get this very specific type of pickles. Even though I doubt anyone but he would have known the difference, I think he was convinced that if he didn't have the right pickles it would just ruin his whole buffet. He was so totally Felix! I was just cracking up."

Morgan observed that Lemmon was oblivious to his pal's predicament. With beer in hand, he laughed and waved when someone he knew appeared on-camera. "Meanwhile, Walter was missing all this, and Jack was yelling at him, 'Waltz, Waltz, get in here. Quit fussing with the food!'"

On this occasion, Morgan first grasped the intensity of Matthau's gambling. "I didn't realize you could call Las Vegas or your bookie or wherever and place big money on the Oscar race," she said. "I remember Walter making a comment that he had wagered money on the Oscars. So as we were watching the television, I wasn't sure if he thought he was watching an awards show or a horserace. Come to think of it, maybe the big buffet fiasco wasn't about pickles. For all I know, Walter was placing last-minute bets. Who knows, maybe his bookie's name is Pickles."

Gambling remained a vice with Matthau to the end of his days, but at this stage of his life another bad habit was creeping into his personality: a growing emphasis on sex in his humor. "He would pinch tushies and say things," reported Charlie Matthau. "He liked to shock people." Added Robert Carradine, "He really had something to say to everybody—especially the female members of the crew. He was a flirt, but it was all bark and no bite." Of his come-ons, Lana Morgan noted, "I saw it as being an icebreaker. But he never meant to offend. He knew when to be that way, and when not to be—and that's why he would constantly tell everybody about Carol."

In 1994, Matthau asked a female journalist, "Do you like kinky sex?" before noting, "You'll notice that I am preoccupied with sex. That's because I'm seventy-four years old. I figure if I'm going to die soon, I might as well talk about an interesting subject." During their conversation, he asked if she could spell the word "titillate." Two years later, he joked that only when he saw "girls" was he afflicted with a severe case of wandering hands. "You know, when you reach seventy-six, you develop a hand problem—among other things." Of Martha Coolidge, his *Out to Sea* director, he quipped, "Never noticed she was female, until one day when I grabbed her by the chest and then I said, 'Oh, excuse me, forgot you were female.'" (During this same conversation, he declared that "the best actors in the world are hermaphrodite Catholics.") The following year, while publicizing *Odd Couple II*, he eyed an attractive female journalist, sat down next to her, and asked, "So, when's the last time you had sex?" "Too long," she responded. "Well," he retorted, as he beckoned her closer, "as long as you're clean." Around this time he noted, "Women sense my passion. It's a basic animal thing. In their eyes, it's either me or Bill

Clinton." Without missing a beat, he added, "Even Paul Newman is no threat to me. He's a seventy-year-old pretty guy with washed-out blue eyes. Now me and Jack Lemmon, we're real men."

Of his sexual humor, Christina Collins, who appeared with Matthau and Carol Burnett in the 1998 television movie *The Marriage Fool*, declared, "He was totally politically incorrect, like a really dirty old man. But he got away with it. A younger guy trying it, and you would have gone, 'Oh, God.' [He could do it] because he was an icon. And his delivery—his delivery was unbelievable. He'd be really trashy, to try to make us laugh.

"I found the best way to handle him was to joke right back in his face. Some people found it difficult to deal with his right-in-your-face sexual flirting. I wasn't too bothered by it. He was just a crusty old dog." Collins added that Matthau "flirted with anything in a skirt. He would come up to you and say, 'Don't you dare kiss me! Don't you dare kiss me on the mouth!' That kind of stuff. Carol Burnett was on set too, and she handled him very well. There were times when he had to be put in his place, and Carol was good at that. And he liked that. He respected that."

While Matthau relished the role of dirty old man and alleged lusty stud, he was a devoted—and monogamous—husband. Charlie Matthau reported that his father was faithful to his mother. Explained Lana Morgan, "He said that he didn't feel whole unless Carol was around. He was like a one-legged man without her. I remember at the *Odd Couple II* premiere, the screening was on the Paramount lot and the reception was outdoors. People were gathering around Walter, and talking to him, and he just started to look like the little boy who got lost at the grocery store. He was looking around, and it was like 'Where's my wife? Where's my wife?' As soon as he had her in his eyeline, he went back to mingling. He would chat, smile at her, and keep talking. He just wanted her near him.

"When he was on the set, he wanted her there. He wanted everybody to know that she was his wife. He wanted her taken care of."

Despite his propensity for telling risqué jokes and making sexual references to women, Matthau was a self-described puritan. "I know it's funny, but I'm a prude," he said. "I will say coarse and vulgar things, but I don't like it." Not all his jests centered around sex. Some were so innocent that they might have emanated from an eight-year-old. "Do you know Lincoln's Gettysburg address?" he might ask, and then follow with the punchline: "I didn't know he moved."

Anyway, Matthau knew all too well that he was too old for sexual improprieties. Once, in his dressing room while filming *Out to Sea*, he removed his trousers in the presence of a female assistant and quipped, "Don't get excited. There's nothing to worry about anymore."

CHAPTER 28

"My Best Friend"

In 1991, Matthau acted in a television movie, *Mrs. Lambert Remembers Love*. His role: the best friend of a grandmother-on-the-run (Ellen Burstyn) who is in danger of losing custody of her grandson. It was an extra-special project for Matthau, because it was directed by an extra-special filmmaker: his son Charlie.

Charlie Matthau had been born twenty-nine years earlier. That same year, 1962, proud papa Walter had his *A Shot in the Dark* Tony Award engraved, "To Carol Matthau for having a baby and for Walter Matthau for 'A Shot in the Dark.'"

From that point on, Charlie became a fixture in press reports citing Matthau's off-screen life; he frequently was mentioned by his father, and not just when the two were appearing together to plug a movie. It was as if Walter's and Carol's children from their previous marriages had faded to the background.

Carole Shelley recalled little Charlie during the Broadway run of *The Odd Couple*. "He was about three," she said. "He used to come around with Carol, in his little short pants and cap. [He was] the apple of Walter's eye. I met his other children a couple of times, but that was not happy. None of that was happy." Lucy Saroyan, Carol's daughter, then was working as her stepfather's dresser. "That was at a time when Lucy was in favor," Shelley added. "I really didn't know the personal side of it all firsthand, but I would hear stuff from Lucy. Apart from Walter and Carol and Charlie, it didn't seem to be the happiest of family situations."

"Walter married Carol, and they had Charlie," noted Anna Berger. "Charlie became his whole world, which I could not understand. He had other children, too. He did not give them the attention he gave Charlie."

When David and Jenny were little, their dad was involved in career building; when Charlie came along, Walter was on the edge of superstardom and comfort. David and Jenny were the products of an unsuccessful marriage; Charlie was a love child. When David was small and Jenny was an infant, their parents split, which made Walter a weekend father. Charlie, on the other hand, was born into a tightly glued marriage. He saw his father any day Walter was not off on location; he literally could roll out of bed, and be with his dad. While offering David and Jenny support and financial generosity, Matthau's time with them was based on a schedule.

David Matthau offered a thoughtful analysis of his father's parenting skills. "His whole parental image was based on my grandmother," he noted, "and my grandmother was really somewhat crazy. Emotionally unstable, I think, is a nice way to put it. And so consequently, my father never really understood a lot about being a parent, and was unable to really be the kind of a parent emotionally in a lot of ways and to certain degrees with me and Jenny—and, whether he knew it or not, with Charlie, too.

"He was always extremely supportive, and was there for us with money for school and clothes and whatever, if we needed something or whatever, doctors and everything like that. We always really knew strongly that our father loved us. But even until the later stages of his life, he was never able to really say 'I love you' to us. We always knew it before then, but he could never really [tell us so]. And so he was not really too good emotionally in terms of parenting skills."

David added, "I don't walk around with a grudge. I just accept it, and look at it as a reality that he did not have that particular fortitude. I think that we always had the sense that he was there for us, and loved us, and especially even after our mother died [in 1982], and there was this sense that he was our only parent, he was there for us even more so. There were times and stretches when we would not see him for a whole year because he would be working, but we'd speak on the phone. It was nice to be able to have that."

Conversely, there is no way to overstate the intimacy that existed between Charlie and his parents. Charlie grew up in the company of celebrities who were as fascinating as they were famous; yet, unlike celebrity offspring who are pawned off on nannies and housekeepers, he was the center of his parents' lives. Walter and Carol eschewed Hollywood nightlife, and spent quality time with their son. In this regard, Charlie enjoyed a princely life.

Jack Lemmon described the connection between Walter and Charlie as "one of the great father-son relationships." Publicist Murray Weissman noted, "Never in my life, with the possible exception of how I feel about my own son, Benjamin, have I ever witnessed such love and devotion between a father and son as existed between Walter and Charlie. He took Charlie to every film set. I saw them sitting in the front row of Laker basketball games."

Having fathered Charlie, Walter reevaluated his feelings about religion. Walter married Geri, a non-Jew, and they chose not to raise their children with any religious affiliation. Even though his mantra remained "I'm Jewish, but I'm not an organized-religion man," he began attending synagogue with Charlie. "[He did so] because he thought it would be good upbringing for me," Charlie explained. "I don't think he was interested so much for himself in being a member of a temple."

When Charlie was a youngster, Matthau became friends with Jerry Cutler, a rabbi who, in the early 1970s, organized what he described as a "show business synagogue," called Synagogue for the Performing Arts. After leaving this synagogue, Cutler's new affiliation was the Creative Arts Temple. Matthau was a member of both. "He was always [in synagogue] for the High Holidays," reported Cutler, "and once in a while he'd come during the year. In temple, I would have him come up for readings all the time. He always looked forward to reading for the congregation."

Cutler described his synagogues as "liberal," related neither to the Conservative nor Reform movements of Judaism. "Our services are very warm, very *haimish* (Yiddish for down-home). We do our own thing, and he really felt very much a part of it. He wasn't intimidated by our approach, which is certainly farther away from organized religion than most temples, and I think that's what brought him back."

Some of Matthau's extracurricular activities involved religion. Occasionally, in order to raise funds, the synagogue sponsored member-authored one-night-only shows. Matthau was a regular participant. In one, he played a Yiddish-accented Catskill Mountain hotel owner. As usual, Matthau's humor abounded. Once, Cutler asked him if he would be in town for High Holiday services. "I hate to tell you, but Charlie and I have converted to Hinduism, and we'll be in the Himalayas," was his response.

Unlike his older half-brother, Charlie Matthau was Bar Mitzvahed. "At [the affair], Walter was wonderful," Cutler remembered. "He was incredibly proud, so terribly proud."

Cutler reported that he met David and Jenny Matthau. "They're both nice, very very nice," he said. "But Walter's life was enveloped with Charlie. Both worshipped the ground each other walked on. I used to go over to the house and we would play games, ping-pong and so forth. [Walter] always would say, 'He's the best, isn't he? The very best.' He never stopped talking in platitudes about this kid." While shooting *I'm Not Rappaport*, Matthau and Ossie Davis chatted about their families, and Davis noted that he "talked mostly about Charlie. We might have discussed the other kids in passing, but it was Charlie." Added Jayne Meadows, "I don't know one other star who loved his child as much as Walter. When he would mention Charlie, his eyes would fill up with tears, but he was smiling. He even said to me one day, 'I love him so much I want to bite his cheeks.' That to me is the measure of the man."

Jean Longacre, manager of the Beverly Hills Tennis Club, recalled that when Matthau joined, his first thought was Charlie. He wanted his son to have a locker, in case he felt like swimming. He was delighted by the presence of a ping-pong table, so that he and Charlie could play. The caring was reciprocal. Longacre noted that Charlie would call the club and say, "My father's coming over today. Now he likes [a specific brand of] frozen non-fat yogurt. If you don't have it, I'm gonna run over a little container, cause I always want him to have what he likes."

Matthau's unabashed love for Charlie directly influenced Richard Benjamin and Paula Prentiss's views toward parenthood. The couple observed how Walter would grab Charlie, and plant big kisses on his cheeks. "It didn't matter if Charlie was trying to wriggle out of it," Benjamin reported. "Walter's gonna love him so much, until he can't stand it anymore. We saw that, and decided that that's how we were going to be with our [children].

"He was so great with Ross, our son. He would grab him and hold him and plant big kisses on the side of his face. So we asked if he would be [our daughter's godfather], and he said yes." Added Prentiss, "One of the most wonderful things about Walter was that he did what he said." Once, their daughter was giving a ballet recital at her elementary school, and Prentiss invited Matthau. She assumed he would forget about it, but on the day of the recital Matthau arrived wearing shorts, tennis shoes, and a baseball cap worn backwards. "Well, I'm ready," he announced. "People turned around, all the parents," Prentiss concluded. "He took his seat and stayed for the performance. That was the kind of person he was."

"He was so sweet to come and see her," Benjamin observed. "That's what really endears you, and makes you love somebody."

Piper Laurie was another who identified with Walter and Charlie's relationship. "Individually, each told me that the other was his best friend," she declared. "Some people might think, 'Oooh, there's something a little weird here.' I have an extraordinary relationship with my own daughter, so I really understood that—and loved them for that, and was happy that they had that."

The closeness and affection between father and son is evident from Charlie's early childhood. In the late 1960s, the two appeared together on Australian television, resulting in a visual record of Walter kibitzing with and coaxing his small son. Charlie called Walter "Poppy," and "Poppy" lovingly kissed Charlie on the cheek. Around this time, the two were offered roles in a remake of *The Champ*, about a broken-down boxer and his loyal son. "I wouldn't do it because he would die in the picture and I wouldn't have any part of that," Charlie recalled. "He respected that."

When the Matthaus were renting Paul Newman and Joanne Woodward's Beverly Hills home, journalist Judy Stone came by for an interview. She was greeted by Walter and five-and-a-half-year-old

Charlie. As Walter left momentarily, the boy sheepishly eyed Stone and announced that his name was Mozart. "I'm eighty-two-years-old," he declared, "and the father of that fellow in the other room." He waved his hand, blurted out a hearty "Abracadabra," and disappeared.

"*Bubbala*, go get dried," Walter told Charlie after the latter's swim. "Poppy, darling," the boy said. "Yes, Charlie, darling, are you crying or breathing?" his father responded. "Matthau made it sound very funny," Stone reported, "but there was also a world of tenderness in his voice every time he spoke to the boy." Later on, Charlie asked his father, "Poppy, what's your wish?" "Just a little kiss out of my boy's face, that *shana punim* (pretty face)," was the response.

Stone asked Matthau if he wished to project the image of the Jewish mother. "I'm a *terrific* Jewish mother," he cracked. "I just want to eat those babies up. Only make it a Methodist mother. Wherever I say Jewish, make it American. It'll broaden your piece and the Jews will know what you're talking about anyway." (Stone later ran into Matthau at a film premiere. The two got to talking about Jewishness, at which point Matthau pronounced, "Everyone's Jewish." As proof, he asked a cop standing nearby to divulge his first name—which turned out to be Adolph! The journalist next encountered the younger Matthau almost thirty years later, when she interviewed him at the 1995 Toronto International Film Festival. She began the conversation by telling him, "The last time I saw you, you were naked.")

A couple of years later, after purchasing his Pacific Palisades home, Matthau was serving a guest chopped liver when Charlie and a little girl named Maura entered. The boy asked his father if he could have some of the chopped liver. His father said yes. Then Charlie requested a beer. He settled for club soda.

When Charlie was in the third grade, his school moved to a new facility in Bel Air. Walter attended the dedication, held on the campus's basketball courts, and was asked to toss up a ceremonial shot. Rather than dribble to the hoop and make an easy basket, or stand under the rim and toss up a shot, he took what Charlie described as "this Jerry West special" from the backcourt. The ball "just swooshed right in. Everybody who was there still talks about it, but at the time it didn't strike me as unusual because I thought my father could do anything. That's what it was like growing up with him. He was Superman."

In April 1974, Walter and Charlie chatted with Mike Wallace on *60 Minutes*, in a segment titled "Matthau and Son." The precocious lad appeared to know all about his dad's gambling habits, declaring "There, you just lost all your bookies" after Matthau claimed, "Oh, I still gamble now, but I don't gamble heavily. I'll bet $20 on a ball-game, maybe a hundred." Charlie revealed that Walter left a $5 tip for an order of a cup of coffee and purchased suits "when his pants are dirty." Charlie even noted, with regard to his father and Barbra Streisand, "I mean, he doesn't like working with her, that's all." That December, the Matthaus dressed up as clowns for a Ringling Bros. and Barnum & Bailey Circus charity performance. "If I move to New York for two weeks, I guess I can leave Charlie home," he declared the following year, while shooting *The Sunshine Boys* on location. "But it hurts. I miss him."

One disturbing incident occurred in late July 1978, when Charlie was fifteen. An eighteen-year-old Canoga Park college student sent Walter a letter in which he threatened to murder Charlie if he did not receive $150,000 in cash. Walter was instructed where to drop the loot; as the suspect opened a suitcase that had been left for him on the Pacific Coast Highway, he was arrested by FBI agents and the Los Angeles police. He was released on $5,000 bail, and eventually sentenced to one year in county jail.

On a happier note, in December of that year, Charlie and Walter shared two very different television credits. One was sweet and inno-cent: *The Stingiest Man in Town*, an animated musical adaptation of Charles Dickens's *The Christmas Carol*, which aired two days before Christmas. The elder Matthau voiced Ebenezer Scrooge; his son was heard as "the boy." The other was, for Charlie at least, an unbilled appearance on *Saturday Night Live*. Walter was guest host, and Charlie may be spotted in a skit titled "Bad News Bees," a parody of *The Bad News Bears*. The teenager and the male *SNL* regulars were dressed as bees, and inhabited a bunkhouse. Enter Walter the coun-selor, garbed in a St. Louis baseball cap. In a bit that dated from *The Odd Couple* on stage, he opened a beer can, splattering the brew about. The humor degenerated from there, with a subtle but clear allusion to the bees collectively masturbating after the bunkhouse lights were doused.

In 1997, *Saturday Night Live* director Dave Wilson spoke about the skit during a Museum of Television & Radio seminar. "We had a lot of trouble getting it past the censors, I'll tell you that," he noted. "Matthau thought it was very funny, and he sort of went to bat [against the censor] for us. When an actor of his stature is on your side in your arguments with standards and practices, it helps a lot."

Like his older half-brother, Charlie followed his father into the entertainment industry—but not as an actor. "I didn't stand in his way," Walter recalled. "All I did was give him the odds on becoming a successful actor. I told him that 83 percent of the members of the acting union are unemployed at any given time. Armed with those facts, he decided he'd be happier behind the camera rather than in front." While Walter endorsed his son's career choice, he noted that it might have been more practical, according to Charlie, to "get a news-stand somewhere and find a husky woman who, at the end of a day's work, can carry me home." Actually, Walter would have been delighted if his son had wanted to become a doctor.

While still a child, Charlie shot films with Walter's super-8mm movie camera. For his eighth birthday, he was presented with his own camera. He often watched his father work. "On the set of *Hello, Dolly!*" Charlie recalled, "I used to sort of follow Gene Kelly around, and he kept saying, 'Let's let Charlie direct the scene.' And I'd say, 'Yeah, yeah, yeah, let me do it.'"

Charlie was especially impressed with Don Siegel, who directed Walter in *Charley Varrick*. "I wanted to be just like him," Charlie exclaimed. "I thought he had the most interesting job in the world." The elder Matthau may not have savored directing—for the rest of his life he lambasted *Gangster Story*, the one feature film he helmed—but he did direct one scene in *Charley Varrick*. It featured nine-year-old Charlie as a boy who rushes up to a sheriff after a bank robbery and reports the getaway car license number. Matthau senior took over when Siegel left the set, allegedly to make a long-distance phone call. Ever-protective, the father began over-coaching the son. "Stop acting and just do it," he admonished. "Don't make a big

Academy Award scene out of it. Just be as natural as you can." The boy grew increasingly flustered. Finally, he blurted out, "When's the real director coming back?"

When it came time for Charlie to select a college, Walter accompanied him to the campuses he was considering. In February 1980, the two spent several days flying around the East Coast in a small airplane, visiting Brown, Vassar, Wesleyan, and other universities. Upon touring Harvard, they were joined by Jack Lemmon, Class of 1947. At the time, Matthau noted that he lamented not getting a college education. In yet another of his tongue-in-cheek declarations, he claimed that instead of being a famous movie star, he "would really like to be a nice quiet doctor some place in a small town in Minnesota."

Ultimately, Charlie chose the University of Southern California. "I'd rather go [there]," he said, "mainly because they have the best film program. Also, I'll be near my parents."

Charlie graduated from the USC film school and, in 1988, directed *Doin' Time on Planet Earth*, a science fiction parody/teen comedy. Cannon Films honcho Menachem Golan tapped him for *Planet Earth* after viewing a student film he directed, a short titled *I Was a Teenage Fundraiser*. While filming in the Los Angeles area, Charlie's dad visited him, which made him "very nervous. But he was very supportive, told me I was doing a good job. Of course, he's biased."

Charlie's feature debut was less than a resounding success. "I think eleven people in the United States saw the film," he observed. Then in 1989, father and son formed The Matthau Company, their own production outfit, with Walter becoming chairman and Charlie president and CEO. "Obviously, one of the goals was to develop projects that we could work on together," Charlie explained. "It would have been terrible not to have worked together. So what if it's nepotism? So it's nepotism. If the film is good, it doesn't matter." Of establishing oneself in Hollywood, he stated, "You are definitely a target of derision before you even get started, especially in this town where people tend to be mean-spirited about other people and wanting them to fail."

Around this time, Charlie became Walter and Carol's neighbor.

He had long-promised to do so, because he loved them so much and never wanted to be too far away. While his parents were in Rome for the filming of *Il piccolo diavolo*, Charlie's grandfather died. The same day Charlie Marcus's inheritance came out of probate, a "For Sale" sign appeared on the house next door. The younger Matthau purchased it, and Walter and Carol had a new neighbor.

On a visit there eight months after Walter's death, Charlie's house was decorated with family photos: Walter and Charlie at various stages of Charlie's life; Walter, Charlie, and Carol; Walter at Dodger Stadium, dressed in a Hollywood Stars uniform with his lanky frame winding up to toss a pitch; Walter, Charlie, and Jack Lemmon, including inscriptions to Charlie signed "Jack" and "Velvul." ("Velvul" was Matthau's Yiddish name. As a youngster, Charlie called him "Papa" or "Poppy" and, as he explained, "then at a certain point I started calling him 'Velvul.'") "You can see who's important in this house," noted Ray, the Matthaus' longtime housekeeper, who had been with the family for over thirty-five years. She was pointing to the many photos of Walter.

In addition to *Mrs. Lambert Remembers Love*, Charlie directed his dad in one other television movie: *The Marriage Fool*, broadcast in 1998. Matthau played Frank Walsh, a quiet-living Queens, New York, widower who becomes romantically involved with Florence (Carol Burnett), a wise, high-spirited widow. Fittingly, Matthau's character shares a close, caring relationship with one of his sons, Robert (John Stamos). He speaks two lines that might as well have been autobiographical: "I know a lot of parks that are pretty noisy. Belmont Park, Central Park . . ." and "Well, I figure I'll sell the house, put the money in the bank or take it to the track." The sentiment of another, spoken by Florence to Robert, directly relates to Charlie, and his wish for his dad: "Your father's gonna live a hundred years."

During the shoot, Walter often arrived on the set and greeted Charlie with a kiss on the lips and a pinch on the cheek, admonishing his son to "give daddy a kiss" and rhetorically asking Burnett, "Isn't he delicious?" While being made up, Matthau regaled cast and crew with raunchy jokes before putting on, and singing along with, CDs of his favorite operas.

Even though it was not to be aired for several months, Matthau plugged *The Marriage Fool* while a surprise guest on a June 1998 *Late Show with David Letterman*. Throughout the program, he was shown getting a haircut from his longtime barber. At the end, Letterman asked Matthau, "What are you gonna do now?" The answer was matter-of-fact: "I'm gonna get on the phone, call my bookie, and see what kind of action is on for tonight's baseball."

Walter and Charlie's most enduring co-credit came three years earlier. It is *The Grass Harp*, based on an autobiographical novella by Carol Matthau's friend, Truman Capote, a story about a young boy's coming-of-age in a pre–World War II Southern town. The elder Matthau played Charlie Cool, a wizened, white-haired widower-retired judge who idles away his hours sitting in the town barbershop and drugstore. Filming on location for two months in Wetumpka, Alabama, the younger Matthau directed a who's who of actors: Jack Lemmon (playing a slick entrepreneur), Piper Laurie, Sissy Spacek, Edward Furlong, Mary Steenburgen, Nell Carter, Sean Patrick Flanery, Charles Durning, Roddy McDowall, and Doris Roberts.

Laurie recalled that, before shooting began, Matthau insisted on wearing a white wig for the role. One and all disagreed, telling him, "No, no, no, you should use your own hair," which was dark. To emphasize his intention to don the wig, Matthau picked up an electric razor and, with one fell swoop, zipped off the first three inches of the front of his hairline. So of course, now he had to wear it. "He got exactly what he thought he needed for the part," Laurie concluded.

Charlie confirmed that his father never dyed his hair, and was determined to wear the wig. "I was afraid [it] would look artificial," he explained. "But ever since Pauline Kael accused him of dying his hair, every time he would get a haircut he would put the hair in an envelope and mail it to her and tell her to take it to a lab."

On the first day's shooting, the entire crew looked on as Charlie cautiously approached Walter and spoke in an undertone while offering up some directorial instructions. Then Walter yelled out, for one and all to hear, "Bullshit! I'm not doing that!" Everyone then let out a collective chuckle. This was Walter's way of cutting through the tension, and easing himself and Charlie into the daily routine of making a film.

Actually, the two did strike a deal. "He'd listen to my directions,"

Charlie recalled. "However, at any time, if so ordered, I'd put on a sweater."

During the shoot, Laurie observed a great deal of respect—not just love—between Walter and Charlie. "On the set, Walter was like a beginning actor who didn't indulge or condescend in any way," she said. "He was just normal. He took direction and criticism, and was like all of us. He loved that Charlie didn't overdirect the actors, as we all did. I just thought it was a very respectful relationship."

She described Walter as "this dear, funny guy who would come into the trailer in the morning and sing. He liked to hear opera in the trailer every morning, [and] we always played it for him." She added that Matthau "kept himself, it seemed to me, alive as an actor—or maybe it was just his love of life and humor—by talking and joking right up to the instant the scene started. Through the first A.D.'s call and 'roll it' and the 'action' from the director, he was overlapping all of that with his own personal communication with whomever he was working with in the scene. [He'd be] telling some jokes that had nothing to do with the scene, something about bagels or something on the Lower East Side. Then we'd go into the scene. There was no separation."

Matthau was, indeed, Matthau. One day, upon returning to the set after a break in filming, he grumbled, "My mother-in-law's dying and I just lost $50,000 at the track. And how was *your* Christmas?"

Despite all the on-camera talent associated with the film, Charlie had difficulty getting it made. Of its limited budget, Walter observed, "I could've made five pictures in the time it took [Charlie] to raise the money for this one. Finally, New Line put up $4.75 million, and a foreign distributor called Mayfair, whatever that is, put up another $4 million." He added, "Hell, Jack and I are working for one five-thousandth of what we usually get just for living expenses," and "Well, [the studio suits are] not gonna beat the hell outta my kid because all he needs is an extra million. Schwarzenegger gets that much for bottled water on the crap he makes.

"On most films you demand every nickel you can get, because you know you're doing a piece of shit anyway. That's the story of my career—*beaucoup de* shit. This one is so full of poetry and over-whelming literacy I would have done it for anybody."

Added Lana Morgan, "The only time I ever knew of him getting really angry was when the studio pulled a huge sum out of the budget of *The Grass Harp* after they were already halfway through the shoot. Walter was not happy with the way they were giving Charlie a bad time, and yet they had this big long list of amazing actors—Oscar winners—all working for scale. In the meantime they were cutting donuts in half on the set to save a few pennies. How strange is that?

"Executives think nothing of spending a bundle on explosives or some new face with little acting experience. You hear about studio jets flying executives to Aspen to luxury houses owned and staffed with studio money. But it isn't for the talent, it's for the execs. This sort of thing annoyed Walter."

The Grass Harp was screened as a Gala Event at the 1995 Toronto International Film Festival, with father and son in attendance and Matthau junior looking like a younger, less craggy version of his dad. The on-podium rapport between Walter and Charlie during a festival press conference was sweet and loving, but not without good-natured bits of humor. When asked if Walter took his direction, Charlie quickly responded, "Most of the time." "I listened to Charlie when he was very young," chimed in Walter. "He went 'aaaaah'—and so I changed his diaper. He went 'aaaaah,' and so I gave him some kasha."

When asked if he ever offered Charlie advice, Walter responded, "I don't remember." "Did I ever give you any advice?" he asked Charlie. The son answered, "Whatever it was, I followed it." Walter added that Charlie constantly offered him counsel on matters unrelated to moviemaking. "'Watch your diet,' he's always telling me. Also, don't use cellular phones, because they cause cancer. Take a lot of Vitamin E, which is good for my heart. My mother used to give me a lot of butter. She'd say that butter would smooth my heart."

Walter, of course, rated Charlie highly as a director. "He's among the tops," the senior Matthau explained. "It depends upon how the director works, but it also depends upon genetics. For instance, I like Charlie better than I do Billy Wilder. Charlie I compare to Harold Clurman. He directed only one picture, but he directed me in two plays [*The Ladies of the Corridor* and *A Shot in the Dark*]. One time I asked him, 'How do I play this part? You haven't said a word to me.' And he said, 'Talk English and walk fancy.' That's the kind of direction Charlie gives. He doesn't bite into you. He doesn't have the need to bolster his own ego; he doesn't worry whether you're going to change an 'if' or a 'but.' He gives you a sense of character, and lets you go."

Some of the film's most tender moments come when Walter's Judge Cool talks of his late wife, and the meaning of love and how difficult and elusive it is to find. These sequences are gifts that a devoted director/son would aspire to present to a beloved actor/father.

As Walter observed, "I'm very happy that he's a friend of mine, and that he's my son." One of the photos in *The Grass Harp* press kit speaks volumes about their closeness. It features Walter, in costume as Judge Cool, beaming proudly, with his arm around his director son.

At the film's screening at Toronto's spacious Roy Thomson Hall, both Matthaus came onstage. "I've wanted to be a director since I was seven years old," Charlie told the throngs. "I've always wanted to direct my dad. I've always dreamed of seeing [our film] shown in such a big hall. I'll remember this night the rest of my life." His parting words to the audience were, "I've got to be the luckiest guy in the world."

Years later, Charlie recalled, "Right after the Gala, the president of Fine Line, who was not expecting the film to get good reviews, read this [glowing] review [in *Variety*]. That was a great relief, because of all the difficulty making the film. [The situation] was like a bad movie, with this review coming out while the movie was [being screened]."

Matthau did all in his power to promote *The Grass Harp*. In addition to attending the Toronto festival, he hyped it on *Larry King Live*. "Walter was so thankful when we put Charlie on [the show] that time, when he did that movie," King recalled. "He was really appreciative." How did Charlie get to be on the show? "Because Walter asked," King noted. "Walter asked personally. And Walter was not the kind of guy to say, 'Put me on the air.'"

Despite its share of critical acclaim and festival circuit success, and Walter's efforts to publicize it, the film barely registered at the box office. Matthau, ever the proud papa, had a ready-made explanation. The film wasn't the beneficiary of "$50,000 advertising every half-minute" because it didn't "have any exploding sex symbols." After its theatrical run, Matthau added, "Now of course [Charlie's] looking for a job because his last movie didn't do $100 million. It couldn't because the production company didn't spend $4 on advertising it, and sometimes you need some help. You've got to advertise what you've got.

"I did bring him up for the new *Odd Couple*, but they were afraid because he's never had a 'success' picture, one that has made more than was put into it. He's only had two pictures, and if you're a director and you're not successful, you work once every ten years."

Charlie believed that Walter's feeling for *The Grass Harp* was little more than a father's pride in his son. After Walter's death, he and Carol looked through his wallet. Aside from credit cards and money, its sole content was a glowing review of the film, published in *Entertainment Weekly*.

Jerry Cutler once asked Matthau to appear on *For Goodness Sake*, a television show he co-hosted with a Presbyterian minister. Cutler explained, "We're doing sixty-five shows, it's a minister and myself, it's being shown all over the world, there are contracts in every major city in the country, it's being syndicated." Matthau's response: "Cut the crap, Jerry, this is for the pilot, isn't it?" Cutler admitted as much, and Matthau told him, "I'll be there." He showed up at the taping with Charlie and, when asked about the goodness in his life, Walter pointed to his son and said, "This is it. This is the best thing that ever happened to me." He likened Charlie to a circus: "He's the acrobats. He's the lion tamer." Tears started welling up in his eyes.

"We did everything together," Charlie recalled in 1996, "and that, I think, is rare in Hollywood. People say I'm really lucky to be the son of Walter and Carol Matthau. They're right, but not for the reasons they think. I'm lucky because my parents have been together for thirty-seven years and they are still madly in love with each other. They've been great role models. They were not strict; they led by example. Because they are such decent people, I didn't have the kinds of problems that other children of famous people have had."

CHAPTER 29

On the Decline

Matthau's work during the 1990s was not confined to feature films. In 1995, he recorded "Chava," a Sholem Aleichem short story, for broadcast on the National Yiddish Book Center's radio series, *Jewish Short Stories from Eastern Europe and Beyond*. During the recording session, he kept halting his work to tell jokes in Yiddish and offer a favorite recipe for kasha varnishkes. He recorded several radio dramas, including *The Hole in the Top of the World*, by Fay Weldon, and *Mastergate*, by Larry Gelbart. When asked why he did the Weldon piece, he responded, "Like all megalomaniacs, I thought it would be nice for posterity, but radio is the kind of fake acting I don't like." During the recording session, Matthau was more interested in reminiscing (about how he lost his virginity, among other subjects) than performing.

The following year, Aviva Kempner interviewed him for her documentary, *The Life and Times of Hank Greenberg*, in the Beverly Hills home of director Arthur Hiller, the actor's friend and Kempner's cousin by marriage. Kempner loves Yiddish, and asked Matthau if he could sprinkle some of the language into his remarks. He responded by answering completely in Yiddish, before offering an English translation. "Answering in Yiddish was quintessential Walter, as I understand it," she concluded.

Not surprisingly, Matthau's enthusiasm for sports remained unabated. One Sunday in the fall of 1996, he was faced with a dilemma as he turned on one of his TV sets: Be patriotic, and watch a pre-election debate between Bill Clinton and Bob Dole, or view a football game. Matthau chose the latter. "It was more interesting," he rationalized, "because you didn't know how it would turn out."

In his advancing years, the overriding circumstance of Matthau's life was his health. He now sat down and rested between takes. A golf cart transported him between dressing room and set. He took naps during lunch breaks. During the filming of *Out to Sea*, Ellen Geer noticed that he "didn't have the strength he once had. I remember that he was concerned about his eyes."

What he did not alter—at least for the time being—were his eating habits. Counsel him about the need for nutrition, and the importance of monitoring diet, and Matthau responded with a glare, and a declaration: "If you eat celery and lettuce, you won't get sick. I like celery and lettuce, but I like it with pickles, relish, corned beef, potatoes, peas. And I like Eskimo Pies, vanilla ice cream with chocolate covering." While sharing a ham sandwich with a Jewish journalist, he offered to split a glass of milk. She refused. "You have scruples about drinking milk after eating ham?" he asked. She responded that, no, she had no scruples. "I do," Matthau grinned, as he drank the milk. "I feel guilty as hell right now."

Once he downed a Bloody Mary, leaving nothing but a celery stick. As a follow-up, he savored a beer. "Ummm-mmm," he uttered. "It's good. It would *have* to be good, since it's poison." Prior to enjoying a portion of lobster ravioli, followed by espresso and chocolate cake, he explained, "Castor oil can cause constipation. The bowel cannot absorb water. I think that's my problem. I can no longer have a bowel movement without a lot of help. . . . I'm sure that will be the [headline]: 'Walter Matthau unable to crap without help from Fleet's enema.'"

Another time, he unbuttoned his shirt and displayed a scar left over from his bypass surgery—but not before extolling the virtues of a certain homemade ice cream ("You can just taste that cherry vanilla"); scolding a companion for not joining him in his salmon lunch ("We are going to eat and you are not eating. You can't eat this marvelous can of salmon? I love it"); offering dessert ("Do you want a cookie?"); and commenting on Italian food and Toronto ("There are 500,000 Italians there and a million-and-a-half restaurants, it seems"). "Wait till you see what they serve for lunch around here," he declared, when admonished for enjoying an ice cream bar early one morning on the set of *Out to Sea*. "All those fancy diets don't appeal to me. Who knows what's better, margarine or butter? One gives you cancer, the other gives you a heart attack."

He had suffered his first heart attack in 1966, when Charlie was a toddler. "I vaguely remember that my father was in the hospital," he noted after Walter's death, "and my mother [said] words to the effect of 'I hope he's gonna make it. I hope we see Poppy again.'" Charlie added, "I grew up with this angst that today might be the last day. . . . The worst nightmare I ever had was that a spaceship came and took my father away."

A decade later, Matthau had the quadruple bypass. Then, beginning in the second half of the 1980s and lasting for the rest of his life, his physical state became increasingly fragile. Charlie was determined to do all in his power to keep his father alive. He monitored Walter's diet, with mixed success. Walter might heed his son's advice regarding an entree, but would cheat on dessert. "Every morning, I would go over to his house and throw out all the food that had fat in it, and I'd buy all sorts of fat-free products," Charlie explained. "He'd get mad as hell. This went on for years. One of his nicknames for me was 'Fat-Free.'" In 1996, Matthau met Dr. Neil Parker, who became his doctor as well as friend. "He was always eating something from Barney's [Beanery, a Los Angeles restaurant], chopped liver or this or that," Parker recalled. "You'd say, 'This is not good for you, Walter,' and he'd say, 'Yeah, right, okay, I'll only eat a little of it.'" That same year, while interviewing Matthau, Leonard Maltin observed that the supporting cast of *Out to Sea* was "far from chopped liver." "You know, that term 'chopped liver,'" Matthau interrupted. "I don't know why not being chopped liver is good. I love chopped liver. You ever have it? Chopped with onions and hard-boiled eggs. . . . It's great. Little olive oil."

Beverly Hills Tennis Club waiter Artoro Alfaro noted that Matthau's favorite lunch was a "macho salad": lettuce, olives, tomato, avocado, and a creamy Italian house dressing. "If he came six days to the club," Alfaro reported, "he'd have six days a macho salad. For dessert, he liked cappuccino ice cream." Rene Mendez, who noted that Matthau was "all the time making jokes," added that the actor also "liked a salad with king salmon on top, and vegetables. He'd have ice cream—when Charlie wasn't around."

"Part of him was with the program," Charlie added. "He tended to avoid red meat, although he liked corned beef. And part of him was, 'Aw, fuck it. This is a great part of life.' He'd say that people on low-fat diets don't really live longer. It's just so boring that it seems longer."

If Charlie remained at his father's side in health, he also did so in sickness. When it came to dealing with his dad's—and his mom's—ailments, he was in complete command. "He'd be on the phone with the doctors discussing this and that treatment," noted Lana Morgan. "He'd be looking after Walter, and his mom. He has this calendar, and on it he has everybody's medical appointments—when they had their mammography, when they had their colonoscopy."

Charlie vividly recalled his father's myriad health crises. "Then in '86, [his heart] was blocked again, and he had an angioplasty," Charlie reported. "He had another one in '87, and another in '88. Then in '93, he had a heart attack. It was during [the filming of] *Grumpy Old Men*. He almost died. I got on the plane to Minnesota, and when I landed I didn't know if he was going to be alive."

Ossie Davis, who appeared in the film, described Matthau and Jack Lemmon as "walking medical examples of men growing old. I remember Lemmon might have had a small heart attack while the shooting was going on. And I do know that the three of us were booked to do a scene shooting in Minneapolis, a scene with Walter, Jack, and myself in a bait shop. On that last day, Walter had a heart problem. And so we couldn't shoot the scene." The set eventually was rebuilt in Los Angeles, where the sequence was filmed after Matthau's recovery.

"Later that year, he was home and his heart kept stopping," Charlie continued. "I drove him to the hospital. His cardiologist at the time lived down the street so he was close by, thank God. He came over and manually started [my dad's] heart in the back seat as we drove to the hospital. So he almost died twice in '93."

Matthau's next major health emergency came in December 1995. "He had been tired," Charlie noted. "He had done two movies back-to-back. He kept getting sicker and sicker, and I kept trying to get him to go to the doctor." When Walter came to the office, Charlie would trick him by telling his secretary, "Say Dr. Gold is on the speaker phone, that he's calling for me." Then Charlie would pretend to be speaking to the doctor, exclaiming, "Rick, you gotta get my father in to see you. He's very weak. Let me take him in right now." "It was an ongoing battle to get him to go to the doctor," he added. "Everyone thought it was his heart. Finally, he became so weak that the doctors thought they would have to do another angioplasty.

"Then they discovered that he was anemic, so they did a colonoscopy and discovered a tumor in his colon. He actually had a colonoscopy only a year and three-quarters before. So it was very strange that he had this tumor. Quite possibly—I would say quite probably—the doctor had missed it during the first colonoscopy. I think it's kind of unusual to have it grow the size that it grew in a year and three-quarters."

Matthau underwent surgery to have it removed. During the operation, Charlie explained that the surgeon felt a lump on his father's liver, which he removed. "When they did the biopsy, it was consistent with the primary tumor, which meant that it had entered his bloodstream and metastasized to his liver, which meant that it was stage D colon cancer."

As he weighed the success rates of treatments for this and Walter's other ailments, Charlie clearly was the son of a man who spent his life calculating the odds. "The cure rate with surgery is at best 25 percent," he said, "but it's actually less than that when it's discovered the same time as the primary tumor. The cure rate odds go down. The most optimistic rate was one-in-five. It was almost a sure thing that the cancer would recur, but by some miracle it did not. Once two years had gone by, it was pretty much given a 90 percent cure rate. But for two years, it was pretty much of a sure thing that he would die of colon cancer. That actually was the worst nightmare of my life. It was like an exquisite form of torture, and actually much more difficult [to endure than his] death was.

"All I did for three months was research colon cancer, and try to find new [cures]. I'd go and meet doctors all over the world [who were experts] in colon cancer. When he would have these CAT-scans and blood tests, waiting for those results would be like a life-and-death situation. The odds were not good, about 3.5 percent; the best odds were one out of five. I would be calling the doctors, driving them crazy. My father knew that if it was good news, I would tell him right away. I think he also knew if it wasn't good news, I would have probably waited to tell him. I certainly wouldn't have been in a rush to tell him."

In the end, the Matthaus opted to fight the cancer with chemotherapy. "He was very, very brave," Charlie declared. "Certain people in his life advised him against doing the chemotherapy, including two of his doctors. He ended up doing [it], and fortunately replacing those doctors. I think it really saved his life."

Because of the nature of his illnesses, Matthau was in the care of multiple doctors, one of whom was Neil Parker, whose specialty is general internal medicine. "He'd worry about [them]," Parker noted, "and [say], 'I'll never do this again.' But with him, it was never, 'Oh, poor me.' It was always, 'OK, I'll do whatever Charlie says. If Charlie wants me to take chemotherapy, I'll take chemotherapy. If it was up to me, I won't.' He was doing it for his family; it was more about his love for his family than him."

Matthau was in decent enough shape to continue working. "It was only in his posture that he showed how old he was," recalled Arlene Mazerolle, who appeared in *The Marriage Fool*, filmed during the summer of 1998. "He had curved shoulders, and a stiff body; I got a sense that his body was giving way, but his mind and his spirit were very young." It was that very spirit that kept him in front of the camera. "Walter didn't put up with his illness interfering with his acting," noted Neil Parker. "He loved acting, and being with people. If it was a choice between 'I may lose my life; I have a medical problem,' and 'I have to go do a film,' there was no question which had priority. It wasn't his medical health; he didn't want these problems to interfere with his living. If I believed it was risky for him to go, then he usually didn't. But you'd have to push, and say, 'No, this is not the time,' and you'd have to get Charlie and Carol involved."

It is not without irony that in his final feature, *Hanging Up*, released in 2000, Matthau played an aged, ailing old codger: Lou Mozell, an irascible screenwriter whose daughters (Diane Keaton, Meg Ryan, Lisa Kudrow) deal with his imminent death. During the shoot, his colleagues were in awe of his presence. "That face," blurted Diane Keaton, Matthau's director and co-star. "It's a great face. It's beautiful." Then she added, "His time on earth, living, is reflected in his face." Added Larry King, "As we'd say in Jewish, it's a *punim*. It's a face you'd want to squeeze. Even when he was sick, he was still . . . Walter."

While creating the character, Matthau improvised under Keaton's direction, drawing from his own life experience. The process allowed Matthau to express himself to Keaton on a deep, personal level. "He has an ability to be very romantic, which is a very surprising aspect of his personality," Keaton remarked prior to the film's release. "He's been married like thirty [actually, forty] years to his wife Carol, and he really deeply loves her. He would go on and on about his wife and it was beautiful. Another time he talked about his love of Mozart. I was just shocked at how rhapsodic he was."

It also is fitting that Charlie Matthau appears fleetingly onscreen, cast as "Young Lou" in several flashback sequences.

Matthau's next health crisis came in the summer of 1999, when he had just about completed *Hanging Up*. "During that time, he came about as close to dying without actually dying," Charlie explained. "The doctors gave him a 10 percent chance to survive. He had pneumonia, congestive heart failure, a urinary tract infection, sepsis, and ARDS [acute respiratory distress syndrome] all at the same time. [ARDS] is about as scary as it gets. About half the people who get it die. And to have sepsis at the same time! The sepsis cure rate is about 50 percent, too. Not to mention a compromised immune system, and colon cancer. And he also had lymphoma. He had a low-grade lymphoma. That was discovered in '96."

The crisis began, explained Neil Parker, when "the decision was made by his pulmonary doctor that it was important to do a test to see what was going on with his lungs because he had some shadows in there, and he's had multiple cancers. He came in for that, and ultimately developed the pneumonia [and all that followed]." The ARDS required Matthau to be on a respirator. "He needed a respirator put into his throat," explained Charlie, "but he was given too many drugs in the rush to restore breathing and get the thing working." He became comatose, and remained so for three months. "Even after he was off the respirator," Parker noted, "he basically was in what I would call a vegetative state." Of his role in *Hanging Up* and his real-life health crisis, Lana Morgan noted the irony of Matthau's playing a film-industry character who ends up ill and in a coma in the UCLA hospital ICU—which was precisely his own plight.

"For somebody to come back from that is amazing," added Parker. "But this comes back to Charlie and Carol, but Charlie in particular." Charlie acknowledged, "We don't know what my father can hear," so he played a Mozart CD for Walter, turned the TV set to a ballgame, or simply read or talked to his dad. "Charlie, you can go home now," Parker would advise, and Charlie would respond, "My father's more interesting not saying anything than most people I work with all day long."

Charlie described Walter's recovery as "almost like being born again. It was thought that he was going to be a vegetable—and his mental functioning didn't recur for a very long time. But then he slowly started to come back, and [eventually] he was as sharp as ever. It was a miracle.

"I would say that the first month was touch-and-go. Then it looked as if he was going to survive physically, which was at one point about a one-in-ten shot. And then the mental thing, they gave him about a 20 percent chance to recover fully. And he beat those odds.

"As great an actor . . . and all the other incredible qualities he had . . . you just cannot imagine the courage. . . . Just the whole way he dealt with it, without any self-pity. Just incredible . . . Heroic. I don't care if he's my father or not. I would say that about anybody. If he wasn't a famous actor—if he was a postal worker—the story of how he triumphed medically would be really inspiring."

During the coma stage, Charlie was called to the hospital for a meeting where it was suggested that the time had come to stop the "heroic effort." Charlie recalled, "Someone—I won't say who it was—said that they had spoken with [my father], and that they had a kind of secret pact, and that he did not want to go on if he wasn't going to be his old self. That person believed that if he had to have kidney dialysis three times a week, that would not be an acceptable lifestyle. I'm always very mild-mannered, pretty much of a pussycat to get along with, but at this point I completely lost it. I said to this individual, 'My father and I also had a secret pact. That pact is that you're a fucking idiot. And I don't care if he has twelve heart attacks, three more cases of ARDS, and Mad Cow Disease. All of the doctors' marching orders are to work 120 percent. If any other doctors felt they had a problem with that, just let me know and I would find a medical team that had the same philosophy.'" Of Charlie, Neil Parker noted, "He was in there, always pushing this and pushing that. Until it was clear that God [was ready to] take Walter, he was gonna do everything possible to have Walter for as many days as he could. He never took 'no,' or 'we might not be able to' for an answer. That was not Walter. That was Charlie."

While Carol's approach to Walter's condition was altogether different, it was no less loving. "Carol wanted Walter home," Parker explained. "She needed him close to her. When Walter was in the hospital, she felt that we were imprisoning him, and harming him, and doing things that we shouldn't be doing. She'd see a man coming in who'd look good, and then he'd go home weak. This guy who once was strapping now couldn't do things for himself. I think she really looked at that portion of the man, where Charlie looked at the intellect." Parker reported that Carol once wanted to sign Walter out of the hospital. "I told her he needed [to be in] ICU. Her response was, 'Tell me what we need to do. We'll get a respirator in the house. We'll get nurses—and I'll have Walter home with me.' It was a different kind of love."

Matthau healed to the point where he completed voice-overs for *Hanging Up*, and even insisted, "They had nothing to worry about." "He's fine now," reported Diane Keaton. "He's ready to work." Yet Parker soberly declared, "He'd come back from an illness that most people much younger wouldn't have come back from." The doctor used the word "exhaustive" in reference to all of Matthau's ailments, adding, "That's why I called Walter 'the cat'—A cat has nine lives."

Of his health problems, Matthau noted in 1997, "I've had other little things like polyps and diverticulitis and hemorrhoids." He figured that all these ailments resulted from "eating what I want to eat."

Despite his infirmities, his humor never wavered. Even though he was seventy-three, he told Roger Ebert in 1993 that he still thought of himself as twenty-eight, except that he refused to fight with anybody because he had just had a heart pacemaker put in. Then he offered an anecdote about how, the day after the surgery, he kicked an unruly German shepherd who had been bothering his own dog. Of his 1999 hospital stay, Charlie reported that a nurse would tell him, "I have to change your line." Walter's retort: "I'll try to think of one for you." While rolling by in a stretcher, Matthau offered a friendly "Hi" to passersby. Of the institutional hospital food, he joked that he may be eating Jell-O but was thinking deli. Added Neil Parker, "I would kid around with him. We always liked to kibitz. He told me I had the delivery of Groucho Marx. I don't know if that was true, but I believed it. That was part of him. It wasn't about him. It was about you—and that's not how many people are. With him, it was always, 'Have something to eat.'"

If Matthau ever felt depressed about his physical condition, he never let on. "He never looked down, never said anything negative," noted Jean Longacre of the Beverly Hills Tennis Club. "He was just himself. He was so graceful with it all." Added Marian Seldes, "I suppose a lot of people who only saw him in the later movies would think, 'Oh, what a grouchy man he must be.' Well, if he was, he didn't show it. And if he had periods of depression, which I tend to think he did, he did not show that. He did not burden you with that, ever."

Ossie Davis recalled that, while filming *I'm Not Rappaport*, Matthau "showed me his special medical equipment, his defibrillator. I think there was a young lady on set [who was] prepared just to grab old Walter in case his heart went wild. So he had a gallows-humor attitude toward himself, and toward life. [I was] aware that he had a problem, that he was in essence living on borrowed time. But he was never maudlin."

Matthau aggressively learned about his illnesses. He and Carol took CPR classes at the tennis club, so that they could handle any unforeseen emergency. On one occasion, he interrupted an interview to phone his doctor and ask, "Is coffee a vaso-dilator or a vasoconstrictor? Check it out, will ya? You have the book right on your desk."

Another harsh reminder of Matthau's mortality: His older brother Henry, who throughout his life maintained the Matthow surname, died on May 21, 1995, in Lido Beach, located on New York's Long Island.

On one level, Walter and Henry's relationship was cordial. One New Year's Eve, Anna Berger was at Henry's house when Walter called, to wish him a Happy New Year. Yet their association was complex. "I know my father loved Henry very much," declared Charlie, "but they didn't have a lot in common. Whenever he'd go to New York, he'd always see [Henry]. And I do know that, growing up, they were quite close. My father looked up to Henry. Henry was the tough older brother." Added William Schallert, "He and Henry had an ambivalent relationship. Henry would sometimes irritate him. I don't know what [that] was about." Yet when Henry died, Schallert recalled that Matthau was bereft. "I've lost my older brother," he declared. "I've lost the guy who got me through the Depression. I've lost the key person in my life." Schallert added, "He'd never said that before, but the loss was devastating to him. This surprised me, because I had no idea of how close they must have been. Underneath it all, there must have been a real bond."

For years, Syd Preses organized reunions of members of the Stuyvesant Settlement House. Neither Walter nor Henry had been members, but one year she invited Henry. He was reluctant to attend, telling her that he would not know anyone, but finally in 1994 he came. "He sat at the table, and he looked at one fellow, Carl Greenberg, and he said, 'I know you. You lived in my building.' With that, he went around—and he knew everyone! He had such a good time, and he couldn't wait until the next year. But unfortunately, he died." It was around this time that Henry also attended a Seward Park High School reunion. "We sat around and chatted," recalled Leon Birns, "and soon after, he died."

Even though he was in his seventies, Henry remained physically active, regularly playing handball. According to Preses, his doctor told him that at his age he should ease up, but he refused. Milt Berger added that he went swimming almost every day. To the end, he remained a likable guy. "I loved Walter," noted Marvin Silbersher, "but

I think that Hank was one of the dearest and straightest people, a real sweetheart."

Right after his passing, Preses sent Walter photos of Henry. On June 24, 1995, Walter wrote her back. "Yes, it was a terrible shock to hear that Henry was dead," he noted. "He was the picture of a healthy man."

If Henry's passing merited attention only from friends, associates, and family, Walter's health status became fodder for the tabloids. This was particularly distressing for actors like him and Jack Lemmon, aging stars who preferred full work schedules but were susceptible to being written off within the industry as health risks. Given Matthau's fragile physical condition, hiring him of course *was* precarious.

The June 25, 1996, issue of the *Globe* announced, "STUNNED PALS BARE GRUMPY OLD MAN'S SECRET OPERATION: Frail Walter Matthau felled by deadly illness." Yet the piece ended with an "eyewitness" spotting Matthau having lunch with three friends at the Beverly Hilton Hotel, and "holding court as only Walter can . . . cracking jokes with his buddies all through lunch, and after his meal [leaning] back and contentedly [lighting] up a big fat cigar." The following day, the *National Enquirer* chimed in with "Frail Walter Matthau fights secret illness." "Walter looks like death warmed over," the omnipresent, unnamed "source close to Matthau" reported.

It likely was this paper that Leon Birns's wife spotted one day in the supermarket. She purchased it to show to her husband, who passed it on to Matthau. His response: "Dear Leon, Thanks for your interest, but that's all a lot of baloney. If you get a pimple on your ass, they write up the whole thing." He added, "Tell your wife to stop buying that horseshit paper." (For one sequence in *Buddy Buddy*, Matthau was sprawled out on a bed with his rear end sticking up. During the filming, he requested that the still photographer not take pictures. His rationale: "You know and I know where they will end up: on the front page of the *National Enquirer*.")

Three months later, on September 17, the *Enquirer* ran an upbeat piece headlined "WALTER MATTHAU: I'M WINNING FIGHT TO REGAIN MY HEALTH." The artwork included a photo of the actor walking on a treadmill. But a year later, on November 4, 1997, the

Globe ran a piece headlined "WALTER MATTHAU HEART DRAMA"; on December 16, the *Star* followed with "WALTER MATTHAU HEALTH DRAMA: He risks blindness from deadly eye tumor." The June 8, 1999, *Globe* had Charlie "confiding" to the paper that his dad was battling "deadly pneumonia." The story's headline was "Walter Matthau's son: Please pray for my dad." Three days later, the *National Enquirer* headlined "WALTER MATTHAU'S BRAVE LAST DAYS." Just over a year later, on June 27, 2000, the *Star* announced, "WALTER MATTHAU: END IS NEAR."

When the tabloids were not reporting that Matthau was breathing his last, they had him squandering his possessions. The March 9, 1997, issue of *The Star* pronounced, "WALTER MATTHAU'S WIFE THREATENS TO KILL HIM AFTER HE GAMBLES AWAY $1m IN THREE WEEKS." The accompanying article quoted the actor as declaring, "Carol came at me with a gun recently. She was talking in a hysterical way, and said, 'This is loaded—if you make another bet this year, I'm going to put a bullet right between your eyes.' She wasn't joking. I said, 'OK.' She was out of control. Every time I take a bad loss I say I'll never do it again. It affects my mood. I've been psychotic. My wife is a depraved spender and I'm a degenerate gambler." Actually, this last sentence originally appeared in a Matthau profile in *Entertainment Weekly*, published on January 28, 1994. Within the context of the article, it is clear that the remark was meant as a wisecrack.

Then the March 18, 1997, *Globe* announced in a headline, "Holly-wood legend's shocking confession . . . Walter Matthau: I'm addicted to gambling." Of course, he freely admitted to his betting decades earlier. In a July 4, 1971, *New York Times* article headlined "What the OTB Bettor Can Learn from Walter Matthau," Thomas Meehan wrote, midway through the first paragraph, "And if he's nothing else, Walter Matthau, the fifty-year-old stage and movie actor, is a compulsive gambler."

Of his betting, Matthau now occasionally swore abstinence. "Gave it up after the Super Bowl," he declared in 1994. "I had Buffalo [over the triumphant Dallas Cowboys], and I just quit, cold turkey." But he never totally abandoned the pastime. "I like to lay eleven-to-ten on a football game," he told Roger Ebert the previous year. "It's really an even-money shot, with the points. But I lay eleven-to-ten because I know the bookie needs that 5 percent that I give him, otherwise he wouldn't be able to make a living and go down to Florida with his family.

"I take it easy now," he added. "I bet, maybe, $20 a game." Then he elicited what Ebert described as a mournful chortle. "If you believe that," he added, "I have a bridge in New York which I'd like to sell you."

In September 1996, he cracked, "I lost my ass last weekend with nine out of ten football games." Noted son Charlie, that same year, "He still loves to gamble, but let's just say the amount he bets hasn't gone up in a commensurate fashion with the amount of money he's making—thank God."

In the mid-1980s, Matthau began working on his autobiography with his friend, *New York Times* sportswriter Ira Berkow. The project never was completed. He also began racking up career awards and accolades. In March 1982, he was honored with a star on the Hollywood Walk of Fame. It is located in front of an unmarked, undistinguished building at 6353 Hollywood Blvd., between the stars for Dave Garroway and, appropriately, Jack Lemmon. In 1987, he was a presenter at the First Annual American Comedy Awards, where Lily Tomlin introduced him by noting, "If a group of aliens from outer space landed in my backyard searching for signs of intelligent life and said, 'We're looking for some laughs. Take us to your leader,' I'd take them to meet Walter Matthau." In 1993, he won the ShoWest Convention Lifetime Achievement Award. Four years later, he was honored by the American Comedy Awards, joining Lemmon, Milton Berle, Johnny Carson, Doris Day, and Phyllis Diller. Goldie Hawn presented him with the prize. Also in 1997, he, Carol, and Charlie shared a new trophy, the American Film Institute Associates Platinum Circle Award, honoring them as "an entire family of talented artists." They were feted at a luncheon, held at the Regent Beverly Wilshire Hotel. Matthau co-stars Hawn, Sophia Loren, and Ann-Margret, who presented the award, were the honorary co-chairwomen.

On November 1, 1996, *The Hollywood Reporter*, an industry trade publication, honored Matthau with a special issue devoted to his half-century in show business. Later that month, Elaine May interviewed him for a short, humorous piece published in *The New Yorker.* The article ended with May querying, "Is there a question you'd like to answer that I haven't asked?" Matthau's response: "Yes. Tell me I've been an actor for fifty years and ask me where the time has gone." May did as ordered. Matthau's response: "Don't ask."

Actor-agent Marty Ingels met Matthau at an Actor's Fund cocktail party in Beverly Hills. "It was not too long before he died," Ingels recalled, but it was before his 1999 health crisis. "He looked like he was failing some. That is, until we spoke. We were both circling the buffet table with our hungry plates."

"Walter, Walter, how ya' doin'?" Ingels exclaimed.

"I'm alive," was the reply.

"Try those little pancake things. They're great," Ingels continued.

There was no response. Determined to keep the conversation going, Ingels noted, "That little green dish over there has the Viagra pills. You use 'em?" Upon "walking away with a mountainous plate-full," Matthau answered Ingels by declaring, "Just to keep from rolling out of bed."

Prior to the March 1999 Academy Awards ceremony, Matthau revealed that he wished he was winning a prize. His reasoning: Elia Kazan, the legendary, controversial stage and screen director—who had directed Matthau in *A Face in the Crowd*—was receiving a special Oscar. The award was hotly debated because of Kazan's decision to name Communist Party members decades earlier, when called before the House Un-American Activities Committee. Had Matthau won, he explained, he would begin his acceptance speech, "There are many people I would like to thank, but I don't want to name names."

In the 1990s, Matthau's old friend and colleague Ossie Davis remarked, "Walter has chosen to grow old, but not grow old gracefully. Walter is still a combatant. Walter still has power in his punch. The joy of being alive, which is so important to the human spirit, is appreciated by Walter Matthau." A year after Matthau's death, Davis recollected, "Walter responded to being alive in a humorous fashion. He was basically a humorous man."

Lana Morgan recalled that her fondest memories of Matthau were when he called her on the phone and attempted to trick her into thinking he was someone else. He employed an accent, or asked for something ridiculous. She knew it was him, but did not want to disappoint him by saying so and ruining his fun. So she played along, and after a few minutes blurted out, "Waaaaalter!"

Once he called and launched into some gibberish, asking Morgan, "Flender schmar blumbleknot derk slem?" She recognized his voice, and came right back with "Muffledar snar dort mem." They volleyed back and forth a couple times, asking "Flootus lumpnus?" and answering "Snortle bem car." Then Matthau grew silent, started chuckling, and said, "I didn't know you spoke Schmendeldar." Morgan's retort: "Oh, yes, I'm very fluent in Ka Marbleschlu and Snismar." She added, "He was just delighted if you could recognize what he was doing and jump into the game with him."

Another time, Morgan received a phone call from a "guy who had a really odd name and a suspiciously deep voice. He's asking me for some script submission information, and I'm not buying it. The name and the voice were just too goofy, so I'm sure it's Walter. I decide to have a little fun so I'm giving this guy a hard time. 'Oh, *Mr.* Schwing-hammerstan,' or whatever the name was. And I launch into some nonsense. 'Of course I remember you. You're the one with bells for dentures. You want to send us a script? Are you kidding? I am not reading anything from you until you pick up the purple spotted sloth you left hanging on our verb compactor.'"

To Morgan's embarrassment, the caller was a real person. "In a way," she added, "this was Walter's best phone trick on me ever, because he set me up and didn't even have to be around for the payoff. When I told Walter about this, he loved it.

"On one occasion, he comes by the office. He walks over to me and gives me a hug—except he doesn't let go. I'm thinking, 'Hum. This is a little unusual.' He wasn't flirting. It was a father kind of hug, but he wasn't letting go. I'm wondering, what is this about?" Morgan kept hugging him, and patting him on the back. Matthau made no indication that he was ready to let go, and soon rested his head on Morgan's head. "I decide I'm going to wait this out and see what happens," she continued. "I'm not going to pull away. So more time goes by. Neither of us moves. Finally, I can't stand the suspense but I'm not going to pull away, so I say, 'Walter, did you just need a little hug?'

And he barks back, 'What are you talking about? I was asleep!'"

Post–*Hanging Up*—and post-coma—Matthau expressed the desire to continue making movies. Perhaps his next might be that second *Grumpy Old Men* sequel, if only the powers-that-be could come up with a suitable script. "I'm the only person talking about it," he noted. Yet again, Matthau colorfully decried the dearth of good scripts. "There are no more stories in the movies," he said, "no more human stories about interesting characters. They're all coming from outer space or they're monsters from within which explode out of you into cellular Internet telephones or something. All kinds of goofy ideas."

Nor did Matthau choose to spend all of his time at home. "One of the things that amazed me," noted Lana Morgan, "was that, after the coma—and you didn't think he was going to make it through that— he would come over to the office, or go for a walk. You would see this guy, and you could not believe that he had just gone through what he had."

While his humor remained wry, his illnesses did effect him spiritually. "He was deeper," Charlie recalled. "He would tell me things. There were certain things he told me that he wouldn't want anyone to know about."

On Father's Day 1999, Charlie felt compelled to compose an extra-special note to his dad. "You are a giant," he wrote. "The most loyal and patient husband, and as a father, a volcanic and infinite explosion of unconditional love, universal wisdom, and a supernova of everything that is right and good in this world."

Then Charlie added a punchline that surely cracked Walter up. "Aside from that, however, I'm not very pleased with you!"

Walter readily returned the teasing. Not long before he died, he was resting in bed when Charlie videotaped him. Charlie began by asking, "What do you want to talk about?"

"I don't have much to talk about," Walter replied.

Then Charlie asked, "What's the smartest and dumbest thing you ever did?"

"Smartest and dumbest at the same time?"

"No. No. Different times, I assume."

"Well, how about in November and in June."

"What do you mean?"

"I have no idea."

"No, I mean in your life, looking back."

"Smartest thing I ever did? I did that without trying. I . . . I . . . put the sperm in your mother's egg, and you showed up."

"That's nice, Velvulah," Charlie cooed.

Walter managed a smile as he retorted, "That's the dumbest thing I ever did."

CHAPTER 30

A Good Life

At a Christmas party sometime in the mid-1990s, Lia Waggner kid-dingly asked Walter, "What thing would you really like to have some day?" Matthau responded, "Oh, Lia, I've had the most wonderful life. There's nothing else I really could hope for." "Except for the last year," added Waggner's husband, William Schallert, "he was a really happy guy."

Despite all he had to live for—beginning with his love for Charlie and Carol—Matthau "was suffering so badly during that last year," according to Schallert. "I remember that last year before he died he came to the house for Thanksgiving. He couldn't stay, but he made the effort. We went [to his house] for Christmas. Then on New Year's Eve, he took a bunch of us down in the canyon to Giorgios. It was amazing. I couldn't get over the fact that he could do this because by then his kidneys had gone and he was on dialysis. That was a terrible experience for him, very painful." Matthau used the word "cold" to describe to Schallert the feeling of having blood passed in and out of his body during dialysis. "It surely did not please him to know that he would have to go through this for the rest of his life."

Matthau also invited Neil Parker and his wife out at Christmas-time. "It wasn't because I was his doctor," he noted. "It was because we had a closeness."

As Matthau settled in at home post-coma, Schallert noted that it appeared as if he was going to recover. He was doing a little walking, and visiting The Matthau Company—but then he fell out of bed and cracked a couple of vertebrae. "That became very painful," Schallert stated. The date was April 10, 2000, and Matthau landed back in the hospital. He returned home after a several-week stay.

"Then toward the end of his life they were giving him massive doses of painkillers, just to make it possible for him to make it through the day," added Schallert. "And he began to slip away. Because of the painkillers, he was less alert, and sometimes he wouldn't recognize me for awhile."

Several months before his death, Matthau had one last conversation with Marvin Silbersher, who noted that his final words were, "Marvin, we've done this and that. We've done Shakespeare and Moliere. But Marvin, I hope we can meet again under happier circumstances."

"When Walter was very, very sick, I called," said Anna Berger. "When he didn't call back, I knew he was dying. Also, Michelle [Matthau's niece] visited him, and she told me that he didn't recognize her. He didn't recognize anybody anymore. The only one he called for was Henry. I feel that he was calling for Henry to escort him to the next stage."

Added Leon Birns, "One thing about Walter, he always responded when you wrote him a letter. I had written him last year [in 2000], just before we went up north [from Florida] for the summer, and he didn't acknowledge it. I said to my wife, 'This is very strange.' We didn't know he was already sick."

On Friday evening, June 30, Matthau was resting quietly at home. He was in the company of Carol and Teresa DiDiego, his nurse for eighteen months, when he suffered a full cardiac arrest. The paramedics were called, and he was brought to St. John's Health Center in Santa Monica. He was pronounced dead at 1:42 A.M. on Saturday.

On the afternoon before, Lana Morgan had stopped by to see Carol, but Walter heard them talking and wanted to say hello. "He was just recently home from the hospital and was on around-the-clock nursing care," she reported. "There was a hospital bed in his room and all sorts of medical equipment and IVs, but Carol had made certain it felt as much like home for him as it could. There were beautiful Porthault sheets on the hospital bed. I thought it was so sweet because it was the little pink heart pattern. It was perfect and what Walter loved."

He carried on as if it was an ordinary day, making no reference to his condition. "What really astonished me was that despite Walter's thin body and deteriorating condition, his skin and hair were extraordinarily healthy. Absolutely radiant, actually."

Morgan was wearing what she described as one of her Holly Golightly hats, which Walter recognized. He was delighted, and had Carol model it. "We all started getting pretty silly and then Walter wanted to play a game where we all do imitations of people we know and then decide who was the funniest. Carol won hands-down, doing an imitation of Charlie doing an imitation of Walter. That really tickled Walter. These were the kinds of things that would entertain him.

"Walter asked me to sing him a song. I wished I knew the words to a Mozart aria but I don't so instead I sang an old torch song I love, 'Blue Moon.' Then Carol sang a fun tune from *Guys and Dolls* in an interpretation that sounded remarkably like Judy Holiday.

"Walter and Carol were flirting and joking with each other. Carol was holding Walter's hand and kissing it. Walter mischievously complained that I hadn't kissed him yet. So I kissed him on the forehead. Before I left, he fell asleep. It was a nice afternoon. I was so happy that I had a chance to say good-bye."

Another visitor was William Schallert. A physical therapist was present, and was leading Matthau through a series of exercises. The two old friends passed the time. Before Schallert went home, he gently kissed Matthau goodbye.

"He was in pretty good spirits when I saw him on Friday night," Charlie Matthau told the media just after his father's death. Charlie described the phone call informing him of the cardiac arrest as the one he had been dreading all his life. As he arrived at the hospital, he "was definitely fearing the worst. They said they were working on him. Then the doctor came out." Charlie asked, "Is he still alive?" The doctor said, "No."

"I don't know what the doctors are going to do now for business with Dad gone," Charlie added, as he struggled to keep his composure. Charlie also noted, "I've lost my hero and my best friend. He gave the world many gifts, but he gave me everything." Neil Parker reported that he spoke to Charlie two to three hours after Walter's death. "I was concerned that Charlie wouldn't be able to handle it," Parker recalled. "He was sad, of course, but was understanding, and glad for all the time they had, all the great years." The doctor explained that Charlie was able to separate the difference between "I'm gonna keep him alive" and the reality of his death.

In Pacific Palisades, Matthau's passing signified the loss of more than a beloved celebrity. "On the day he died, I went over to see Carol, to ask if there was anything I could do," recalled William Schallert. "So many of the neighbors were out in the street, offering their best wishes.

"At least he died peacefully," Schallert added.

On several occasions over the following days, Charlie told the press that, intellectually, he understood that his father would not live forever. Given his age and the precarious state of his health, Walter might pass away at any time. Still, the emotional impact of the event floored him.

One of the ads in the 1996 *Hollywood Reporter* Matthau tribute was designed as a letter: "Dear Waltz, My congratulations to the best of the best. Just keep including me in the next 50 years. Love, Jack." Now, four years later, Jack Lemmon issued a statement in which he declared, "I have lost someone I loved as a brother, as a closest friend and a remarkable human being. We have also lost one of the best damn actors we'll ever see." Added Billy Wilder, "He was so natural. He was himself, with all the quirks that a human being has. He was a guy who made great friends. Whether you played cards with him or whether you talked football bets with him, he was a full-blown man. He was good at everything he did. Sometimes I messed it up as a director. But he was absolutely perfect, always."

When Matthau died, Leon Birns was in Atlantic City. On Friday evenings, their hotel ran movies. "One of the ones they were showing was *Hanging Up*," he noted. "It was strange, because the next morning people came up to us and said, 'I heard Walter died.'" Birns eventually wrote of Matthau, in the Seward Park High School Alumni Association newsletter, "He still wanted his old friends to be part of his world. He never failed to answer my letters or return my calls. . . . We will miss him because he added something to this world."

On the day of his death, flowers were placed on Matthau's star on the Hollywood Walk of Fame. The following day, he was buried in the Memorial Gardens section of Pierce Brothers Westwood Memorial Park, a small cemetery located behind the high-rises lining Wilshire Blvd. in the Westwood section of Los Angeles. Matthau's plot is nearby that of another comedy legend, Fanny Brice. Over fifty mourners were present, including Matthau's immediate family and his closest friends in the acting community. According to his wishes, he was buried in a simple pine casket. "The service was traditional," explained Rabbi Jerry Cutler, who presided, "but unfortunately he was not buried in a Jewish cemetery."

One of the movie stars interred at Westwood is Marilyn Monroe. "Knowing my father," recalled Charlie Matthau on the day of the funeral, "he'll insist on alphabetical billing." Scores of celebrities are buried there, from Eve Arden, Jim Backus, and John Cassavetes to Natalie Wood and Darryl Zanuck. Buried nearby are Matthau friends and colleagues, including Truman Capote, Carol's childhood pal; Norma Crane, who appeared in the *Mister Peepers* pilot; Nancy Kelly, of Broadway's *Season in the Sun* and *Twilight Walk*; Burt Lancaster, of *The Kentuckian*; and Franklin Schaffner, who directed Matthau on television.

Jack Lemmon eulogized his buddy by noting that Walter, Carol, and Charlie were as much a part of his family as his own wife and children. Matthau's home was teeming with bouquets from a star-studded array of colleagues, including Diane Keaton, Meg Ryan, Goldie Hawn, and Sophia Loren.

Upon his death, film critics, historians, and journalists collectively gushed as they paid homage to him, using the most colorful and descriptive language. Their essence was summed up by Roger Ebert, who wrote that Matthau's face was "mapped with laugh lines. . . . In comedy he never tried to be funny, and in tragedy he never tried to be sad. He was just this big . . . shambling, sardonic guy whose dialogue had the ease and persuasion of overheard truth."

Scant days after Matthau's death, Charlie Matthau, Jack Lemmon, Carol Burnett, and Dyan Cannon reminisced on a *Larry King*

Live tribute. Charlie described in detail the night his father died. "Charlie's description of his last night, that was tough," King recalled several months later. One of the most poignant moments came when Lemmon revealed how he learned of Matthau's demise: "I was sitting on the throne. Felicia, my bride, knocked and came in and bent over and gave me a kiss." Lemmon began crying as he noted what Felicia told him: "You're not gonna smile anymore."

A couple of days later, Charlie noted, "When I start to get sad, I think, 'Well, what am I getting sad for? The only problem was that he didn't live forever.' Everybody wants their father to live longer, but he had a great life."

Carole Shelley, his *Odd Couple* co-star, caught a Matthau interview that was rebroadcast on television. "He was being interviewed maybe six, seven, eight months before he died," she recalled. "He looked old and frail, and the interviewer said, 'What are you, eighty-three now?' and he said, 'OoooUhhhh, I'm seventy-nine.' And I thought, 'Oh, God bless you for being vain.' I just loved him for being vain at that point in his life."

After Walter's death, Carol presented a number of his friends with his favorite *chatchkas*. Larry King received a sterling silver yo-yo. Zubin Mehta's gift was a small silver dish. "Glenda Jackson gave it to Walter," he explained. "There's a Mozart coin at the bottom of the dish. Walter took it everywhere with him. It was one of his favorite things."

Then on Sunday, August 20, a memorial service was held in Matthau's honor at the headquarters of the Directors Guild of America. Charlie was the host, and the event was a love feast to Walter's memory. Over 500 of his friends, colleagues, and relatives attended, including Sophia Loren, Richard Benjamin, Gregory Peck, Norman Lear, Doris Roberts, Carl Reiner, Piper Laurie, Daryl Hannah, Angie Dickinson, Richard Lewis, Kevin Pollak, Howard Koch, Walter Mirisch, and Jack Klugman. Charlie began by declaring, "Well of course we're sad that he had to die. We're here to celebrate his life in the spirit which he would have appreciated, namely with joy and laughter." The speakers included Diane Keaton (who noted that Matthau possessed an "ironic dignity" and described his face as "not handsome but magnificent"); Jack Lemmon; Neil

Simon; Lauren Bacall; Leonard Hirshan; Larry King; Neil Parker; and Jerry Cutler. Collectively, they focused on Matthau's sense of humor and his humanism and fellowship. Cutler got the event's biggest laugh as he recalled dining with Matthau at the Beverly Hills Tennis Club. The rabbi's spinach salad came topped with bacon bits, and the actor went from table to table and feigned auctioning it by asking "How much for a spinach salad blessed by Walter Matthau's rabbi?"

Bacall read a message from Carol Matthau, who penned, "We had lots of fights and perfect love." Lemmon used the phrase "magic time"—an exclamation he invoked before each take on a film set—to describe his moments with Matthau. He sobbed at the end of his tribute. He might have smiled had he recalled that Matthau once joked that he employed the term whenever he had to pass wind, "so that you wouldn't hear anything."

Filmmaker Chuck Workman assembled a series of Matthau film clips, which was screened. Once decades earlier, Matthau trekked to Coney Island to savor kosher hot dogs at the original Nathan's eatery. A cab driver, shocked to see a celebrity among the Brooklyn masses, asked him, "What the hell are you doing in a place like this?" Matthau responded, "What's the matter? Are you a snob? Do you think this is a place for only people like you?" Among the edibles at the memorial were Nathan's hot dogs and beer, served from a Nathan's hot dog stand, complete with bright yellow and red umbrella and the green company logo. Among the edibles were fortune cookies, served in Chinese food take-out packaging labeled "Whiplash Willie's Fortune Cookies." Inside were lines uttered by Matthau screen characters. At the end of the memorial, Charlie invited the guests to enjoy this "health food."

A *Chicago Tribune* homage to Matthau, written by Michael Wilmington, was printed inside the program. It was headlined "Extra Ordinary: Odds Are Walter Matthau Will Always Be One of the Greats." "In a town filled with too many male swans and peacocks," observed Wilmington, "Matthau was a proud and unregenerate crow. He was a supercrow: secure in his homeliness, confident in his earthly antiglamour, mostly unconcerned with fine feathers—and capable of stealing the screen (and the entire movie) from any peacock, anytime."

The program included a solicitation to anyone interested in helping fund a life-size bronze sculpture of Matthau, "to be installed in a public area in Los Angeles." The project to raise funding continues. Those interested in learning more about it can read about its progress on a Matthau website (www.matthau.com/sys-tmpl/door/).

On the back of the program was "Walter's Pre-Season line for Conference Championship and Super Bowl XXXV." His call was that the reigning champion St. Louis Rams would repeat as champs. Predictably, the Rams made a quick exit from the playoffs.

In September, Carole Matthau sold their beach house, purportedly for more than $5 million. Then in April 2001, she closed a deal on the Pacific Palisades home for a similar price tag. The following month, she moved back to Manhattan. At the end of June—almost a year to the day after Matthau passed away—Jack Lemmon died of complications from cancer. "They were great, lifelong friends," declared Charlie Matthau, on a *Larry King Live* tribute to Lemmon. "And they're together again."

Those who knew and loved Matthau never will forget him. "I miss him," declared Jerry Cutler nine months after his passing. "I treasured his friendship greatly, as I do Charlie's. He left me Charlie. I had him for the [then just-concluded Passover] Seder. We sat together with Madonna, of all people, and Guy Ritchie and a few others."

"We broke all the rules about how one is supposed to separate from a parent," declared Charlie Matthau. "We both took some criticism for it. I made my choice of where to go to college, where to buy my house, what films to direct, in order to maximize the time we could spend together. I treasured every moment, and I always will.

"I don't regret a day of it because while we were going to Laker games and concerts and making movies and walking our dog around [Pacific] Palisades and playing *Jeopardy!* against the TV contestants, or betting at the track, he was teaching by example how to live with humor and compassion and love and strength."

CREDITS AND AWARDS

Motion Pictures

The Kentuckian (1955) (United Artists) Dir: Burt Lancaster. Cast: Burt Lancaster, Dianne Foster, Diana Lynn, John McIntire, Una Merkel, John Carradine, Donald McDonald, John Litel. WM plays *Sam Bodine*

The Indian Fighter (1955) (United Artists) Dir: Andre de Toth. Cast: Kirk Douglas, Elsa Martinelli, Walter Abel, Diana Douglas, Lon Chaney Jr., Edouard Franz, Alan Hale Jr., Elisha Cook. *Wes Todd*

Bigger Than Life (1956) (Twentieth Century-Fox) Dir: Nicholas Ray. Cast: James Mason, Barbara Rush, Robert Simon, Christopher Olsen, Roland Winters, Rusty Lane, Lee Aaker, Jerry Mathers. *Wally Gibbs*

A Face in the Crowd (1957) (Warner Bros.) Dir: Elia Kazan. Cast: Andy Griffith, Patricia Neal, Anthony Franciosa, Lee Remick, Percy Waram, Paul McGrath, Marshall Neilan, Howard Smith, Kay Medford, Rip Torn. *Mel Miller*

Slaughter on Tenth Avenue (1957) (Universal) Dir: Arnold Laven. Cast: Richard Egan, Jan Sterling, Dan Duryea, Julie Adams, Charles McGraw, Sam Levene, Mickey Shaughnessy, Harry Bellaver, Nick Dennis. *Al Dahlke*

King Creole (1958) (Paramount) Dir: Michael Curtiz. Cast: Elvis Presley, Carolyn Jones, Dolores Hart, Dean Jagger, Liliane Montevecchi, Paul Stewart, Vic Morrow, Brian Hutton, Raymond Bailey. *Maxie Fields*

Voice in the Mirror (1958) (Universal) Dir: Harry Keller. Cast: Richard Egan, Julie London, Troy Donahue, Ann Doran, Mae Clarke, Max Showalter, Arthur O'Connell. *Dr. Leon Karnes*

Onionhead (1958) (Warner Bros.) Dir: Norman Taurog. Cast: Andy Griffith, Felicia Farr, Erin O'Brien, Joe Mantell, Ray Danton, James Gregory, Joey Bishop, Roscoe Karns, Claude Akins, Tige Andrews. *"Red" Wildoe*

Ride a Crooked Trail (1958) (Universal) Dir: Jesse Hibbs. Cast: Audie Murphy, Gia Scala, Henry Silva, Joanna Moore, Leo Gordon. *Judge Kyle*

Gangster Story (1960) (Releasing Corp. of Independent Producers) Dir: Walter Matthau. Cast: Carol Grace (Carol Matthau), Bruce McFarlan, Gerrett Wallberg, Raikin Ben-Ari. *Jack Martin*

Strangers When We Meet (1960) (Columbia) Dir: Richard Quine. Cast: Kirk Douglas, Kim Novak, Ernie Kovacs, Barbara Rush, Virginia Bruce, Kent Smith, Helen Gallagher, Nancy Kovack. *Felix Anders*

Lonely Are the Brave (1962) (Universal) Dir: David Miller. Cast: Kirk Douglas, Gena Rowlands, Michael Kane, Carroll O'Connor, William Schallert, Karl Swenson, George Kennedy. *Sheriff Johnson*

Who's Got the Action? (1962) (Paramount) Dir: Daniel Mann. Cast: Dean Martin, Lana Turner, Eddie Albert, Nita Talbot, Margo, Paul Ford, John McGiver, Dan Tobin, Jack Albertson, Ned Glass. *Tony Gagoots*

Island of Love (1963) (Warner Bros.) Dir: Morton DaCosta. Cast: Robert Preston, Tony Randall, Giorgia Moll, Betty Bruce, Michael Constantine, Titos Vandis. *Tony Dallas*

Charade (1963) (Universal) Dir: Stanley Donen. Cast: Cary Grant, Audrey Hepburn, James Coburn, George Kennedy, Ned Glass, Jacques Marin. *Hamilton Bartholomew*

Ensign Pulver (1964) (Warner Bros.) Dir: Joshua Logan. Cast: Robert Walker Jr., Burl Ives, Tommy Sands, Millie Perkins, Kay Medford, Larry Hagman, Gerald S. O'Loughlin, Al Freeman Jr., James Farentino, James Coco, Diana Sands, Jack Nicholson. *Doc*

Fail-Safe (1964) (Columbia) Dir: Sidney Lumet. Cast: Henry Fonda, Dan O'Herlihy, Frank Overton, Edward Binns, Fritz Weaver, Larry Hagman, Russell Hardie, Russell Collins, Sorrell Booke, Hildy Parks, Dom DeLuise, Dana Elcar. *Groeteschele*

Goodbye Charlie (1964) (Twentieth Century-Fox) Dir: Vincente Minnelli. Cast: Tony Curtis, Debbie Reynolds, Pat Boone, Joanna Barnes, Ellen McRae (Ellen Burstyn), Martin Gabel, Roger C. Carmel. *Sir Leopold Sartori*

Mirage (1965) (Universal) Dir: Edward Dmytryk. Cast: Gregory Peck, Diane Baker, Kevin McCarthy, Jack Weston, Leif Erickson, Walter Abel, George Kennedy, Anne Seymour. *Ted Caselle*

The Fortune Cookie (1966) (United Artists) Dir: Billy Wilder. Cast: Jack Lemmon, Ron Rich, Cliff Osmond, Judi West, Lurene Tuttle, Les Tremayne, Marge Redmond, Ned Glass, Sig Rumann, Howard McNear. *Willie Gingrich*

A Guide for the Married Man (1967) (Twentieth Century-Fox) Dir: Gene Kelly. Cast: Inger Stevens, Sue Ane Langdon, Jackie Russell, Robert Morse, Elaine Devry, Majel Barrett, Linda Harrison, Lucille Ball, Jack Benny, Polly Bergen, Joey Bishop, Sid Caesar, Art Carney, Wally Cox, Jayne Mansfield, Hal March, Louis Nye, Carl Reiner, Phil Silvers, Terry-Thomas, Ben Blue, Ann Morgan Guilbert, Jeffrey Hunter, Marty Ingels, Sam Jaffe. *Paul Manning*

The Odd Couple (1968) (Paramount) Dir: Gene Saks. Cast: Jack Lemmon, John Fiedler, Herbert Edelman, David Sheiner, Larry Haines, Monica Evans, Carole Shelley, Iris Adrian, Heywood Hale Broun. *Oscar Madison*

The Secret Life of an American Wife (1968) (Twentieth Century-Fox) Dir: George Axelrod. Cast: Anne Jackson, Patrick O'Neal, Edy Williams. *Charlie, the Movie Star*

Candy (1968) (Cinerama) Dir: Christian Marquand. Cast: Charles Aznavour, Marlon Brando, Richard Burton, James Coburn, John Huston, Ringo Starr, Ewa Aulin, John Astin, Elsa Martinelli, Sugar Ray Robinson, Anita Pallenberg, Florinda Bolkan, The Byrds, Steppenwolf. *General Smight*

Hello, Dolly! (1969) (Twentieth Century-Fox) Dir: Gene Kelly. Cast: Barbra Streisand, Michael Crawford, Louis Armstrong, Marianne McAndrew, E. J. Peaker, Danny Lockin, Tommy Tune. *Horace Vandergelder*

Cactus Flower (1969) (Columbia) Dir: Gene Saks. Cast: Ingrid Bergman, Goldie Hawn, Jack Weston, Rick Lenz, Vito Scotti, Irene Hervey. *Julian Winston*

A New Leaf (1971) (Paramount) Dir: Elaine May. Cast: Elaine May, Jack Weston, George Rose, William Redfield, James Coco, Graham Jarvis, Doris Roberts, Renee Taylor, David Doyle. *Henry Graham*

Plaza Suite (1971) (Paramount) Dir: Arthur Hiller. Cast: Maureen Stapleton, Barbara Harris, Lee Grant, Louise Sorel. *Sam Nash/Jesse Kiplinger/Roy Hubley*

Kotch (1971) (Cinerama) Dir: Jack Lemmon. Cast: Deborah Winters, Felicia Farr, Charles Aidman, Ellen Geer, Darrell Larson, Lucy Saroyan, Jane Connell, Jessica Rains, Larry Linville. *Joseph P. Kotcher*

Pete 'n' Tillie (1972) (Universal) Dir: Martin Ritt. Cast: Carol Burnett, Geraldine Page, Barry Nelson, Rene Auberjonois, Lee H. Montgomery, Henry Jones, Kent Smith, Whit Bissell. *Pete Seltzer*

Charley Varrick (1973) (Universal) Dir: Don Siegel. Cast: Joe Don Baker, Felicia Farr, Andy Robinson, John Vernon, Sheree North, Norman Fell, Benson Fong, Woodrow Parfrey, William Schallert, Tom Tully, Donald Siegel, Charles Matthau. *Charley Varrick*

The Laughing Policeman (1973) (Twentieth Century-Fox) Dir: Stuart Rosenberg. Cast: Bruce Dern, Louis Gossett, Albert Paulsen, Anthony Zerbe, Val Avery, Cathy Lee Crosby, Joanna Cassidy, Louis Guss, Clifton James. *Jake Martin*

The Taking of Pelham One Two Three (1974) (United Artists) Dir: Joseph Sargent. Cast: Robert Shaw, Martin Balsam, Hector Elizondo, Earl Hindman, James Broderick, Dick O'Neill, Jerry Stiller, Kenneth McMillan, Doris Roberts, Tony Roberts, Anna Berger, Marvin Silbersher, Lucy Saroyan, Michelle Matthow. *Lieutenant Zachary Garber*

Earthquake (1974) (Universal) Dir: Mark Robson. Cast: Charlton Heston, Ava Gardner, George Kennedy, Lorne Greene, Genevieve Bujold, Richard Roundtree, Marjoe Gortner, Barry Sullivan, Lloyd Nolan, Victoria Principal, John Randolph, Donald Moffat. *Drunk Man* (billed as Walter Matuschanskavasky)

The Front Page (1974) (Universal) Dir: Billy Wilder. Cast: Jack Lemmon, Susan Sarandon, Vincent Gardenia, David Wayne, Allen Garfield, Austin Pendleton, Charles Durning, Herbert Edelman, Martin Gabel, Harold Gould, Cliff Osmond, Dick O'Neill, Paul Benedict, Allen Jenkins, Carol Burnett. *Walter Burns*

The Sunshine Boys (1975) (United Artists) Dir: Herbert Ross. Cast: George Burns, Richard Benjamin, Lee Meredith, Carol Arthur, Rosetta LeNoire, F. Murray

Abraham, Howard Hesseman, Ron Rifkin, Phyllis Diller, Steve Allen. *Willy Clark*

The Gentleman Tramp (1975) (Audieff) Dir: Richard Patterson. *Co-Narrator*

The Bad News Bears (1976) (Paramount) Dir: Michael Ritchie. Cast: Tatum O'Neal, Vic Morrow, Joyce Van Patten, Ben Piazza, Jackie Earle Haley, Alfred W. Lutter, Brandon Cruz. *Morris Buttermaker*

House Calls (1978) (Universal) Dir: Howard Zieff. Cast: Glenda Jackson, Art Carney, Richard Benjamin, Candice Azzara, Dick O'Neill, Thayer David, Jane Connell, Lloyd Gough, Gordon Jump, Charlie Matthau. *Dr. Charley Nichols*

Casey's Shadow (1978) (Columbia) Dir: Martin Ritt. Cast: Alexis Smith, Robert Webber, Murray Hamilton, Andrew A. Rubin, Stephan Burns, Michael Hershewe, Harry Caesar, Joel Fluellen, Whit Bissell. *Lloyd Bourdelle*

California Suite (1978) (Columbia) Dir: Herbert Ross. Cast: Alan Alda, Michael Caine, Bill Cosby, Jane Fonda, Elaine May, Richard Pryor, Maggie Smith, Herbert Edelman, David Matthau, Army Archerd, Dana Plato. *Marvin Michaels*

Little Miss Marker (1980) (Universal) Dir: Walter Bernstein. Cast: Tony Curtis, Bob Newhart, Lee Grant, Sara Stimson, Brian Dennehy, Kenneth McMillan, Joshua Shelley, Jessica Rains. *Sorrowful Jones*

Hopscotch (1980) (Avco Embassy) Dir: Ronald Neame. Cast: Glenda Jackson, Sam Waterston, Ned Beatty, Herbert Lom, David Matthau, Lucy Saroyan, Severn Darden. *Miles Kendig*

Portrait of a 60% Perfect Man (1980) (Action Film) Dir: Annie Trescot. *Himself*

First Monday in October (1981) (Paramount) Dir: Ronald Neame. Cast: Jill Clayburgh, Barnard Hughes, Jan Sterling, James Stephens. *Supreme Court Justice Dan Snow*

Buddy Buddy (1981) (MGM/UA) Dir: Billy Wilder. Cast: Jack Lemmon, Paula Prentiss, Klaus Kinski, Dana Elcar, Miles Chapin, Ed Begley Jr. *Trabucco*

I Ought to Be in Pictures (1982) (Twentieth Century-Fox) Dir: Herbert Ross. Cast: Ann-Margret, Dinah Manoff, Lance Guest, Lewis Smith, David Faustino. *Herbert Tucker*

The Survivors (1983) (Columbia) Dir: Michael Ritchie. Cast: Robin Williams, Jerry Reed, James Wainwright, Kristen Vigard, Annie McEnroe, Anne Pitoniak, John Goodman. *Sonny Paluso*

Movers and Shakers (1985) (MGM/UA) Dir: William Asher. Cast: Charles Grodin, Vincent Gardenia, Tyne Daly, Bill Macy, Gilda Radner, Michael Lerner, Joe Mantell, William Prince, Nita Talbot. *Joe Mulholland*

Pirates (1986) (Cannon) Dir: Roman Polanski. Cast: Cris Campion, Damien Thomas, Olu Jacobs, Richard Pearson, Charlotte Lewis, Roy Kinnear, Ferdy Mayne, Tony Peck. *Captain Thomas Bartholomew Red*

The Couch Trip (1988) (Orion) Dir: Michael Ritchie. Cast: Dan Aykroyd, Charles Grodin, Donna Dixon, Richard Romanus, Mary Gross, David Clennon, Arye Gross, Victoria Jackson, Chevy Chase. *Donald Becker*

Il piccolo diavolo (*The Little Devil*) (1988) (Columbia Pictures Ital/Yarno Cinematografica/Cecchi Gori Group/Tiger Cinematografica) Dir: Roberto

Benigni. Cast: Roberto Benigni, Nicoletta Braschi, Paolo Baroni, Stefania San-
drelli, John Lurie, Franco Fabrizi. *Father Maurice*

JFK (1991) (Warner Bros.) Dir: Oliver Stone. Cast: Kevin Costner, Sissy Spacek,
Kevin Bacon, Tommy Lee Jones, Laurie Metcalf, Gary Oldman, Michael
Rooker, Joe Pesci, Donald Sutherland, John Candy, Jack Lemmon, Edward
Asner, Vincent D'Onofrio, Jay O. Sanders. *Senator Russell Long*

Beyond 'JFK': The Question of Conspiracy (1992) (Embassy) Dir: Barbara Kopple,
Danny Schechter. *Himself*

Dennis the Menace (1993) (Warner Bros.) Dir: Nick Castle. Cast: Joan Plowright,
Mason Gamble, Christopher Lloyd, Lea Thompson, Robert Stanton, Amy
Sakasitz, Kellen Hathaway, Paul Winfield, Natasha Lyonne, Arnold Stang. *Mr.
Wilson*

Grumpy Old Men (1993) (Warner Bros.) Dir: Donald Petrie. Cast: Jack Lemmon,
Ann-Margret, Burgess Meredith, Daryl Hannah, Kevin Pollak, Ossie Davis,
Buck Henry. *Max Goldman*

I.Q. (1994) (Paramount) Dir: Fred Schepisi. Cast: Tim Robbins, Meg Ryan, Lou
Jacobi, Gene Saks, Joseph Maher, Stephen Fry, Tony Shalhoub, Frank Whaley,
Charles Durning, Lewis J. Stadlen. *Albert Einstein*

The Grass Harp (1995) (Fine Line) Dir: Charles Matthau. Cast: Piper Laurie, Sissy
Spacek, Edward Furlong, Nell Carter, Jack Lemmon, Mary Steenburgen, Sean
Patrick Flanery, Joe Don Baker, Charles Durning, Roddy McDowall, Scott
Wilson, Bonnie Bartlett, Mia Kirshner, Doris Roberts, Charles Matthau. *Judge
Charlie Cool*

Grumpier Old Men (1995) (Warner Bros.) Dir: Howard Deutch. Cast: Jack
Lemmon, Ann-Margret, Sophia Loren, Burgess Meredith, Daryl Hannah,
Kevin Pollak, Ann Morgan Guilbert. *Max Goldman*

I'm Not Rappaport (1996) (Gramercy) Dir: Herb Gardner. Cast: Ossie Davis, Amy
Irving, Craig T. Nelson, Boyd Gaines, Martha Plimpton, Guillermo Diaz, Elina
Lowensohn, Ron Rifkin, Ranjit Chowdhry, Irwin Corey. *Nat Moyer*

Out to Sea (1997) (Twentieth Century-Fox) Dir: Martha Coolidge. Cast: Jack
Lemmon, Dyan Cannon, Gloria DeHaven, Brent Spiner, Elaine Stritch, Hal
Linden, Donald O'Connor, Edward Mulhare, Rue McClanahan. *Charlie
Gordon*

Walter Matthau: Diamond in the Rough (1997) (Wombat Productions) Dir: Gene
Feldman. *Narrator*

The Life and Times of Hank Greenberg (1998) (Cowboy Booking International) Dir:
Aviva Kempner. *Himself*

The Odd Couple II (1998) (Paramount) Dir: Howard Deutch. Cast: Jack Lemmon,
Christine Baranski, Barnard Hughes, Jonathan Silverman, Jean Smart, Lisa
Waltz, Mary Beth Peil, Rex Linn, Jay O. Sanders, Alice Ghostley, Ellen Geer,
Doris Belack. *Oscar Madison*

Hanging Up (2000) (Columbia) Dir: Diane Keaton. Cast: Meg Ryan, Diane Keaton,
Lisa Kudrow, Adam Arkin, Cloris Leachman, Edie McClurg, Charles
Matthau. *Lou Mozell*

Television Films

The Incident (1990) (CBS) Dir: Joseph Sargent. Cast: Susan Blakely, Robert Carradine, Peter Firth, Barnard Hughes, Harry Morgan, William Schallert, Ariana Richards, Norbert Weisser. *Harmon Cobb*

Mrs. Lambert Remembers Love (1991) (CBS) Dir: Charles Matthau. Cast: Ellen Burstyn, Ryan Todd, William Schallert, Kathleen Garrett, Sherry Hursey. *Clifford*

Against Her Will: An Incident in Baltimore (1992) (CBS) Dir: Delbert Mann. Cast: Harry Morgan, Susan Blakely, Ariana Richards, Brian Kerwin, Barton Heyman. *Harmon Cobb*

Incident in a Small Town (1994) (CBS) Dir: Delbert Mann. Cast: Harry Morgan, Stephanie Zimbalist, Nick Stahl, Bernard Behrens. *Harmon Cobb*

The Marriage Fool (1998) (CBS) Dir: Charles Matthau. Cast: Carol Burnett, John Stamos, Teri Polo, Michael McMurtry, Kevin Frank, Charles Matthau, Arlene Mazerolle, Christina Collins, Sally Willis. *Frank Walsh*

Television Series

Mr. I. Magination (1950) (CBS) Dir: Donald Richardson. Cast: Paul Tripp, Red Tiller, Ruth Enders, Donald Harris. *Various Roles* (WM appeared for thirteen weeks)

Mister Peepers (1952) (NBC) Dir: James Sheldon. Cast: Wally Cox, Norma Crane, Joseph Foley, Leonard Elliott, Betty Sinclair, Helen Wagner, Penny Santon, Georgia Harvey. *Mr. Burr* (WM is billed as "David Tyrell"; he appeared in episodes during the show's summer tryout)

Tallahassee 7000 (1960–1961) (Syndicated) Twenty-six half-hour episodes: "Cold-ball"; "Man Bait"; "The Kale Boys"; "Danger Road"; "Loan Shark"; "The Alibi"; "The Violent Night" (part 1); "The Violent Night" (part 2); "Prince Hal"; "Billy the Kid"; "Vendetta"; "The Reunion"; "Early in the Morning, Far into the Night"; "Document of Death"; "The Crossroads"; "The Hostage"; "Best Laid Plans"; "The Meet"; "Undercover Man"; "The Fugitive"; "Scared Witness"; "Punch Drunk"; "Trial and Error"; "Interrupted Journey"; "Lady Killer"; and "Man from Tallahassee". *Lex Rogers*

Acres and Pains (1962) (CBS pilot) Dir: Perry Lafferty. Cast: Anne Jackson, Edward Andrews, Alice Pearce, Phillip Coolidge, Jerry Stiller, David Doyle. *Tom Dutton*

Television Appearances

Matthau made guest appearances on many talk shows, awards shows, and specials. He had acting roles in scores of television dramas and comedies. Here is a selected list of credits:

Lux Video Theatre (CBS), "Shadow on the Heart," October 16, 1950. Dir: Fielder

Cook. Cast: Veronica Lake, Gene Lyons, Roy Fant, William Kemp, Robert Allen, Myron (Mike) Kellin. WM plays *First Coast Guardsman*

Lux Video Theatre (CBS), "Mine to Have," October 30, 1950. Dir: Fielder Cook. Cast: Nina Foch, Andrew Duggan, Muriel Landers, Eileen Page, Jim Davidson, Maxine Stuart, Janet Fox, Rosalind Ivan. *Cop Number One*

Studio One (CBS), "The Last Cruise," November 13, 1950. Dir: Paul Nickell. Cast: Don Dickinson, Richard Webb, Robert Wark, Richard Carlyle, John Alberts, Walter Storkey, Harry M. Cooke, DeForest Kelley. *Jacobs*

Lux Video Theatre (CBS), "Manhattan Pastorale," January 22, 1951. Dir: Fielder Cook. Cast: Teresa Wright, Francis Lederer, Myron (Mike) Kellin, Murvyn Vye, Harold Stone. *Inspector*

Lux Video Theatre (CBS), "The Speech," April 30, 1951. Dir: Fielder Cook. Cast: Fredric March, Florence Eldridge, Roland Winters, Eileen Heckart, Martin Newman, Rex O'Malley, Dan Frazer. *Extra*

Lux Video Theatre (CBS), "Cafe Ami," November 15, 1951. Dir: Fielder Cook. Cast: Robert Preston, Maria Riva, Rod Steiger, Frances Fuller, Susan Wayne, Andrew Duggan, Rosemary Murphy. *Craig*

Lux Video Theatre (CBS), "For Goodness Sake," January 28, 1952. Dir: Fielder Cook. Cast: Jack Carson, June Lockhart, Edgar Stehli, Fredd Wayne, Victor Thorley, Dan Frazer. *Extra*

Goodyear Theatre (NBC), "Tour of Duty," February 3, 1952. Dir: Gordon Duff. Cast: Neva Patterson, Gerald S. O'Loughlin, Louise Erickson, Maxine Stuart, Norma Crane, Halliwell Hobbes.

Lux Video Theatre (CBS), "Man at Bay," April 7, 1952. Dir: Fielder Cook. Cast: Broderick Crawford, Anthony Ross, Carmen Matthews, George Roy Hill, Gloria McGhee, Jack Weston, Leo Bayard, Louisa Horton. *Extra*

Armstrong Circle Theater (NBC), "The Darkroom" (some sources list the title as "The Straight Forward Narrow"), April 15, 1952. Cast: Louise Albritton, John Newland, Glenda Farrell.

Philco Television Playhouse (NBC), "The Basket-Weaver," April 20, 1952. Dir: Gordon Duff. Cast: Robert Keith, Sho Onodera, Robert Alan Aurthur.

Schlitz Playhouse of Stars (CBS), "Doctors Should Never Marry," May 2, 1952. Cast: Diana Lynn, Jamie Smith.

Danger (CBS), "A Buck Is a Buck," May 20, 1952.

Kraft Television Theatre (NBC), "The Death of Kid Slawson," June 18, 1952. Cast: Jamie Smith, Duncan Baldwin, Geoffrey Lumb, Vaughan Taylor, Dan Morgan, Olive Blackeney.

Philco Television Playhouse (NBC), "Three Sundays," August 24, 1952. Cast: Murray Matheson, Malcolm Keen.

Omnibus (CBS), sequence titled "The Abracadabra Kid," April 19, 1953. Dir: Andrew McCullough. Cast: Maria Riva, Ian Tucker, Jane Rose, J. C. McCord. *Thomas Turningout*

Danger (CBS), "Hand Me Down," April 21, 1953. Dir: Sidney Lumet. Cast: Nina Foch.

Suspense (CBS), "F.O.B. Vienna," April 28, 1953. Cast: Jayne Meadows.

CREDITS AND AWARDS

Plymouth Playhouse (ABC), "Nightmare Number Three" (an episode in "Four Sto-
ries," also known as "Sketch Book"), May 24, 1953. Dir: Sir Cedric Hardwicke.
Storyteller
Goodyear Theatre (NBC), "Nothing to Sneeze At," July 12, 1953. Cast: Elaine
Stritch, Maxine Stuart.
Goodyear Theatre (NBC), "The Cipher," August 2, 1953. Dir: William Corrigan.
Cast: Edward Binns, Ernest Truex, Stefan Gierasch, Addison Richards, Martin
Balsam, Ross Martin.
Goodyear Theatre (NBC), "The New Process," August 23, 1953. Dir: Delbert Mann.
Cast: Ernest Truex, Geoffrey Lumb, Carole Matthews. Introduced by Hedda
Hopper. Presented as a double feature, under the title "Hollywood Tandem."
Campbell Television Soundstage (NBC), "Wonder in Your Eyes," August 28, 1953.
Cast: Clifford Sales, Nancy Coleman.
Philco Television Playhouse (NBC), *Othello*, September 6, 1953. Dir: Delbert Mann.
Cast: Torin Thatcher, Olive Deering, Gene Lyons, Jack Manning, Marian
Seldes, Basil Langton. *Iago*
Studio One (CBS), "Dry Run," December 7, 1953. Dir: Franklin Schaffner. Cast:
Frances Starr, Catherine McLeod, James Broderick, Dorothy Maruki. *Captain
Robert I. Olsen*
Philco Television Playhouse (NBC), "The Glorification of Al Toolum," December 27,
1953. Dir: Arthur Penn. Cast: Betsy Palmer, Murray Hamilton, Maxine Stuart,
Van Dyke Parks. *Al Toolum*
Danger (CBS), "Night of Reckoning," January 5, 1954. Cast: Edward Binns, Con-
stance Ford.
The United States Steel Hour (ABC), "Late Date," April 13, 1954. Dir: James Sheldon.
Cast: Patty McCormack, Barbara Baxley, Jessie Royce Landis, Vaughn Taylor,
Howard St. John, Lin McCarthy.
Motorola Television Hour (ABC), "Atomic Attack," May 18, 1954. Dir: Ralph Nelson.
Cast: Phyllis Thaxter, Robert Keith, Patsy Bruder, Patty McCormack, Audrey
Christie. *Dr. Spinelli*
Philco Television Playhouse (NBC), "Adapt or Die," June 13, 1954. Dir: Arthur Penn.
Cast: John Qualen, Hildy Parks, Geoffrey Lumb, Guy Raymond, Stefan
Gierasch. *Stuart Benson*
Center Stage (NBC), "The Human Touch," June 29, 1954. Cast: Polly Rowles,
Patricia Smith, William Redfield. *Charles*
Goodyear Theatre (NBC), "Flight Report," November 7, 1954. Cast: E. G. Marshall,
Bill Gideon, Richard Carlyle, Addison Powell, Charles Aidman. *Lieutenant Joe
Burch*
Robert Montgomery Presents (*The American Tobacco Theatre*) (NBC), "Dr. Ed,"
December 6, 1954. Cast: Lucie Lancaster, Audra Lindley, Pud Flanagan, Julian
Nea, Reuben Singer, Peg Hillias. *Dr. Edward Conner*
Philco Television Playhouse (NBC), "Walk Into the Night," January 9, 1955. Cast:
Neva Patterson, Ford Rainey, William Hansen, Virginia Kaye, Frank Overton,
Don Keefer. *Charley Putnum*
Robert Montgomery Presents (*The American Tobacco Theatre*) (NBC), "The Lost

Weekend," February 7, 1955. Dir: Norman Felton. Cast: Robert Montgomery, Leora Dana, Edward Andrews. *Nat, the Bartender*

Robert Montgomery Presents (*The American Tobacco Theatre*) (NBC), "A Westerner's Race Prejudice," March 14, 1955. Dir: John Newland. Cast: Anne Seymour, Lin McCarthy, Jo Rabb. *Gart Logan* (Also listed with the title "A Stone for His Son")

Justice (NBC), "Booby Trap," October 23, 1955. Cast: William Prince, James Ward. *Frank*

The Alcoa Hour (NBC), "The Big Vote," August 19, 1956. Dir: Norman Felton. Cast: Ed Begley, Kathleen Maguire, Robert Emhardt, Luis Van Rooten, William Harrigan. *Bill Egan*

Goodyear Theatre (NBC), "A Will to Live," May 12, 1957. Cast: Betsy Blair, Cathleen Nesbitt, Larry Gates, Virginia Kaye, Harold Vermilyea. *Dr. George Morrison*

Goodyear Theatre (NBC), "The Legacy," June 30, 1957. Dir: Fielder Cook. Cast: Melvyn Douglas, Philip Abbott, June Dayton, Roland Winters, Sally Chamberlin. *Julian*

The Alcoa Hour (NBC), "The Trouble With Women," August 11, 1957. Dir: Fielder Cook. Cast: Audrey Christie, Hiram Sherman, Jeff Harris, Shirley Standlee, Nicholas Pryor. *George Berry*

Climax! (CBS), "To Walk the Night," December 19, 1957. Dir: Buzz Kulik. Cast: Richard Boone, Mary Anderson, Judith Evelyn, George Tobias, Joe di Reda, Helen Kleeb. *Charlie Mapes*

Kraft Television Theatre (NBC), "Code in the Corner," January 15, 1958. Dir: Richard Goode. Cast: Howard Morris, Nancy Walker, Barton MacLane, Nancy Gates, Robert Middleton. *Harry*

Alfred Hitchcock Presents (CBS), "The Crooked Road," October 26, 1958. Dir: Paul Henreid. Cast: Richard Kiley, Patricia Breslin, Richard Erdman. *Officer Chandler*

Alfred Hitchcock Presents (CBS), "Dry Run," November 8, 1959. Dir: John Brahm. Cast: Robert Vaughn, David White, Tyler McVey. *Moran*

Play of the Week (syndicated), "Juno and the Paycock," February 1, 1960. Dir: Paul Shyre. Cast: Hume Cronyn, Evans Evans, Liam Clancy, Pauline Flanagan, Luella Gear. *Joxer Daly*

Play of the Week (syndicated), "The Rope Dancers," March 14, 1960. Dir: Jack Ragotzy, Mel London. Cast: Jacob Ben-Ami, Siobhan McKenna, Audrey Christie, Judy Sanford. *James Hyland*

Alfred Hitchcock Presents (CBS), "Very Moral Theft," October 11, 1960. Dir: Norman Lloyd. Cast: Betty Field, Karl Swenson, Sal Ponti. *Harry Wade*

Play of the Week (syndicated), "Two by Saroyan" (adaptations of "Once Around the Block" and "My Heart's in the Highlands"), November 7, 1960. Dir: Kirk Browning. Cast: ("Once Around the Block") Orson Bean, Larry Hagman, Nina Wilcox. *Judah*; ("My Heart's in the Highlands") Kevin Coughlin, Myron McCormick, Eddie Hodges, Nathaniel Frey. *Father*

Our American Heritage (NBC), "Born a Giant," December 2, 1960. Dir: Fielder

Cook. Cast: Bill Travers, Barbara Rush, Farley Granger, Robert Redford, John Colicos, Tom Clancy, Carlos Montalban, Estelle Hemsley. *Dickinson*

Naked City (ABC), "The Man Who Bit a Diamond in Half," December 14, 1960. Dir: Buzz Kulik. Cast: Paul Burke, Nancy Malone, Horace McMahon, Harry Bellaver, Luther Adler, Elizabeth Allen, Michael Conrad, James Tolkan, Casey Allen. *Sam*

Route 66 (CBS), "Eleven, the Hard Way," April 7, 1961. Cast: Martin Milner, George Maharis, Edward Andrews, Guy Raymond. *Sam Keep*

Target: the Corrupters (ABC), "Million Dollar Dump," September 29, 1961. Cast: Stephen McNally, Robert Harland, Peter Falk, Robert Middleton. *Books Cramer*

Alfred Hitchcock Presents (NBC), "Cop for a Day," October 31, 1961. Dir: Paul Henreid. Cast: Glenn Cannon, Carol Grace (Carol Matthau), Bernard Fein, Robert Reiner. *Phil*

Target: the Corrupters (ABC), "One for the Road," January 12, 1962. Cast: Stephen McNally, Robert Harland, Irene Hervey, David Brian, Constance Ford, Simon Scott, Linda Lawson. *Michael Callahan*

Westinghouse Presents (CBS), "Footnote to Fame," February 3, 1962. Dir: Alex March. Cast: Lee J. Cobb, Martin Balsam, Robert Webber, Dina Merrill, Larry Gates, Shepperd Strudwick, Burgess Meredith. *James Martel*

DuPont Show of the Week (NBC), "Big Deal in Laredo," October 7, 1962. Dir: Fielder Cook. Cast: John McGiver, Teresa Wright, Zachary Scott, John Megna, Roland Winters, Dana Elcar, William Hansen. *Meredith*

Naked City (ABC), "Don't Knock It Till You've Tried It," December 26, 1962. Dir: Alex March. Cast: Paul Burke, Nancy Malone, Horace McMahon, Harry Bellaver, Joan Copeland, Pat Englund, Sally Gracie. *Dr. Max Lewine*

DuPont Show of the Week (NBC), "Police Emergency," February 17, 1963. Dir: Julian Claman. *Narrator*

The Eleventh Hour (NBC), "A Tumble from a High White Horse," February 27, 1963. Cast: Wendell Corey, Jack Ging, Telly Savalas, Frankie Avalon, Phyllis Hill. *Charles Thatcher*

DuPont Show of the Week (NBC), "A Dozen Deadly Roses," June 23, 1963. Dir: Robert Allen. Cast: Lauren Bacall, Robert Alda, Vincent Gardenia, Addison Powell. *Martin Pitt*

DuPont Show of the Week (NBC), "Fire Rescue," July 21, 1963. Dir: John G. Fuller. *Narrator*

DuPont Show of the Week (NBC), "The Takers," October 13, 1963. Cast: Shirley Knight, Claude Rains, Nancy Barrett, Larry Hagman. *Harley Downing*

Bob Hope Chrysler Theater (NBC), "White Snow, Red Ice," March 13, 1964. Cast: Jack Kelly, Senta Berger, Grace Lee Whitney. *Gregory*

DuPont Show of the Week (NBC), "Jeremy Rabbitt, the Secret Avenger," April 5, 1964. Dir: Franklin Schaffner. Cast: Frank Gorshin, Brian Donlevy, Jim Backus, Carolyn Jones, Franchot Tone, Phil Leeds. *Tony Maruzella*

The Rogues (NBC), "The Personal Touch," September 13, 1964. Dir: Hy Averback.

Cast: David Niven, Charles Boyer, Gig Young, Gladys Cooper, Robert Coote, Dina Merrill, Alfred Ryder, John Dehner, Marcel Hillaire, Dabbs Greer, John Banner. *Aram Rudescu*

Dr. Kildare (NBC), "Man Is a Rock," September 24, 1964. Cast: Richard Chamberlain, Raymond Massey, Georgann Johnson, Richard Evans, Lana Wood, Ken Lynch. *Franklin Gaer*

Profiles in Courage (NBC), "Governor John M. Slaton," December 20, 1964. Cast: Michael Constantine, Anthony Costello, Betsy Jones-Moreland, Whit Bissell, Alan Baxter, Tyler McVey. *Governor John M. Slaton*

Profiles in Courage (NBC), "Andrew Johnson," February 28, 1965. Cast: Alfred Ryder, Conlan Carter, Paul Fix, John Abbott, Linden Chiles, Joan Tompkins. *Andrew Johnson*

Carol Channing: One Hundred and One Men (ABC) (November 16, 1967). Dir: Alan Handley. Cast: Carol Channing, Eddy Arnold, The Association, The United States Air Force Cadet Chorale, George Burns.

Jack Benny's Bag (NBC) (November 16, 1968). Dir: Norman Abbott. Cast: Jack Benny, Eddie "Rochester" Anderson, Phyllis Diller, Lou Rawls, Dick Clark, Eddie Fisher, Dan Rowan, Dick Martin.

Super Comedy Bowl 2 (CBS) (January 12, 1972). Dir: Marty Pasetta. Cast: Jack Lemmon, Tony Curtis, Jack Klugman, Burt Lancaster, Paul Newman, Burt Reynolds, Kurt Russell, George C. Scott.

Hollywood Television Theatre (PBS), "Awake and Sing!" March 6, 1972. Dir: Norman Lloyd. Cast: Felicia Farr, Ruth Storey, Robert Lipton, Leo Fuchs, Milton Selzer, Martin Ritt, Ron Rifkin, John Myhers. *Moe Axelrod*

A Show Business Salute to Milton Berle (NBC) (December 4, 1973). Dir: Grey Lockwood. Cast: Milton Berle, Sammy Davis Jr., Lucille Ball, Jack Benny, Kirk Douglas, Redd Foxx, Jackie Gleason, Bob Hope, Jack Lemmon, Jan Murray, Carroll O'Connor, Don Rickles, Henny Youngman.

60 Minutes (CBS) (April 14, 1974). *Interviewee*

The Rona Barrett Special (ABC) (March 29, 1976). *Interviewee*

The George Burns Special (CBS) (December 1, 1976). Dir: Bill Hobin. Cast: George Burns, The Osmonds, Johnny Carson, Madeline Kahn, Chita Rivera.

Insight (syndicated), "This Side of Eden," 1977. Cast: Carol Burnett, Edward Asner. *Adam*

Oscar Presents John Wayne and the War Movies (ABC) (November 27, 1977). Dir: Mel Stuart. Cast: John Wayne, Jeff Bridges, Louise Fletcher, Brenda Vaccaro.

The Making of Casey's Shadow (1978) Dir: William Riead. Cast: Martin Ritt, Murray Hamilton, Andrew A. Rubin, Alexis Smith, Robert Webber.

Kraft 75th Anniversary Special (CBS) (January 24, 1978). Dir: Dwight Hemion. Cast: Bob Hope, Leslie Uggams, Bob Crosby, Hal Peary, Edgar Bergen, Milton Berle, Alan King, Donna McKechnie, Roy Clark.

Hollywood Television Theatre (PBS), "Actor," February 7, 1978. Dir: Norman Lloyd. Cast: Herschel Bernardi, Georgia Brown, Jeff Lynas, Barry Robins, Michael Kidd, Howard Duff, Harold Gould, Hildy Brooks, Ezra Stone, Leo Postrel. *Boris Thomashevsky*

Funny Business (CBS) (July 28, 1978). Dir: Richard Schickel. *Host/Narrator.*

Saturday Night Live (NBC), December 2, 1978. Dir: Dave Wilson. Cast: John Belushi, Dan Aykroyd, Gilda Radner, Garrett Morris, Jane Curtin, Laraine Newman, Bill Murray. *Guest Host*

The Stingiest Man in Town (NBC) (December 23, 1978). Dir: Arthur Rankin Jr., Jules Bass. Cast: Tom Bosley, Theodore Bikel, Robert Morse, Dennis Day, Paul Frees, Charles Matthau. *Voice of Ebenezer Scrooge*

The American Film Institute Salute to Jimmy Stewart (CBS) (March 16, 1980).

Magic of the Stars (September 20, 1981). Cast: Milton Berle, Lucille Ball, Carl Ballantine, Ruth Buzzi, Melissa Gilbert, Jack Lemmon, Dick Shawn, Tanya Tucker, Dick Van Patten.

I Love Liberty (ABC) (March 21, 1982). Dir: Bill Carruthers. Cast: Barbra Streisand, Robin Williams, Mary Tyler Moore, Gregory Hines, Jane Fonda, Rod Steiger, Kenny Rogers, Christopher Reeve, Burt Lancaster, Michele Lee, Melissa Manchester, Helen Reddy.

20/20 (ABC) (April 8, 1982). *Interviewee*

Hollywood: The Gift of Laughter (ABC) (May 16, 1982). Dir: Jack Haley Jr. *Co-Host*

The Shakespeare Hour (PBS), 1985–1986. *Host-Commentator*

George Burns' 90th Birthday: A Very Special Special (ABC) (January 17, 1986). Dir: Walter C. Miller. Cast: George Burns, Ann-Margret, Diahann Carroll, Billy Crystal, John Denver, John Forsythe.

Comic Relief (HBO) (March 29, 1986). Cast: Whoopi Goldberg, Billy Crystal, Robin Williams, Gilda Radner, Bob Hope, Sid Caesar, Carl Reiner, Madeline Kahn, Pee Wee Herman, Richard Dreyfuss, Penny Marshall, Dick Van Dyke, Gary Shandling, Henny Youngman, Minnie Pearl, Joe Piscopo.

The American Film Institute Salute to Billy Wilder (NBC) (April 26, 1986). Dir: Don Mischer.

Change of Heart (1987). Dir: William Riead. Cast: Arthur Ashe, Brooke Shields, Rod Steiger.

James Stewart: A Wonderful Life (PBS) (March 13, 1987). Dir: David Heeley. Cast: Johnny Carson, Peter Bogdanovich, Carol Burnett, Nancy Davis Reagan, Richard Dreyfuss, Clint Eastwood, Sally Field, Katharine Hepburn, Gene Kelly, Ronald Reagan, Lee Remick, James Stewart.

The American Film Institute Salute to Barbara Stanwyck (ABC) (May 29, 1987). Dir: Dwight Hemion.

A Beverly Hills Christmas (FOX) (December 22, 1987). Dir: Woody Fraser. Cast: James Stewart.

We the People 200: The Constitutional Gala (CBS) (September 17, 1987). Dir: Dwight Hemion. Cast: Walter Cronkite, Gregory Peck, Lloyd Bridges, Rich Little, Barry Manilow, E. G. Marshall, George Peppard, Stefanie Powers, Eli Wallach.

The American Film Institute Salute to Jack Lemmon (CBS) (May 30, 1988). Dir: Louis J. Horvitz.

American Masters: Neil Simon: Not Just for Laughs (*Simply Simon: A Neil Simon Retrospective*) (PBS) (April 21, 1989). Dir: Amram Nowak.

Reflections on the Silver Screen with Professor Richard Brown (syndicated) (1990).

Laurel and Hardy: A Tribute to the Boys (The Disney Channel) (1992).

How the Grinch Stole Christmas! (1992). *Narrator*

The First Annual Comedy Hall of Fame (NBC) (1993)

Elvis: His Life and Times (syndicated) (1993)

What Is This Thing Called Love? The Barbara Walters Special (ABC) (1993)

A Menace Called Dennis (CBS) (June 22, 1993). Dir: John Pattyson, Michael Meadows. Cast: Mason Gamble, Lea Thompson, Joan Plowright, Nick Castle, John Hughes, Hank Ketcham. *Host*

Biography, "Jack Lemmon: America's Everyman" (Arts & Entertainment) (1996)

The GI Bill: The Law that Changed America (PBS) (1997) Dir: Karen Thomas. *Interviewee*

An American Masters Special: Billy Wilder: The Human Comedy (PBS) (1998) *Narrator*

Private Screenings: Lemmon and Matthau (Turner Classic Movies) (1998)

Biography, "Neil Simon: The People's Playwright" (Arts & Entertainment) (1999)

Hollywood Remembers Walter Matthau (Fox Movie Channel) (2001) Cast: Charles Matthau, Richard Benjamin, Dyan Cannon, Rabbi Jerry Cutler, Tom Dixon, Mason Gamble, Jack Lemmon, Piper Laurie, Zubin Mehta, Kevin Pollak, Neil Simon, Brent Spiner, Kevin Thomas.

Stage

Matthau's work as an extra in Yiddish theater productions, his roles in New School for Social Research Dramatic Workshop productions, and his summer theatre appearances are cited in the manuscript. His Broadway appearances and pre-Broadway tryouts include:

Anne of the 1000 Days, Shubert Theatre, New York. Dir: H. C. Potter. Cast: Rex Harrison, Joyce Redman, Percy Waram, John Williams, Robert Duke, Viola Keats, Harry Irvine, Louise Platt. WM plays *Candle Bearer; Understudy* Opened December 8, 1948. 288 performances.

The Liar, Broadhurst Theatre, New York. Dir: Alfred Drake. Cast: Alfred Drake, Paula Lawrence, William Eythe, Russell Collins, Barbara Moser, Philip Coolidge, Melville Cooper, Joshua Shelley, Martin Balsam. *Venetian Guard* Opened May 18, 1950. 12 performances.

Season in the Sun, Cort Theatre, New York. Dir: Burgess Meredith. Cast: Richard Whorf, Nancy Kelly, Eddie Mayehoff, Anthony Ross, Joan Diener, Paula Lawrence, King Calder, Jack Weston. *John Colgate (Understudy, before taking over role)* Opened September 28, 1950. 367 performances.

Twilight Walk, Fulton Theatre, New York. Dir: Paul Stewart. Cast: Nancy Kelly, Ann Shoemaker, Charles Proctor, Virginia Vincent, Walter Brooke, Anna Berger. *Sam Dundee* Opened September 24, 1951. 8 performances.

Fancy Meeting You Again, Royale Theatre, New York. Dir: George S. Kaufman. Cast:

Leueen MacGrath, Glenn Langan, Ruth McDevitt, Margaret Hamilton. *Sinclair Heybore* Opened January 14, 1952. 8 performances.

One Bright Day, Royale Theatre, New York. Dir: Michael Gordon. Cast: Howard Lindsay, Glenn Anders, Marian Russell, Bess Winburn, Phillip Pine, Bart Burns, Addison Richards. *George Lawrence* Opened March 19, 1952. 29 performances.

In Any Language, Cort Theatre, New York. Dir: George Abbott. Cast: Uta Hagen, Joe De Santis, Eileen Heckart, Gloria Marlowe, Nita Naldi, Dino Terranova, Maurice Gosfield. *Charlie Hill* Opened October 7, 1952. 45 performances.

The Grey-Eyed People, Martin Beck Theatre, New York. Dir: Morton Da Costa. Cast: Virginia Gilmore, John Randolph, Sandra Deel, Brandon Peters, Katherine Anderson, Walter Klavun, Rosemary Prinz, Mary Grace Canfield. *John Hart* Opened December 17, 1952. 5 performances.

A Certain Joy, pre-Broadway tryout. Dir: Daniel Mann. Cast: Margo, Ruth Warrick, Arthur Cassel, Jeff Silver, Joe De Santis, Roger Stevens. *Andrew Lamb* Opened February 12, 1953, at the Playhouse Theatre, Wilmington, Delaware. Closed February 21, 1953, at the Locust Theatre, Philadelphia.

The Ladies of the Corridor, Longacre Theatre, New York. Dir: Harold Clurman. Cast: Edna Best, Betty Field, Shepperd Strudwick, Frances Starr, June Walker, Vera Allen, Margaret Barker, Lonny Chapman. *Paul Osgood*, Opened October 21, 1953. 35 performances.

The Burning Glass, Longacre Theatre, New York. Dir: Luther Kennert. Cast: Cedric Hardwicke, Scott Forbes, Maria Riva, Isobel Elsom, William Roerick. *Tony Lack* Opened March 4, 1954. 28 performances.

The Wisteria Trees, City Center Theatre, New York. Dir: John Stix. Cast: Helen Hayes, Cliff Robertson, Lois Smith, Ella Raines, Bramwell Fletcher, Will Geer, Ossie Davis, Alonzo Bosan, Jonelle Allen, Warren Oates. *Yancy Loper* Opened February 2, 1955. 15 performances.

Guys and Dolls, City Center Theatre, New York. Dir: Philip Mathias. Cast: Helen Gallagher, Ray Shaw, Leila Martin, Martin Wolfson, Oggie Small, Al Nesor, Murray Vines. *Nathan Detroit* Opened April 20, 1955. 15 performances.

Will Success Spoil Rock Hunter?, Belasco Theatre, New York. Dir: George Axelrod. Cast: Orson Bean, Martin Gabel, Jayne Mansfield, Harry Clark, Carol Grace (the future Carol Matthau), Tina Louise, Michael Tolan, David Sheiner. *Michael Freeman* Opened October 13, 1955. 444 performances.

Maiden Voyage, pre-Broadway tryout. Dir: Joseph Anthony. Cast: Melvyn Douglas, Mildred Dunnock, Tom Poston, Lee Hays, Colleen Dewhurst, Bruce Gordon. *Odysseus* Opened February 28, 1957, at the Forrest Theatre, Philadelphia. Closed there on March 9, 1957.

Once More, With Feeling, National Theatre, New York. Dir: George Axelrod. Cast: Joseph Cotten, Arlene Francis, Paul E. Richards, Leon Belasco, Dan Frazer. *Maxwell Archer* Opened October 21, 1958. 263 performances.

Once There Was a Russian, Music Box Theatre, New York. Dir: Gene Frankel. Cast: Francoise Rosay, Albert Salmi, Julie Newmar, Sig Rumann, Carol Grace

(Matthau), Eric Christmas, Louis Guss, Marvin Silbersher, Roger C. Carmel. *Potemkin* Opened February 18, 1961. 1 performance.

A Shot in the Dark, Booth Theatre, New York. Dir: Harold Clurman. Cast: Julie Harris, William Shatner, Gene Saks, Diana van der Vlis, Louise Troy. *Benjamin Beaurevers* Opened October 18, 1961. 389 performances.

My Mother, My Father and Me, Plymouth Theatre, New York. Dir: Gower Champion. Cast: Ruth Gordon, Lili Darvas, Anthony Holland, Dorothy Greener, Sudie Bond, Heywood Hale Broun, Henry Gibson. *Herman Halpern* Opened March 23, 1963. 17 performances.

The Odd Couple, Plymouth Theatre, New York. Dir: Mike Nichols. Cast: Art Carney, Nathaniel Frey, Paul Dooley, Sidney Armus, John Fiedler, Carole Shelley, Monica Evans. *Oscar Madison* Opened March 10, 1965. 964 performances.

Juno and the Paycock, Mark Taper Forum, Los Angeles. Dir: George Seaton. Cast: Jack Lemmon, Maureen Stapleton, John Glover, Sean McClory, William Schallert, Laurie Prange, Mary Jackson, Mary Wickes. *Captain Jack Boyle* November 7–December 22, 1974.

Awards

New York Drama Critics Circle Award, *Twilight Walk*, 1951.

New York Drama Critics Circle Award, *Once More, With Feeling*, 1959.

Tony Award nomination, Supporting or Featured Actor [Dramatic], *Once More, With Feeling*, 1959.

Tony Award: Best Actor, Featured or Supporting, *A Shot in the Dark*, 1962.

Film Daily Award, *Lonely Are the Brave*, 1962.

Emmy Award nomination, Outstanding Single Performance by an Actor, "Big Deal in Laredo," *DuPont Show of the Week*, 1963.

Tony Award, Best Actor, Dramatic, *The Odd Couple*, 1965.

New York Drama Critics Circle Award, *The Odd Couple*, 1965.

Academy Award, Best Supporting Actor, *The Fortune Cookie*, 1966.

Golden Globe Award nomination, Best Motion Picture Actor—Musical/Comedy, *The Fortune Cookie*, 1966.

Golden Globe Award nomination, Best Motion Picture Actor—Musical/Comedy, *The Odd Couple*, 1968.

British Academy Award nomination, Best Actor, *Hello, Dolly!* and *The Secret Life of an American Wife*, 1969.

Academy Award nomination, Best Actor, *Kotch*, 1972.

Golden Globe Award nomination, Best Motion Picture Actor—Musical/Comedy, *Kotch*, 1972.

Golden Globe Award nomination, Best Motion Picture Actor—Musical/Comedy, *Pete 'n' Tillie*, 1973.

British Academy Award, Best Actor, *Charley Varrick* and *Pete 'n' Tillie*, 1973.

Golden Globe Award nomination, Best Motion Picture Actor—Musical/Comedy, *The Front Page*, 1975.

CREDITS AND AWARDS

Golden Globe Award, Best Actor in a Musical or Comedy, *The Sunshine Boys*, 1976.

Academy Award nomination, Best Actor, *The Sunshine* Boys, 1976.

British Academy Award nomination, Best Actor, *The Sunshine Boys* and *The Bad News Bears*, 1976.

American Heart Association Heart of the Year Award, 1977.

Golden Globe Award nomination, Best Motion Picture Actor—Musical/Comedy, *Hopscotch*, 1981.

Golden Globe Award nomination, Best Motion Picture Actor—Musical/Comedy, *First Monday in October*, 1982.

ShoWest Convention Award, Lifetime Achievement, 1993.

American Comedy Awards, Lifetime Achievement, 1997.

American Film Institute Associates Platinum Circle Award (shared with Carol and Charles Matthau), 1997.

BIBLIOGRAPHY

Books

Bentley, Eric. *What Is Theatre?* New York: Hill and Wang, 2000.

Bergman, Ingrid, and Alan Burgess. *Ingrid Bergman: My Story*. New York: Delacorte, 1980.

Curtis, Tony, and Barry Paris. *Tony Curtis: The Autobiography*. New York: William Morrow, 1993.

Douglas, Kirk. *The Ragman's Son*. New York: Simon & Schuster, 1988.

Ebert, Roger. *A Kiss Is Still a Kiss*. Kansas City: Andrews, McMeel & Parker, 1984.

Edelman, Rob. *Great Baseball Films*. New York: Citadel, 1994.

Matthau, Carol. *Among the Porcupines*. New York: Turtle Bay, 1992.

Munn, Michael. *Stars at War*. New York: Robson, 1995.

Ross, Lillian, and Helen Ross. *The Player: A Profile of an Art*. New York: Simon & Schuster, 1962.

Sikov, Ed. *On Sunset Boulevard: The Life and Times of Billy Wilder*. New York: Hyperion, 1998.

Spada, James. *Streisand: Her Life*. New York: Ballantine, 1995.

Periodicals

Reviews and feature articles from several dozen publications were consulted while preparing this book. Among them: the *New York Times; New York Daily News; New York American; New York Journal-American; New York Daily Mirror; New York World-Telegram & Sun; New York Herald-Tribune; New York Post; Brooklyn Eagle; Newsday; Photoplay; Boston Globe; Morning Telegraph; Newark Evening News; Entertainment Weekly; Los Angeles Times; International Film Guide; Washington Post; Chicago Sun-Times; Chicago Tribune; Jerusalem Post; San Diego Union; The Observer; Louisville*

Courier-Journal; Variety; TV Guide; Soho Weekly News; Calgary Sun; Hollywood Reporter; Buffalo Evening News; Drama-Logue; Philadelphia Inquirer; Time; Premiere; Long Island Traveler; San Jose Mercury News; The Evening Star; Boston Traveler; Long Island Traveler–Mattituck Watchman; Cue; Theatre Arts; Suffolk Times; Boston Herald; Interview; Boston Daily Record; Boston Record American; US; Newburgh News; American Film; Louisville Courier-Journal & Times; People; Christian Science Monitor; Toronto Sun; Entertainment Today; Los Angeles Daily News; The New Yorker; and *Current Biography.*

Ann Lewis's and Tom McMorrow's summer theater reminiscences originally were published in the *Long Island Traveler* (August 2, 1973) and New York *Daily News* (December 28, 1975).

INDEX

ABOUT THE AUTHORS

Rob Edelman is the author of the acclaimed *Great Baseball Films* (1994) and *Baseball on the Web* (1997), which Amazon.com cited as one of the Top 10 Internet books of 1998. He is a contributing editor of *Leonard Maltin's Movie and Video Guide*, *Leonard Maltin's Movie Encyclopedia*, and *Leonard Maltin's Family Film Guide*. He has written essays and entries in several other books (from *A Political Companion to American Film* and *St. James Film Directors Encyclopedia* to *The Total Baseball Catalog*); and his work has appeared in dozens of periodicals (from *American Film* to *Variety* and the *Washington Post*). He is director of programming of Home Film Festival (which rents select videotapes and DVDs throughout the country); offers film commentary on WAMC (Northeast) Public Radio; and teaches film courses at the University at Albany (State University of New York).

Audrey E. Kupferberg is a film and video consultant, archivist, and appraiser. She has been director of the Yale Film Study Center, assistant director of the National Center for Film and Video Preservation at the American Film Institute, and project director of the American Film Institute Catalog. She is a contributing editor of *Leonard Maltin's Family Film Guide*, and has written for *Women Filmmakers and Their Films*, *International Dictionary of Films and Filmmakers*, and *St. James Encyclopedia of Popular Culture*. She teaches film history at the University at Albany (State University of New York), and works as film consultant to The Peary-MacMillan Arctic Museum at Bowdoin College.

Rob and Audrey have co-authored several books, including *Angela Lansbury: A Life on Stage and Screen* (1996) and *Meet the Mertzes* (1999), a dual biography of Vivian Vance and William Frawley. They are married, and live in upstate New York.